THE WESTERN



**Mark Stoyle** is Professor of History
An expert on Tudor and Stuart Brit
including *Soldiers and Strangers* and
*Dog*.

Further praise for *The Western Rising of 1549*:

'An excellent new book ... Stoyle brings a fresh eye and much new material to the fore.'
Martin Empson, *Agricultural History Review*

'A local history with national ramifications ... A must-read for anyone interested in the mid-Tudor rebellions.'
Heather Falvey, *Local Historian*

'A compelling new narrative of a revolt that threatened the very heart of the Tudor regime and almost halted the English Reformation in its tracks.'
Debbie Kilroy, *Get History*

'Tells the gripping story of the ill-fated rising in 1549 of the people of Devon and Cornwall against the English government of Edward VI. Full of new insights, the book is beautifully written with great clarity and sensitivity and an unrivalled grasp of the source material.'
Michael Wood, author of *The Story of England*

'In the summer of 1549, as this book's gripping and authoritative account proves, a spontaneous rising in Devon and Cornwall came much closer than we have imagined to bringing the whole English Reformation to an abrupt end – and 4,000 of them paid for the effort with their lives. Now, at last, in Mark Stoyle's book, they have a fitting scholarly memorial.'
Alec Ryrie, author of *Protestants: The Radicals Who Made the Modern World*

‘A fresh and detailed retelling of the Western Rising . . . Over many years, Professor Mark Stoyle has made the history of early modern Cornwall and Devon his own, and this book, with its sparkling prose and telling insights, adds further to his brilliant repertoire.’
Philip Payton, University of Exeter and Flinders University

‘Comprehensive in its command of the evidence, judicious in interpretation and salted with a controlled sympathy for place and people, this book offers a compelling reinterpretation of the Western Rising.’
John Walter, University of Essex

‘A riveting new account . . . Combining empirical rigour and high narrative powers, Mark Stoyle stylishly recasts our understanding of an episode that has too often been written off as doomed to failure from the start.’
Alexandra Walsham, author of *The Reformation of the Landscape*

# THE WESTERN RISING OF 1549

MARK STOYLE

YALE UNIVERSITY PRESS
NEW HAVEN AND LONDON

First published in paperback in 2024



For information about this and other Yale University Press publications, please contact:
U.S. Office: sales.press@yale.edu yalebooks.com
Europe Office: sales@yaleup.co.uk yalebooks.co.uk

Set in Adobe Caslon Pro by IDSUK (DataConnection) Ltd
Printed in Great Britain by Clays Ltd, Elcograf S.p.A

Library of Congress Control Number: 2023947207

ISBN 978-0-300-26632-0 (hbk)
ISBN 978-0-300-27688-6 (pbk)

A catalogue record for this book is available from the British Library.

10 9 8 7 6 5 4 3 2 1

*For George Bernard*

# CONTENTS


*List of Illustrations* *ix*
*Acknowledgements* *xi*
*List of Abbreviations* *xv*

Introduction 1

PART I *The Background*

1 Presages: The West Country under Henry VIII 11

2 Foreshocks: The Disturbances of 1547–48 44

PART II *The Rising*

3 Outbreak: June 1549 79

4 Escalation: 1–15 July 1549 114

5 Flood Tide: 15–31 July 1549 144

6 Defeat: August 1549 181

PART III *The Aftermath*

7 Retribution: September 1549 219

8 Aftershocks: October 1549 to January 1550 255

Conclusion 289

*Endnotes* *298*
*Bibliography* *331*
*Index* *345*

# ILLUSTRATIONS

## Plates

1. Portrait of Edward VI, possibly by William Scrots. The Royal Collection © London Metropolitan Archives.
2. Portrait of Edward Seymour, Duke of Somerset, by an unknown artist. The Picture Art Collection / Alamy Stock Photo.
3. Title page of *The Order of the Communion* (1548). Cambridge University Library.
4. St Keverne Church, Lizard Peninsula, West Cornwall. David Chapman / Alamy Stock Photo.
5. Launceston Castle, site of Cornwall's county gaol. John Husband / Alamy Stock Photo.
6. Title page of *The Book of Common Prayer* (1549). Granger Historical Picture Archive / Alamy Stock Photo.
7. Sampford Courtenay Church, Devon. Photograph by the author.
8. View from the Church Tower, Sampford Courtenay. Photograph by the author.
9. Portrait of Sir Peter Carew, after Gerlach Flicke. ART Collection / Alamy Stock Photo.

10. The City of Exeter, map drawn by Remigius Hogenberg, 1580s. Album / Alamy Stock Photo.
11. Pendennis Castle, Cornwall. James Eate / Alamy Stock Photo.
12. Portrait drawing of John, Lord Russell, by Hans Holbein, *c.* 1532–43. Royal Collection Trust / © Her Majesty Queen Elizabeth II 2022.
13. Portrait of the Lady Mary, by Master John, 1544. © National Portrait Gallery.
14. Portrait drawing of Sir Gawen Carew, by Hans Holbein, *c.* 1532–43. Royal Collection Trust / © Her Majesty Queen Elizabeth II 2022.
15. Portrait drawing of 'the Lady Ratclif', by Hans Holbein, *c.* 1532–43. Royal Collection Trust / © Her Majesty Queen Elizabeth II 2022.
16. Gravestone in Sampford Courtenay churchyard. Photograph by the author.

## Maps

1. Devon and Cornwall: main physical features xvii
2. Devon and Cornwall: towns and villages xviii
3. Exeter in the 1540s xix
4. The Cornish commotion of April 1548 xx
5. The Western Rising in Devon, June 1549 xxi
6. The Western Rising in Cornwall, July–August 1549 xxii
7. The defeat of the western rebels, July–August 1549 xxiii

# ACKNOWLEDGEMENTS

I first became interested in the Western Rising as a schoolboy, almost 40 years ago, when I had a summer job as a tour-guide at Bickleigh Castle: the jewel-like fortified manor house which slumbers beneath a wooded hill in the heart of Devon's Exe Valley. One of the treasures of the house is an ornate stone mantlepiece, dating from the 1600s, upon which a series of vivid depictions of people and places is carved. During the early 1900s, it had been suggested by several local antiquarians that the scenes on the mantelpiece were intended to memorialise the role played by Sir Peter Carew – a sixteenth-century gentleman whose family had once owned the house – in suppressing the Western Rising: a major revolt against the Crown's religious policies which had broken out in Devon in 1549. This possibility was duly flagged up in the standard spiel delivered to the summer visitors during the 1980s and, in my head, I can still hear the voice of Noel Boxall – the charming and urbane man who then owned the castle – declaiming, in the serene tones of one who is repeating a familiar litany, 'And above the fire we see the mantelpiece, with a series of carvings which are thought to depict events from the Western Rising, or Prayer Book Rebellion'. I quickly learned to incorporate this phrase into the talks that I gave to the visitors myself and, as I cycled home from Bickleigh to my own village of Thorverton in the evenings – effortlessly propelling myself, in those far-off days, up the lanes that switchback their way over the steep hill which separates the two – I would sometimes ponder on the sudden eruption of violence some four centuries ago that had shattered the calm of the countryside I knew so well, and wonder how I might find out more about it. Four decades later, this book is the result.

I have incurred a host of debts during the many years in which I have been pursuing the history of the rebellion, and it is a great pleasure to be able to acknowledge some of them now. First, I would like to thank the shades of Noel and his wife, Norma – both long since departed, alas – for the kindness and encouragement that they showed me as a budding historian, and for giving me the opportunity to take my first faltering steps as a public speaker in such a magical setting. Second, I would like to thank the former staff of the Exeter Museums Archaeological Field Unit for the invaluable experience I gained while working with them during the later 1980s and the 1990s: I could not have asked for a better – or more enjoyable – historical apprenticeship. Third, I would like to thank those who taught me as an undergraduate and postgraduate student, especially the late Gerald Aylmer, Alastair Duke and Greg Walker, for helping me to hone my historical skills, and for being such generous and humane mentors.

In 2012, I was fortunate enough to visit some of the chief sites connected with the Western Rising in the company of Michael Wood, who was then making his documentary film about the past lives of ordinary people, *The Great British Story*. It was in the wake of these visits that I first began to sketch out in my mind how a new history of the rebellion might conceivably look, and I am most grateful to Michael for his encouragement. I also owe a huge debt of thanks to the staff of the record offices and libraries that I have visited while carrying out my research, including: the Bodleian Library; the British Library; the Cornish Record Office (now Kresen Kernow); the Dean and Chapter Archives in Exeter; Exeter College, Oxford; King's College, Cambridge; Longleat House; the National Archives; the North Devon Record Office; the Royal Cornwall Museum and Courtney Library; the Somerset Heritage Centre; the West Devon Record Office; and, most important of all, the Devon Heritage Centre. Extracts from the Thynne Papers appear in the following pages by kind permission of the Marquess of Bath, Longleat, and extracts from John Hooker's unpublished narrative of the rebellion – MS. Rawl. C. 792 – by kind permission of the Bodleian Library, Oxford. I am grateful to Oxford University Press and to Cambridge University Press, respectively, for permission to publish in altered form material that first appeared in the following articles: 'Fullye Bente to Fighte Oute the Matter: Reconsidering Cornwall's Role in the Western Rebellion of 1549', *The English Historical Review*, vol. 129, no. 538 (June 2014), pp. 549–77; 'Kill all the Gentlemen?: Misrepresenting the western rebels of 1549', *Historical Research*, vol. 92, no. 255 (February 2019), pp. 50-72; and 'The Execution of Rebel Priests in the Western Rising of 1549', *The Journal of Ecclesiastical History*, vol. 71, no. 4 (October 2020), pp. 755–77. I am also most grateful to John Draisey, not only for his expert advice, on many occasions, but also for his permission to reproduce portions of several articles that originally appeared in the journal *Devon and Cornwall Notes and Queries*.

I thank my colleagues in the History Department at Southampton – especially David Brown, Mark Cornwall, Julie Gammon, Maria Hayward, Tony Kushner, Sarah Pearce and Helen Spurling – for their warm friendship over many years. I thank the several hundred former students who have taken my 'Tudor Rebellions' course – especially Mike Hunkin, Lucy Joyner, Joe McArdle and Sacha Robson – for all that I have learned from them. I thank the authors of the unpublished PhD theses I have read – most notably, A.R. Greenwood, Amanda Jones and Helen Speight – for the crucial insights I have gained from their splendid research. While writing this book, I have turned, again and again, to the works of Eamon Duffy and Diarmaid MacCulloch, and I am indebted to them both for their intellectual inspiration. I would also like to express my gratitude to the late Harry Guest, for words on the page, and to Susan Ballion, Rose McDowall and Laufey Soffia, for voices on the air. Many generous people have provided me with information, assistance and advice, including David Appleby, Simon Baker, Angela Broome, Emma Challinor, Sara Charles, Wendy Clarke, Martin Conway, John Cooper, Jannine Crocker, Alistair Dougall, Guy Edwards, Glenn Foard, Todd Gray, Mark Hailwood, Cheryl Hayden, Charlotte Hodgman, Andy Hopper, Oliver House, Alice Hunt, Ronald Hutton, Christine Linehan, Peter Marshall,

Joanna Mattingly, Ian Mortimore, Oliver Padel, Philip Payton, Ismini Pells, Alec Ryrie, Nick St Aubyn, Dan Spencer, Matthew Spriggs, my father Ian Stoyle, Retha Warnicke and Andy Wood. Lloyd Bowen, in particular, has been a wonderful comrade-in-arms. I am especially obliged to Peter Clarke, Diarmaid MacCulloch, Anthony Musson, Jonathan Vage, John Walter and my sister, Kate Tobin, all of whom read earlier drafts of portions of the text, and to the two anonymous readers for Yale University Press, who made many extremely helpful suggestions for improvements to the manuscript. Finally, I would like to thank Felicity Maunder and Lucy Buchan for overseeing the production of the book, Robert Shore for copy-editing the text, Katie Urquhart for her invaluable help with the illustrations, and Trixie Gadd for compiling the index.

I have three more very special debts: to my dear wife, Lynn, who supported me, in so many different ways, while I was researching and writing this book; to Heather McCallum, my editor at Yale and a much valued friend, who spurred me on into finishing it; and to my former tutor George Bernard, who not only read the text in draft, but who also did more than anyone else to inspire it. It was George who introduced me to the academic study of the Tudor period, and who first encouraged me to believe that I might one day become a Tudor historian myself; this book is dedicated to him.

Mark Stoyle
Caerruthe
5 April 2022

# ABBREVIATIONS

| | |
|---|---|
| ***APC*** | *Acts of the Privy Council of England* |
| **BL** | British Library, London |
| **Bod.** | Bodleian Library, Oxford |
| **Carew** | J. Chynoweth, N. Orme and A. Walsham (eds), *The Survey of Cornwall, by Richard Carew* (DCRS, New Series, 47, 2004) |
| ***CPR*** | *Calendar of the Patent Rolls* |
| ***CSPD*** | *Calendars of State Papers, Domestic* |
| ***CSPS*** | *Calendar of State Papers, Spanish* |
| ***D&C*** | Dean and Chapter Archives, Exeter |
| ***DCNQ*** | *Devon and Cornwall Notes and Queries* |
| **DCRS** | Devon and Cornwall Record Society |
| **DHC** | Devon Heritage Centre, Exeter |
| **ECA** | Exeter City Archives |
| **EETS** | Early English Texts Society |
| ***EHR*** | *English Historical Review* |
| ***FRDK*** | Anon. (ed.), *Fourth Report of the Deputy Keeper of the Public Records* (London, 1843) |
| **HMC** | Historical Manuscripts Commission |
| **Holinshed** | R. Holinshed, *The Third Volume of Chronicles . . . Now Newlie Recognised, Augmented and Continued . . . to the Yeare 1586* (London, 1587) |
| ***HR*** | *Historical Research* |

| | |
|---|---|
| ***JBS*** | *Journal of British Studies* |
| ***JEH*** | *Journal of Ecclesiastical History* |
| **Jones** | A.C. Jones, 'Commotion Time: The English Risings of 1549' (unpublished PhD thesis, University of Warwick, 2003) |
| ***JRIC*** | *Journal of the Royal Institution of Cornwall* |
| **KCC** | King's College, Cambridge |
| **KK** | Kresen Kernow, Redruth |
| ***L&P*** | J.S. Brewer, J. Gairdner and R.H. Brodie (eds), *Letters and Papers, Foreign and Domestic, of the Reign of Henry VIII* (21 vols, 1862–1932) |
| ***ODNB*** | *Oxford Dictionary of National Biography* |
| ***P&P*** | *Past and Present* |
| **Pocock** | N. Pocock (ed.), *Troubles Connected with the Prayer Book of 1549* (Camden Society, New Series, 37, 1884) |
| **RHS** | Royal Historical Society |
| **Rose-Troup** | F. Rose-Troup, *The Western Rebellion of 1549: An Account of the Insurrections in Devonshire and Cornwall against Religious Innovations in the Reign of Edward VI* (London, 1913) |
| ***RTDA*** | *Report and Transactions of the Devonshire Association* |
| **SHC** | Somerset Heritage Centre, Taunton |
| **SP** | State Papers |
| **Speight** | H.M. Speight, 'Local Government and Politics in Devon and Cornwall, 1509–1549, with Special Reference to the South Western Rebellion of 1549' (unpublished PhD thesis, University of Sussex, 1991) |
| **TNA** | The National Archives, Kew, London |
| ***TRHS*** | *Transactions of the Royal Historical Society* |
| ***TRP*** | P.L. Hughes and J.F. Larkin (eds), *Tudor Royal Proclamations: Volume I, The Early Tudors, 1485–1553* (New Haven and London, 1964) |
| **WCSL** | West Country Studies Library, Exeter |
| **WDRO** | West Devon Record Office, Plymouth |

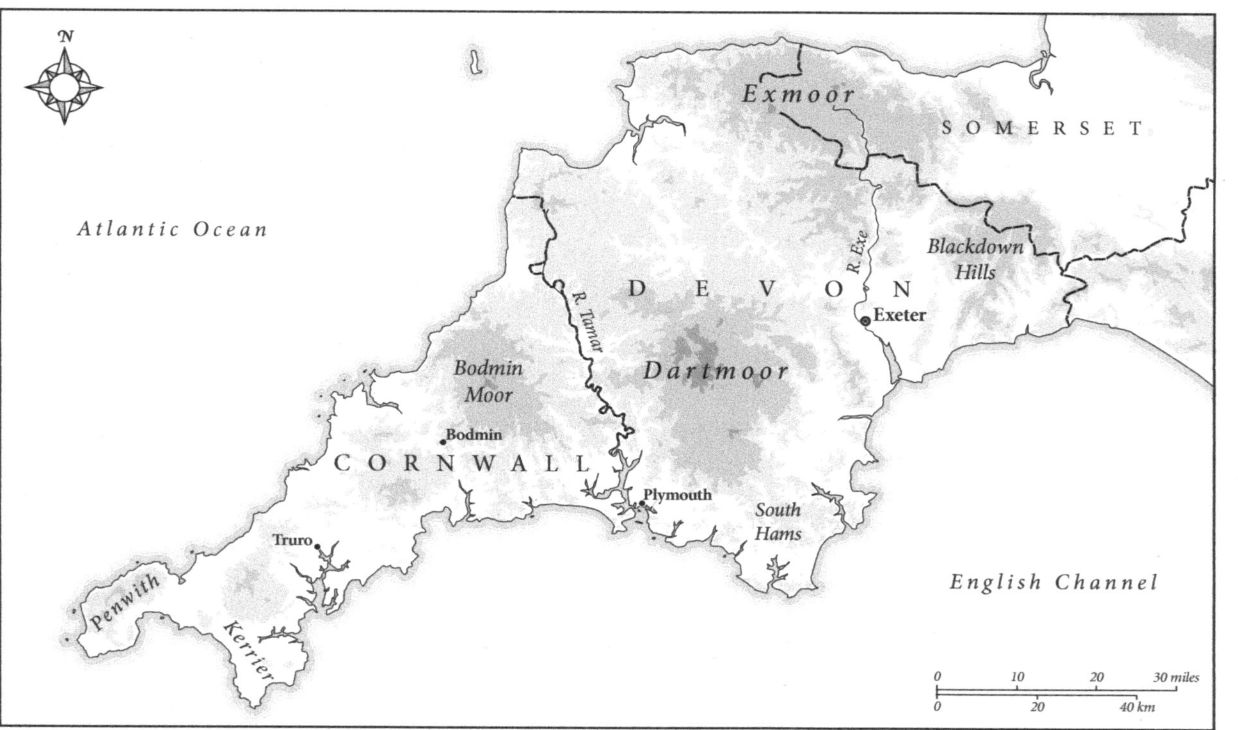


Map 1 – Devon and Cornwall: main physical features

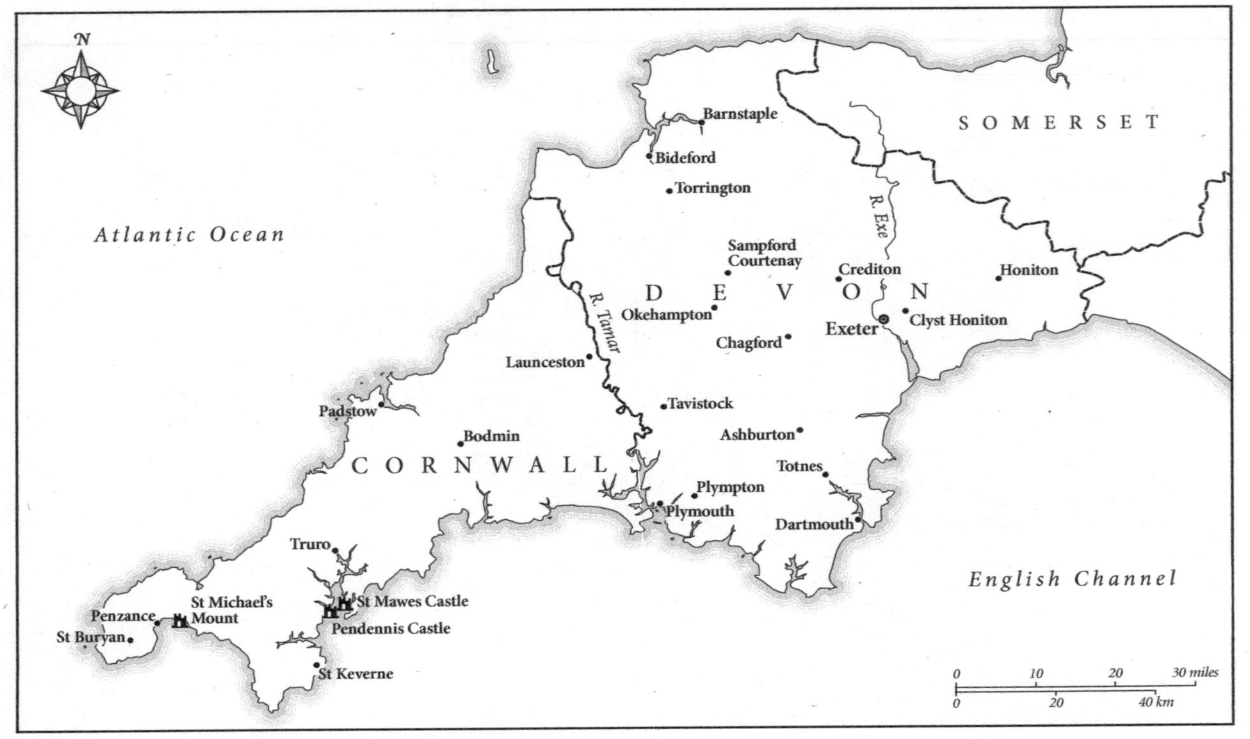


Map 2 – Devon and Cornwall: towns and villages

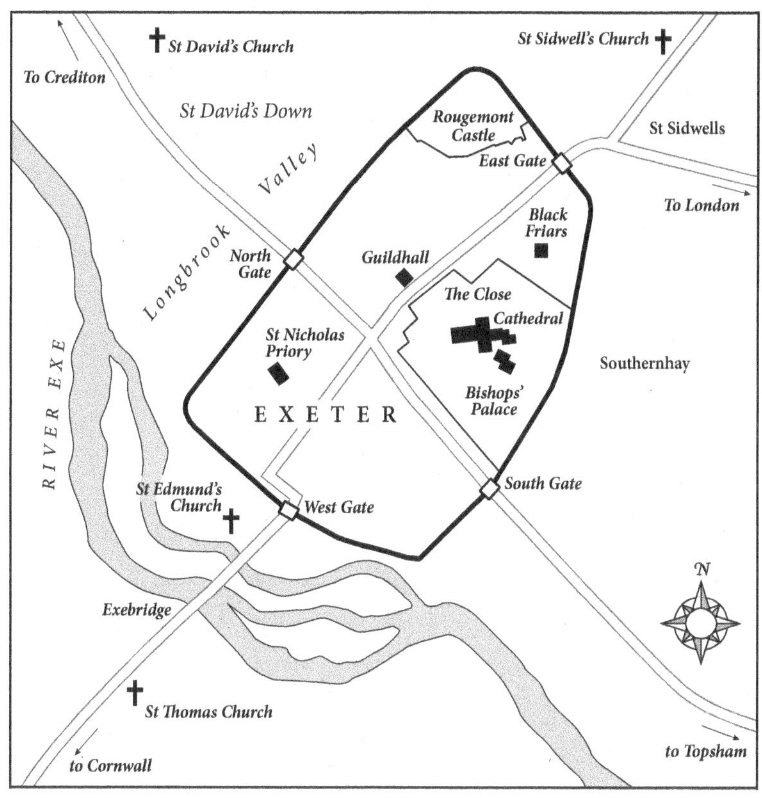


Map 3 – Exeter in the 1540s

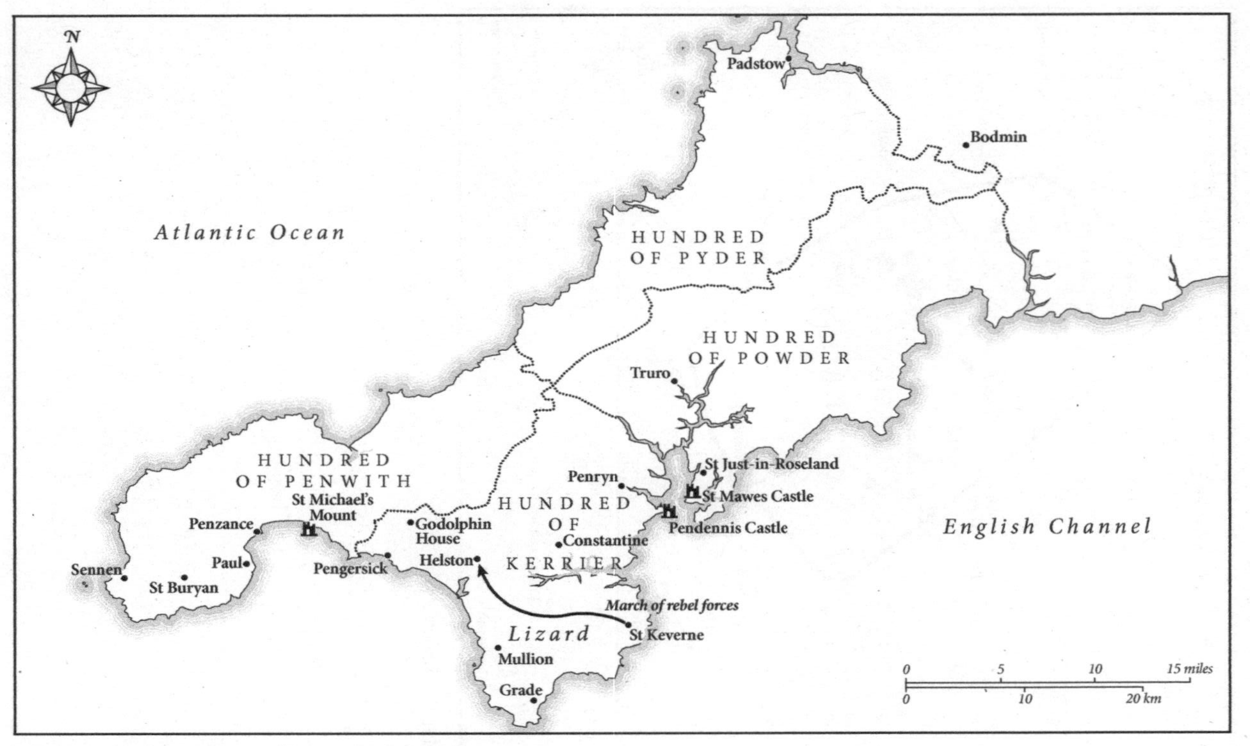


Map 4 – The Cornish commotion of April 1548

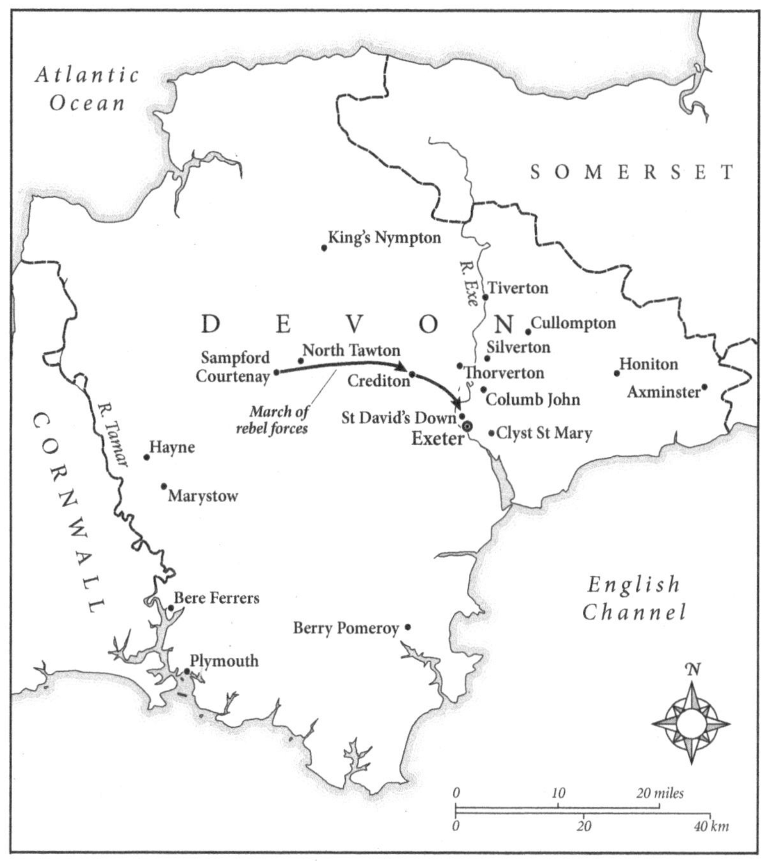


Map 5 – The outbreak of the Western Rising in Devon, June 1549

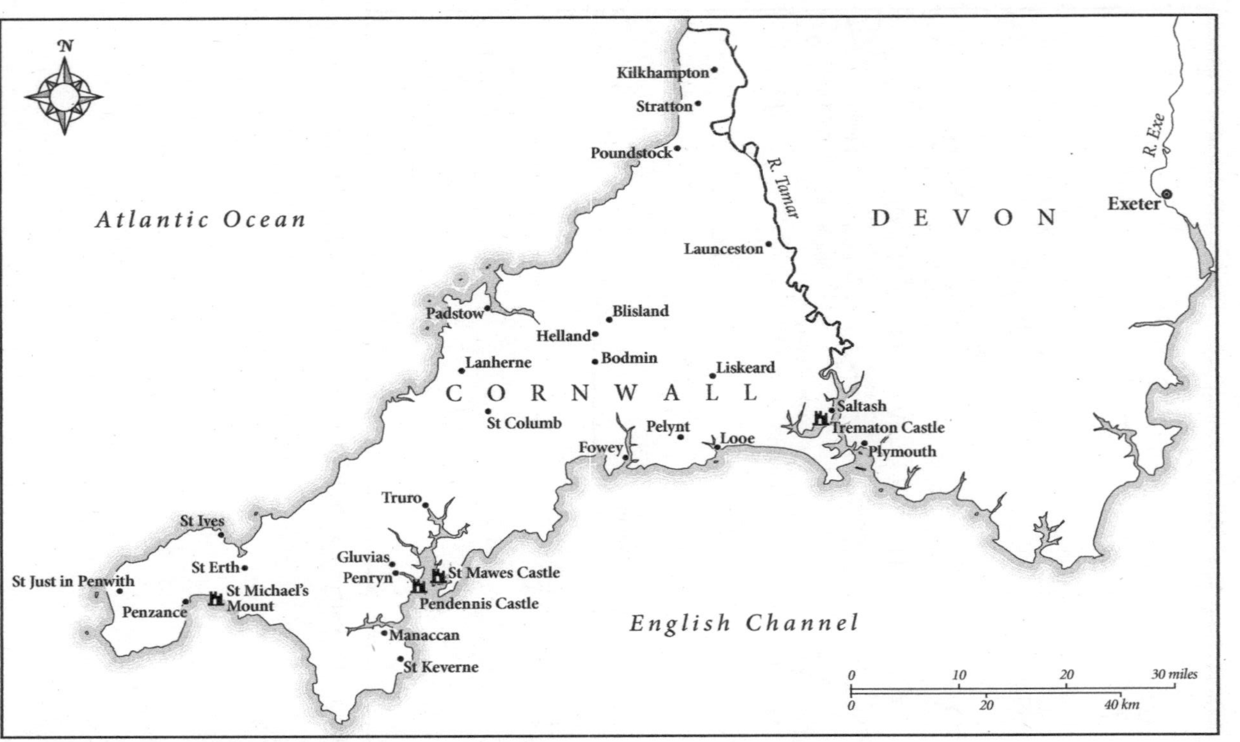


Map 6 – The Western Rising in Cornwall, July to August 1549

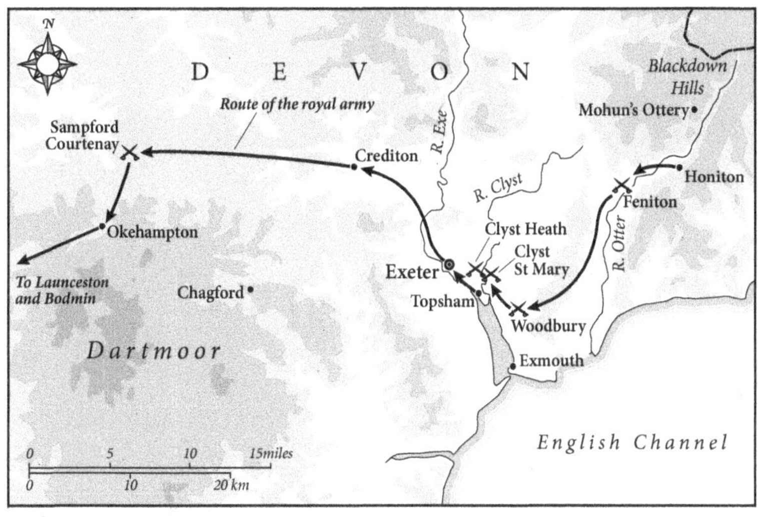


Map 7 – The defeat of the Western Rebels, July to August 1549

# INTRODUCTION

On Whit Monday 1549, two respectable inhabitants of the remote Devon parish of Sampford Courtenay got into an argument with their vicar outside the village church. The quarrel was about the religious service which the clergyman had held in that church the day before: a service he had conducted – as all parish priests across the kingdom had been enjoined to do – along the lines laid down in the new Book of Common Prayer which had recently been issued by the government in London. Within a week of this initial dispute, the church had become the focal point of a major popular protest, or 'stir'; within a fortnight, a large body of men from Sampford Courtenay and the surrounding parishes had set off to the nearby market town of Crediton with the aim of expressing their displeasure at the new service book and at various other matters, and of seeking redress; and within a month, the whole of Devon and Cornwall was in uproar. So serious did the disturbances in the West Country eventually become that the councillors of the boy-king, Edward VI – who had come to the throne at the age of just nine, two years before – were forced to send an army to put them down. During July and early August, a series of savage military encounters took place in the East Devon countryside, as the protestors – most of them agricultural workers, rural craftsmen, tin miners and other ordinary folk – battled it out with the forces sent against them by the Crown: forces that were largely composed of gentlemen's retinues and bands of professional mercenary soldiers. Having been badly worsted in these encounters and driven from their positions around the regional capital of Exeter – which they had besieged for some five weeks – the protestors rallied again at Sampford Courtenay. Here, the royal army advanced upon them on 18 August and, after another desperate battle, cut them to pieces. By the end of that month, order had finally been restored throughout the whole of Devon and Cornwall – and perhaps as many as 4,000 local men had been killed.

The disturbances that took place in the West Country during the summer of 1549 may be regarded, collectively, as the most catastrophic episode to have occurred in the region between the Black Death of 1348–49 and the English Civil War of 1642–46. In addition to the thousands of local families that had been shattered as a result of their menfolk being killed or injured in the fighting, there were also thousands more whose members had been robbed, fined or threatened, either during the course of the protests themselves or during their subsequent, brutal suppression. Nor was this all, for local communities were left fractured and deeply divided after the disturbances had come to an end, with people throughout the region remembering all too well which of their neighbours had participated in the protests or helped to further them, on the one hand, and which had stood back from those protests or actively helped to suppress them, on the other. So divisive was the memory of the events that had occurred during the summer of 1549, indeed, that, for decades to come, when local people found themselves obliged to refer to that troubled season, they tended to allude to it as 'the commotion': a conveniently neutral term that – like the phrase 'the Troubles', which is generally used today by the people of Northern Ireland to refer to their recent experiences – has the merit of acknowledging the fact of civil strife without apportioning blame to any particular party. But the episode came to be known by other, far more condemnatory names as well. Within weeks of the first stir at Sampford Courtenay, the government and its most committed local supporters had begun to refer to the demonstrators as 'rebels', and to the protest in which they were engaged as 'a rebellion' or 'an insurrection', and it was by such names as the 'insurrection in the West' or 'the rebellion in the western parts' that the affair was generally referred to by those who were seeking to distance themselves from it, both at the time and subsequently.

John Hooker, the Exeter man who lived through the disturbances, and went on to become their first and most important chronicler, described the episode as 'the Commotion, or Rebellion, in the Counties of Devon and Cornwall': a choice of words that nicely reflects the fact that Hooker himself was both a local man and a zealous loyalist.[1] Later generations of historians would know it as 'the Devonshire Rebellion' or 'the Western Rebellion', but, at around the time of the First World War, a shift in the established nomenclature seems to have taken place, for, in 1916, a local antiquarian named Beatrix Cresswell claimed that the rising was 'usually known as "The Prayer Book Rebellion"'.[2] How long the term had been circulating when Cresswell wrote these words is unclear, but the name rapidly caught on, especially among West Country folk, and it is as the 'Prayer Book Rebellion' that the episode is generally remembered in the region today. This is certainly the name by which it was first introduced to me, as a schoolboy, many years ago. However, in the title of this book, I have chosen to refer to it as the 'Western Rising' instead, in deference to the fact that the protestors would scarcely have regarded themselves as rebels at the time, however posterity may have chosen to view them.

The aim of my book is a simple one. It sets out to provide a new history of the Western Rising, and to consider the disturbances afresh: beginning with the preliminary tremors which may be seen, in retrospect, to have provided a series of ominous warnings – or 'fore-halsenings', as the expressive contemporary dialect term had it – of the great explosion of popular anger that was soon to come, and concluding with the series of major political aftershocks that occurred in London after the protests had been suppressed.[3] I am all too conscious of the fact that, in choosing to go over this ground again, much of it well trodden, I am following in the most illustrious of footsteps, for the Western Rising has attracted the attention of some of our greatest historians: not only of the West Country, but of the Tudor period in general. My debt to their collective endeavour is enormous, as will be apparent from my notes. Nevertheless, despite the wealth of research that has already been carried out on the rising, I hope that readers of this book will find it has new and interesting things to say about an episode that remains obscure and mysterious in many respects, and which has been well described, by the authors of the best overall survey of popular protest in sixteenth-century England, as 'this curiously perplexing rebellion'.[4]

The book is divided up into three parts. The first part is designed to set the scene, and begins with a chapter, 'Presages', that provides an introduction to the Tudor West Country, while at the same time considering the dramatic impact that the major religious reforms undertaken by Edward's pugnacious father, Henry VIII, during the 1530s and 1540s had upon the region and its inhabitants. This chapter is followed by one that demonstrates how the tempo of religious change quickened – across the West Country, just as across England as a whole – during the two years that followed Henry's death and his son's accession, in January 1547. This chapter, 'Foreshocks', also revisits 'the Cornish commotion' of 1548 – a short-lived but, from the Crown's point of view, deeply troubling *émeute* which flared up in West Cornwall in April that year, during the course of which a royal commissioner who was overseeing the removal of images from local churches was killed – and argues that the stir may well have owed something to Cornwall's unique cultural heritage, as well as to its deep-seated religious conservatism.

The second part of the book, which forms its core, concentrates on the events of the Western Rising itself, and is divided into four chapters. Chapter 3, 'Outbreak', explores how the protests at Sampford Courtenay were initially kindled, and how the flames of popular dissent then spread rapidly to envelop much of Devon by the end of June 1549. It also considers how the government of Edward Seymour, duke of Somerset – Edward VI's uncle, and the man who had been appointed to act as lord protector of England and governor of the king's person during his nephew's minority – initially reacted to these alarming events. Chapter 4, 'Escalation', investigates how the disturbances spread into Cornwall during early July, how the protestors in Devon assembled under 'captains' and began to besiege Exeter – whose civic leaders had resolved to hold out for the Crown – and how the government in London scrambled to deal with what was rapidly becoming a military emergency. Chapter 5,

'Flood Tide', shows how the rising reached its zenith during the second half of July, as an army of Cornishmen surged across the Tamar to join the Devonian protestors before the walls of Exeter, while Lord Russell – the nobleman who had been sent down from London by Protector Somerset with orders to suppress the disturbances, and who was then hovering uneasily on the borders of Devon and Somerset – briefly contemplated an ignominious retreat in the face of the thousands of insurgents who were by now massing just a few miles to the west. Chapter 6, 'Defeat', shows how the rising was eventually crushed in August, after Russell, who had by now received substantial reinforcements, first overcame the protestors in a series of pitched battles fought in East Devon, thereby enabling him to relieve the siege of Exeter, then scattered the insurgent forces that had regrouped at Sampford Courtenay and finally advanced into Cornwall itself, at the head of a large army, in order to stamp out the last remaining embers of resistance there.

The third and last part of the book focuses on the aftermath of the rising and is divided into two chapters. Chapter 7, 'Retribution', tells the grim story of what happened to the defeated insurgents after the protests had been crushed, as Russell and his subordinates identified the chief leaders of the rising and sent them up to London for interrogation by the king's Privy Council in preparation for their eventual trial, while scores of lesser 'rebels' suffered summary justice on the ground. As its title suggests, the final chapter of the book, 'Aftershocks', considers some of the consequences of the rising. The scene now shifts away from the West Country as we turn our gaze, instead, upon the bitter factional struggles that raged in London between October 1549 and January 1550. In early October, Protector Somerset was toppled from power. His fall was a direct consequence of the terror that the popular protests of the previous summer – protests that had occurred, not just in the West Country, but in many other parts of England, too – had inspired in the hearts of the ruling elite. The Western Rising had already helped to usher in dramatic political change, then, despite the insurgents' defeat, but its consequences could well have been more momentous still, for, in the wake of Somerset's fall, religious conservatives at court battled to take control of the boy-king's government and to install his Catholic half-sister, Mary, as regent. Had this happened, the imprisoned captains of the western rebels – now incarcerated in London and gloomily awaiting trial and surely inevitable execution – could well have seen their fortunes change overnight. The final chapter of the book therefore traces how this desperate battle for power at the heart of government played out, as the rebel captains – who possessed close links, as we shall see, to several of the key contestants in that battle – looked on, helpless, from the Tower: suspended, as it were, halfway between life and death.

As I hope that this brief prospectus has made clear – despite the fact that I am a proud West Country man myself, and have long felt a particular affinity with the local men and women who were unfortunate enough to find themselves caught up in 'the commotion' – I regard the story of the Western Rising as one that possesses a national, as well as a regional, significance. Most of the impulses that destabilised West Country society during the early years of the sixteenth century, and which were eventually to spark off the cataclysm of 1549, appear to have emanated from outside the region – and particularly from the political centre – rather than to have been generated organically, as it were, from within the region itself. While many scholars have, quite rightly, stressed the remote and inward-looking nature of local communities during the early 1500s, moreover, the surviving evidence makes it hard to doubt that at least some of the ordinary people who rose up in protest in the West Country – in both 1548 and 1549 – were fully aware of the currents of political and religious opposition to the Edwardine regime that existed in other parts of the kingdom, and eager to make common cause with allies elsewhere. Nor should we forget that, if many West Country folk were keeping a close eye on politico-religious developments beyond the borders of their region, then many outsiders were keeping a similarly watchful eye on politico-religious developments within the West Country itself. In Wales, in the North, in London and even on the continent, religious traditionalists watched the protests in Devon and Cornwall develop with bated breath during the early summer of 1549, as they wondered where those events might lead, while religious reformists did precisely the same thing: albeit with a sense of deep apprehension, rather than one of keen anticipation. Even the stories of those who stood at the very apex of Tudor society, of the members of the royal family itself, were intertwined with the stories of those who rose up in Devon and Cornwall in 1549, moreover, for – as the following chapters will show – Edward VI's own position was gravely imperilled by the insurgency, and on one occasion the boy-king came face to face with the western rebel captains who had challenged the regime of which he was the titular head. Similarly, the future Queen Mary may well have toyed, at least briefly, with the notion of installing herself as regent at the point of rebellious West Country swords during the summer of 1549 – and she possessed intriguing links with several of those who were regarded as the insurgents' backers. The Tudor world was a surprisingly small world, in other words, and, as this book hopes to show, it was a world that the West Country insurgents of 1549 came much closer than is generally realised to turning upside down.

# *Part I*
## *The Background*

# 1

## Presages
### The West Country under Henry VIII

The Western Rising of 1549 was not a storm that burst from a clear blue sky. On the contrary, it was the product of a general sense of suspicion, unease and resentment that had been building up across the kingdom for many years and which appears to have been especially strong among the people of Devon and Cornwall. We will turn to examine how this general sense of malaise developed in a moment, but first we should consider the particular terrain in which it took root: the terrain of the south-western peninsula, which, then as now, contained some of the most rugged, varied and beautiful landscapes in the entire kingdom. What would a traveller have seen if he or she had decided to ride the 150 miles or so from the eastern borders of Devon to Land's End in Cornwall during the reign of King Henry VIII? Fortunately, it is possible to answer this question with a certain degree of confidence, for the antiquarian John Leland journeyed through both counties during the late 1530s and early 1540s and the detailed notes that he made along the way provide us with a vivid impression of how the region then appeared to an inquisitive and sharp-eyed outsider.

Most people travelling into the West Country at this time would have made their approach along the ancient Roman road known as the Fosse Way and then followed the line of the present-day A303 over the high, rolling Blackdown Hills which separate Somerset from Devon. Once arrived in Devon, the traveller would then have continued along the main highway from London, passing first through the market town of Honiton, at the foot of the Blackdowns, and then over Fenny Bridges. Leland describes these as three 'fair stone bridges', which had been built to carry the highway over separate arms of the River Otter, at a place where it had been divided in order to power a series of mills used in the process of cloth manufacture, then Devon's most important industry.[1] From Fenny Bridges, the highway ran on, first to the little village of Clyst Honiton, and then across another stone bridge over the River Clyst. After crossing the bridge, the traveller would then have skirted around an area of open, uncultivated land known as Clyst Heath before, 3 miles later, reaching the city of Exeter, the regional capital of the West Country and one of the most populous communities in Tudor England. Some 8,000 people lived here during the reign of Henry VIII.[2]

Exeter was governed by a group of twenty-four townsmen known as 'the Chamber', the 'Council of Twenty-Four' or simply 'the Twenty-Four', who governed the city's affairs from their headquarters at the Guildhall. The city was divided up into four wards, or administrative districts, and boasted no fewer than seventeen separate parishes. Most of these were contained within the circuit of the ancient city wall, a formidable structure more than a mile in compass, studded with towers and castellated gates, but there were several suburban parishes as well. The most populous of these was the parish of St Sidwell's, on the eastern side of the city, which the traveller would have ridden through in order to enter the city via the East Gate, from which a gilded statue of Henry VIII's father gazed impassively down. Exeter was the chief centre of local government in Devon, and the magistrates of the county – the justices of the peace, or JPs – convened four times each year at Rougemont Castle, in the north-eastern corner of the city, to attend the judicial meetings known as the 'quarter sessions'. Exeter was also the seat of a bishopric, and for much of Henry's reign the diocese of Exeter – which included both Devon and Cornwall – was overseen by Bishop John Veysey, whom the king had appointed to that post in 1519.[3] The cathedral was the most splendid building in Exeter, its two great towers soaring skywards above the much smaller towers of the many parish churches that lay huddled in their shade. The cathedral was governed by the dean and Chapter, a group of senior clerics, whose substantial townhouses stood in the Cathedral Close. It was to the cathedral that most travellers visiting Exeter for the first time would initially have directed their steps.

After having explored Exeter, and perhaps stayed for a night or two in one of the great inns that lay in the centre of the city, the traveller would then have saddled up once more and ridden out through the North Gate, passing through the suburb of St David's – or, as Leland terms it, 'St David's Down' – on the way to Cowley Bridge. Here, the road crosses the River Exe – often considered to separate the lowland zone of England from the highland zone beyond – and passes on to Crediton, 7 miles to the north-west. Leland clearly enjoyed this stretch of his own journey, describing 'the ground betwixt Exeter and Crediton' as 'exceeding fair [in] corn, gresse [i.e., grass] and wood'. He also appears to have been favourably struck by Crediton itself, where, he noted, there was 'a praty [i.e., pretty] market'. The town 'usith clothing', he went on to observe – in other words, it was a cloth-making town – 'and most [of the inhabitants] therby lyvith': a remark that could have been made about most Devon towns at this time.[4] Sheep abounded in Tudor Devon as a consequence, and flocks of them were to be seen grazing on every side. As one leaves Crediton behind, the road begins slowly to rise, and the traveller would now have been able to glimpse the great granite mass of Dartmoor looming up some 10 miles to the south-west, while, if it was a clear day, it would also have been possible to pick out the hazier outline of Exmoor, some 20 miles to the north-east. Exmoor, which straddles the north-east Devon–Somerset border, was sheep-farming country par excellence. Sheep were also grazed round the edges of Dartmoor, but during the sixteenth century this wild upland district was better known as the centre of the Devon tin-mining industry. Tin miners, or 'tinners', followed their arduous trade all over the moor, and were renowned as some of the toughest men in the kingdom. The four so-called 'Stannary towns' of Chagford, Ashburton, Plympton and Tavistock, one set at each corner of Dartmoor, formed the chief centres of the Devon tin trade.[5]

Skirting the northern edge of Dartmoor, the traveller would next have passed through the villages of Copplestone and Bow, before arriving at the market town of Okehampton, where the formidable remains of a

Norman castle still lie just outside the town. From each of these places, roads radiated off towards the major towns of North Devon, Torrington, Barnstaple and Bideford – the last two were busy seaports, with many local people engaged in fishing and maritime trade. North Devon was also the home of the Bourchiers, earls of Bath, whose mansion house lay at Tawstock, just outside Barnstaple. From Okehampton, the traveller would have pressed on to Tavistock, the largest town on the western edge of the moor.[6] From here, one main road led south to Plymouth, which was a thriving port and one of Devon's most populous communities, with perhaps as many as 2,500 inhabitants.[7] Leland observed that 'the toun of Plymmouth is very large . . . [yet] there is but one paroch chirche', before going on to add that, in recent years, this overflowing church had been much improved, for a local merchant had paid for the making of a brand new steeple.[8] Beyond Plymouth, to the south-east, lay the district known as 'the South Hams', with the town of Totnes at its centre and the port of Dartmouth lying on its eastern seaboard. The traveller heading for Land's End would not have had time to visit this rich and fertile region, however, but would have sped on instead from Tavistock to the west, making for Greystone Bridge, 6 miles away, on the wooded banks of the River Tamar.

The Tamar, the river that separates Devon from Cornwall, was already an ancient administrative boundary by the time Henry VIII came to the throne. Indeed, according to a medieval chronicler, King Athelstan had driven the West Britons, or 'Cornwallish' – the indigenous inhabitants of the south-western peninsula – out of the lands to the east of the Tamar as long ago as 926 and had decreed that, henceforth, that river would serve as the line of demarcation between them and the encroaching Saxons.[9] During the sixteenth century, relations between the Cornish and their Devonian neighbours were far more harmonious. Nevertheless, under the Tudor monarchs, just as today, when one crossed the Tamar one was conscious of passing through a liminal zone: of moving, in a sense, from one cultural realm into another. The first thing the traveller would have seen, after clattering over the four elegant arches of the fifteenth-century Greystone Bridge, would have been the outline of the walled town of Launceston rising on the skyline beyond, with the great keep of its castle rising higher still above that. Leland, like most who passed this way, was highly impressed by Launceston. He began his description of it by noting that 'I went up by the hille through . . . [a] long suburbe ontylle I cam to the toun waul and gate, and so passed through the town . . . [ascending] the hille ontylle I cam to the very toppe of it'. Here, he feasted his eyes on what he termed 'the large and auncient castelle of Launstun [which] stondith on the nappe of the hill', before going on to note that 'this castel yet stondith, and the . . . [mound] that the kepe stondeth on is large and of a terrible hight, and the *arx* [i.e., the citadel] of it, having 3 severale wards, is the strongest . . . that ever I saw in any auncient worke'.[10] Coming from a man who had castle-crawled his way across much of the kingdom, this may be regarded as high praise indeed. Launceston was the administrative centre of eastern Cornwall. It was to Launceston Castle that the royal judges came on circuit from London twice a year, in order to preside over the judicial proceedings known as the assizes at which the most serious crimes committed in Cornwall over the preceding six months were tried; and it was at Launceston Castle, too, that 'the common Gayle [i.e., gaol]' for Cornwall was kept.[11]

From Launceston, the road led westwards: first ascending to cross the district of high granite moorland known then as 'Fowey Moor', but today as Bodmin Moor, before descending once more to Bodmin. This was the largest town in Cornwall, which is typically a county of scattered settlements: between 1,000 and 2,000 people lived here in the early sixteenth century.[12] Leland noted as he passed through that 'Bodmyn hath a market on every Saturday [which is] lyke a fair for the confluence of people', adding that 'the paroch church standith at the est end of the town and is a faire large thing'.[13] There were no fewer than thirty-five religious 'guilds', or 'devout fraternities', in Bodmin at this time, which had been set up by the inhabitants for various pious purposes: some measure, perhaps, of the town's populousness.[14] Richard Carew – himself an East Cornish gentleman and the author of *The Survey of Cornwall*, first published in 1603 – described Bodmin as 'the convenientest and usuall place of assembly for the whole County', and noted that it was also the town in which the JPs for the eastern division of Cornwall held their regular quarter sessions.[15] Ten miles to the north of Bodmin, on the sea coast, lay the 'fischar toune' of Padstow, one of Cornwall's major ports. Leland remarked that 'there use many Britons [i.e., Bretons] with smaul shippes to resorte to Padestow with commoditees of their countery and to b[u]y fische'.[16] As this comment suggests, the links between Brittany and Cornwall remained extremely strong during the early sixteenth century, not least because the Cornish and Breton languages were practically identical. Indeed, many parishes in the far west of Cornwall boasted substantial Breton populations, with no fewer than fourteen Breton families living in Constantine alone in 1544.[17]

We may note here that, while Cornish had once been spoken throughout practically the whole of Cornwall, during the medieval period the language had slowly begun to retreat in the face of English. As a result, by 1500 or thereabouts, Bodmin stood a little to the east of a linguistic boundary: a boundary that divided the west of Cornwall, where most of the common people still spoke Cornish, from the east, where both the common people and the gentry all spoke English. (In West Cornwall, at least some Cornish gentlemen and women were bilingual.)[18] As the traveller passed out of Bodmin and rode still further to the west, therefore, he or she would have noticed the Cornish cultural influence growing steadily stronger and might well have encountered increasing difficulty when needing to ask local people for directions, or to enquire about the price of food or lodgings. The writer Andrew Boorde compiled a helpful collection of translations of everyday Cornish phrases into English for visitors to Cornwall who found themselves in this situation in a book published in around 1542.[19]

There can be no doubt that there existed, at least at times, an undercurrent of ethnic tension between the Cornish – and perhaps especially the Cornish-speaking West Cornish – and their English neighbours. Writing half a century after Leland's time, Carew was to observe of the Cornish that

> one point of their former roughnesse, some of the Western people doe yet still retaine, & therethrough, in some measure, verifie that testimonie which Matthew of Westminster giveth of them, together

> with the Welsh, their ancient countrimen; namely, how fostering a fresh memories of their expulsion [from the rest of ancient Britain] long agoe by the English, they second the same with a bitter repining at their fellowship; and this the worst sort expresse in combining against [them]; and working them all the shrewd turns which with hope of impunitie they can devise.[20]

It is interesting to note that, in the original medieval text to which Carew here refers – a text that had been transcribed and published in London in 1567 – the attitude of those who were described as 'the miserable relics of the Britons' towards their English conquerors had been portrayed as more hostile still. Thus the medieval chronicler had written of the Welsh and Cornish 'that they always regard the nation of the Angles, even to this very day, with mortal hatred, as if it were owing to them that they were banished from their proper country, and they are not more willing to associate with them than with dogs'.[21] Having read this passage, Carew had clearly concluded that, while it was still possible to recognise the sense of ethnic alienation which the chronicler had described among the Cornish people in his own day, that sentiment was by now less strong and was confined to only 'some' of Cornwall's inhabitants – and that, even among these irreconcilables, it was only 'the worst sort' who were prepared to turn hostile thoughts into hostile actions. Carew's final comment on this subject, moreover – that the sense of bitter discontent which he had just described 'shooteth not to a like extremitie in all places and persons, but rather by little and little, weareth out unto a more milde and conversable fashion' – bears witness to his conviction or, at the very least, to his pious hope, that these long enmities would soon fade away.[22] Yet Carew's words also betray a recognition that the sentiment which a later writer would describe as 'a conceyled envye agaynste the Englishe' was stronger in some parts of Cornwall than it was in others – and it seems overwhelmingly probable that, during the reign of Henry VIII, just as during the reign of his youngest daughter, it was in Cornish-speaking West Cornwall that such sentiment was chiefly concentrated.[23]

From Bodmin, the main road led on towards Truro, some 25 miles further to the west. As Leland noted, however, a few miles to the north of that road lay the mansion house of Lanherne, which was the seat of the Arundells, the most powerful family in Cornwall. Leland refers to them simply as the 'great Arundale[s]', while Carew, writing half a century later, was more expansive, noting that 'the Country people entitle them "The great Arundels"' and adding that, not long since, they had enjoyed 'the greatest . . . love, living and respect in the Countrey'.[24] The head of the family in 1540 – the man whom Leland refers to as 'old Arundale of Lanheron' – was Sir John Arundell, the closest thing that Cornwall possessed to a resident peer.[25] His two adult sons were Sir John, his heir, and Sir Thomas. Both were highly influential in their own right, and Thomas, in particular, was well connected at court; Leland noted both men's names in his journal as he explored the countryside near Lanherne. He also noted the name of another locally significant figure, their cousin 'Humfre Arundale', the son of old Sir John Arundell's brother, Roger, whom Leland describes as 'a man of mene [i.e., many] lands, [and] nephew to [Sir John] Arundale'.[26] Humphrey Arundell – who was about twenty-seven years old in 1540 and lived in the parish of Helland, near Bodmin – was not as socially exalted as his cousins, but, as Leland's comment suggests, he was a man of considerable wealth: indeed, it has been calculated that he was among the twelve richest men in Cornwall.[27] Even so, Leland would doubtless have been flabbergasted to learn that, within ten years, the young Cornish gentleman whose name he had touched on so briefly in his text would be leading an armed host over the River Tamar.

Having made the journey from Bodmin to Truro, the traveller might well have been tempted to stop for a couple of nights. This would have made time for an excursion to the south to admire the twin artillery forts which had recently been erected – at enormous expense – on either side of Carrick Roads, the estuary of the River Fal, in order to protect the haven of Falmouth from attack by foreign enemies.[28] Work on these 'blockhouses', as they were originally known, had been going on since at least 1536, and by the time Leland visited, they were already extremely impressive.[29] At the western mouth of the haven, Leland wrote, was 'an hille wheron the king hath buildid a castel . . . caullid Pendinant [i.e., Pendennis] . . . [which] belongith to Mr Keligrew'.[30] (This was a reference to John Killigrew, of nearby Arwennack, the gentleman who had been associated with the fort since its inception.)[31] The headland on which Pendennis stands, Leland went on, 'is almost environed with the se[a], and where it is not [so surrounded] the ground is so low, and the cut to be made so little, that it were [practically] insulated'.[32] Looking out across the sparkling waters of the Fal from the demi-island on which Pendennis stood, it was possible to see the round central tower of a twin structure lying on the further shore, its banners waving lazily in the breeze: this was Pendennis's twin castle of St Mawes.

After having inspected Pendennis and returned to Truro, the traveller would then have been ready to proceed on the final stage of their journey, into the furthest extremities of Cornwall. Leaving Truro, the road passed through the two westernmost hundreds of Kerrier and Penwith, both still almost entirely Cornish-speaking during the 1540s. On this ride, the traveller would have glimpsed numerous tinworks, for the economy of Cornwall – to a much greater degree than that of Devon – was built on tin and, in this district in particular, there were thousands who laboured in that industry. In the midst of the richest workings lay Godolphin House, the home of Sir William Godolphin, a leading West Cornish gentleman whose family had grown rich on the profits of tin.[33] Next, the road led on to what was without doubt the most famous place in sixteenth-century Cornwall: the great fortress of St Michael's Mount. Long a place of pilgrimage, St Michael's Mount is an exquisite medieval castle and chapel combined, built on a rocky tidal island which stands on the edge of Mount's Bay. Few travellers could have resisted waiting until the tide went out and then passing over the glinting sands to explore this fabled place, which had withstood so many storms, both natural and man-made, over the previous centuries. From the Mount, the road led on to the little fishing town of Penzance and from there over the hills beyond into West Penwith, the curving arm of granite that forms the most westerly tip of Cornwall. Riding ever westwards, the traveller would next have seen the tower of St Buryan church, the tallest in the district, beckoning ahead, with the Atlantic light shining on the towers of the smaller churches scattered round about. Of these, the little church of Sennen, 4 miles on from St Buryan, is the most westerly of them all. From here, the weary traveller would have ridden on one further mile – over springy green turf, dotted with grey granite boulders and flecked with yellow gorse – before finally dismounting at the high cliff's edge overlooking the endlessly rolling breakers beyond. At which point, as Carew was later so elegantly to put it, 'your journey endeth with the land . . . whose promontory [is] . . . called . . . by the Cornish *Pedn an laaz* and by the English The lands end, [and] because we are arrived, I will here sit me down and rest'.[34]

The population of the jagged peninsula whose length and breadth we have just mentally traversed would, to modern eyes, appear remarkably thinly spread during the early sixteenth century; it has been estimated that there were some 40,000–50,000 people living in Cornwall at this time and Devon's population was probably three times as big.[35] In the West Country, as in early modern England as a whole, most ordinary people – the 'commons' or 'commoners', as they were termed – made their livings from working the land. But, as we have seen, there were also many thousands of local folk engaged in cloth-making and tin-mining, and in trades connected with the sea, while in the towns there would have been many artisans and makers of specialist wares. Exeter, of course, was a society all to itself and, as befitted a regional capital, possessed an unusually diverse and specialised economy. About matters of government, it seems fair to suggest, most people, most of the time, thought relatively little. It was clear to all that the king ruled the kingdom, that the nobles who were his right-hand men oversaw the governance of the regions of the country in which they dwelt, and that the senior gentlemen whom the monarch had selected to serve on the commission of the peace, that is to say, as JPs, both governed and oversaw the administration of the counties in which they lived. In addition, each county possessed a high sheriff: a local gentleman who had been 'pricked', or selected, to serve as the king's judicial representative in that shire for a single year. Whenever the monarch wished to have a particular task performed in a county or region, moreover, he would appoint a group of 'commissioners' to carry it out; once again, these individuals tended to be wealthy local gentlemen.

The role of Parliament at this time was chiefly to act as an advisory and tax-granting body. The monarch was free to summon and dissolve it at will, while the MPs who sat for the various constituencies were usually selected in advance from among the members of the local ruling elite and then returned unopposed, rather than being elected as the result of a genuine electoral contest as they are today. And, needless to say, all of those who were chosen as MPs were gentlemen – or, at the very least, wealthy merchants or lawyers.

It will be seen from what has already been said that a tiny, wealthy elite held all the levers of power in sixteenth-century Devon and Cornwall. But this is not to say that those below the level of the great gentry possessed no power at all. Middle-ranking gentlemen and even minor gentlemen – 'hedge gentry', as we might term them – were frequently appointed to the less important local offices, and most commanded considerable respect in their own neighbourhoods. In the towns, moreover, successful merchants and traders could rise to become mayors, aldermen, bailiffs and portreeves, and, in these roles, could exercise genuine power within their own communities. And in the countryside, too, those just below the level of the gentry – the yeomen, or richer farmers – could take on responsible and respected offices in their own parish: like that of constable, for example, or of churchwarden.

Mention of this last office reminds us that, running alongside the power of the state, and helping to bolster it, was the power of the Church. When Henry VIII acceded to the throne, the Church in England was still a branch of the universal Catholic Church, of which the pope in Rome was the supreme head. More important than the pope in terms of the routine governance of the Church in this country, however, were the archbishops of Canterbury and York, and, beneath them, the bishops of the nineteen individual dioceses. We have already met John Veysey, who became bishop of Exeter in 1519 and was supposed, in theory, to govern the diocese from his palace beside the cathedral. But Veysey was a busy man and was sometimes required to carry out other duties elsewhere. In 1526, for example, he was appointed president of the Council of the Marches and governor of the ten-year-old daughter of Henry VIII and Catherine of Aragon, the Lady Mary: who, it was later recalled, 'dyd [always] honor and reverense hyme' thereafter.[36] In Veysey's absence, many of his pastoral and administrative duties were carried out by deputies.

Beneath these deputies came other senior churchmen, the middle managers of the Church, and below them again came the parochial clergy: the incumbents of the 530 or so parishes into which the diocese was divided.[37] It was these parish priests who would conduct divine service in the local church, perform christenings, marriages and burials, and generally act as spiritual fathers to the members of their flock. Nor did this exhaust the list of the region's churchmen because, beneath the parish priests, came the unbeneficed clergy: those who had taken holy orders, but who did not possess a permanent post. There were hundreds of these 'stipendiary priests' in the early sixteenth-century West Country, and they served in many different roles, most notably as curates and as chantry priests, who said prayers for the souls of the dead. Last but by no means least, there were several hundred members of religious orders – monks, canons, nuns and friars – who lived in the various monasteries, friaries and collegiate churches that were scattered across the region.[38]

The religious life over which these churchmen presided was an extraordinarily rich and diverse one, and, as scholars are increasingly coming to realise, in the early 1500s most ordinary folk remained deeply attached to their traditional faith. Most of the parish churches in the West Country were not only elegant on the outside at this time but were beautifully embellished on the inside as well. Upon entering a typical parish church during the early sixteenth century, one's eye would immediately have fallen upon vibrant wall paintings; jewel-like stained-glass windows; elaborately carved crucifixes, the largest of them all mounted in the rood loft, above the painted rood screen; gilded images of saints; and the 'lights', or candles, which were left constantly burning before these figures. The fact that all of this ornamentation and much more besides, as well as the routine maintenance of the church itself, was paid for by the parishioners speaks volumes for the depth of their devotion, as does the alacrity with which so many people took part in religious festivals of all sorts, observed the regular saints' days, or 'holy days', and joined parish guilds. There were some who questioned elements of the traditional faith, of course, and during the twenty years or so before and after 1400, religious dissenters, known as 'Lollards', had created a considerable stir. Lollards disliked many of the practices of the Catholic

Church. In particular, they were often sceptical about the doctrine of transubstantiation – that is to say, the belief that the body and blood of Christ were actually present in the bread and wine that were used in the Church's central act of worship, the religious ceremony generally known as 'the mass'. Lollards also advocated the reading of the Bible in the vernacular – that is to say, in English rather than in Latin – and were scathing about some popular religious practices, particularly those of praying to saints and going on pilgrimage to shrines.[39] Yet the Lollards had been fiercely persecuted as heretics and, while Lollardy had clung on in certain parts of England for over a century after 1400, there is no sign that it ever put down strong roots in Devon or Cornwall.[40]

At the dawn of the 1520s, then, the West Country was a remote but generally well-ordered and well-governed part of the realm. If the inhabitants of the region were divided by geography, by social rank and sometimes by language and culture, too, they were nevertheless united in their devotion to the king, to God and to the practice of their traditional faith. Yet over the succeeding years an uncomfortable suspicion would begin to grow in many local people's minds that it might no longer be possible to cleave to all three of these unifying pillars at once. The opening stages of the Reformation in Europe – which saw Martin Luther and other reformist thinkers angrily denouncing almost every aspect of the Catholic Church – appear to have created few ripples in Devon and Cornwall. Instead, life here went on much as usual, though one appointment fraught with future significance was made. In 1527, Reginald Pole – a nobleman's son, as well as an excellent scholar – was chosen by the king as dean of Exeter Cathedral. Pole does not appear to have resided in Exeter for any appreciable length of time, but he soon won local admirers. This was to have important consequences when Pole and Henry VIII himself later, spectacularly, fell out.

It was also in 1527 that the king first began to have 'scruples' about his marriage to Catherine of Aragon. Having managed to persuade himself that the marriage had been illegitimate – because Catherine had previously, albeit briefly, been married to his brother, now dead – and that this was why God had not blessed them with a male heir, Henry reached the conclusion that the match must be annulled. This would leave him free to marry Anne Boleyn, the much younger woman with whom he was already, conveniently enough, conducting a romantic dalliance. Henry therefore demanded that the pope grant him an annulment. When this was not forthcoming, he began to put pressure on the supreme pontiff to accede to his request by attacking the power of the Church in England, and the so-called 'Reformation Parliament' of 1529 was probably called with precisely this aim in mind.[41] Meanwhile, under the influence of events on the continent, reformist – or 'evangelical' – religious ideas were beginning to circulate increasingly widely in England.[42] Evangelicals were men and women who wished to return to the true spirit of the scriptures, as they had been preached by Christ, and who were convinced that this could be achieved by stripping the Church of all of the erroneous, non-scriptural accretions that had grown up around it during the medieval period. Individuals who embraced these beliefs saw themselves as reformers, or revivers, who were purifying the Church of centuries of corruption, but those who took the opposing view saw them simply as heretics: enemies of God and of the true Christian faith.

In October 1531, a frisson of horror ran through the streets of Exeter when several handwritten notices declaring that 'The Pope is Anti-Christ and we ought to woorship God oenly and no Saintes' were found nailed upon the doors of several city churches. The leading churchmen in Exeter at this time – prominent among them, according to a later account, Dr John Moreman and Dr Richard Crispin – subsequently preached from their pulpits against the heresies contained in the 'bills' and also consulted with 'the officers ... of that citie' about the best means through which the 'enormious heretique, whiche had pricked up those Bylles, might be espied and knowen'. Suspicion eventually fell on Thomas Benet, a schoolmaster who had recently moved to the city, and he was duly arrested and interrogated. When Benet refused to recant, he was tried as a heretic, found guilty and sentenced to be burned at the stake. Accordingly, in January 1532, Benet was handed over to Sir Thomas Denys of Holcombe Burnell, near Exeter. Denys was one of Devon's most important gentry governors, who was then serving as sheriff and was thus responsible for overseeing the punishment of heretics. Denys accordingly conveyed Benet to Livery Dole, in Heavitree parish, just beyond the city boundaries. Once Benet had been tied to the stake and had said a last prayer, the officials standing by 'caused the wood & furses to bee set a fire' and the condemned man went to his terrible end. The members of the crowd that had assembled to watch this ghoulish spectacle clearly felt little sympathy for Benet. On the contrary, as an evangelically minded writer later sorrowfully recorded: 'such was the devilishe rage of the blynd people, that wel was hee or shee that coulde catche a sticke or furse to cast into the fire'.[43]

The violent popular hostility that was expressed against Benet may well have been, at least in part, a product of local unease about the direction of government policy. In London, Henry VIII – furious that his unfortunate matrimonial problem, tactfully dubbed 'the king's great matter', had not yet been resolved – had been stepping up his campaign against the Church and had even begun to hint that he might become a 'Lutheran' himself if his demand for an annulment was not met. In 1530, he had accused the churchmen of England of *praemunire* – that is to say, of breaching the acts designed to secure the rights of the Crown against encroachments by the papacy – and in 1531, through the so-called 'submission of the clergy', they had been forced to pay almost £120,000 to secure a pardon for this supposed offence. During the following year, Henry forced convocation, the clerical parliament, to surrender some of its key legislative powers. Many were alarmed by the king's assaults on the Church, but few dared to speak out openly against them. One of the boldest critics of Crown policy during these years was a young woman named Elizabeth Barton, the so-called 'Nun of Kent'. Barton claimed to have been visited by an angel, who had told her that Henry 'was not to take away any of the pope's rights' and that he should extirpate all those who espoused 'the new learning' instead. In addition, Barton's celestial visitor had allegedly foretold that, if the king married Anne Boleyn, 'the vengeance of God would plague him'.[44] Needless to say, there were many who took heart from Barton's visions, and several friars and monks from Canterbury later confessed that they had gone 'to sundry places ... and made secret relation of them' to a string of prominent individuals. Among them were the Lady Mary; 'the lady

Marques of Exeter' (this was Gertrude, the wife of Henry Courtenay, marquess of Exeter, who possessed huge estates in the West, though he did not reside there); Sir Thomas Arundell; and John Arundell.[45] Barton was eventually executed for treason by a vengeful king, but the fact that both the Courtenays and the Arundells had been contacted by her emissaries is a straw in the wind: a hint that both families were already beginning to be seen as defenders of the traditional faith.

Henry VIII, meanwhile, was pressing ahead with both his marriage plans and his assault upon the Church. In 1532, Thomas Cranmer, a churchman of strongly reformist leanings, was made archbishop of Canterbury, and in 1533 Cranmer conducted a ceremony of marriage between the king and Anne Boleyn and declared Henry's previous marriage to be null and void. When the pope refused to consent to this, Henry – assisted by his chief minister, Thomas Cromwell, whom many contemporaries also believed to be a 'heretic' – initiated a wave of new measures designed still further to reduce papal influence over the English Church. Henceforth, it was forbidden to make appeals to the pope, for example, or to send any payments to Rome, and Henry issued a proclamation directing that the pope's name should be struck out of all prayer books, so that it should be 'never more . . . remembered, but perpetually suppressed and obscured'.[46] At the same time, reformist churchmen were continuing to expound their message, and in June 1534 the fiery theologian Hugh Latimer was sent to deliver what may well have been the first evangelical sermons ever to have been heard in Exeter.[47] Huge numbers of people turned out to listen to Latimer, and although many of the churchmen of Exeter reviled him, and one local gentleman attempted to drag him out of the pulpit, calling him 'heretic knave', Latimer also made converts in the city.[48] From now on the reformist message would begin to be heard with increasing frequency in West Country communities, which had hitherto been almost entirely free from such evangelising currents of thought.

Later that same year, Parliament passed the Act of Supremacy, which set the seal upon all of the measures that had gone before it, and formally declared that the king, rather than the pope, was 'supreme head of the Church of England'.[49] Having brought the Church completely under his control, Henry was now determined to take revenge on the religious orders, which he regarded as the chief centres of resistance to the royal supremacy. In January 1535, the king appointed Cromwell as his vicar-general and ordered him to institute 'visitations', or formal inspections, of all the religious houses in the kingdom.[50] Cromwell was deeply unpopular with religious traditionalists, many of whom believed that it was his influence and that of other 'heretics' about the throne that had persuaded the king to launch his assault upon the Church in the first place. This was as true in the West Country as it was everywhere else, and in March 1535 one of Cromwell's local correspondents informed him that Sir Thomas Arundell and his father, old Sir John of Lanherne, 'little regard[ed]' the new vicar-general's 'authority' and that one of their associates 'makes many cracks in your name at Launson [i.e., Launceston]'.[51] Later that year, Sir Thomas's brother, John Arundell the younger, had the audacity to restore the former abbot of Hartland Abbey to his place by force, despite the fact that he had previously been dismissed on Cromwell's orders.[52] During that same year, moreover, it was reported from Bodmin that Roger Arundell of Helland – the brother of old Sir John and the father of Humphrey – was unlawfully retaining many men 'which yn . . . tavarnes bost & crake that it is nat Cromwell that shall rule there mast[er]'.[53] Taken together, these snippets of evidence suggest that the Arundells may by now have been adopting a covertly critical stance towards at least some of the regime's religious policies.

The following year, 1536, saw further momentous changes. In January, first of all, Catherine of Aragon died. Then, in March, Parliament passed an act directing that the smaller religious houses should be dissolved and their property given to the Crown. In May, Anne Boleyn was accused of multiple adulteries and executed for treason, leaving Henry VIII free to marry his third wife, Jane Seymour (who, within the year, died in giving birth to Henry's son and future heir, Edward). In July, convocation passed the Ten Articles, the Church of England's first statement of independent doctrine, followed by an act ordering that the dedication feasts of all churches should henceforth be held in early October, and that their traditional patronal festivals, or 'church holy days', should no longer be

observed.[54] In August, finally, the first set of 'royal injunctions' was issued to the clergy, ordering them to expound the royal supremacy and to preach against the 'usurped power ... of the Pope'; to ensure that the recent order concerning the reduction in the number of dedication feasts was obeyed; to ensure that all children were now taught 'their *Pater Noster*, the Articles of our Faith and the Ten Commandments in their mother tongue', rather than in Latin; and to ensure that a copy of the Bible in English was placed in every parish church.[55]

Dr John Tregonwell, a Cornish lawyer, was one of the visitors who had been appointed to inspect the religious houses during the previous year. He also appears to have been tasked by Cromwell with overseeing the introduction of the injunctions in the West Country, perhaps because it was feared that they might cause particular resentment in this highly traditional part of the realm.[56] The news that Tregonwell was on his way with new directives relating to the governance of the Church certainly caused considerable apprehension in Cornwall. After he had arrived at Penryn, in the far west of the county, in September 1536, Tregonwell wrote to Cromwell, informing him that 'before my coming ynto this Contrie, hit was (by some light persons) reportyde that I shulde come hither with the kingys graces authoritye ... to take away the crosses, challyshes and other ydells of the churches'.[57] The fact that, even as early as this, many Cornish people had already begun to fear that the Crown's agents were bent on removing the crucifixes and the images of saints that stood in their churches, and on confiscating the chalices and other pieces of silver plate that parishioners had donated to those churches over the years, is significant, and reveals the extent to which royal policy was now starting to impact local communities. Tregonwell hastened to add that, notwithstanding these rumours,

> at my commyng into this sheire, I fownde as myche conformytye emongeste men and as reddye to obbaye the kynges authorytie yn inuncycons and other orders ... as ever I sawe ... yn soo myche that I dare affyrme ... that this contrye ys as quiet and trewe to the king ... as any sheire w[ith]yn his graces realme

– words that may be said to protest too much and which, again, hint that the regime had been expecting the reforms to provoke some sort of backlash in Cornwall. Tregonwell went on to observe that the people were 'mervelowsly well pleasyde' to have been recently assured by Sir William Godolphin that the king had agreed, at Cromwell's intercession, that they should still be permitted to celebrate their parochial dedication feasts. These words show that the order for the abrogation of the holy days had also caused unhappiness in Cornwall: so much unhappiness, indeed, that Godolphin had gone so far as to declare – on whose authority is uncertain – that that order had been revoked.[58]

If Tregonwell encountered unease about the Crown's religious policies in Cornwall, he encountered open opposition to them in Exeter. According to a later account by the Exeter chronicler John Hooker, following the Act of Parliament ordering the dissolution of the smaller monasteries, Tregonwell, Sir Thomas Arundell and others

> were apoynted to be commissioners for the same yn the west partyes, who came to this cittie yn the somer tyme to exequte theire commissyon and begynnynge first with the priorie of St Nicholas, after that they [had] viewed the same they went thense to dynner and commanded . . . [a man] in the tyme of theire absence, to pull downe the Rood lofte in the churche.

Word of what was happening at the priory was beginning to spread through the neighbouring streets, however, 'and before they dyd returne', Hooker continues,

> certayne women and wyffes yn the cittie, namely Jone Reeve, Elizabeth Glandfeld, Agnes Collaton, Alys Myller, Jone Reede and others myndinge to stopp the suppressing of that house, came yn all hast[e] to the said church, some with spykes, some with shovells, some with pykes, and some with such tooles as they could geyte.

Finding the door to the priory shut fast, the women now smashed it open and, running to the rood loft, began to throw stones at the man who was dismantling it. He fled into the tower of the church, 'yet they pursued hym so egerlye that he was enforced to leape out at a wyndo[w] . . . to save hymselff'. John Blackaller, one of the city aldermen, now appeared on the scene and attempted to pacify the enraged women. 'But how so ever he talked with theym, they werr playne with him,' Hooker goes on, 'and the foresaid Elizabeth Glandfield gave hym a blowe and sent him packinge'. The women now blockaded themselves into the priory, and 'bestowed theym selffes yn places meet as they thoughte to stand to their defense.' Yet eventually, the mayor and his officers broke in upon the protestors, apprehended them and committed them to prison.[59]

This was one of the most determined protests against the king's religious policies to have occurred anywhere in the kingdom so far, but the visitors proved surprisingly lenient towards the demonstrators. Hooker tells us that, after they had been told what had happened, Tregonwell, Arundell and the others simply thanked the mayor for what he had done, continued with the suppression of the priory and 'before their departure entreated the mayor for releasynge of the women'.[60] Confirmation that the visitors had, if anything, sought to play down the whole affair comes from a quite independent document, written some time later, in February 1537.[61] This is a letter sent by Sir Thomas Denys and another JP, together with the mayor of Exeter, to Henry Courtenay, marquess of Exeter. The writers began by observing that they had recently received letters from Courtenay in which he had stated that it was understood – presumably at court – that 'there shuld be dyvers men assembled and disguised in womyns apparel at the late unlawfull assemble at the priory of Saynt Nicholas'. Courtenay had therefore ordered Denys and the others to make further enquiries into the matter, so 'that the kynges grace maybe advertised of the trouth'. Clearly sensing an implied rebuke here, the writers hastened to inform Courtenay that the matter had already been investigated some time ago 'by us and by Sir Thomas Arundell . . . who promised us to make relacion to the kings grace . . . of all the said unlawfull assemblie, else we would . . . have certified his grace ... ourselves with all celerity before this tyme'.[62] The question of why Arundell had not fulfilled his promise was left hanging in the air. Was it because he had not considered this all-female riot to present a genuine threat, perhaps? Was it because he had feared that he and the other visitors might be blamed for failing to prevent the disturbances? Or was it because he himself felt a secret sympathy for the protestors' cause?

Denys and the others now hurried to assure Courtenay that, according to his orders, they had, the day before, summoned before them in the Guildhall 'a great nombre of women which were amonge other the chief doers of the said unawfull assemblie and also dyvers of thaier husbands', swearing them 'apon a boke' to make truthful answer to a series of questions. Had they had 'any trayterous entent towards the Kynges grace or any of his councell' at the time that 'they dyd advance themselves to do the said unlawfull actc', for example? Had there been any men dressed in women's clothes among the rioters? Had they been encouraged by their husbands, or by any other men, to take part in the riot? Had they been 'prevy to the letting falle and setting up of dyvers sedicious billes ayenst the mayre of the said cety for the Imprisonment of the said offenders'? Did they know who had written or set up these bills? And finally, 'what was the ... cause and entent of thaier said unlawfull assembl[i]e'? Unsurprisingly, the women who had been summoned before the magistrates answered all of the first five questions in the negative. To the sixth, they replied that their only intent had been to stop the activities of two Breton carpenters who, they said, had 'made theire advaunte that they wuld pull downe the crucyfx of the sayd church ... withal the saynts there naming them to be Idolls'.[63] Here again, we see clear evidence of the passionate devotion that West Country people felt for the crosses and the images of the saints that stood in their churches – and the animosity which they felt for those who bragged that they would pull them down.

It appears to have been someone at court who had directed Courtenay to institute an investigation of the riot that had occurred in Exeter during the previous summer and this may well have been because, during the intervening months, a huge popular demonstration known as the 'Pilgrimage of Grace' had taken place in the North of England. Most historians agree that these protests were primarily fuelled by popular hostility to the Crown's religious policies and by a general desire to preserve the monasteries. It is interesting to note that one of the Pilgrims' demands was that the twenty-year-old Lady Mary, well known to be devoted to the old ways in religion, should be made legitimate again, after her father had declared her a bastard.[64] The Pilgrimage was the greatest internal challenge that Henry VIII ever faced, and for a week or two his very grip on the Crown seemed to hang in the balance. Yet the Pilgrims, fatally for their cause, took the decision not to move south but to remain in their northern strongholds instead, thus giving Henry time to gather his forces and regain the initiative. Henry Courtenay, like other noblemen, raised large numbers of troops to assist the king at this time, although it is hard not to suspect that the marquess, a religious conservative, may have felt some sympathy for the protestors.[65] Eventually, Henry was able to trick the Pilgrims into believing that he would both accede to their requests and grant them pardons. Then, after they had disbanded their forces, several new risings occurred in the North, and this gave Henry the chance to strike, causing many of the protestors to be executed, including a number of monks.

One of the most disturbing things about the Pilgrimage, from the king's point of view, was the fact that the protestors had contemplated seeking the assistance of both the Holy Roman emperor, Charles V of Spain, and the pope. To Henry's intense chagrin, Reginald Pole – the man whom he had long ago caused to be elected dean of Exeter – had first gone into self-imposed exile in Italy as a result of his disapproval of the king's divorce proceedings, and had then, in mid-1536, published a treatise in which he had denounced the divorce and denied the royal supremacy. Goading the king into further transports of fury, the pope had then made Pole a cardinal and, in February 1537 – by which time it was already too late – had charged him with sending help to the Pilgrims from the continent. Henry had every reason to strip Pole of his offices, and on 6 April 1537, the king wrote to the Chapter at Exeter, 'recommending' that they appoint a new man, Simon Haynes, as dean.[66] Haynes, a fiery evangelical, was cut from a wholly different cloth from the conservative cathedral canons at Exeter – and, indeed, Henry probably selected him as Pole's successor for precisely this reason.[67] Soon afterwards Haynes sent his servant, Richard Chambers, down to Exeter to present the king's letters of recommendation to the Chapter and to get his household ready. Chambers soon realised that he had arrived in a region in which resentment against the Crown's religious policies was simmering just beneath the surface, and in which he and his master were unlikely to receive a warm welcome. In an undated letter to Haynes, penned soon after his arrival, Chambers observed that people in Exeter were 'half afraid of a privy insurrection of Cornishmen'.[68]

It seems probable that these rumours of an imminent Cornish rising had been sparked off by the investigation which Sir William Godolphin – who was both a reformist and a close associate of Cromwell – was then conducting into whispers of trouble in the Lizard, the remote and wind-blown peninsula that forms the southern part of the hundred of Kerrier. On 22 April, Sir William wrote to Cromwell from his house at Godolphin, informing him that a friend, a local painter, had warned him about a worrying conversation that he had recently had with a man named Carpyssacke, 'dwellyng yn the parysche of Sent Keveron'.[69] St Keverne – the largest and most populous parish in the district in the south-east of the Lizard known as 'the Meneage' (i.e., the monks' land) – was a place with a distinctly uncomfortable history from the point of view of the local gentry. It was the inhabitants of St Keverne, as Godolphin pointedly reminded Cromwell, who had been 'the firste that steryd the Cornyshmen to rysse' in 1497, when a major insurrection against Henry VII had taken place in Cornwall, and, indeed, as Godolphin went on to note, it was in St Keverne that the most noted leader of that rebellion, Michael Joseph, 'the blacksmith', had lived.[70] It was not surprising, then, that St Keverne was a parish on which Sir William kept a weather eye.

According to Godolphin's informant, Carpyssacke had come to see him in order to commission him to paint a devotional 'banner for the said parysche'. He had then gone on to furnish him with a precise description of the devices that 'they' – presumably the parishioners of St Keverne – wished to see represented upon this ensign. Carpyssacke had specified that the banner should have 'the pyct[ure] off C[hri]ste w[i]t[h] hys wounds abrode' on one side, and on the other 'the Kynges grace & the quene knelyng, And al the commonaltie knelyng, w[i]t[h] scripture above ther hedds makyng ther petisyon to the pict[ure] off C[hri]ste that hyt wolde plesse the kyngs grace that they myght have ther holy dayye'.[71] This was an extremely subversive image to have commissioned at this particular time. What Carpyssacke and his fellow parishioners were clearly envisaging was a picture showing the common people praying to Christ to persuade the king to reverse the recent decision to move all parochial dedication feasts to a single, 'standard' day in October: a decision that had evidently resulted in the feast day of St Keverne being shifted away from its time-honoured date. That the parishioners of St Keverne should have considered such a plea necessary, moreover, strongly indicates that they had by now come to realise that – although Godolphin had assured local people they would continue to be allowed to celebrate their traditional dedication feasts during the previous year – this assurance had subsequently turned out to be either false, or else merely a one-off concession, designed to quell any initial muttering at the time the cull of the holy days was first announced.

Yet what made the proposed 'devyce[s]' so peculiarly threatening, from the authorities' point of view, was the fact that, by representing the common people appealing to divine authority against the king's religious policies, those images were strongly redolent of the ideology of the Pilgrimage of Grace: all the more so as it was under the banner of the five wounds of Christ that the Pilgrims had marched just months before.[72] The resemblance between Carpyssacke's planned banner and those that had been carried by the Pilgrims was clearly no coincidence, moreover, for, according to Godolphin's informant, Carpyssacke had not only been aware of the protests in the North but had been strongly supportive of them. After Carpyssacke had first approached him, the painter told Godolphin, he had asked him 'wher fore he wolde have such a banner', to which Carpyssacke had replied that he and a certain John Treglosacke had recently

> bene at Hamell besyd Sowthe hampton [i.e., Southampton] sellyng of ther fysche, [when] ther came to them ii men ... whyche demaundyd off them why they [i.e., the Cornish men] rose not when the Northern men dyd ... And now, sayd he, we have power to helpe

> them, and to thys thay [had] swore . . . apone a booke [all those] who ar yn thyr minde . . . [to] cary thyr baner on Pardon Monday and there hyt schallbe schowyd amonge all the peppyll that wylbe there how [i.e., who] wille follow thyr banner.[73]

Carpyssacke's reported words are fascinating, not only because they demonstrate that he was anxious to further the Pilgrims' cause, but also because they reveal that he was part of a larger group of individuals who had sworn a secret oath to put the banner that they were planning on public display. The fact that Carpyssacke and his associates were intending to 'show' their new banner to 'all the people' on 'Pardon Monday' is also extremely significant. 'Pardons' were religious festivals which were held annually in Brittany at this time on the feast day of the saint to whom an individual church was dedicated. On that day, the image of the saint would be removed from its normal place in the church and borne aloft at the head of a procession, past the crowds of local people who had gathered to watch, to worship and eventually to take part in a communal feast. Later paintings of Breton pardons depict many hundreds of men and women carrying candles and painted banners – as, indeed, participants in Breton pardons still do to this day.[74] The fact that the inhabitants of sixteenth-century St Keverne celebrated an annual pardon feast is another sign of Cornish cultural difference, therefore – and of the close cultural links that existed between this part of the West Country and Brittany.

How dangerous was the demonstration that Carpyssacke and his associates were planning? It could be argued that the banner they had commissioned was intended for intercessory purposes and nothing more; that they had genuinely believed that, by carrying their standard with its heartfelt message through St Keverne on the forthcoming 'Pardon Monday', they might be able to persuade Christ Himself to intervene directly on their behalf and to change Henry VIII's mind on the question of their holy day.[75] Godolphin, however, was plainly extremely alarmed by what he had learned. The former 'Pardon Monday' had, presumably, been shifted – along with all of the other dedication feasts – to October after all, so, by planning to process in front of the people on the traditional feast day, Carpyssacke and his fellows were plotting to proclaim a subversive message at an outlawed festival. The fact that Godolphin specifically mentioned the 1497 rising at the beginning of his letter to Cromwell, moreover, indicates that he feared that another such 'stir' might well be in the offing at St Keverne – and some of his later comments strongly reinforce this impression.

'I have layde in secret wysse to knowe yff any steryngs be among them,' Godolphin assured Cromwell at one point, for example, going on to explain that although he had not arrested Carpyssacke straight away, this was simply because, so far, he only knew of two witnesses who could testify against him: namely, the painter and his wife. Instead, Godolphin gave Cromwell to understand, he was playing the long game. He had therefore instructed the painter that 'yf they [i.e., the conspirators of St Keverne] come to hym agen', he was 'to follow ther myndes And to geve me knowledge and to cawse the best of ther sect to come and specke w[i]t[h] hym'. Godolphin's use of the word 'sect' here reveals his conviction that he was now on the trail of an organised group of people who were opposed to the Crown's religious policies, rather than just a handful of isolated individuals. His subsequent aside to Cromwell, moreover – that he had instructed the painter to inveigle 'the best' of the plotters into coming to talk to him because 'ther is no hedy man [i.e., head man, or gentleman] dwelling yn the sayd paryshe' – underscores Sir William's conviction that the plotters were, without exception, humble folk. One of the most striking things about the letter is the sheer rage that Godolphin exhibits against the plotters. 'By the precious body off God,' he assured Cromwell towards the end of his missive, 'yff they ster, or any off them, I will ridde [i.e., kill] as many as wil [a]bide aboute ther banner by the helpe of my friends and the Kyngs Graces servants in that part, or ellys I and a gret many wyll dy for hyt,'[76] That these violent words should have been occasioned by what appeared, on the face of things, to have been the simple commissioning of a devotional banner shows how polarised society in West Cornwall had already become by the spring of 1537.

Cromwell was equally alarmed. As soon as he had received Sir William's letter, he ordered him to arrest both Carpyssacke and

Treglosacke, to examine them and then to send them directly to the king. Godolphin was not able to act upon these orders straight away, because by the time he received them, Carpyssacke was back at Southampton again: presumably on another sales trip.[77] The unfortunate fisherman was clearly apprehended soon afterwards, however, for – in a subsequent letter – Godolphin not only assured Cromwell that he had recently been to the assizes in order to give evidence against 'the traitor Carpyssacke', but also asked him to intervene in person with the judge in order to make sure that the fisherman received the sentence that he, Sir William, believed he deserved. Carpyssacke should be 'hanged in chains' on the outskirts of Helston – the most populous town in Kerrier – Godolphin declared, 'wher alle hys parys[h]men and many more off that quarter schalle dayly see hym'.[78] This particular form of punishment was reserved for those who were held to have committed especially heinous crimes and, significantly enough, several of the Northern Pilgrims had recently been executed in precisely the same way.[79] The condemned man was first hanged on a pair of gallows. The dead body was next cut down and wrapped in chains. Finally, the iron-bound corpse was hoisted up again in some prominent place, and left on display until it eventually fell to pieces. Hanging in chains was a practice that was specifically designed to intimidate the people of the surrounding district, therefore, as well as to punish the individual offender, as Godolphin's final words reveal. He was evidently convinced that there were more potential 'traitors' in the Lizard Peninsula, and that the ghastly sight – and smell – of Carpyssacke's rotting corpse would have a salutary effect upon them. We do not know for certain that Carpyssacke met with the fate that Godolphin prescribed for him, but it seems all too probable that he did.[80] If this was indeed the case, then he was the first West Cornish man to be executed in this grim fashion for his loyalty to his traditional faith. He was not to be the last.

Meanwhile, back in Exeter, the members of the Cathedral Chapter were bracing themselves for the advent of their new dean. In June 1537, Simon Haynes was admitted to the canonry that had formerly been held by Pole.[81] A month later, Haynes was formally admitted as dean of Exeter, and in August he entered into residence at the cathedral.[82] No sooner had he arrived in Exeter than it was forcibly borne in upon him, just as it had been upon Chambers in April, that he was now entering distinctly hostile territory. Writing to Cromwell on 21 August, Haynes reported that 'on my arrival here, I enquired of my brethren in the chapter house for the injunctions left by the king's visitors [in 1536] in order to put them into execution'. To Haynes's evident outrage, however, 'no one present knew who had them, and [even] if I had them (it was said) that they imported nothing else but that we should do as we have done in times past and live after the old fashion'. The effect that these cheerful words would have had upon the new dean – an evangelical firebrand, who emphatically came not to bring peace but a sword – can only be imagined. Haynes now asked Cromwell to send him a replacement copy of the injunctions, promising, grimly, that 'I will see them executed within this closs [i.e., close]'. Later in his letter, Haynes made the distaste which he felt for his new colleagues crystal clear, observing that 'I like the people of this town very well, but, as far as I have yet seen, the priests of this country are a strange kind, very few of them well persuaded [in the matter of the recent religious reforms] or anything learned'. In a subsequent comment, moreover, he went further still and gave Cromwell to understand that he believed the entire region to be shot through with disaffection to the regime, warning him: 'This is a perilous country, for God's love let the King's grace look to it in time'.[83]

Haynes brought a much more radical and combative spirit of reform to the West Country and religious traditionalists now found themselves increasingly forced to make at least a show of conformity to the new order. In May 1538, for example, Bishop Veysey – who, while no friend of radical reform, was a regime loyalist – issued his own set of injunctions to the clergymen of his diocese, echoing and reinforcing the royal injunctions of 1536. Veysey, an old West Country hand, was clearly conscious of the fact that the new orders emanating from London – with their emphasis on the provision of English Bibles in churches, and on the use of the English tongue in some prayers – had the potential to antagonise the many Cornish-speakers in his diocese and, in his own injunctions, the bishop went out of his way to guard against this. Veysey directed, for example, that, every Sunday, each parish priest should read the epistle for that day or the Pater Noster, creed, etc, 'in the English tongue, *or in the Cornyshe tonge where the English tonge is not used*'. He also took care to specify that children were to be taught the Pater Noster, Ave Maria, creed and commandments in English '*or in the Cornishe . . . wheare the English tongue is not used*'.[84] Veysey could only go so far in accommodating the spirit of Cornish 'cultural defensiveness', however, for, when local practices went against the king's clearly expressed wishes, the bishop's hands were tied. Elsewhere in his injunctions, therefore, Veysey ordered that superstitious devotional practices, not justified by scripture, should cease 'espetiallie within the Archdeakenrie of Cornwall'.[85] In an order issued in 1539, moreover, Veysey ordered the clergy to stamp out the superstitious observance of holy days by ordinary people: an order that is bound to have stoked up further resentment in Cornwall, in particular – and which could well have revived memories of the Carpyssacke affair.[86]

In the months that followed, the West Country was to witness further dramatic changes. The larger monasteries were now following the smaller ones into ruin, for example, and in September 1538 the houses of the Grey Friars and the Black Friars at Exeter were both suppressed.[87] Later that month, Cromwell issued a second and still more reformist set of royal injunctions which directed, among other things: that a sermon based on 'the very Gospel of Christ' should be preached in every church each quarter; that the people should be exhorted 'to the works of charity, mercy and faith . . . commanded in scripture', rather than putting their trust any longer in 'works devised by men's phantasies . . . as in wandering to pilgrimages, offering of money . . . to images or relics . . . [or] saying over of . . . [mass] beads'; and that all 'feigned images . . . abused with pilgrimages and offerings' were forthwith to be 'take[n] down'.[88] Dean Haynes at once set about enforcing these orders with the utmost zeal in the cathedral, and – following his appointment as one of the royal commissioners for the implementation of the injunctions – was able to extend his iconoclastic reach across the entire diocese as well, ordering the destruction of images that had allegedly been 'abused' in both Devon and Cornwall.[89] Towards the end of that year, moreover, catastrophe befell the Courtenays, whose senior members had long been hostile to the reformist agenda. In November 1538, the marquess of Exeter and his wife were arrested for allegedly conspiring against the king. They were tried and condemned and the marquess himself was executed soon afterwards, while Gertrude Courtenay was immured for some time in the Tower.[90]

Within months of Courtenay's fall, Henry VIII created a new regional magnate to oversee affairs in the South-West. In March 1539, the king elevated the rising courtier Sir John Russell to a barony, and at the same time endowed him with a huge estate, based on the former lands of Tavistock Abbey, in order to underpin his newly acquired noble status. In April, the now-Lord Russell was appointed president of the Council in the West, a new administrative body which had been set up to oversee the governance of the four south-western counties of Cornwall, Devon, Dorset and Somerset, and to ensure that they were as well prepared as possible to resist any potential foreign attack.[91] In July, Russell was made lord warden of the Stannaries in order to boost his status in the region still further, while during that same month he was also given the former house of the Black Friars, in the heart of Exeter, to serve as his permanent residence in that city.[92]

All was not well in Russell's new fiefdom, however, for, by 1539, deep divisions had begun to emerge among the local gentry governors: divisions that were based, in part, on simple rivalry for local power and influence but which also reflected diverging religious attitudes. In Cornwall, the key rift was that which existed between the Arundells of Lanherne, who were associated with the old ways in religion, and the Godolphins of Godolphin, who were associated with the new.[93] As early as 1537, Sir William Godolphin had written to Cromwell to complain that 'John Arundel, son and heir to Sir John', was boasting that Godolphin 'shall never have' an estate at Tywardreath that he particularly coveted.[94] Godolphin may well have hoped that the Arundells would fall from grace as a result of their religious conservativism and, at some point in either 1537 or 1538, this did indeed seem to be briefly on the cards, when Henry VIII sent a furious letter to Sir Thomas Arundell, scolding him and other Cornish JPs for, among other things, failing to bring to justice 'the privy mayneteynors of that papisticall faction, the most cancred and venomous worms that be in our commonwealth'.[95] Sir Thomas must have been terrified to receive this stinging rebuke from his suspicious and ruthless monarch, but he had somehow managed to scrabble his way back into favour again, and his brother, John, was subsequently knighted by the king. It was not long before John, too, was feuding with the Godolphins. In March 1539, he and two other gentlemen made 'grete sutte' against the appointment of Godolphin's son, William Godolphin the younger, as knight of the shire for Cornwall.[96] And though old Sir John Arundell died a few years later, young Sir John now succeeded him as master of Lanherne, from where he kept up the feud with the Godolphins, and with Sir Richard Grenville of Kilkhampton in East Cornwall, another rising, and vaguely reformist, gentleman with a keen appetite for power.[97] Russell, who preferred to remain at court rather than to spend much time in the region of which he was now the nominal overlord, did little to diffuse these tensions.

After a decade of bewildering change, the final years of Henry VIII's reign saw a measure of stability return, on the surface of things at least, as the king – fearful of irredeemably alienating the great Catholic powers of Europe – signalled his determination to call a halt to religious innovation and thereby to consolidate his reformation. In June 1539, Parliament passed 'An Act Abolishing Diversity in Opinions', popularly known as 'the Six Articles', which affirmed traditional religious teaching in a number of respects, and which, in particular, directed that anyone who denied that the body of Christ was really or substantially present in the bread consumed in the eucharist – as some of the more radical reformers, or 'sacramentarians', did – was to be burned as a heretic.[98] Several evangelical bishops resigned in the wake of the passage of this act, though Cranmer remained firmly in place.[99] A year later, moreover, Cromwell was arrested and executed: ostensibly for heresy and for plotting against the king, but probably, in fact, because Henry was infuriated with his chief minister for having encouraged him to marry Anne of Cleves, who had turned out to be not at all to Henry's taste, and because Cromwell's death would send out a useful signal, just then, to the rulers of Catholic France and Spain.[100]

There are signs that, in the West Country, these changes at the top encouraged a cautious fightback by those who favoured the old learning.

In 1539, for example, Bishop Veysey – who was by now around eighty and living, most of the time, in his home town in Warwickshire – appointed John Blaxton, a senior local churchman who would later reveal himself to be a highly combative religious traditionalist, as one of his deputy vicars-general. Over the following years, Blaxton would rise still further to become Veysey's 'commissary', in which capacity he would institute many clerics to local benefices.[101] Meanwhile, the cathedral canons had been emboldened to strike back against their overbearing dean. In July 1540, they revoked the procuratorial powers that they had previously granted to Haynes, while in September they noted that the dean had recently caused great damage to the cathedral by, among other things, tearing down images of saints, ripping up choir books, and removing the candles that had formerly burned at the high altar.[102] When Haynes refused to make reparations for the damages, the dispute went to formal arbitration and, in 1542, the canons upped the stakes by declaring the dean to be no longer resident in Exeter, and therefore not entitled to claim his normal fees.[103] A year later, some of the canons appear to have gone further still and accused Haynes of heresy. In 1543, he was committed to the Fleet prison in London, and he later appeared before the Privy Council accused of 'lewd and seditious preaching' – though, after being reprimanded, he was released 'with a declaration of the king's mercy and goodness towards him'.[104]

Another religious radical who found himself in trouble in London during the latter years of Henry's reign was a headstrong young man named Peter Carew.[105] The third son of Sir William Carew of Mohun's Ottery in East Devon, Carew had, according to his contemporary biographer, been born in around 1514, gone abroad to serve as a soldier in the Italian Wars and, upon his return, presented himself to Henry VIII, who had so liked the cut of Carew's jib that he had promptly appointed him as a 'henchman' at the royal court.[106] Carew – like a number of other ambitious young West Country gentlemen, including Sir William Godolphin the younger, Sir Richard Grenville and Sir Hugh Paulet of Hinton St George in Somerset – had gone on to serve in the ruinously expensive wars that Henry had waged against the French during the following decade and, like them, had been able to use his record of military service to the Crown to further his own advancement. In 1545, Carew had been knighted, together with his uncle, Gawen Carew, by John Dudley, the lord admiral of England, for the part which they had played in the English attack upon Le Tréport in Normandy.[107]

Dudley was later to become a leading evangelical, and Carew's association with the lord admiral may well have helped to stoke his interest in reformist ideas; in December 1545, Sir Peter, then in London, was found in possession of what appears to have been a heretical book.[108] His punishment for this offence was a token one: he was first committed to the keeping of Lord Russell – who may well have been Carew's patron, and who had almost certainly had a hand in helping to secure Sir Peter's recent election as an MP for Tavistock – then transferred to the keeping of another nobleman and, finally, released.[109] This escapade did nothing to halt Carew's upward progress, therefore: a progress that was unexpectedly accelerated still further when – following the accidental death of his brother, Sir George Carew, in the sinking of the great warship the *Mary Rose* in 1545 – Sir Peter inherited all of the Carews' extensive estates in Devon. Carew had spent little time in the West Country since leaving the region as a boy, but he now possessed a rich patrimony there, as well as many powerful allies at court, and it has been persuasively argued that it was thanks to his links with Dudley, with Edward Seymour, the earl of Hertford, and with other powerful members of the evangelical faction that was growing in power during the final months of Henry VIII's reign that Sir Peter Carew found himself being pricked as sheriff of Devon in November 1546.[110] As we shall see in the following chapter, Carew's year in office was to prove a controversial one – and would result in the growing religious divisions that already existed in the West Country becoming wider still.

# 2

## Foreshocks
### The Disturbances of 1547–48

On 28 January 1547, the old king finally breathed his last. In accordance with the conventional dictates of heredity, Henry's crown now passed, not to his adult daughter, Mary, let alone to his fourteen-year-old daughter, Elizabeth, but rather to his nine-year-old son, Edward. England therefore found itself with a child upon the throne: a situation that would have been fraught with potential danger even if it had not been for the deep religious fissures that had opened up in the country as a result of 'the king's Reformation'. Henry had been preparing for this eventuality long before his death, of course, and in his will he had named sixteen 'executors' who were to make up Edward's Privy Council and to assist the boy-king in governing the kingdom until he attained the age of eighteen.[1] Henry had directed that each of these individuals was to enjoy equal status and authority, but, within days of his demise, the executor-councillors had decided that 'some special man' from among their number should be declared *primus inter pares* and Edward Seymour, earl of Hertford – the brother of Henry's dead wife Jane Seymour and thus the new king's uncle – had persuaded his colleagues that this role should fall to him.[2] On 31 January, therefore, a majority of the councillors agreed to Seymour's appointment as 'protector of the realm' and, a few days after this, as part of a general distribution of honours to the new king's councillors, Seymour was created duke of Somerset: the title by which he will be referred to from now on.[3]

Somerset promptly set about strengthening his power still further. On 6 March, the chancellor, Thomas Wriothesley, earl of Southampton, was dismissed from the Council – almost certainly because he had opposed Somerset's elevation to the rank of protector – while, later that month, Somerset gained the right to control new admissions to the Privy Council.[4] As a result, he became ruler of England in all but name.

The policies of the new regime of which Edward was the titular head but Somerset was the driving force may be swiftly summarised. First and foremost – as befitted a man who had made his name as a soldier and who had recently won a glorious military victory against the Scots – Somerset was determined to pursue Henry VIII's ruinously expensive war against his northern neighbours.[5] Needless to say, the continuance of this conflict would require the extraction of further large sums of money from the English people, who had already been bled white by the ceaseless financial demands made of them during the closing years of the old king's reign. Second, and potentially more destabilising still, Somerset was intent on driving through a radical religious policy, on jettisoning the 'middle-way' approach that had been adopted by Henry VIII during the 1540s and on moving instead in the direction of full-blown Protestantism. Somerset's motives for championing the new learning remain unclear. It is possible, even probable, that he was himself a committed reformist.[6] He certainly possessed evangelical allies on the Council, including Thomas Cranmer, the archbishop of Canterbury. And if, as most historians believe, the boy-king, too, was already an ardent reformer – having had the tenets of the new faith drummed into him by his childhood tutors – then this would have been another good reason for Somerset to tack with what appeared to be the prevailing wind.[7] Whatever the truth may have been, the shift in religious emphasis at the centre was soon to make itself felt in the provinces.

In the West Country, as in the rest of England, many must have been unsettled by the death of Henry VIII – who had reigned, after all, for as long as anyone under forty could remember – and anxious to learn more about the priorities of the new regime. In the immediate aftermath of Henry's demise, the Council had entrusted the maintenance of 'good order' in the West to four local notables: John Bourchier, earl of Bath;

Sir Thomas Denys; Sir Hugh Pollard; and Sir Hugh Paulet.[8] This might well have been thought to herald a policy of 'steady as she goes' at the centre, for all of these individuals were well-established regional authority figures, and Paulet is the only one who appears to have had reformist sympathies.[9] Yet, once Somerset was firmly in the saddle, very different signals began to emanate from London. In early May, for example, it was announced that another royal visitation of the Church would shortly take place. It subsequently emerged that the team of commissioners, or 'visitors', who had been chosen by Cranmer to carry out this task in the West Country would include Exeter's radical dean, Simon Haynes.[10] Neither Haynes nor his colleagues were likely to prove at all sympathetic to traditional religious practices. More troubling still, for many local conservatives, may well have been the fact that, when new commissions of the peace for Devon and Cornwall were issued by the government on 26 May, the lists of county magistrates contained some highly significant additions and omissions. In Devon, for example, Haynes himself, as well as Sir Gawen Carew and Sir Peter Courtenay, both well-known evangelicals, had been appointed as JPs, together with a string of lesser reformists.[11] Even more telling was the fact that Sir John and Sir Thomas Arundell, the two most powerful men in Cornwall, had been removed from their accustomed places on the Cornish bench – for reasons that remain unclear but which were surely linked to Sir John's reputation for staunch religious conservatism.[12] With the Arundells gone, their old rivals Sir William Godolphin and Sir Richard Grenville – who may well have helped to engineer their dismissal – now became the most senior Cornish JPs.[13]

These alterations in the complexions of the commissions of the peace provided the gentry governors of Devon and Cornwall with a clear indication of the direction in which the new government was moving, and we may presume that the politico-religious significance of the changes would have been glimpsed by many other local people as well. Even before this time, moreover, it is evident that – in the West Country, just as in London – the shift in the mood music at court had already begun to embolden religious radicals on the ground. On 24 March, for example, a fiery young reformer named Philip Nicolles had attended a sermon given by Richard Crispin, one of the cathedral canons and a leading religious conservative. According to his own later account, Nicolles had been infuriated by the traditionalist views which Crispin had expounded on that day in front of a large and socially prestigious congregation. Within hours, he had composed a confrontational letter to the canon, in which he had criticised his doctrine and demanded that he answer several theological questions. On 30 April, Nicolles had sent this missive to Crispin, and soon afterwards he had written to him again, this time 'desireinge hym to send me an answere'. Crispin, understandably cautious, had replied 'that he would not writ, but commune wyth me him selfe'. Accordingly, Nicolles went on, he had twice come to debate matters with Crispin face to face at the latter's benefice of Harberton in mid-June. Nicolles admitted that he had found 'Mayster Chrispyne verye gentle and charitable to talke withal', but, predictably enough, there had been no meeting of minds. On the contrary, the two men had parted with their differences completely unresolved and, according to Nicolles, rumours had afterwards started to circulate – presumably at Crispin's instigation – 'yt I came to him for non other purpose, but to have matter to talk of, and to accuse him' to the authorities as a spreader of seditious doctrine.[14] Thus was bred a quarrel that was to have increasingly bitter ramifications as the year went on.

In the far west of Cornwall, meanwhile, considerably more forceful steps were being taken against another local cleric. In the household book of Edward VI, it is recorded that a payment of £2 was made in June 1547 to one 'Henry Edwards, servant to Sir William Gwidolphin . . . for his charges in commyng up [to London] with the vicar of Saint Pol, by west [of] the Mount, and his retorne agayn with the same'.[15] It is hard to be sure whether Edwards was a retainer of Sir William Godolphin the elder, who is known to have died in *c.* 1547, or of his son, Sir William Godolphin the younger, who succeeded to his father's estate.[16] Both the Godolphins were favourers of the new learning, though, so it seems reasonable to suspect that the reason that one or other of them had caused the vicar of Paul – a parish that lies on the coast of Penwith, overlooking Mount's Bay – to be escorted up to the capital was because he was alleged to have expressed religious opinions that would be regarded as subversive or dangerous by England's new rulers. That this was indeed the case is confirmed by the Privy Council's original warrant authorising the payment, dated 24 June, which notes that the £2 was to be given 'in rewarde to a servant of Sir William Godolphins, who had the bringing up of a lewde preeste owte of Cornewayle sent to the Lord Protectours Grace and Counsail to be examyned'.[17] Taken together, these two scraps of evidence make it hard to doubt that, within six months of Edward coming to the throne, fresh whispers of disaffection were beginning to circulate in West Cornwall.

If religious conservatives were already muttering in corners in the spring of 1547, the events of that summer can only have made their apprehensions worse. On 31 July, the regime published a new set of royal 'injunctions' for the governance of the English Church, which, the preamble declared, were intended for 'the advancement of the true honour of Almighty God, the suppression of idolatry and superstition . . . and to plant true religion'.[18] As one historian has observed, while the injunctions at first sight looked like an extended reprise of those issued by Henry VIII in 1538, they were in fact a full-blown 'charter for revolution', because they made it impossible for religious conservatives to cling on to many of the traditional practices that had continued to be permitted during the final years of the old king's reign.[19] The injunctions laid down, for example, that praying with rosary beads should be forbidden; that religious processions should be discontinued; that images within churches which had been 'abused' by people making offerings to them should be removed; and that 'all shrines . . . pictures, paintings, and all other monuments of feigned miracles, pilgrimages, idolatry and superstition' should be 'take[n] away, utterly extin[guished] and destroy[ed] . . . so that there remain no memory of the same in walls, glass windows, or elsewhere'.[20] These were radical directives, which struck at the heart of many ordinary people's faith. It is worth noting, too, that, in their insistence that all clerics should ensure that their parishioners could recite the Lord's Prayer and the Ten Commandments *in English*, the royal injunctions of 1547 may have particularly offended the sensibilities of Cornish-speakers, for there is no evidence to show that Bishop Veysey went on to stipulate that it would be equally acceptable for these things to be learned and recited in the Cornish tongue, as he had done in the wake of the injunctions issued in 1536.[21]

Within two months of the new injunctions being published, the visitation that had been announced in the spring finally got under way.[22] The commissioners for the diocese of Exeter soon began their work in the West Country: summoning representatives from every parish to appear before them, so that they could question them on the extent to which the religious directives that had recently been promulgated had been enforced and order them to ensure swift and full compliance.[23] While religious conservatives viewed the arrival of the visitors with deep trepidation, fervent evangelicals, by contrast, welcomed them – and one man who was especially eager to assist the commissioners in their task of furthering godly reformation was Philip Nicolles. Following his dispute with Crispin, Nicolles had become extremely unpopular among local traditionalists, who had claimed, as we have seen, that he had been deliberately baiting his antagonist in order to provoke Crispin into making pronouncements that would get him into hot water. Nicolles was undeterred. Far from drawing in his horns, he had continued to monitor the activities of those whom he considered to be 'blynde, wycked and sediciouse ... preachers', and, at some point during the late summer or autumn of 1547, he drew up a list of 'articles' against several local churchmen whom he believed to be preaching unlawful doctrine and presented it to the commissioners.[24] Predictably enough, Nicolles's actions confirmed his local adversaries in their animosity towards him, and – as he himself subsequently confessed – 'they begin to byte me privily . . . for exhibityinge certayne Articles preached of oure learned men, and would perswade ... [others] that I dyd it of a pretended malice, sekeinge their destruction'.[25]

Who were the 'learned men' whose doctrine Nicolles had impugned in his 'articles offered to the visitours'?[26] He does not tell us in the self-penned pamphlet – printed in London at some point after the original text was completed on 7 November – in which he provides a vivid account of his struggle with his local adversaries. It is possible to guess at the identities of at least two of the individuals whom Nicolles had denounced, however. As we have seen, it was the preaching of Richard Crispin that had provoked his indignation in the first place, so it seems unlikely to be a coincidence that – at around the time Nicolles finished writing his narrative – both Crispin and John Moreman, another of the leading traditionalists among the cathedral canons, were arrested and sent up to London.[27] Here, the two clerics were imprisoned in the Tower, as it was later noted, 'for preaching in the West country, by the accusement of the Dean of Pauls and other commissioners there'.[28] The dean of St Paul's Cathedral at this time was Dr William May, who, in early 1547, had been appointed as one of the commissioners for the visitation in the diocese of Exeter.[29] That it was May and his fellow commissioners who had ordered the arrest of Crispin and Moreman, therefore, makes it seem overwhelmingly likely that the two canons had been among the 'learned men' whose theology Nicolles had denounced to those same 'visitours'. Indeed, it is tempting to suggest that Nicolles's decision to write and publish an account of his dispute with Crispin in late 1547 may have been motivated not only by a desire to justify his own actions, but also publicly to celebrate the downfall of the two canons.

Nicolles's pamphlet merits careful study, for it sheds much light on the religious situation in the South-West in 1547. Entitled *The Copie of a Letter Sente to One Maister Chrispyne for that he Denied ye Scripture to Be the Touchstone or Trial of Al Other Doctrines*, the tract makes its evangelical sympathies plain from the very first. The fact that Nicolles chose to dedicate it to the man whom he describes as 'his singular good Maister Syr Peter Carewe' may be said to have underscored its religious allegiance, moreover, for, as we have seen, Carew, who had been chosen as sheriff of Devon during the preceding year, was also a fervent reformist. Nicolles began his work with a geographical simile, observing that, 'among so manie hudg Rockes and wylde seas as oure weste partes are compassed with', it was a blessing to find 'some ... haven wher Christs shippes mought cast ancre and for a space have succoure'. These words were obviously intended to praise Carew, as one who could be relied upon to provide a port in a storm for local evangelicals, but, by noting the particular need for such a haven amidst the rockiness and wildness of 'oure weste partes', Nicolles was also gesturing towards the fact that Devon and Cornwall represented quite unusually intractable terrain for advocates of the new learning. This point was made more forcefully still a few lines further on, when Nicolles referred in passing to 'my contrey . . . where most daynger appeareth to be'.[30] The nature of this 'daynger' was not specified, but, in the context of the overall discussion, it is hard to doubt that the threat Nicolles had in mind was that posed to the further progress of godly reformation by the strength of religious conservatism in the South-West, a conservatism which he believed to be fostered and upheld by traditionalist churchmen like Crispin. We are reminded of Haynes's characterisation of the diocese of Exeter ten years before: 'this is a perilous country'.[31]

Having set the scene, Nicolles subsequently went on to emphasise that Carew was not just his patron in a general sense but that he had also been directly involved in his dispute with Crispin. This had already been hinted at on the second page of the dedicatory epistle, where Nicolles had praised Carew for 'your pure . . . zeale towards gods truth, and paynefull labours in defendynge innocentes', thus implying that Sir Peter had stepped in to protect Nicolles after the challenge he had issued to Crispin had brought down the wrath of the latter's allies upon his head. Yet, in subsequent passages, Nicolles reveals that Carew's involvement had gone much deeper than this. By referring to 'your yerneste desire to thys my small laboure in writing to maister Chrispyne a simple letter', for example, Nicolles appears to be suggesting that it was Sir Peter who had been responsible for deliberately inciting the quarrel between him and Crispin in the first place. By noting that 'I perceyved that you were determinately mynded to put it [i.e., the original letter] in print', moreover, Nicolles makes it plain that it was Carew who had originally conceived the plan of bringing the controversy to the attention of a much wider audience by publishing it, and that – in writing the pamphlet and sending it off to the printer – Nicolles had therefore simply been following his patron's wishes. His subsequent aside – that he had 'set it [i.e., the pamphlet] forthe in . . . [Carew's] name chiefely to purg me from that evel suspicion that is lyke to ensue the printing of it' – shows that Nicolles was well aware of just how much anger the publication of the pamphlet was likely to provoke.[32]

There is no reason to doubt Nicolles's claim that Carew had been deeply involved in his quarrel with Crispin. Carew is certainly known to have been in the West Country at around the time that the controversy between the two men was raging, for, on 3 October, he had stood as surety for another of his local clients and evangelical allies, William Gibbs of Feniton, in the Exeter mayor's court.[33] Nor does it seem implausible to suggest that Carew – as one of the leading figures in the West Country's now ascendant evangelical faction – might have decided to make use of Nicolles as a theological attack dog, in order to force local opponents of continued godly reformation out into the open where they could be intimidated, sanctioned and, if necessary, arrested. The imprisonment of Crispin and Moreman for refusing to renounce their traditionalist religious views formed part of a broader national pattern, after all. On 25 September, Stephen Gardiner, bishop of Winchester – and the man who was generally regarded as the most subtle and influential opponent of the new learning in England – had been committed to the Fleet prison in London for refusing to confirm his unconditional support for the royal injunctions, and for suggesting that the state of religion should remain as Henry VIII had left it until Edward attained his majority.[34] Carew's eagerness for Nicolles's letter to Crispin to be published at this particular time almost certainly reflected a desire to intervene in national affairs as well as local ones, moreover, for the first parliament of Edward's reign opened in London on 4 November 1547, with Sir Peter sitting as MP for Dartmouth and his uncle, Sir Gawen, sitting as one of the knights of the shire for Devon.[35] It would obviously have been useful for the Carews to have had Nicolles's pamphlet to hand as the MPs foregathered, in order to demonstrate how hotly reformation was being promoted on their 'patch' and how thoroughly its local opponents were being confounded.

Behind the personal quarrel that had broken out between Nicolles and Crispin in April 1547, then, it is possible to glimpse the broader, factional conflict that was simultaneously being waged between reformists like the Carews and Haynes and their traditionalist rivals in the West Country – and, behind that again, the still greater conflict that was being fought out between Somerset's radicalising regime and its conservative opponents across the entire kingdom. The calling of Edward's first parliament was inextricably tied up with that wider struggle, of course, for one of Somerset's main purposes in summoning the assembly was to repeal those pieces of Henrician legislation that – as Gardiner had unhelpfully pointed out – constituted a block to further religious reform. Once the new parliament had opened, the existing laws against heresy were swiftly abolished.[36] Particularly significant was the repeal of the totemic statute of 1539 known as the Act of Six Articles, which had reaffirmed Henry VIII's adherence to the basic tenets of the Catholic faith and had emphasised his continued determination to ensure that those who dared to deny the real presence in the sacrament of the altar would 'suffer as . . . heretics'.[37] Its presence on the statute book had served to reassure religious conservatives of the old king's implacable opposition to Protestant heresies and, even after Edward's accession, it had continued to be used by traditionalists to check the activities of the most thorough-going evangelicals.[38] Now the act was gone, leaving the reformists' opponents deprived of their most effective legislative weapon. Nor was this the only respect in which the new parliament undercut the conservatives' position, for it also passed an act for the dissolution of all chantries and guilds and the confiscation of their property by the Crown, thus striking another body blow to the world of the old faith.[39]

It is interesting to note that, soon after the new parliament began to sit at Westminster, a public disturbance occurred in Exeter: the first that is known to have occurred in the West Country since Edward's accession to the throne. On 25 November, it was recorded in the Chamber Act Book that, six days before, there had been 'an unlawffull assemblye w[i]thout [the] Estgate' of the city. Clearly alarmed by this episode, the town councillors resolved 'that the Lorde P[ro]tectors grace shalbe thereof advised yn writing by a letter sent by Mr Mayer . . . consernyng the same'.[40] It is possible that news of the tumult had already reached London before this letter was sent, however, for, on the very next day, the Privy Council sent a letter to the cathedral canons in which they taxed them with having winked at, and perhaps even encouraged, a serious affray within 'the precinct of their liberties': almost certainly within the 'fee of St Sidwells', the populous suburban area that lay immediately outside the East Gate and which had long fallen under the cathedral's jurisdiction.[41] The mayor and his officials had recently been endeavouring to 'detect ... such lewde persones as of late had attempted within that cittye moste haynouse offences against ... the Kings Majestye', the councillors observed. Yet when the civic watchmen had tried to conduct a search for these malefactors within the cathedral's 'liberties', the councillors indignantly went on, the inhabitants 'by the instruction of some of them [i.e., the canons] had ... proceeded to a violente and tumultuous repultion of the watchemen of the cittie from ... out of their liberties ... after such a sorte as might have easily growne to a sedition and fraye'.[42] To add insult to injury, moreover, the churchmen had subsequently plotted to indict the mayor himself for causing a riot. Now, the councillors brusquely ordered the canons to leave the mayor in peace and to ensure that there were no further 'occassione[s] of tumulte' until the entire 'matter should at length be heard here [i.e., in London] and such order taken as to unitie and conservac[i]on of quiet should appertayne'.[43]

Jurisdictional conflicts between the city and the cathedral at Exeter were nothing new, of course; on the contrary, there was a long tradition of such 'town versus gown' disputes stretching far back into the Middle Ages. Nevertheless, there are clear hints that the dispute which occurred in November 1547 possessed an unwonted ideological edge. In a subsequent letter, directed to the Cathedral treasurer, Thomas Southron, and the rest of the canons, the privy councillors made it clear that, shortly before the recent 'fraye' within the cathedral's liberties, the mayor had sent a letter to London to inform Somerset and his fellows that 'a nawghtie person ... had affixed to dores and scattered in the streetes [of Exeter] most slaunderous and seditious billes [i.e., notices or placards]'.[44] The councillors had promptly written back, giving 'exprese comaundement ... to the ... maior to devise by all meanes that he might to search for the mallefactor'.[45] Unfortunately, the letter does not go into detail about the precise nature of the subversive literature the anonymous 'mallefactor' had dispersed, but, given the mayor had decided that the incident was serious enough to report to the Council in the first place, and the councillors themselves had then immediately ordered that the offender be tracked down, it seems a fair assumption that the 'billes' had been critical of the regime's policies.[46] We are reminded, here, of the similarly 'seditious' bills that had been dispersed in the city a decade before, following the riot at St Nicholas priory.

Could the placards have contained protests about the recent arrests of Crispin and Moreman? There is nothing to show that they did, but the fact that, in their first letter to the canons, the councillors had declared the repulse of the city watchmen had occurred 'by the instruction of some amongst them [i.e., the canons], *peradventure not unguilty of ye said disorders* [i.e., the scattering of the bills]' certainly appears to hint at a suspicion that the cathedral close at Exeter was a centre of disaffection to the new regime.[47] The fact that, a year after this dispute occurred, a statute was passed that extended the boundaries of the city of Exeter – and in the process transferred jurisdiction over St Sidwell's from the cathedral to the city – can hardly be a coincidence, moreover.[48] The affair of the 'seditious bills' had clearly provided Exeter's town governors with a golden opportunity, first, to persuade the privy councillors that the extensive liberties enjoyed by their clerical neighbours possessed the potential to obstruct the Crown's policies, and, second, to make use of the traction they had thereby gained in order to secure the passage of a statute which greatly curtailed those same liberties – thus leading to a considerable augmentation of the Chamber's local authority and a corresponding reduction in that of the Chapter. The episode had demonstrated that the members of Exeter's ruling elite had much to gain from ingratiating themselves with the new regime in London, in other words, whatever their own private religious sympathies may have been, and this in turn may well have helped to strengthen the pre-existing bonds of affinity between the Crown and the town governors which were shortly to prove of such crucial importance.

Towards the end of November 1547, new sheriffs were pricked for the south-western counties, with Sir Gawen Carew succeeding his nephew, Sir Peter, as sheriff of Devon and John Milliton of Pengersick Castle, near Helston, becoming sheriff of Cornwall.[49] Milliton would soon face an unsettling popular protest in his own back yard. Earlier in the year, a commission had been issued by the Crown to the bishops, ordering them to ensure that inventories were compiled of all of the silver plate, jewels and other valuable ornaments belonging to each of the parish churches in their dioceses. The government had stressed that the creation of these lists was intended to ensure simply 'that the goods might be preserved to the use of the church'.[50] Yet, with the dissolution of the monasteries still fresh in their minds, many people had at once concluded that the drawing-up of the inventories was likely to prove the first step in a process that would lead to the eventual confiscation of their church treasures by the Crown – and had therefore begun to sell off those treasures themselves, before they could be seized. Unsurprisingly, the government had intervened to prevent this from happening, in the West Country as elsewhere, and, on 17 October, the Privy Council had sent a letter to Bishop Veysey ordering him to ensure that no more church plate, jewels or bells were sold by any parishioners within his diocese.[51] Meanwhile, the work of compiling the inventories was beginning to get under way on the ground.

In Cornwall, the oversight of this task had fallen to William Body, a former servant of Thomas Cromwell, and a man who possessed an unsavoury reputation for violence, ill temper and greed. Body, who had started life as a London clothworker, was a layman, but, in 1537 – as he waxed fat in Cromwell's service – he had leased the archdeaconry of Cornwall, together with all of its offices, rents and profits, from Thomas Winter, the illegitimate son of Cardinal Wolsey, who had himself been officially installed as archdeacon just a month before.[52] This was hardly a very edifying state of affairs, and during the early 1540s Bishop Veysey and several of the senior churchmen who served as his deputies in the diocese had made strenuous attempts to deprive Body of his lease, but to no avail. Body had fought back with vigour and had routed his local adversaries, one of whom had died in prison. At the start of Edward's reign, therefore, Body had remained firmly entrenched as deputy archdeacon of Cornwall, in which role he was responsible not only for 'enforcing religious change' in the county, but also for overseeing the compilation of the inventories of 'church-juelles'.[53]

Towards the end of 1547, Body summoned representatives from each of the parishes in the hundred of Penwith to appear before him, so that he could address them on the subject of the forthcoming 'enserch', or survey. But far from persuading his auditors that they had nothing to fear from the exercise, the privy councillors later complained – clearly on the basis of information that had been sent up to them by the local gentry governors – Body had done the exact opposite: 'handel[ing] himselfe after such a mannere as thereby the people were perswaded that the Enserch . . . tended only to [the] effect as yf thereupon a confiscacion [of the church-goods] shuld have ensued . . . much contrary to the Counselles entente'. It seems unlikely that Body addressed his auditors in Cornish, despite the fact that this was a largely Cornish-speaking district: perhaps he made use of an interpreter to get his message across. Whatever the case, his words provoked an angry response and a 'tumulte' now broke out: one that was only stilled after the intervention of three local gentlemen – Sir William Godolphin of Godolphin, John Milliton of Pengersick and Thomas St Aubyn of Clowance.[54]

We must presume that, as soon as the disturbance was over, the three gentlemen sent word to the Privy Council of what had occurred, for on 17 December the councillors wrote to them from London, thanking them 'for their paines taken in appeasinge the tumulteous assembly of the parisheoneres of Penwith' and blaming Body's 'indiscreet' actions for causing it.[55] The councillors ordered that Body should be imprisoned for a week, as a punishment, and then sent up to them 'to answere further' for what he had done. Meanwhile, copies of the councillors' original letter to Body – in which they had not only ordered him to supervise the compilation of the inventories, but had also specifically stressed that the lists were designed to ensure 'the preservacion of the church juelles' – were to be shown 'unto the substanciall persones of every parishe' in Penwith in the pious hope that this would set their minds at rest. Finally – in a directive that was suggestive of a concern that there might have been more to the stir than initially met the eye – the councillors ordered Milliton and his fellow JPs 'further to enquire out ii or iii of the cheefe stirreres upp of this busenes and comitte them also to warde'. Once they had apprehended these ringleaders and interrogated them about their recent activities, the councillors concluded, the Cornish justices were then to get back in touch, 'and of their whole doings to advertice hether [i.e., to send word]'.[56]

No sooner had the anger aroused by the 'enserch' into the church treasures of West Cornwall died down than a new disturbance occurred in Devon, this time occasioned by the activities of those who had been commissioned by the Crown to implement the recent Act of Parliament for the suppression of chantries and guilds. At some point in January 1548, a riot took place in the little town of Ashburton, on the south-eastern fringe of Dartmoor, when around twenty of the parishioners 'attempted to resist the confiscation of lands . . . formerly belonging to the guild of St Lawrence [and] violence was allegedly employed' against one of the commissioner's servants.[57] Little evidence has survived about the fracas in Ashburton, and it is hard to judge how serious it was. Yet what is crystal clear is that, as the regime's drive for religious 'reformation' intensified during the early months of 1548, so levels of tension rose across the realm, with evangelicals and traditionalists becoming involved in a series of local disputes and stand-offs.

One of the most hotly contested topics was that of religious images. As we have seen, the royal injunctions of 1547 had ordered that all images in churches that had been 'abused' by people making offerings to them should be destroyed. The wording of this directive had made it possible for religious conservatives to claim that images that were not being 'abused' in this way should be retained. Yet fervent evangelicals in London and the South-East had swiftly proceeded to smash up *all* of the images in their churches without any sort of discrimination, thus provoking angry protests from their more traditional neighbours. Now, the Council moved to put a stop to such controversies by making a final ruling on the subject. On 21 February, Somerset and his colleagues sent a letter to the bishops in which they observed that dangerous factions were beginning to form in some parts of the kingdom over the question of whether or not certain images might be spared. As a result, the councillors went on smoothly, 'almost no place of this realm is in any sure quietness, *but where all images be wholly take away and pulled down already*'.[58] The king's pleasure, they informed the bishops, was now therefore 'that, immediately upon the sight hereof . . . you shall . . . give order that all the images remaining in any church . . . within your diocese be removed and taken away'.[59] This order had naturally infuriated traditionalists and four days later it was reported from Hampshire that the people were 'murmuring against the destruction of images'.[60] In the West Country, such 'murmuring' was shortly to escalate into outright violence.

Meanwhile, the regime was also pressing ahead with its plans to modify 'the central act of worship of the Church, the mass'.[61] On 13 March, yet another letter was sent out to the bishops, this time noting that, in the wake of a recent Act of Parliament directing that communion should henceforth be distributed to the laity in both kinds, the king had caused 'sundry . . . learned men in the scriptures, to assemble themselves', in order to draw up a new form of words which was to be incorporated within the traditional mass for 'the distribution of the said most holy sacrament'. Now, the letter went on, this new liturgical form had been completed, 'as may appear to you by the book thereof which we send herewith'. The bishops were therefore ordered to ensure that copies of the new text were 'delivered to every parson, vicar and curate' within their dioceses as soon as possible, so that they would have time to familiarise themselves with the modified rite before it was introduced in churches throughout the realm on Easter Day.[62] The 'order of communion', as the new liturgical form was termed, was probably based on texts that Cranmer had penned some time before, and was the first communion service in English. Although the mass was still to begin in Latin, as it had always done, after the celebrant himself had taken communion he was now directed to switch over to English in order to conduct the next part of the service.[63] This change would have been deeply shocking to traditionalists – not least, perhaps, in those parts of the realm where English was a minority tongue – and it is tempting to suggest that the introduction of the new 'order of communion' in the Cornish-speaking parishes of West Cornwall on 1 April 1548 had a part to play in sparking the major popular protest that broke out in that district just four days later.

Piecing together what happened in West Cornwall in April 1548 is a difficult task, because no contemporary narrative of the short-lived uprising, which was variously known at the time as 'the besynys yt was yn the weste parte', 'the . . . commotion in the west part' and 'the Cornish commotion', appears to have survived.[64] Nevertheless, as the Cornish Elizabethan writer, Richard Carew, was later to record in his *Survey of Cornwall* of 1603 – and as several other pieces of documentary evidence have since emerged to confirm – the trouble clearly began in the large and populous parish of St Keverne in the Lizard Peninsula: the very same parish in which a major popular insurrection had broken out once before, in 1497, and in which another had been fearfully anticipated by Sir William Godolphin in 1537, at the time of the Carpyssacke affair. That St Keverne was again the initial seat of the disturbances in 1548 is made clear, first, by a legal document of 1583 – in which a local man referred in passing to St Keverne as the 'place wherein the late insurrexion in Cornewall made in the raigne of . . . Edward the Syxth had his comencement' – and, second, by two letters composed in the immediate aftermath of the rising.[65] The first of these, unsigned and sent to an unknown recipient on 20 April 1548, is a testimonial on behalf of one Hugh Mason of Grade, a parish near St Keverne. Mason, the writer notes, had recently been arrested at Exeter on suspicion of having been 'one of the Sterers off the vilayns off Sent Keverne'. Yet, far from having been one of those who had initially 'stirred' the people to rise, the writer continues, Mason had himself been the target of the protestors' wrath: 'for thay off sent Keverns thretnyd hyme hongyng & burnyng off hys howse unless he wolde do as thay did'.[66]

Having made it abundantly clear that those whom he disparaged as the 'vilayns', or low-born rustics, of St Keverne had been at the centre of the initial stirs, the anonymous correspondent then goes on to relate how Mason had forsaken the protestors' company 'at ther fyrst proceydyng & Came to the Castell off Pendenys', near Falmouth, where 'I met heme & gave heme advysse to get heme estewardes untyll such tyme as the vyllayn Treators ware subdewyd'.[67] The writer's allusion to the protestors as 'traitors' further underlines his own detestation of them, while his account of how, upon being threatened by the insurgents, Mason had at once made his way to Pendennis suggests a conviction, on the latter's part, that the newly completed castle was not only formidable enough to serve as a bulwark against domestic insurrection, but was also in reliably loyalist hands. That Mason's confidence was justified on both counts is amply demonstrated by the fact that John Killigrew junior – the son of the local gentleman who had been appointed as the governor of Pendennis – later sought repayment from the Crown for the monies he and his father had laid out 'for thinterteignment of certayne soldyers [in the castle] & for vituellinge of the same agenst the Rebells at Easter [1548]'.[68] Clearly, then, John Killigrew senior had drawn in men and shut his gates soon after the inhabitants of St Keverne had risen, and had then held Pendennis against the insurgents throughout the stir. Indeed, it was almost certainly Killigrew himself who penned this letter on Mason's behalf: the writer's reference to his having met Mason at Pendennis and then told him to continue his journey to the east – presumably in order to carry first-hand intelligence about the rising to the authorities – makes it clear that he held a position of authority in the castle.

The second of the two letters written in the immediate aftermath of the rising is also a testimonial to Mason's loyalty and is also anonymous. It is shorter but in some ways even more helpful than the first letter, because it allows us to pinpoint exactly when and where the rising began. Perhaps written by Thomas Treffry, the captain of St Mawes – the coastal fortress that lies on the other side of the estuary from Pendennis – this letter certifies that 'at the fyrst off the Rebelyen off thys Rebelles of sent Keveran [on] the vth off thys presents [i.e., on 5 April] the sayd Hugh [Mason] for saveguard off his lyff Repayred to the Weste Castell of Falmothe [i.e., Pendennis] & . . . [from thence was] Convayd to the east castell [i.e., St Mawes] & from thens . . . estward to Exceter'.[69] So, in the course of still further confirming Mason's loyalist bona fides, this letter provides us with firm evidence that the disturbances had indeed begun at St Keverne on 5 April, and that, by the end of the first day, Mason had already been threatened by the protestors and made his escape. While we can be sure St Keverne and its hinterland formed the initial seat of the rising, though, we can also be sure that the main body of the protestors did not remain there for long, for independent evidence shows that, later that same day, an unknown number of men from St Keverne and the surrounding parishes made their way to Helston. This was the most populous town in the hundred of Kerrier and the seat of the local administration. During the Elizabethan period, moreover, Helston is also known to have been the place where the men of the Lizard Peninsula were accustomed to assemble for military musters: on Helston Down, just to the south of the town.[70] If this custom had already been established during the 1540s, it would have been another excellent reason for choosing Helston as a point of rendezvous. And it was at Helston – whether by accident or design – that the demonstrators' path would converge with that of the man who had already provoked angry protest in Cornwall once before: William Body.

We last encountered Body in December 1547, at which time the Privy Council had been criticising him to the gentry governors of Penwith for having been, in their view, 'the verie occasion' of the 'tumulteous assembly' that had occurred in that hundred earlier that month, through his 'indiscreete . . . mishandlinge' of their commission concerning the church goods.[71] As we have seen, at the end of their letter, the councillors had directed that Body should be sent up to London in order to answer for his misdeeds. Yet, if Body did return to the capital and appear before Somerset and his colleagues, it is clear that he swiftly managed to convince them that his offences had been relatively minor ones – or, at the very least, that he was far too useful a servant for the regime to be able to dispense with his services for long – since, by the beginning of April, he was back in West Cornwall again and continuing to advance the regime's religious agenda. Precisely what Body was doing at Helston on the day that the St Keverne men surged into the town is unclear. Many years later, Carew wrote simply that he had been sitting 'in Commission at Helston for matters of reformation in religion'.[72] A letter written by the French ambassador in London, Odet de Selve, on 15 April is more specific, stating that Body and his fellow commissioners 'had gone there [i.e., to West Cornwall] to remove images' and that, at some unspecified point – either just before the disturbances began or on the day of the rising itself – they 'had cut down and broken the crucifix of a church, which the people had insisted should be left'.[73] There is nothing to indicate whether this crucifix was in Helston church, in St Keverne church or in some other local church altogether. What is absolutely clear is that, once the protestors had arrived in Helston, they launched a murderous assault on Body.

Almost everything we know about what happened in Helston on that day comes from the slew of 'indictments', or formal legal charges, that were drawn up in the wake of the rising by the Crown's lawyers as they prepared to accuse the leading protestors of being rebels and traitors. According to the most informative of these documents, on 5 April, Martin Geffrey of St Keverne, a 'clerk' or priest, John Pyers of St Keverne, mariner, Edmund Irish of St Keverne, smith, John William Tribo of St Keverne, mariner, and William Thomas of nearby Mullion, yet another mariner, had, 'at Helston ... in ... Cornwall', through 'outcry, ringing of bells &c, raise[d] and assemble[d] other traitors to the amount of 1,000 men and more, [and] with arms &c levied war against the king ... and ... so continue[d] all that day'.[74] It seems probable that this single charge was designed to encompass both the accused men's alleged incitement of the initial stirs around St Keverne, and the steps that they had then allegedly taken to gather further support after the occupation of Helston. Next, the five men were accused of having 'attacked the house in which William Bodye, Gentleman, dwelt, and assaulted and murdered the said ... Bodye'.[75] This charge clearly implies that, after having been confronted by the protestors – or, perhaps, forewarned of their approach – Body had retreated to his lodgings in the vain hope that he would be able to defend himself against his attackers by barring the doors, but that he had subsequently been dragged out and despatched.

Who killed William Body? We will never know for sure. Carew was later to imply that 'one Kilter' of St Keverne had been at the head of those 'who imbrued their wicked hands in ... [Body's] blood', while, later still, several seventeenth-century chroniclers were to claim that 'a priest' – presumably Geffrey – had stabbed Body to death with a knife.[76] Writing just ten days after the event, however, de Selve reported that the people of Cornwall had 'killed and made into a thousand pieces some commissioners who had gone there to remove images', and while de Selve was surely wrong to state that more than one 'commissioner' had been slain, his report that the protestors had riven their victim(s) 'into a thousand pieces' is suggestive.[77] These words clearly imply that Body had been lynched – that he had died during the course of a mob attack, in which many different attackers had struck and injured their victim – and the fact that the Crown subsequently charged more than a score of men with being involved in Body's murder surely points the same way. At their subsequent trials, all but two of these individuals – William Kilter of Constantine, husbandman, and Pasco Trevian of St Keverne, mariner – pleaded 'not guilty'. That Kilter and Trevian, by contrast, frankly acknowledged themselves to be guilty can only be because they realised that the evidence against them was too strong to be convincingly refuted.[78] It seems reasonable to assume that Kilter and Trevian took a leading role in the attack, therefore, and they may well have been the men who struck the fatal blows, but it is impossible to say for sure that they were the only killers.

The indictments make it plain that, far from feeling any remorse about what they had done, Body's assailants had subsequently gone out of their way, not only to proclaim his killing to the world, but also to present it as a wholly legitimate act which had been carried out in defence of the true religion. The third charge in the indictment against Geffrey and the others states that, after Body was dead, the insurgents had caused a public 'proclamation' to be made 'in the marketplace of . . . Helston' by a local yeoman named John Resseygh that

> They [i.e., the insurgents] would have all such laws as was made by the late King Henry the 8th, and none other, until the King's Majesty that now is, accomplish the age of 24 years, and that whoso would defend Bodye, or follow such new fashions as he did, they would punish him likewise.[79]

Once they had issued this defiant statement of intent, the insurgents had then proceeded to gather in more strength from the surrounding countryside. So much is made clear by the penultimate charge in the indictment against Geffrey and his fellows, which says that, on 7 April, they, together 'with divers other malefactors, to the number of 5,000 men', had continued to remain in arms and had caused a second 'proclamation' to be made. This had stated that, 'on Tuesday next at the General Sessions [of the peace] to be holden at Helston, we will be there with a greater number, to see if any men will be revenged herein'.[80] The insurgents had dared the local governors to punish them for Body's murder, in other words, and the final charge in the indictment states that these 'threats'

– combined, presumably, with the physical presence of the protestors themselves – had proved so effective that 'William Godolphin, knight' and other JPs had been unable to hold the sessions that were scheduled to take place at Helston, as usual, on 10 April.[81] Further indictments provide the names of a dozen more St Keverne men who had taken part in the commotion. Also named in these subsidiary indictments are both William and John Kilter of the nearby parish of Constantine – one of whom, presumably, was the man whom Carew later identified as the leader of the rising – and individuals from a further nine parishes in the hundreds of Kerrier, Pyder and Penwith.[82] The geographical spread of the parishes from which these men were drawn – together with the fact that the indictments refer, first, to 1,000, then, to 5,000 'malefactors' having gathered in arms – suggests that the uprising had gained popular support throughout much of West Cornwall.[83]

Alarmed, and clearly unable to quell the rising through their own strength alone, Godolphin and the other local gentry governors were forced to appeal to their neighbours for aid. Over the following days, armed men were hastily raised in a number of parishes in the eastern half of Cornwall by Sir Richard Grenville and others – as well as in Plymouth by the mayor of that town – and were sent hurrying westwards in order to help suppress those whom the church warden of St Winnow later termed 'the rebellers of the west'.[84] About what happened next, and about precisely how the insurgents were eventually persuaded to disperse, virtually no information has survived. The 'Black Book' of Plymouth – a manuscript volume that contains a chronicle of local events, updated by an anonymous hand soon after 1549 – provides the only near-contemporary account. Under the date 1548, the chronicler observes merely that 'in this yeare was the Fyrst inssurreccyon in Cornwall, where one Bodye was slayne and afterwards the commons were pacified by the gentylemen of the countrey w[i]t[h] small troble'.[85] The insouciance of the last three words reflects the fact that the entry was written several years later, because it is evident that, at the time, not only the local gentry but the Privy Council, too, had been extremely concerned about the rising.[86] That the common people of Cornwall were, indeed, eventually 'pacified' and persuaded to go home by the local gentlemen, however, is made clear by a letter which the councillors sent to Godolphin, Grenville and eight other Cornish gentlemen on 17 April, thanking them for their own letter of four days before, in which they had let them know of 'your good diligence and wise . . . proceding in the stay of the seditious commotion lately stirred up in those parties'.[87]

In the absence of other evidence, we must presume that the local gentry and their retainers – reinforced by the contingents of armed men that had been brought to their assistance from elsewhere – had marched to the outskirts of Helston at some point between 11 and 13 April and had succeeded in facing down the protestors through a mixture of threats and blandishments, eventually persuading them to lay down their arms and go home. The fact that the Plymouth receivers' accounts note a payment of 3s.4d. made to one Thomas Croppe soon after 11 April 'for his costs to cary a l[ett]re to Sir Peter Carew into Cornewall' raises the intriguing possibility that Carew may also have been with the Cornish gentlemen at the time that they negotiated with the protestors, or at least that he had then been hastening to join them.[88] What is clear from the councillors' letter is that, by 13 April, the local governors had already succeeded in apprehending those whom they regarded as 'the most notable offenders' in the stir. It would be interesting to know how these individuals had been persuaded to give themselves up, or how their comrades had been persuaded to abandon them, but – significantly perhaps – the sources remain silent on this point. Now, the councillors directed the local gentlemen to 'send . . . up to us in savegard the priest, Piers the maryner' and four more 'of the chief ringleaders', stressing that it was vital to ensure that these men were kept apart during their journey, so that they would be unable to speak with each other before they were subjected to further interrogation.[89] A fortnight later, the Council directed that two men be paid the considerable sum of £38 'towerd their charges for bringing hyder vi rebelles, prisonniers, out of Cornewall'.[90]

While the councillors' letter of 17 April breathed a tangible sense of relief that the rising had been so quickly suppressed, it also contained more than a hint of apprehension about the possibility of further trouble ahead. After having noted that they understood that 'the simple people remayn so dysmayed as they myght peradventure . . . be eftsones easely stirred to further folly', Somerset and his colleagues directed the local gentlemen 'to declare, or cause to be declared unto them by such persons and means as you shall thinke most convenient', that the king was disposed to be merciful to those who had been 'seduced & brought to this ill attemptate' by 'the spurring and setting forwardes of some ... evill disposed persons'. Having convinced the erstwhile protestors that they would not be harshly punished, and thus 'put them out of dispayre', the councillors went on, the gentlemen were then to strive 'to lern by all wayes and meanes possible the very gro[u]nde and originell of this commotion [and] who wer the chief doars and ringleaders ... in the same'.[91] Further orders instructing the local governors to enquire into the causes of the rising and to pre-empt any future disorder clearly followed soon afterwards, for, on 23 April, Godolphin wrote to another gentleman, John Reskymer of Merthen in Constantine, informing him that he had just 'receved the Kynges majesties commyssyon ... dyrected to you, me and others consyrnyng the Tumulte of the commen people to take an order with them'.[92]

Over the following weeks, the Cornish gentlemen continued to track down those whom they considered to have committed the most serious offences during the insurrection, probably focusing on those who had participated in Body's murder. The apprehended men were imprisoned in Launceston Castle, and among them were the two Kilters: one of whom, Carew later recorded, while 'lying there in the castle green upon his back', performed the extraordinary feat of hurling 'a stone of some pounds wayght' over the top of one of the castle towers.[93] On 16 May, a special commission of oyer and terminer was sent down from London to Godolphin, Sir Richard Grenville and five other local gentlemen, empowering them to try the offenders imprisoned at Launceston on charges of treason.[94] The next day – and in accordance with the policy of relative leniency that had already been trailed in the Council's letter to the local gentry of a month before – a formal royal pardon was issued to the people of Cornwall. This document noted that, although 'many of you, the king's ... commons, dwelling ... in ... Cornwall ... have ... of late attempted and committed manifest and open rebellion', yet the king, 'of his inestimable goodness, replenished with most godly pity and mercy, and at your most humble petitions', was nevertheless now 'pleased to ... grant ... his ... pardon' to all who had taken part in the rising – apart from twenty-eight individuals whose names appeared at the end of the text.[95] Of these, six were the 'notable offenders' who had been sent up to the Council in the immediate aftermath of the rising, while the others were those who were scheduled to be tried at Launceston.

On 21 May, the commissioners sitting at Launceston ordered the sheriff to empanel a grand jury from among the ranks of the Cornish gentry.[96] It was the grand jurors who would decide whether or not the indictments drawn up against the twenty-two alleged rebels and traitors who had been imprisoned locally were 'true bills'. On the evidence of the erasures in the indictments, it would appear that the charges against 10 of the men were dropped, while the cases of the remaining 12 proceeded to trial on 28 May.[97] Of these, two were found not guilty, nine – including William Kilter and Pasco Trevian – were found guilty of high treason and were therefore sentenced to the terrible 'traitor's death' of hanging, drawing and quartering, while one was found guilty of murder alone, and was therefore sentenced merely to be hanged. The sentences were clearly not carried out straight away, however, for, on 3 June, the Council wrote to the Cornish commissioners directing them 'to proceed with as conveniente speede as might be to the executiones of the traitores there ...; albeit some of them thoughte the nomber appointed to be executed there was over greate'.[98] It is evident from this last comment that some of the local gentlemen who had been appointed as commissioners were anxious to temper justice with mercy, perhaps because they feared that excessive harshness might provoke a new rising; it is intriguing, too, that, despite their initial order, the councillors later shifted towards this same point of view. Later in the year, at least four of those who had been condemned to death at Launceston were pardoned, including, remarkably, William Kilter and Pasco Trevian.[99]

Others were clearly less fortunate, for the Plymouth receivers' accounts contain a gruesome series of entries which record the sums of money laid out 'for doyyng th'execuycyon upon the traytor of Cornwalle' on Plymouth Hoe soon after the special commission of oyer and terminer at Launceston had concluded its business. These include payments for building the gallows; for 'leadyng the horse when the traytor was drawen to execucon'; for paying the executioner; for purchasing the faggots with which the victim's entrails were burned after he had been disembowelled; for the purchase of two poles on which to fix his head and one of his dismembered 'quarters'; for two clamps of iron to fix those poles and their bloody burdens in a prominent position on Plymouth's guildhall; and for carrying another quarter to Tavistock, to be similarly placed on public display. Further sums of money laid out 'for the dyner of the undersheryf of Cornewalle, beying here when the traytor was putt to execucyon', and 'for wyne at the recyving of the traytor' suggest that the town governors of Plymouth – an urban community in which there were by now a number of individuals who favoured the new learning – were in holiday mood as they prepared for the punishment of this luckless individual.[100] The fact that John Milliton subsequently received £40 to repay him for 'his charges in takinge and execucion of certeine rebellions in . . . Cornewall', moreover, makes it hard to doubt that similarly grisly scenes were enacted in a number of carefully selected places within Cornwall itself: including, one must surely presume, both Helston and St Keverne.[101]

Meanwhile, in London, preparations were being made to try the 'ringleaders' of the commotion: the men who had been sent up to the Council for interrogation immediately after the disturbances were suppressed. On 7 June, a second commission of oyer and terminer was issued, this time addressed to twelve knights who dwelt in or near the capital, for the trial of these individuals. The next day, the sheriff was ordered to return a grand jury at Westminster, and a letter was sent to the constable of the Tower, ordering him to convey the bodies of five men – Geffrey, Pyers, Thomas, Irish and Tribo – to Westminster by 7 a.m. on 11 June.[102] The trial of the accused men took place later that day; few can have been surprised when all five were found guilty of high treason and sentenced to death.[103] In Geffrey's case, execution would follow within the month. It is clear that, from the moment they first received word about the rising's alleged leaders, Somerset and his colleagues had been convinced that Geffrey – the man whom they simply termed 'the priest' in their letter to the Cornish gentry of 17 April – had been the prime mover of the insurrection; the fact that his name appears first in each of the indictments relating to the five men imprisoned in the Tower is hardly a coincidence. Whether this conviction was based on detailed information which had been sent to the councillors about Geffrey's role in the protests, or simply on their own visceral dislike and distrust of conservative clerics, it is impossible to say. Little can be said about Geffrey for certain, beyond the fact that, rather than having been the incumbent of St Keverne, as is often claimed, he appears to have been an unbeneficed clergyman: in a document compiled during the early 1540s, he had been listed as a stipendiary priest in the parish of St Just-in-Roseland, some 17 miles to the south-east of Truro.[104] How, and in what capacity, he eventually made his way to St Keverne is unknown.

In any event, Geffrey had become emblematic of the rebellion in the councillors' eyes, and it was therefore inevitable that he would now suffer the full horror of 'a traitor's death'. According to a London chronicler:

> [on] the seventh day of Julie, a priest was drawen from the Towre of London into Smythfield and their hanged, headed and quartered, and his membres and bowells brent, which was one of the causes of a commotion in Cornewall, where one Bodie, a gentleman and one of the Kinges commissioners was slaine ... His head was sett one London Bridge and his quarters on fower gates of this cittie.[105]

The men who had been sentenced alongside Geffrey at Westminster must surely have anticipated a similar fate, but, remarkably, all four of them, including Pyers, received pardons later that year.[106] Having made their point through the execution of Geffrey, the councillors had clearly decided that they could now afford to be merciful.

It seems unlikely that the regime's most redoubtable Cornish champion would have concurred with this judgement, however, because – even as Geffrey was being drawn towards the gallows – Sir William Godolphin was taking urgent steps to prevent a recrudescence of popular disorder in Penwith. On 3 July, almost three months after the commotion had been suppressed, Godolphin wrote to Reskymer and another local gentleman, informing them that he had summoned all 'the gentlemen ... off every parishe within the hundred off Penwyth' to assemble before him near the Mount in order 'to consult with them & to knowe what number off trustye men may be yn a redynes uppon a sodayn warnyng to serve the kyng'. After this meeting was over, Godolphin went on, 'I myself with all the gentyllmen that I . . . can gette unto me wyll ryde with . . . as many horse as we can well furnyshe' through the surrounding countryside, 'to th'entent that men shall see that we be hable to do somewhat yff any sedycyous persons wyll offer to sturre'. Godolphin advised his correspondents to take similar precautions, and asked them to meet him soon, so that they could 'furder . . . consult of thes matiers'.[107] The fact that this letter was sent to two gentlemen who lived in the neighbouring hundred of Kerrier shows that Godolphin feared further disturbances right across the west of Cornwall during the summer of 1548, and there are hints that such anxieties continued to persist among the regime's local supporters until well into the autumn.

What lay behind the Cornish commotion of 1548? Because of the prominence that the killing of William Body assumes in the indictments, and in the few contemporary references to the insurrection that survive, there has been a tendency to view the episode as a rising that was primarily fuelled by popular antagonism towards this one man: or even, indeed, as a rising that was not genuinely popular at all, but which had instead been deliberately orchestrated by some of Body's personal enemies in order to act as a smoke screen for his prearranged murder.[108] Yet no one has ever suggested that the similarly short-lived rising which took place in Lincolnshire in 1536, during the course of which Dr Raynes, the bishop of Lincoln's chancellor, was similarly murdered by a mob, was the product of hatred of Raynes alone – and this difference in emphasis surely reflects the fact that, while we have plenty of evidence about the motives of the Lincolnshire protestors, we have practically no evidence at all about the motives of the Cornish protestors, beyond that which is contained in the indictments and the brief comments of de Selve.[109] In fact, it is hard to doubt that the insurrection was, above all, the product of popular outrage at Somerset's religious policies, and that Body was killed not only because of who he was, but also because of what he represented: in the protestors' eyes, the entire evangelical establishment.

The 'proclamation' which the insurgents are recorded to have made in Helston marketplace – 'They would have all such laws as was made by the late King Henry the 8 and none other, until the King's Majesty that now is, accomplish the age of 24 years, and that whoso would defend Bodye, or follow such new fashions as he did, they would punish him likewise' – makes their view of Body as the personification of those who sought to adopt 'new' religious and cultural 'fashions' – that is to say, evangelical ones – absolutely clear.[110] By stating they would 'punish' anyone who dared to adopt such 'fashions' in the same way as they had punished Body, moreover, they were hinting at the view that such persons were heretics, and therefore worthy of the most condign penalties: to be inflicted by the community, if Church and State were no longer willing, or able, to oblige. Furthermore, by declaring that all of the laws made under Henry VIII should remain in force until Edward came of age and that no new laws should be introduced until then, the protestors were demonstrating they were well aware of the similar – though more subtle – arguments which had recently been advanced by Gardiner and other conservative figures elsewhere in the realm to precisely that effect – and that they were therefore conscious of themselves as part of a wider coalition of opposition to the policies of Somerset's regime. A phrase that appears in another of the indictments against the five men tried in London, stating that the insurgents had maintained themselves in arms in Helston, 'believing that a great part of the kingdom would join them', may be said to make exactly the same point.[111] None of these charges would have made any sense if the protestors had been demonstrating against Body alone.

The fact that when Dr Roger Tong, one of the king's chaplains and an ardent evangelical, was sent on a preaching tour of the West Country in the autumn of 1548, he either chose, or was instructed, to speak at St Keverne again hints at a perception, on the part of regime loyalists, that profound religious conservatism had underlain the rising that broke out in that parish just a few months before. A letter sent to John Reskymer at this time not only advised him that 'doctor Tongye entendethe to preache at St Keveran uppon Sondaye next', but also requested him 'to command the baylyff of the hundred [of Kerrier] ... [to] warne all Meneke', that is to say, all of the inhabitants of the twelve parishes of the

Meneage Peninsula, 'to be there at the same sermon'.[112] Clearly, determined efforts were being made by the authorities to ensure that the inhabitants of Kerrier were exposed to the regime's religious message, though it is difficult to say how far the inhabitants of this largely Cornish-speaking district would have understood that message. Earlier that year, Tong had denounced Bishop Gardiner – then newly released from prison – to the Council for contemning those he termed the 'new preachers'. Outraged, the councillors had summoned Gardiner to London, where, a month later, he had been rearrested for other supposed offences and imprisoned in the Tower.[113] As he addressed the sullen throng who had been 'warned in' to St Keverne to hear him speak, therefore, Tong may well have mused on the bishop's fall, and rejoiced that, just as he had witnessed the humbling of Gardiner and other conservative churchmen who had sought to check the progress of godly reformation through the force of their eloquence, so was he now witnessing the humbling of the obdurate western people who had sought to check the progress of that same reformation through the force of their arms.

If we credit de Selve's account, it was a specific act of iconoclasm that served as the final spark for the rising. Yet why should such an action have prompted a full-scale uprising in West Cornwall, when in other parts of the West Country the destruction of images in 1547–48 appears to have met with no open opposition? The district's unique cultural identity may well provide a clue, for the three western hundreds in which the rebellion occurred were those in which most of the common people still used the Cornish tongue. The fact that West Cornwall was Cornish-speaking can only have made its inhabitants even more stubbornly resistant than were other West Country folk to the message of the Reformation – preached as that message invariably was, in English – while the fact that some of the West Cornish regarded themselves as a downtrodden, subject people meant that it was easy for Body to be regarded as an alien oppressor there, in a way that was not possible elsewhere. We should not forget, moreover, that on Easter Day 1548 – just four days before the uprising at St Keverne began – the new order of communion had begun to be used in churches throughout the realm, meaning that many Cornish-speakers attending the Easter services had been confronted with a liturgical form in English for the very first time: an innovation that would inevitably have come as a particular shock in Cornish-speaking communities.

It is interesting to note that, when he later referred back to those who had risen up in 1548, John Killigrew junior termed them 'the Rebells at Easter': a form of words that hints at a perception, on Killigrew's part, that the particular time of year at which the protests had occurred had been significant. The contemporary writer Walter Lynne, moreover, did precisely the same thing in his book of *Chronicles*, printed in 1550, noting, under the year 1548, that 'at Easter was a great coniunction of rustikes in Cornwall, by popysh priestes'.[114] Lynne's reference to 'priestes' shows that he, like Somerset, believed conservative churchmen to have instigated the protests, but the fact that Lynne specifies that the trouble had begun 'at Easter' also raises the possibility that he did not see the conjunction of the church feast and the rising as a complete coincidence. As we shall see, those who rose in arms in Cornwall in 1549 can be shown to have been motivated, at least in part, by their desire to resist the imposition of the new prayer book in English. It does not seem implausible to suggest, therefore, that those who rose in arms in Cornwall at Easter 1548 may also have been motivated, at least in part, by their desire to resist the imposition of the new order of communion in the same tongue. Finally, it is perhaps worth observing that, in one of the handful of copies of the original printed order that still survive – a copy that was originally sent to the curate of Aston, in the diocese of Lichfield – a handwritten 'direction for the removal of images is combined with that for the use of the book': a fact that demonstrates that, in some parts of the kingdom at least, the agents of central government had been ordering images to be destroyed and the new order of communion to be introduced at one and the same time.[115] Might William Body have been doing precisely the same thing – and might this have been what finally triggered the explosion of popular outrage that resulted in his murder?

News of the Cornish commotion had briefly alarmed the evangelical establishment in London, but the swift suppression of the disturbances permitted Somerset and his colleagues to breathe easily once more, and the fact that seven men, at most, appear to have been executed in the wake of the rising suggests that leading figures in the regime now considered the danger from this particular quarter to have passed. In treating those whom they had publicly declared to be 'rebels' with such comparative mildness, though, Somerset and his fellow councillors were almost certainly storing up trouble for themselves, and one historian has suggested that the 'relative leniency' that the government had displayed in the wake of the Cornish commotion – exemplified by the granting of a royal pardon to the majority of the protestors on 17 May – may have helped to trigger the very different protests that broke out in the Hertfordshire parish of Northaw just four days later: protests against the activities of a gentleman who had recently received a royal commission to enclose local common land.[116] The demonstrators – adopting the same line of argument as the Cornishmen at Helston – claimed that the newly issued commission remained invalid until Edward came of age; and although it was not long before their protests, too, were suppressed, the Northaw stirs were to have momentous consequences.

Just a week after the trouble in Hertfordshire came to an end, Somerset issued a new commission to investigate the problem of illegal enclosure in the Midlands: a commission that was led by the passionate anti-encloser John Hales. As a result, an entirely unwarranted conviction began to grow up among ordinary people that Somerset's regime was opposed to the enclosure of common land per se, rather than simply to illegal enclosures, and that the Crown was about to embark on a radical programme of agrarian reform which would lead to the destruction of enclosures across the entire country. Hales was soon being accused by angry landowners of stirring up trouble and, during the summer and autumn of 1548, a number of anti-enclosure riots took place in the Midlands and the South-East, fuelled by the rioters' belief that, in pulling down enclosures, they were simply anticipating Somerset's wishes. In the West Country, where agricultural conditions were very different from those that obtained in other parts of the kingdom, enclosure was scarcely an issue.[117] Nevertheless, sparks from the succession of straw fires that were breaking out in other parts of the kingdom would soon begin to drift westwards, where they would eventually ignite a conflagration greater than any that had been seen so far.

# *Part II*
## *The Rising*

# 3

# Outbreak
## June 1549

### I

On 28 January 1549, the boy-king in London embarked on his third year as England's ruler and – according to the system of reckoning that was generally employed in civil documents at this time – he and his subjects therefore entered upon a new regnal year: 'the third year of King Edward VI' or, as it was commonly written in abbreviated form, 'iii Edward vi'. Over the following days and weeks, scribes across the kingdom would swiftly make the adjustment from the old regnal year to the new one as they wrote and dated financial, legal and administrative documents of all sorts. None of them can have realised that 'the third year of Edward VI' was soon to become a calendric term freighted with grim significance: a term that would be intimately associated, for the rest of the Tudor century, with rebellion, with bloodshed and with death. From the point of view of Protector Somerset and the other evangelically minded councillors who now governed England in the king's name, the future looked bright with promise, rather than dark with foreboding, and they continued to press eagerly ahead with a legislative programme that was designed to meet their twin objectives of victory over the Scots in the North and victory over all lingering remnants of 'papistry' at home. During the early months of 1549, two acts were passed in the second session of Edward's first Parliament, both of which would have far-reaching effects on the kingdom as a whole and on the West Country in particular. The most important of these was the Act of Uniformity, which decreed that the old medieval liturgy in Latin should be abolished, in all of its regional variations, and replaced with a new prayer book in English, to be introduced in parishes throughout the realm by Whitsun that year.[1] The new 'Book of Common Prayer', which had been masterminded by Cranmer, was designed to move the Church still further in an evangelical direction and contained many elements that traditionalists were bound to find deeply objectionable.[2]

In addition to the Act of Uniformity, the Parliament also passed a significant piece of financial legislation. This was the Act for the Relief of Sheep and Cloth: in effect, a statute granting the Crown the right to raise money through a new poll tax on sheep and a new purchase tax on cloth combined.[3] The 'relief' would provide the government with much-needed cash for military purposes. Somerset may also have hoped that the new tax on sheep would tend to discourage sheep farming, and hence the practice of enclosing common land for grazing, though the evidence on this point is unclear.[4] The first part of the act directed that, from May 1549 onwards, all owners of sheep would be required to make a payment of between 1d. and 3d. for each of their beasts to the Crown: the precise amount depending on how many sheep an individual owned, what kind of sheep they were and whether they were grazed on enclosed or common land. It was obvious that this measure would hit counties like Devon, in which sheep grazing was ubiquitous, especially hard. The second part of the act directed that, for each pound in weight of woollen cloth manufactured after 24 June, the sum of 8d. would now be payable to the Crown. In Devon, cloth-making was the most important local industry and employed many thousands of people, so, once again, it was evident that this act would have a particular impact on Devonian pockets.[5]

By the time the parliamentary session came to an end on 14 March, therefore, a series of further religious innovations and financial impositions were hurtling down the track, even as people in the West Country – like people all over the realm – were struggling to absorb the many radical changes that Somerset's regime had already made. As Eamon Duffy has shown in his splendid study of how the Reformation came to the Exmoor parish of Morebath, the Crown's policies had effectively dismantled traditional religious practice during the two years between May 1547 and May 1549, leaving many formerly vigorous parish communities hollowed out and almost penniless.[6] A new commission for drawing up inventories of all church goods had recently been issued, moreover, and as churchwardens throughout Devon and Cornwall reluctantly applied themselves to this task once more, few can have doubted that, in doing so, they were simply preparing the way for the seizure of their cherished 'church juells'.[7] By the beginning of May 1549, a great deal had already happened to make local people angry, resentful and fearful, in other words – and it was at this crucial moment, we may strongly suspect, although the evidence does not permit us to say for sure, that whispers of the stirs taking place in the counties to the east first began to circulate in Devon.

As we saw in the last chapter, demonstrations against the enclosure of common land had occurred in several Midland counties from May 1548 onwards: demonstrations that had possibly been encouraged, in the first place, by the relative leniency with which the Cornish rebels of Easter 1548 had been treated by the Crown, and which had certainly been encouraged, thereafter, by the regime's own actions and by its stated determination to deal firmly with the problem of illegal enclosures. Those demonstrations had now somewhat abated, but in April 1549 the Privy Council issued a new proclamation, stressing once again its intention to 'redress' such enclosures and to punish those who had erected them, and it was evidently this restatement of the imminence of official reform that now prompted unofficial attacks on enclosures to break out anew.[8] On 5 May, a small group of men gathered at Frome in Somerset in order to pull down fences, claiming that 'they had heard of a proclamation sent into the country whereby they and all others were authorised so to do'.[9] Attempts to quell the disturbances backfired, the trouble quickly spread and, by 15 May, enclosure rioting had become widespread throughout both Somerset and Wiltshire.[10]

Among the enclosures levelled in Wiltshire at this time were some belonging to William Herbert, first earl of Pembroke, who was both a leading local landowner and a member of the Privy Council.[11] Herbert, a man of violent passions, who owed his elevated rank chiefly to his prowess as a soldier, responded with fury.[12] According to a contemporary chronicler, he raised '200 men in harness' who 'attacked the commons and slaughtered them like wolves among sheep'.[13] Herbert's savage onslaught cowed the protestors in Wiltshire, but unrest in Somerset continued to simmer. As late as 13 June, Sir Hugh Paulet wrote to his friend Sir John Thynne, the steward of Protector Somerset's household, that he had been obliged to remain at his house at Hinton St George, near Crewkerne, for some time past for 'the more assured staie' of his 'nere neighbours': in other words, in order to ensure that the inhabitants of the surrounding countryside remained quiet.[14] Hinton St George is only 10 miles from the Devon border and overlooks the Fosse Way, the old Roman road that in the 1540s, as for centuries before, was the main route linking Devon to the rest of the country. It is inconceivable that news of the protests in Somerset would not have been carried westwards, along this road and others: first to the East Devon cloth-making towns of Axminster, Cullompton and Tiverton, and from there, further west still, into the heart of Devon. Here, reports of the current 'commotion' in Somerset over enclosure would have reawakened Devonians' memories of what they had heard about the recent 'Cornish commotion' in defence of the traditional religion, and – as stories of popular protest to both east and west collided and converged with new rumours about confiscations of church goods and imminent taxes – would have made it easier for them to conceive of rising in protest themselves. Yet, as we know from the testimony of John Hooker, it was the introduction of the Book of Common Prayer that finally set the spark to the tinder in Devon.

## II

John Hooker was the first, and incomparably the most influential, historian of the series of events that he himself termed 'the Comotion or Rebellion in ... Devon and Cornewall in the Thirde Yere of Kinge Edward the VIth An[no] 1549'.[15] Because we now see those events primarily through Hooker's eyes, it is vital to pause for a moment here in order to introduce him and to consider the kind of man he was.

Hooker was born in Exeter around the year 1527 and was the son of a prosperous city merchant and his wife. He was schooled as a boy by none other than John Moreman – the cleric who was later to be imprisoned by the Edwardine visitors for his traditionalist preaching – and clearly came to feel a genuine affection for him: Hooker was later to recall of his old teacher that he had been 'of a very honest and good nature, loving to all men and hurtefull to none'.[16] Yet, despite his warm feelings for Moreman, Hooker was eventually to tread a very different doctrinal path. Having first gone up to Oxford to study the civil law, Hooker had then – most unusually – travelled to Cologne to continue his legal studies, and from there had gone on to Strasbourg to study theology. The fact that, while he was in Strasbourg, he had stayed with the Italian reformed thinker Pietro Martire Vermigli, better known in England as 'Peter Martyr', makes it clear that Hooker was already a quite unusually committed evangelical.[17] Having returned to Exeter in his late teens or early twenties – where he married Martha Tucker, the daughter of another city merchant – Hooker had been living there at the time that the commotion of 1549 broke out, and had remained in the city throughout the subsequent siege.[18] He was an eyewitness to the rebellion, then, and it is clear that – like so many people who have lived through violent conflicts – he was to be profoundly affected by the experience thereafter.

Throughout the rest of his long life, Hooker would constantly revisit the events of that extraordinary summer: thinking about them, talking about them and eventually composing a series of different accounts of the revolt – accounts that remain, to this day, the chief primary sources on which all subsequent histories of the rebellion have been based. The longest and best-known of these is the narrative that Hooker drew up for inclusion in Raphael Holinshed's *Chronicles* of England, first published in 1587: a narrative he later copied out again and incorporated, with minor changes, into his manuscript volume entitled 'The Description of the Cittie of Excester'.[19] It is the account published in Holinshed's *Chronicles* and then again in the 'Description' that has most often been cited in previous books about the Western Rising. But we should note that Hooker also wrote another, rather shorter account of the rebellion –

almost certainly an earlier draft – which survives in manuscript in the Bodleian Library in Oxford. The Bodleian account is very similar to the one that Hooker published in 1587, but it occasionally differs from it in significant respects, as we shall see.[20] Hooker's accounts of the human drama that unfolded in the West Country during the summer of 1549 are vivid, well informed and beyond price from an historian's point of view. Without them, we would only be able to see these events as through a glass darkly. But it is important to realise that, invaluable as they are, Hooker's accounts also contain biases and distortions.

The first, and most obvious, thing to bear in mind is that these are highly partisan texts. As an evangelical himself, Hooker had no sympathy whatsoever for protests that he believed to be inspired by a wicked desire to restore an entirely discredited set of religious practices, and, although he was able to discern fine personal qualities in some of those who held to the old faith – as his comments about Moreman show – he never doubted that, in spiritual terms, such people were utterly misguided. Hooker's perception of the disturbances he chronicled as a contest between right and wrong – literally between good and evil – inevitably means that he tended to portray the rebels' actions in the worst possible light, therefore, and to put a positive spin on those of their opponents. Second, it is important to remember that, during the 1560s, Hooker became the client of Sir Peter Carew, the swashbuckling evangelical gentleman who had played a major role in opposing the protestors in 1549, and that Hooker greatly admired Sir Peter; indeed, he later went on to write his 'Life', or biography.[21] So, as one would expect, in his treatment of Carew's activities, too, Hooker displays a propensity to accentuate the positive. Third, Hooker was an Exeter man to his fingertips. This means that, on the one hand, his accounts are designed to celebrate Exeter's resistance to the insurgents and to hold it up as a model to the world, while, on the other, his own perspective on events tends to be that of the man on the Exeter city walls. In both respects, his accounts are resolutely Exeter-centric. Fourth, last and perhaps most important of all, we must take care that the very richness and accessibility of Hooker's accounts do not tempt us into simply succumbing to his vision when reconstructing the story of the Western

Rising: especially as so few other contemporary documents relating to the commotion survive. Hooker's testimony is vital, of course, and it is often all we have, but at the same time we need to ponder his words carefully – and to weigh them against other sources wherever we can.

## III

'It is apparant & most certeine that this rebellion first was raised att a place in Devon named Sampford Courtneie, which lieth westwards from the citie [of Exeter] about sixteene miles, upon Mondaie in the Whitsun weeke beinge the tenth daie of June 1549,'[22] It is with these dramatic words that Hooker begins his account of the Western Rising – and it is important to stress that he is the only contemporary commentator not only to ascribe a date and a place to the initial disturbances, but also to provide a clear picture of how they originally broke out. Hooker now sets the scene by observing that, on the previous day – Whit Sunday, 9 June – the new service according to the Book of Common Prayer had been introduced throughout the country as the government had ordered. In the Bodleian manuscript, he then goes on to note that, on that day, 'the people for the most parte in all and through the whole West Countrie' heard the new service without making any protest, 'but the next day as it were of a . . . secreate conspiracie . . . [they] confederated to mislike and renounce the same'.[23] Here, Hooker is clearly hinting that he believed that there had been some sort of prearranged plan for protests against the new service to be staged on 10 June, and that Sampford Courtenay was not the only local community in which hostility to the Book of Common Prayer had been voiced on that day. Interestingly, however, he did not include this sentence in the published version of his account: perhaps because he no longer believed it to be true, perhaps because he feared that it might rattle too many skeletons in the cupboard.

The trouble in Sampford Courtenay itself had begun that Monday, Hooker went on, when 'the priest beinge come to the . . . church' had begun to prepare to read the new service, just as he had done the day before. At this, 'some of the parishioners, namelie one William Underhill a tailor, and one Segar a laborer and others, who had consulted and determined before of the matter', had confronted the priest and 'demanded what hee ment to doo, and what service he would saie?' When the priest had replied that he meant to read the new service, as he was now obliged to do by law, Underhill and his companions had told him

> that he should not do so, saying further that they would keep the old and ancient religion, as their forefathers before them had done, and ... [that] King Henrie the eighth by his last will and testament had taken order, that no alteration of religion should be made untill King Edward his sonne were come unto his full age, and ... [that] he was now but a childe and could doo nothing.[24]

These were extremely bold words. Underhill and the others were not just refusing to accept the new service book. By stating their determination to adhere to all of their traditional religious practices, they were offering a direct challenge to the evangelical establishment in London. By demanding that there should be no religious changes until Edward came of age, moreover, they were echoing the central demand that the Helston protestors had made the year before – and thus demonstrating their awareness of much wider strands of 'oppositionist' thought. By openly expressing the view that Edward himself was 'but a childe and could doo nothing', finally, they may be said to have been striking at the legitimacy of Somerset's entire regime.

According to Hooker, the rest of the parishioners now joined in the debate, making it clear that they were all of the same opinion, and 'willing and charging the priest that he should use and saie the ... [former] service, as in times past he was wont to do', until eventually the priest bent to their combined will and agreed to do as they asked. This decision was a momentous one, and by stating that the priest had taken it 'whether it were with his will, or against his will', Hooker was clearly flagging up the possibility that he might have simply pretended to be acting under duress. A marginal note at this point in the published version of Hooker's text – 'the priest compelled because he *would* be compelled to say masse' – goes further still, and specifically charges the priest with having been secretly more than happy to accede to his parishioners' demands. His decision made, the priest had next donned elaborate clerical vestments of the type that had been discouraged by the visitors in 1547 – or, as Hooker characteristically puts it, had 'ravish[ed] himselfe in his old popish attire' – and had then proceeded to say the Latin mass 'and all such services as in times past accustomed'.[25] It was not only the members of the congregation who were delighted by their priest's volte-face, moreover. Hooker tell us that news of what had happened at Sampford Courtenay was 'carried and noised even in a moment throughout the whole countrie: and the common people so well . . . liked thereof, that they clapped their hands for joie, and agreed . . . to have the same in everie of their severall parishes'.[26]

Sampford Courtenay lies at the centre of Devon, in the deep countryside to the north of Dartmoor. At the heart of the parish stands an exceptionally beautiful – and unspoilt – village, which still retains many houses built of the local whitewashed cob and thatch, while in the middle of the village stands an equally beautiful church, built of grey granite and ashlar stone: the same church outside which Underhill and Seagar held their fateful disputation with the priest over 470 years ago. Sampford Courtenay is a relatively large parish and contains many scattered farms; of the 500 or so people who lived here in 1549, most would have been employed in agriculture or in various rural trades.[27] As many visitors have observed over the years, it seems an unlikely place for a major rebellion to have begun – though this is true of St Keverne, too, of course, and of other seats of rebellion elsewhere in the country, such as Louth in Lincolnshire. Why should it have been in Sampford Courtenay, of all places, that popular protest suddenly erupted in 1549? Some have pointed to the fact that, as its name still testifies, the village had formerly belonged to the Courtenay family, whose most eminent member, Henry Courtenay, marquess of Exeter, had been widely regarded as well affected to the old faith until he was executed by Henry VIII for treason in 1538. But while there are, indeed, signs of 'a polarisation of forces' in Devon in 1549 'between on the one hand the radically Protestant Carew circle, and on the other the remnants of the old

Courtenay affinity', there is no hard evidence to prove that it was a residual affection for the Courtenay family that caused the people to reject the new prayer book in June that year.[28]

An alternative possibility that has sometimes been advanced is that a 'church ale', or parish feast, was being held in Sampford Courtenay on 10 June, that many people from nearby had assembled to take part in it, and that it was this large popular gathering that had bred the initial protests.[29] It is an attractive theory. The two days after Whitsun, 'the Whitsun holidays', certainly were the most common times for church ales to be held during the sixteenth century – and Whit Monday, in particular, is known to have remained the customary day for Whitsun revels in North Devon until as late as the 1890s.[30] This particular season of the year is known to have been regarded with keen apprehension by those in authority during the early modern period, moreover, because of their fear that 'the summer games' with which it was so intimately associated might breed rebellion. When the sheriff of Kent wrote to the Council expressing his fears of popular disorder in his county in May 1550, for example, they at once commanded him to assemble forces to deal with any potential trouble on the next Whit Sunday, while, three years later, the government went so far as to ban May Games in Kent altogether, on the grounds that they might lead to popular unrest.[31] The fact that the royal visitors had specifically banned the holding of church ales in the West Country in 1547, on the other hand, together with the fact that, across England as a whole, such parish feasts seem to have practically disappeared during Edward's reign, rather militates against the suggestion that an ale had been in progress in Sampford Courtenay in 1549 – and certainly no contemporary source refers to one.[32]

What of the priest who had been at the centre of the protests? As we have seen, Hooker insinuates that he had merely feigned reluctance to abandon the new service book and to return to the mass, when in fact this was precisely where his own inclinations led him, so is it possible that the priest had somehow contrived to start the trouble at Sampford Courtenay? Protector Somerset certainly convinced himself that that was the case later, at least for a while – but this may simply have reflected his own intense suspicion of 'seditious priests'.[33] Hooker never once mentions the name of 'the priest' to whom he refers in his narratives. Yet later historians have discovered that the incumbent of Sampford Courtenay in June 1549 was William Harper, a former clerk of the closet to Henry VIII's last wife, Catherine Parr, who had presented him to the living in 1546 – by which time Harper may well have been quite an elderly man.[34] There seems no reason to doubt that Harper was the man with whom Underhill and Seagar debated at Sampford Courtenay church on 10 June 1549. No evidence survives about Harper's religious views, though it is possible that he knew the Lady Mary, to whose household Parr had once belonged. It is interesting, too, to note that Harper was instituted to his living by Bishop Veysey's commissary, John Blaxton: a religious traditionalist whom the Council would later accuse of having helped to promote disaffection among the clergy of the diocese.[35] The fact that Harper survived the Western Rising, however, and that he continued to hold on to his living until his eventual resignation in 1559 surely suggests that he was either innocent of any part in fomenting the disturbances, or that he had concealed his tracks remarkably well.[36] Had the Crown found any evidence to suggest that he had deliberately caused the stir, he would undoubtedly have been executed.

There is no clear evidence to show that the protests against the new service book had been orchestrated in advance by gentlemen belonging to the old Courtenay affinity, therefore, or by the parish priest, or that they had sprung from a communal meeting for a church ale. Instead, if we return to the words of Hooker, our only contemporary source, it would seem that those protests occurred, first, because some of the parishioners of Sampford Courtenay had 'consulted' together about the new service and had 'determined' to make their distaste for it clear, and, second, because two of them, Underhill and Seagar, had not only been courageous enough to turn those words into actions on the following day, but had also been forceful enough to persuade the priest to go along with their wishes. Hooker acknowledges the two men's primacy in the opening stages of the commotion by noting that 'Underhill and Segar [were] the first captains', while at the same time seeking to reassure his presumed gentry readers that the pair were too low-born to possess any genuine pretensions to authority; he states that Underhill was a tailor and Segar a labourer.[37] Yet, as historians have since discovered, Underhill and Seagar were by no means as humble as Hooker suggests.

William Seagar, in particular – almost certainly the 'Segar' to whom Hooker refers – far from being a labourer, appears to have been comparatively wealthy: he had been assessed at no less than £8 for the subsidy of 1544. The Underhills, too, were evidently prosperous yeoman farmers. William Underhill had been assessed at £4, while Gilbert Underhill had been assessed at £10 and two Thomas Underhills at £3 apiece.[38] A survey of the parish drawn up some years later, in 1568, reveals that the Seagar family owned the two substantial tenements of Brook and Lower Incott, to the south of the village, while the Underhill family owned the tenement of Frankland, to the north, near the hamlet of Honeychurch.[39] Underhill and Seagar were not men from the bottom of the parochial pile, in other words, but from the top, only one step below the minor gentry: the very kind of men who most often led Tudor rebellions.[40] And having already sent a wave of excitement pulsing through the surrounding countryside by persuading their parish priest to restore the traditional mass, they and their neighbours were about to show their mettle once more.

## IV

It is evident that, after the service had ended on 10 June, the people who had attended it did not disperse and return to their homes as normal but remained gathered together, in or near the church. Hooker now resumes his story by telling us that, soon after the dramatic events at Sampford Courtenay had taken place, the local magistrates were told of what had happened and informed 'that the common people were ... assembled together to continue and to maintaine their lewd and disordered behaviour'. Accordingly, four of the justices – Sir Hugh Pollard, Alexander Wood, Mark Slader and Anthony Harvey – now 'came & met' at Sampford Courtenay, 'minding to have had conference with the chiefe players in this enterlude'.[41] Hooker's description of the stir as an 'enterlude', or stage play, and of Underhill and Segar as the 'chiefe players', or actors, in it, is significant, for, by making these comparisons, he is not only ridiculing the protests themselves, but is also, once again, seeking to convey the impression that those who led them were 'mock-captains': devoid of any legitimate authority. The supposed resemblance of episodes of popular protest to pageants, plays and other dramatic productions was a familiar contemporary trope, and, as we shall see, one loyalist writer was later to deride the entire Western Rising as 'a midsummers game'. Yet, as these words make clear, there can be little doubt that Hooker's description of the initial stir at Sampford Courtenay as an 'enterlude' was also partly inspired by the fact that the disturbance had broken out at a time of year that was traditionally associated with plays, games and other communal festivities. And more specifically, we may note that in Hooker's home town of Exeter it had long been the custom for civic dramas to be staged at Whitsuntide – the very week in which the trouble at Sampford Courtenay began – while the city's waits, or retained minstrels, were required to perform every year 'att mydsomer'.[42]

Of the JPs who rode out to Sampford Courtenay, Sir Hugh Pollard of King's Nympton, 15 miles away, was by the far the most important and had, indeed, been one of the four local notables to whom the maintenance of good order in the West had been entrusted in the wake of Henry VIII's death. Alexander Wood lived at North Tawton, just 2 miles from Sampford Courtenay; while Mark Slader, who was his son-in-law, lived at the manor of Bath, in the same parish; they would both have been familiar figures to the protestors.[43] Anthony Harvey, by contrast, lived at Columb John, near Exeter, and therefore seems to have been some way from his home turf when he rode out to meet the protestors. It is conceivable that he had been engaged on other business in the area at the time: perhaps in his capacity as one of the Devon chantry commissioners.[44]

Hooker tells us that the magistrates' plan was first to speak to the chief protestors, then to 'redresse . . . the disorder already committed' – presumably by arresting those who had taken a leading part in the rejection of the new service – and finally 'to persuade and pacifie the rest of the people'. It was a familiar script for sixteenth-century local governors; indeed, we may suspect that the insurrection in West Cornwall had eventually been 'pacified' through the adoption of broadly the same procedure. This time, the protestors would not prove so easy to disperse. The people assembled at Sampford Courtenay had been forewarned that the justices were on their way, Hooker records, and had 'fullie resolved themselves . . . to mainteine what . . . they had begun'.[45] When the JPs arrived, therefore, the protestors informed them that they were not prepared to speak with them unless Pollard and the others would agree, first, to leave their retainers behind them in the village and, second, 'to walke into a . . . large close which was a little distant from the town with them' and there to 'conferre' face to face. (We may presume that the protestors' demand that the JPs should dismount from their horses before walking with them into this field reflected a desire to ensure that the two parties were conversing more or less as equals.) The magistrates agreed to do as they had been asked and, during the course of their subsequent conference with the protestors, 'perswaded [them] what they might that they should yield themselves and bee obedient to the Kinge and his lawes but they little avayled' and in the end, Hooker concludes, exasperatedly, 'without any good done they went away'.[46]

Hooker was contemptuous of the way in which the four magistrates had behaved, and he plainly believed that it was the JPs' spinelessness, as he saw it, that was above all to blame for the fact that a minor village protest had subsequently escalated into a major regional demonstration. 'The gentlemen . . . and their men were the greater number,' Hooker alleged, 'sufficient to have repressed the small companie of commoners then & there assembled' if they had been prepared to resort to force. Yet Pollard and his companions do not seem to have contemplated the use of violence, even after it had become plain that the protestors were unwilling to disperse. Why had they been so reluctant to go down this route? Hooker advances three different explanations. First, he suggests that the JPs had acted as they did on grounds of policy: 'because they thought in such a case to use . . . the . . . quietest way for the pacifieng of them'. Second, he alleges that they had simply been too frightened to attack the protestors, railing against the magistrates as 'white-livered' cowards, who had been 'afraid of theire owne shadowes'. Third, last and most serious of all, Hooker raises the possibility that 'some of them [i.e., the JPs], being like affected as they were [i.e., the protestors], did not like the alteration [i.e., in religion], as it was greatlie suspected' and that they had therefore made only a token effort to quell the demonstrations against the new service book.[47] In his unpublished account, Hooker goes further still, observing that, 'to saye the trueth, the Justices, although some of them would doe something [to quell the protests] and were verie forward, the greater parte being not well acquainted with, nor yet liking, the alteracion of the Religion were the lesse earnest and careful to represse the same'.[48] Here, it will be noted, Hooker appears to slide from suggesting that the four individual justices who had met with the insurgents at Sampford Courtenay had been secretly sympathetic to the protestors and therefore unwilling to quell them, to suggesting that this had also been true of *most* of the Devon justices: an extremely grave allegation.

Are there any other grounds for suspecting that the four gentlemen who met with the protestors at Sampford Courtenay on or soon after 10 June secretly shared their hostility to the new service book – and to the regime's religious policies in general? Later in his account, Hooker would again cast very similar aspersions against Pollard, as we shall see, while there is no sign that either Wood or Slader made any further move to pacify the protests – though Harvey certainly did. Not much can be read into all this, but it is interesting to note that when, fifteen years later, Bishop William Alley asked Sir Peter Carew and others to let him know which of the Devon JPs should be regarded as disaffected to Elizabeth I's Protestant Church settlement, Mark Slader was the one man who was picked out by them as 'hostile' and 'not counted worthy to be [a] Justice'.[49] This piece of evidence suggests that it is at least possible that Slader had felt some sympathy for the protestors at Sampford Courtenay in 1549 – though, of course, it was Pollard who would presumably have had the loudest voice in determining which course of action the four justices should adopt. Whatever the truth may be, the JPs' decision to depart from the scene without having persuaded the 'small companie' of protestors at Sampford Courtenay to disperse clearly acted as a green light to the inhabitants of the surrounding countryside. Because the JPs had failed to lance the boil at Sampford Courtenay while they still could, Hooker laments, 'within verie short time [it] grewe to such a scabbe as passed their cure, for the people foorthwith . . .

did assemble and confederate themselves throughout the whole shire in great Troopes and Companies'.[50]

It is customary, at this point in accounts of the Western Rising, to tell the story of William Hellions, a minor gentleman, or perhaps a yeoman, who, according to Hooker, was bold enough to come and remonstrate with the protestors at Sampford Courtenay.[51] In fact, Hooker does not tell us when this incident occurred, so it is impossible to be sure whether Hellions came to the village within a day or two of the protests breaking out, or rather later – though it does seem reasonable to assume that his visit occurred after that of the justices. After having come to Sampford Courtenay with the intention of first talking to the protestors and then 'pacifieng of them in their due obedience', Hooker relates, Hellions was taken prisoner 'at the townes end' and 'carried to the churchhouse'.[52] The fact that Hellions was conveyed at once to this particular building – which still stands in the middle of the village – suggests that the church house may, at this point, have functioned as the protestors' local headquarters: something that suggests, in its turn, the close connection they felt to exist between their cause and that of the church itself. As the church house was the place in which church ales and other parish festivities were traditionally held, this conjunction may also have helped to inspire Hooker's ironic description of the protests as a whole as an 'enterlude'.

Upon being brought to the church house, where a number of the protestors were gathered, Hellions had then 'so earnestlie reproved them for their rebellion', Hooker tells us, '& so sharplie threatened them with an evil successe that they all fell in a rage with him'. If Hellions had indeed castigated the villagers as 'rebels' – a term which they themselves would certainly have rejected – and predicted that their actions were bound to fail and to result in their own harsh punishment, then it is not altogether surprising that his outburst provoked an angry response. The protestors at once 'with evill words reviled him', Hooker goes on, and then, as Hellions 'was going out of the churchhouse & . . . downe the staires' – a turn of phrase, incidentally, that rather undermines the idea that he had initially been brought to the place as a prisoner – one of those present, a man named Lithbridge, struck him in the neck with a bill, a curved iron blade mounted on a wooden pole. At this, Hooker continues, 'notwithstanding his pitifull ... lamentations, a number of the rest fell upon him, slue him and cut him into small peeces'.[53] The picture that Hooker paints here – that of a violent killing, by a crowd, of a single hated individual – is strikingly reminiscent of that which other sources paint of the assault upon William Body. It is hard to doubt, moreover, that Hellions, like Body, was seen by his attackers as representative of those who embraced 'new fashions'. Hooker concludes by noting that, though the protestors 'counted him for an heretike, yet they buried him in the church-yard there, but contrarie to the common manner, laieng his bodie north and south'.[54] Christians were customarily buried facing towards the east, so this was a way of underscoring the protestors' view that Hellions had been an enemy of the true faith.

The fact that a man named Hellions was indeed 'slayne' by the protestors at Sampford Courtenay – in part, at least, because they disliked his religious beliefs – is confirmed by a source quite independent of Hooker: a loyalist ballad, published in London during the autumn of 1549, which refers, in passing, to the death of 'Wyllam Hilling that marter truly, whiche they killed at Sandford mowre in the playne'.[55] It will be noted that, while this source confirms the main thrust of Hooker's story, and demonstrates that the balladeer regarded Hellions as a 'martyr' for the evangelical cause, it also suggests that he had been cut down in the large area of common ground to the south of the village known as 'Sandford More', rather than at the church house.[56] Unfortunately, the anonymous author of the ballad provides no more indication than Hooker does of precisely when the killing occurred, for the murder clearly marked a significant escalation in the protests. If we presume that Hellions was killed within a day or two of the initial 'disorders' in Sampford Courtenay on 10 June, as all previous accounts have done, then we must presume that the protestors were in an ugly mood from the very beginning – and that it was they who drew first blood. If we allow for the possibility that Hellions might have been killed a week, or even a fortnight, after the protests began, however, things would look rather different. For the moment, at least, the evidence does not permit us to determine where the truth lies.

## V

All that we know about the first five days of the stir at Sampford Courtenay comes from the pen of John Hooker: apart, perhaps, from the scrap of information about Hellions noted above. From mid-June onwards, however, evidence starts to emerge in contemporary sources to show that the disturbances in mid-Devon were beginning to cause ripples of anxiety elsewhere. On Saturday, 15 June, for example, it was noted in the Exeter Chamber Act Book that, 'for dyvers considerac[i]ons att this present', the 'common watch' – the collective title given to the series of splendid parades by armed members of the local craft corporations, which were traditionally held in Exeter, as in many other towns and cities, in late June – 'shalbe omitted & leyft for this yer'.[57] There can be little doubt that this decision was taken because, having learned of the trouble that was stirring to the north-west, the town governors had decided that it would be unwise to permit large numbers of armed men to assemble within the city walls, some of whom might well share the protestors' grievances.[58] Instead of holding the traditional – and largely ceremonial – 'common watch', therefore, the Chamber now ordered that ten 'honyst house holders' in each of the city's four quarters should be selected to hold an extraordinary watch each night instead, and that this watch should be maintained 'every nyght betweene this & the feist of Seynt Michell [i.e., 29 September]'.[59] The fact that the new watch was ordered to be kept up for three months is indicative of the town governors' growing sense of unease.

Meanwhile, the first tidings of the stir in Devon had reached the government in London. According to Hooker, the Council's immediate response was to send for both Sir Peter Carew, who was then in Lincolnshire – where his wife, Lady Margaret Tailboys, whom he had married in 1547, possessed extensive estates – and his uncle, Sir Gawen Carew, who was already 'attendant at the court'. Hooker's claim that the councillors had at once summoned the Carews when they learned of the disturbances in Devon seems plausible. Not only were they fervent evangelicals with many local links, but they were also regime loyalists and, as we have seen, it seems likely that Sir Peter, at least, had been involved in the 'pacifying' of the Cornish rebels during the preceding year. Once the two men had appeared before the Council, Hooker goes on in the earliest of his accounts, they were commanded 'to departe forthwith and in all haste into Devon and there to use ... the best meanes they might for the quieting of the people'. If the protestors 'would not be satisfied', on the other hand, then the Carews were authorised 'to use such other meanes as they best might for the suppressing of them'.[60] It was not the clearest set of instructions, perhaps, and it is interesting to note that, in a later account, Hooker was careful to state that the Carews had been issued with a formal 'commission under the king's hand ... for their doing of all such things as to this service did appertain, and they should think good'.[61] If such a commission was indeed issued, no trace of it now appears to survive – and it is possible that Hooker exaggerated both the degree of authority that Somerset vested in the Carews in June 1549 and the extent to which the protector was relying on them alone to take the initial lead in quelling the protests.

We do not know when Sir Peter and Sir Gawen left the court and spurred their horses westwards, though it seems probable that their departure took place around a week after the disturbances in Devon began: perhaps on 17 or 18 June.[62] Even as the Carews set off, the councillors – increasingly alarmed by the reports which were now coming in from the West, as well as from other parts of the realm, where enclosure riots and other 'tumults' were still raging – had taken the decision to send Lord Russell, by now lord privy seal as well as the greatest landowner in the South-West, in their wake. Hooker notes that the councillors ordered Russell to 'follow [the Carews] and dispatch himselfe into Devon' adding that Russell had been given 'a commission ... for the pacifienge of the said tumults'.[63] Warrants authorised at Richmond Palace on 20 June for the payments of monies for the 'dyetes' of 'the Lord Pryvey Seale, sent westwards', suggest that Russell had already embarked on his journey by then.[64] Two days later, the 'commissions' that had hastily been drawn up in order to provide him with full authority in the West were sent on to Protector Somerset, and two days after this, the councillors drafted a 'memoriall' – or a set of detailed instructions – for

Russell.[65] These noted that it had been decided that he should 'reside for a time in the west partes' for the 'good governance' of the south-western counties, and expressly commanded him 'to se[e] his majesties proceedings touching matters of religion well obeyed'.[66] Around the same time, Russell received his commission and was also formally appointed as 'the King's Lieutenant in the West'.[67] Meanwhile, three of the councillors went to visit Bishop Gardiner in the Tower in a vain attempt to persuade him to make a public demonstration of support for the new service book; presumably in the hope that this would show the protestors that they could not regard the bishop as a covert backer of their cause.[68]

What was happening on the ground in Devon during the third week of June remains extremely obscure, but it is possible that, through soft words and hints of concessions, the more conservative local governors were contriving both to contain the protests and secretly to pursue their own agenda. As we have seen, Hooker was extremely critical of the way in which Devon's gentry governors had reacted to the initial disturbances, effectively accusing them of collusion with those who had rejected the new prayer book. He was especially critical of the JPs who had taken part in the parley at Sampford Courtenay, but he also alleged that most of the Devon justices had disliked the government's religious changes and had therefore been 'less earnest' to suppress the stirs.[69] The impression that Hooker gives us, therefore, is not one of a magisterial class that was determined to ensure that the regime's religious policies were imposed, but rather of a magisterial class that – having been apprised of a popular protest against religious change with which many of its members were in secret sympathy – had largely decided to sit on its hands. In another manuscript that remained unpublished during his own lifetime, moreover, Hooker went further still, declaring that the relatively obscure men who began the rising had enjoyed 'the countenance of some ... of the best, who did both favour their course and secretly encouraged them therein'.[70] These words are intriguing and remind us of one historian's observation that, if early modern crowd actions 'did not question the local power structure' but were directed instead against unpopular policies emanating from the centre, local governors who themselves disliked those policies might well be tempted to permit the demonstrations to continue, at least for a time, in the hope of pressurising the Crown into thinking again.[71] Was this what happened in Devon in June 1549?

Possibly it was, for, on 20 June, the councillors composed a draft 'memorial' to the Devon JPs which indicates that they had reason to believe that the protests were on the point of subsiding. This document began by noting that some local people had 'rebelled' against the new service book and therefore 'deserve[d] most extreme punishment'. Nevertheless, it went on, 'at the sute of diverse gentlemen', the king was now pleased to grant all such 'offenders' a pardon. This being the case, the JPs were ordered, first, to 'promulgate' the news of the pardon and, second, severely to punish anyone who should dare to oppose the king's laws in future.[72] On the day this document was drawn up, therefore, it would seem that the councillors believed – conceivably on the strength of assurances that had recently been received from the JPs – that the worst of the trouble was over.[73] Yet such hopes were built on sand, because, although the JPs may, perhaps, have succeeded in temporarily 'quietening' the disturbances, it seems highly unlikely that they had managed to persuade the protestors to accept the new service book. On the contrary, we may suspect that any temporary success which the JPs had enjoyed had been achieved as a result of some of them having given the protestors to understand that, if they agreed to go home, then the religious innovations would cease: an outcome with which, if we credit Hooker, the more conservative magistrates would themselves have been secretly well pleased.

If some of the Devon JPs proved less than zealous in enforcing the reading of the new service book in the wake of the initial protests, then one Cornish gentleman went even further than this and openly caused the mass to be reinstated. As we have seen, Sir John Arundell of Lanherne was the most powerful man in Cornwall and a staunch religious conservative. In June 1549, he does not appear to have been living at Lanherne, but was rather – as he was later to testify before the Privy Council – staying away from home and 'a stranger in the countrey where he [then] lay'.[74] The best guess is that Sir John was at Shaftesbury in Dorset, where his brother, Sir Thomas, possessed large estates.[75] While sojourning in this part of the world, as Sir John subsequently acknowledged, 'upon occayson of the light talk of the people at the fyrst rising of Rebells in Devonshire he [had] caused two masses to be sayd . . . to appease the people'. Nor was this all, for he went on to admit that, a few days later, 'upon Corpus Christi day' (i.e., 20 June) he had caused a 'procession' to be held.[76] The feast of Corpus Christi, with its elaborate religious processions, had traditionally been one of the highlights of the sacred year, but in 1548 Edward's government had abolished it.[77] By not only causing masses to be said soon after 10 June, therefore, but by going on to cause a procession to be held on Corpus Christi day, Sir John had all but acknowledged his sympathy for the protestors. He had later compounded his offence, moreover, by twice failing to obey a summons from Lord Russell to join him as he desperately tried to raise forces on the Devon–Somerset border. It is therefore hardly surprising that the Council ordered Arundell to be apprehended and brought up to the capital for questioning in July – and, as we shall see, both Sir John and his brother were to resurface later in the story of the rebellion.[78]

## VI

Either on or around 20 June, Sir Peter and Sir Gawen Carew rode into Exeter. No sooner had they arrived than they were informed that 'a great number [of countryfolk] from out of Sampford Courtenay, where the storm first began, and from the other places thereabouts' had come 'and assembled themselves . . . [in Crediton]', the market town that lies 7 miles to the north-west of Exeter.[79] We do not know what had prompted the protestors to set off along the ancient highway that runs between Sampford Courtenay and Crediton but, from the point of view of the Carews, the decision of 'the Sampford men' to move towards the regional capital must have seemed ominous. They immediately summoned Sir Piers Courtney, the sheriff, and 'all the justices' to join them in the city so that they could discuss the best way forward. At the meeting that followed, Hooker tells us, it was concluded that Sir Peter and Sir Gawen should ride out with 'a competent party' to meet the protestors, which they accordingly did on Saturday, 22 June.[80] It was to prove a fateful mission – and a turning point in the history of the Western Rising.

According to Hooker, the Carews had originally intended to parley with the protestors, but, when they reached the outskirts of Crediton, they found that 'the Commoners' had erected strong earthen ramparts 'on the high waye att the Townes end ... and had hanged upp great plough chaines uppon them and fortefyed the same'. They had also occupied the buildings on either side of the road and broken loopholes through the walls for firing 'their shott'.[81] It was a strong position, and the protestors knew it. Despite the fact that the Carews and their followers now dismounted from their horses 'and went on foot unto the rampart', the commoners refused to negotiate with them. An impasse had clearly been reached and at this point, as Hooker notes in a studiedly bland phrase, 'the gentlemen thought it best to make way over the Rampyre into the Towne', in which 'adventure' they were badly 'galled' by the protestors' shot.[82]

Hooker's account is constructed in such a way as to leave the reader with the impression that it was the defenders who had fired first during the course of this fracas, but in fact it seems just as likely that it was the attackers who had done so, as they launched themselves against the rampart. In any case, it is evident that it was the Carews who had made the first aggressive move. This is highly significant, because the encounter at Crediton is the first occasion on which blood is known to have been shed during the Western Rising, with the possible exception of the attack upon Hellions (though, as we have seen, there is no secure date for that incident). After the gentlemen had been driven back by the defenders' fire, Hooker goes on, a serving man in their party set light to one of the barns from which the protestors were shooting. This sparked a panic, causing the commoners to abandon their defences and flee for their lives, and enabling the gentlemen to ride into the now-deserted town immediately afterwards.[83] Having driven away those with whom they had initially hoped to negotiate, and thus won what would soon turn out to be a Pyrrhic victory, the Carews then rode back to Exeter. According to Hooker, the attackers suffered 'the losse of some, and the hurte of manie' during this engagement, but John Fry, a Devon gentleman who took part in the skirmish, paints a rather different picture.[84] In a subsequent letter to Thynne, Fry observed that 'our fyrst fight with ... [the protestors] was at Kyrton ... wheare were slayne of the rebelles about tenne & of our men none'.[85] His words indicate that the loyalists had enjoyed an easy victory, and this, in turn, tends to confirm the justice of the charge that was later levelled against the Carews by Protector Somerset, that they had waded into an unnecessary fight and had thus 'provoked the escalation of the disorder'.[86]

That Hooker himself felt some embarrassment about the Carews' decision to assault the rampart is demonstrated not only by the way he passes swiftly over this incident in his various accounts of the rising, but also by the fact that he omits the episode altogether from his 'Life' of Sir Peter. Here, no mention at all is made of any fighting at Crediton, and the protestors' flight from the town is again attributed solely to the fact that a servant in the Carews' party, 'unawares of the gentlemen, did set one of the barns on fire'.[87] What Hooker is clearly attempting to do here is to suggest that the Carews were in no way to blame for the general panic which – as he freely admits – spread rapidly across the county in the wake of their attack upon Crediton. Instead, he implies, it was the reckless and unauthorised action of a single 'serving man' that had resulted in this unfortunate outcome. Significantly, Hooker was careful to note that the man who had fired the barn was a certain 'Fox', a servant of Sir Hugh Pollard, the senior magistrate whom he had already castigated for his failure to 'repress' the initial protests at Sampford Courtenay.[88] In the earliest of his accounts, moreover, Hooker specifically states that Pollard had been in Exeter on the day that the Carews rode out to Crediton but that he had not accompanied them.[89] Hooker thus left his readers to assume, at best, that Sir Hugh had been unable to join the expedition for some reason and that his servant's overzealousness had then caused a public-relations disaster, or, at worst, that Pollard had, for a second time, refused to confront a company of protestors whose cause he secretly favoured.

Even Hooker's reference to the burning of the barn is less straightforward than it initially appears. While he states in his published narrative that a single barn was set ablaze, in a marginal heading on the same page he switches from the singular to the plural, stating that 'the barns at the townes end' were torched. In the earliest version of his text, Hooker makes a similar, but opposite, switch: first including a heading which notes that 'The barnes [were] fiered', but later altering this to read 'A barne fiered'.[90] In the account he supplies of the awkward interview that later took place between Sir Peter and the privy councillors, moreover, during which they criticised him for his conduct during this affair, Hooker notes that Protector Somerset himself told Carew that the fact that '*he* had caused the *houses* to be burned at Crediton . . . was the onelie cause of the commotion'. Here, we note, the 'barn' allegedly fired by Fox without Carew's consent has been transformed into several 'houses' fired at Carew's own direction. And, significantly, in Hooker's rendition of things at least, Carew made no attempt to correct Somerset on either point, but instead simply insisted on 'the necessities of that service'.[91]

A sudden assault upon a market town, ten protestors killed; barns and, possibly, houses set on fire: reading between the lines of Hooker's own accounts and considering Fry's evidence, it is not hard to see why the Carews' expedition to Crediton should have caused a wave of alarm to spread across the mid-Devon countryside and, in the process, supercharged the protests, leading the common people to 'swarme togeather in great multitudes, some in one place, and some in another'.[92] News of the violent reaction that the Carews' actions had provoked clearly reached Exeter within hours, for, later that same day, it was noted in the Chamber Act Book that, 'for the better savegarde & good order in the . . . Cetie', the craft corporations should supply ten armed men to watch each night. It was further specified that these watchmen should be either 'householders of the . . . Cetie or [h]onest & dyscret p[er]sons inhabitynge within the . . . Cetie': a nod to the many local gentlemen who were then gathered in Exeter with their retinues. Finally, it was directed that the city constables should accompany the watchmen as they went about their duties every night.[93] This was the last entry to be made in the Act Book for almost three months, a clear indication that 22 June was the day on which normal routine in Exeter suddenly came to a halt in the face of the gathering storm. Formal meetings of the Cathedral Chapter ceased on that same day, while business in the mayor's court was suspended shortly afterwards.[94]

The protests were by now spreading to other local villages and news soon reached Exeter that at Clyst St Mary, 2 miles to the east of the city, 'the commons of those parts' had fortified the bridge on the main road leading towards London.[95] This was a threat that could not be ignored, and on Sunday, 23 June, a party of gentlemen including the Carews, Courtenay, Pollard and Sir Thomas Denys set out for Clyst St Mary, 'there to use the best means they might for the pacifying . . . of the said commoners'.[96] The expedition started inauspiciously when the protestors refused to deal with Sir Peter and even threatened to kill him. They were prepared to negotiate with Denys and Pollard, however, so the two JPs made their way into the village with another justice and took part in a lengthy conference. Much later that day, the three men returned to meet their companions, who eagerly enquired of them how the discussions had gone and 'howe they had sped', to which they replied: 'well enough'. For the time being, the other gentlemen had to be content with this brief response, but after they had returned to Exeter that night, and all reconvened for supper, Carew returned to the charge.[97]

Sir Peter now 'demanded of [Denys and Pollard] what agreement they had made', notes Hooker, to which the JPs replied that the protestors had promised 'to proceed no further in their attempts, so that [i.e., on condition that] . . . the councell would not alter the religion, but suffer it to remaine . . . as king Henrie the eight left it . . . untill the king . . . came to his full age'. To the evangelicals in the party this must have seemed an outrageous answer. How could Denys and Pollard possibly have believed that they had fared 'well enough' in their negotiations with the protestors if all they had managed to do was to persuade them to agree to disperse in return for an assurance that their central demand – that there should be a complete halt to religious changes – would be met? The divergence between the approach to the disturbances which was being adopted by the conservative local governors, and that which was being adopted by their reformist colleagues was now laid bare. Furious, both Carew and Piers Courtenay turned on Denys and Pollard, berating them 'for their slender dealings in so weightie a cause, wherein they . . . ought . . . to have used all meanes to have suppressed their [i.e., the commons'] outrages, [rather] than to have maintained their follies'. An argument then ensued, with heated words being exchanged 'on each side', until the company eventually broke apart. It had become obvious that the local governors were unable to agree on a concerted course of action and within hours, Hooker tells us, 'everie man shifted for himselfe'.[98]

This is a story that is familiar from Hooker's published narrative but, in the Bodleian manuscript, he provides a slightly different account of the argument, stating that Courtenay not only inveighed against Denys and Pollard, but '*also against the commoners whom he termed to bee rebells*'.[99] Hooker clearly saw the sheriff's decision to brand the protestors with this opprobrious label as a highly significant development because, in one of the marginal headings that he used to indicate key passages in his text, he highlighted the episode with the words 'The commoners termed rebelles'.[100] In the context of the local governors' approach to the disturbances, it is easy to see why Courtenay's utterance should have been regarded by Hooker as a key turning point. Hitherto, after all, the Devon JPs – though not the Carews – had been adopting much the same policy towards the protestors as Somerset was simultaneously adopting towards the demonstrators who had risen in many other parts of the realm: attempting to conciliate them and promising pardons in return for their agreement to disperse. They had been treating the protestors as petitioners, in other words – albeit unruly ones – with whom peaceful accommodation might yet be reached. Courtenay's angry denunciation of the protestors as 'rebels', by contrast, showed that he had now come to regard them as outright enemies of the king: as 'traitors' who could only be dealt with by force. And from late June onwards, it was as 'rebels' that those who took part in the Western Rising were generally referred to by their enemies, a fact that justifies the periodic use of that term to denote, though not to denounce, the protestors from this point onwards in the present book.

## VII

Following the collapse of consensus among the local gentry governors, Hooker tells us, Sir Peter Carew left Exeter early on the morning of 24 June and rode swiftly eastwards: travelling first to meet Lord Russell, who had already reached Sir Hugh Paulet's house at Hinton St George, and then on towards London in order to report back to the Privy Council.[101] It is hard not to suspect that Carew's decision to return to the capital within a week of leaving it was prompted by his keen desire, not only to 'advertise the king and council of the whole matter', as Hooker puts it, but also to be at court in person when the news of the debacle at Crediton arrived, so that he could effectively 'spin' his own part in it. This Carew subsequently managed to do when he made his breathless reappearance before the Council board, probably within three days of his hasty departure from Exeter, convincing Somerset that, despite all appearances to the contrary, he deserved, not only to be commended for his actions so far, but also to be 'willed to return with speed into the [West] country ... there to follow the service for the suppression of the rebellion'.[102] Having successfully vindicated himself, Sir Peter was soon on his way to rejoin Russell. Meanwhile, back in Devon, the county's local governors had been scattered to the four winds.

On the same day that Carew left Exeter, Courtenay and Denys – two of the chief antagonists in the argument of the night before – had, together with Anthony Harvey, written to the Council to report on the deteriorating situation.[103] These letters are unfortunately lost, but two days later, on 26 June, the councillors wrote back to the three men, noting how concerned they were to learn that 'those lewd personnes of whom you wrote before, being ons well quieted by your good meannes, bee now agayne assembled in a farre greatter nombre'.[104] It is possible, as we have seen, that this reference to the JPs having previously reported that the protestors had been 'quieted' relates to a lost letter that had described an otherwise unrecorded agreement, arrived at between the JPs and the insurgents at some time prior to 22 June. Yet we should not dismiss the possibility that it might refer, instead, to a lost letter containing wholly mistaken assurances that the protestors had been dispersed by force, which had been sent to the Council in the immediate aftermath of the fray at Crediton. In any event, after having treated the JPs to a good deal of rather general advice, the councillors went on to observe that 'as for the delay of ... th'execution of the statute of the shepe & cloth we have written more amply to you by our former letters'.

These words show that the JPs had previously requested that the implementation of the relief be delayed, clear evidence that they believed that resentment against the new tax was helping to fuel the disturbances, and, as we shall see, the protestors' own public pronouncements would shortly demonstrate that this was indeed the case. The councillors concluded their letter by urging Courtenay, Denys and Harvey 'to joyn wisely and man[full]y together' in pacifying the stir: a form of words which suggests that – hardly surprisingly – they had sensed both division and disheartenment in the latest despatch from the local gentry governors.[105]

It seems unlikely that this exhortation ever reached its intended recipients, for even as the councillors were drafting their letter, most of the gentlemen who had gathered in Exeter to meet the Carews were already either in captivity, in hiding or in flight. Hooker notes that, as the protests had begun to spread – and as fears had begun to grow that Exeter might soon be cut off – the mayor had warned the assembled gentlemen that there was not enough food in the city to support them and their retinues as well as the inhabitants. After the acrimonious supper on 23 June, therefore, a general exodus from the city had begun, as the gentlemen had set off for their own homes. For those who had not had the foresight to depart that night or early the next morning, an unpleasant surprise was in store. The terror aroused by the attack upon Crediton had clearly caused the inhabitants of many other local communities to erect barricades to defend themselves, just as the people of Clyst St Mary had done, and these hurriedly erected roadblocks now served, not just as fortifications, but also as traps for the unwary gentlemen as they tried to make their way home. Hooker records that 'all the high-ways everie where were . . . entrenched, and great Trees felled and layd in the midle . . . [of] the same, by meanes whereof many gentlemen were in their departure taken and kept *in duras* [i.e., imprisoned] during the whole time of the Rebellion'. In a subsequent comment, Hooker again reveals his conviction that at least some of the local governors had made use of claims of constraint to mask their secret collusion with the rebels: 'some were taken because they would be taken', he cynically observes, and these were soon 'lett loose att libertie again'.[106]

Among the gentlemen who were captured at this time was the sheriff of Devon himself, Piers Courtenay, who can hardly be suspected of nursing a secret sympathy for the protestors. At his funeral sermon, many years later, the congregation were reminded that Courtenay had been 'taken prisoner, and [was] in extreme peril to be cruelly handled [i.e., in danger of being roughly treated] by the rebels in the Western Commotion'.[107] The apprehension of Courtenay was a signal triumph for the insurgents as he was the most important royal official in the county as well as a key member of Devon's evangelical faction. Hooker notes that Walter Raleigh, another reformist JP, also fell into the rebels' hands in late June and that he was subsequently imprisoned 'in the towre and church of St Sidwells', in the suburbs of Exeter.[108] Other captured gentlemen were similarly imprisoned in churches elsewhere.[109] All of these individuals had clearly refused to join the rebels, but the case of John Bury, a gentleman from Silverton in the Exe Valley, was very different. During his subsequent examination in the Tower of London, Bury deposed that he was a servant of Sir Thomas Denys, and that he had come to Exeter – presumably when the JPs had been summoned to the city by the Carews – 'to abyde there with his harnes[s] [i.e., his weapons] and ... wayted uppon his sayd master and after returned to his house at which tyme ... [he] was taken by fyve hundred rebells'.[110] Bury was clearly trying to give the impression that, after he had left Exeter, he had been intimidated into joining the protestors, but, as he was widely believed to have become one of the rebels' chief captains, his explanations cut little ice with his interrogators. The fact that Bury's widow, Margery, subsequently testified that her late husband had been executed for 'hys offences manyfe[s]tly comytted & don yn the last commocyon', moreover, and that John Chubbe – a yeoman of Ugborough in South Devon – had been one of Bury's 'under Capytayne[s]' can only be said to reinforce the impression that Bury had been involved in the rebellion up to his neck.[111] The defection of one of Denys's senior retainers must surely have raised fresh doubts in loyalists' minds about the reliability of Sir Thomas himself – not least because Denys, like Pollard, simply fell off the radar after 24 June. Had these two senior magistrates been captured and imprisoned, like Courtenay? Had they hidden themselves away in remote parts of the countryside, as Hooker tells us some other loyalist gentlemen did? Or had they been among those who had been first apprehended by the rebels and then, for whatever reason, released? No evidence to help us answer these questions appears to have survived.

Another longtime follower of Sir Thomas Denys – Philip Furse of Raddon, near Thorverton, a wealthy yeoman – was certainly imprisoned by the insurgents at around this time. We know this from a manuscript memoir of the Furse family, written by Robert Furse of Dean Prior during the 1590s. Here, Robert records that Philip Furse had been 'by the rebells longe [kept] a prisoner at Samford and very evell intreated & in grett hasarde'.[112] The fact that Furse had been dragged all the way to Sampford Courtenay by the insurgents, and there 'longe' imprisoned, is significant, because it provides us with our first indication that the village in which the protests had begun had continued to act as a key rebel headquarters throughout the entire course of the commotion. A subsequent aside by an early Stuart antiquarian – that the rebels had 'imprisoned divers gentlemen in the church & tower there' – points very much the same way.[113] And the continued importance of Sampford Courtenay during the early stages of the rising is underscored still further by a crucial letter sent by Somerset and the other privy councillors to Lord Russell on 29 June: a letter that provides us with a few precious scraps of information about what was happening in the rebels' camp.

The councillors began by informing Russell that they had lately received severall 'letters out of the west . . . brought by one Stowell, of whome we harde [i.e., heard] at length the hole state and procedyngs of the busie people in Devonshire'.[114] Unfortunately, they did not state when these missives had been written, but, as it was possible for a letter sent post-haste from Devon to reach the capital within two or three days at this time, it seems unlikely that the communications were more than a week old. We know that the councillors had already received other letters written from Exeter on 24 June, moreover, so the advice they then proceeded to dispense to Russell must surely have been based on relatively up-to-date information. The fact that the first thing they directed Russell to do was to advance with his forces 'for the appeasing the multitude assembled at Sampford Courtenay' is intriguing, therefore. These words show that, on 29 June, the councillors continued to regard that village as the epicentre of the commotion and – if they were indeed doing so on the basis of information received after 22 June – then this in turn would suggest that, following the skirmish at Crediton, most of the protestors had fled westwards and regrouped at Sampford Courtenay. It is possible that the letters which the Council were chiefly relying on for their information had been written *before* the protestors first advanced to Crediton, of course: that is to say, at some point in mid-June. But it seems unlikely that Somerset and his colleagues would have been quite as far behind the curve as this. In any case, the councillors' letter to Russell certainly conveys an impression of the picture that Somerset and his colleagues had built up of what was happening at Sampford Courtenay at some point prior to 29 June.

First, the councillors had learned that the village, like Crediton and Clyst St Mary, had been barricaded: that 'in the utter partes of the towne . . . they have cheyned up their passages'. Second, they had learned that many rumours were circulating among the rebels. Apparently, the latter were claiming that 'after the payment for shepe thay should pay for theyr geese and pigs and such like', for example, and complaining that, because of the religious changes, their children could only now be baptised on Sundays. Needless to say, Somerset and his colleagues angrily rebutted these claims. Third and last, the councillors had plainly learned something about the rebels' command structure, for they impressed upon Russell that, once he had defeated the insurgents, 'we dyssyer especyally those Syxe men w[hi]ch do soly[cit] the causes of theyr compl[a]y[n]ing unto one especiall man in the Steple in the same towne, and the same man also may be apprehended, to be ponyshed above all others, for example sake'.[115] Towards the end of their letter, moreover, the councillors returned, obsessively, to this same point, telling Russell that, 'yf the man kepyng his fonde office in the steple and [the] vi other[rs] w[hi]ch be referanderies of causes to hym maie be conveniently apprehended', they should be sent up to London, so that they might be interrogated and made to reveal the 'authors and begynnynges' of the commotion.[116]

The precise meaning of these two sentences is a little hard to pin down, but their overall sense is clear. A group of six men were by now presenting the people's grievances to a single overall leader, who had taken up his station in the church tower at Sampford Courtenay. Ironically enough, the term that the councillors used to describe this individual – 'one especiall man' – is precisely the term that had previously been used to describe Somerset himself when he had first assumed the role of lord protector some two years before. In the councillors' scathing reference to the rebel leader as one who was keeping his 'fonde [i.e., foolish] office' in the church tower, moreover, it is possible to sense their outrage at the fact that a mere commoner should have taken it upon himself to pose as someone possessed of true authority. Here, we are reminded of Hooker's characterisation of the rebel leaders as 'players', strutting for a few brief moments upon an all-too-temporary stage.

Who was the 'especiall man in the steple'? The letter does not say, but Hooker's identification of the protestors' 'first captains' as William Underhill and William Seagar means that these two men are the most likely candidates, and the fact that, as we shall see, Underhill would shortly become the most notorious of 'the Sampford men' means that he is the likeliest candidate of all. Why should the 'especiall man', whoever he was, have chosen to install himself in the church tower? Several possible answers present themselves. To begin with, the church was the largest and most easily defensible building in the village; it would not have taken much work to have transformed it into a miniature castle. Second, the tower of Sampford Courtenay church is particularly tall and elegant, and contains – rather unusually – not just one, but two rooms in its upper stages, as well as a spiral stair leading up to a roof that commands far-reaching views over the countryside beyond. As the councillors' sour comment implies, the fact that the rebel leader was 'kepyng his . . . office' within this impressive structure would have given him a certain gravitas. Third, the tower was the place in which important documents were sometimes housed in early modern churches and might therefore have seemed an appropriate place for business to be transacted and records kept.[117] Here, the lists of complaints that were being submitted to the 'especiall man' via his six 'referendaries' could well have been stored, for example, and here, too, the 'writinges' that the protestors are later known to have sent out in the king's name, summoning local people in to join them, could perhaps also have been composed.[118] Fourth and last, as has already been noted, the fact that the protestors believed themselves to be rising in defence of their traditional faith made a church the ideal place for their headquarters in a symbolic sense.

During the great 'commotion' that took place on the other side of England, in Norfolk, in July, Robert Kett's followers are known to have gathered under the tree that they named the 'Oak of Reformation' in order to watch Kett dispense justice across the whole of rebel-held East Anglia. The councillors' garbled words permit us to glimpse the possibility that, in Devon in June, the followers of Underhill and Seagar may have similarly gathered around Sampford Courtenay church in order to watch their 'especiall man' assume precisely the same sort of judicial role as he addressed the grievances that had been brought to his attention by the people of the surrounding countryside. They permit us to glimpse the possibility, in fact, that, in June 1549, Sampford Courtenay may – for the first, and presumably the last, time in its history – have found itself the de facto seat of government in Devon.

It would not be long, moreover, before the protestors would attempt to take control of the official seat of local government: of the city of Exeter itself. Hooker now takes up the story once more, recording that, during the last week of June:

> The commons, advertised of the departure of all the gentlemen from out of the citie, take hearte of grace and nowe thinking the game to bee on their side doe openlie shewe themselves to be Traitors and rebells, and assembling themselves togeather doe appoint out captaines: the chiefest of them att the first were Underhill a Tayler, Maunder A shoomaker, Seager A husband laborer and Ashenrydge a fishedriver.[119]

This is a revealing passage because it suggests that, in the wake of the encounter of 22 June, the protestors had assumed a far more menacing and warlike demeanour than they had exhibited hitherto; a fact that, again, tends to indicate just how far the Carews' assault on Crediton had inflamed the situation. It is interesting, too, to note that, of the four men whom Hooker names as the rebels' chief captains, 'att the first' two – Underhill and Seagar – were definitely Sampford Courtenay men, while a third – Maunder – probably was as well. (Ashenrydge's place of residence is unknown.) This fact again tends to suggest that, during the final week of June, Sampford Courtenay had remained the centre of the protestors' activities. At some time during this week, the rebel captains sent a message to the mayor of Exeter, John Blackaller, demanding 'that he should ioyne with them'. Blackaller – bolstered by the support of most of the town governors, a hard core of reformist citizens and a small group of loyalist gentlemen who had remained behind in Exeter on 24 June – refused and ordered the city's gates to be firmly closed against the protestors instead. The die was thus cast. Now, wrote Hooker, 'the foresaid Captaines, stomaking att this answere, doe agree . . . to besiege the cittie and to assayle the same', and they prepared to march on Exeter with all of their followers – presumably from the vicinity of Sampford Courtenay.[120] By 25 June, the citizens were already beginning to work on their defences, and a later comment of Hooker's suggests that Saturday, 29 June may have been the day on which Exeter was finally cut off from the outside world.[121] And as the city from which the South-West had traditionally been governed was suddenly rendered incommunicado, so the inhabitants of Devon and Cornwall found themselves entering upon a period of unparalleled excitement, turbulence and dread: a period that they would ever afterwards remember as 'the commotion time'.

# 4

# Escalation
## 1–15 July 1549

### I

The decision of Exeter's town governors to reject the overtures of the rebel captains, and to place the city in a defensive posture instead, was a critical one in the history of the Western Rising. If the governors' decision had gone the other way – and the protestors had received the enormous accretion of strength, both material and reputational, that possession of the fifth-largest city in the realm would at once have conferred upon them – the rising would almost certainly have spread even further and faster. So, what were the considerations that prompted the members of the Council of Twenty-Four to make the crucial choice that they did? Hooker, who was himself in the city at this time, tells us that, upon receiving the initial communication from the rebels, the mayor 'straight awayes conferr[ed] with his brethren' – almost certainly in the council chamber at the Guildhall – and submitted the message to their joint consideration, at which they, 'respecting their dueties to God, their obedience to the Kinge, the safetie of the Cittie and of themselves, give their directe answeare that they would not make nor medle with them, but would repute them as rebells and enemies to God and the kinge'.[1] The impression of unanimous resolve that Hooker's words create is almost certainly misleading, for, as he himself admits, most of Exeter's inhabitants favoured the insurgents and they had their supporters in the Chamber too.[2] Even so, it is clear that a majority of the councillors eventually agreed that the rebels should be rebuffed, and Hooker's words indicate that the town governors had come to this decision for three main reasons.

First, they had concluded that, by opposing the new service book, the insurgents were going against the will of the king, and that – as the king was God's anointed – this could only be said to be going against the will of God himself. (Any of their number who believed that it was not, in fact, Edward's wishes that the regime was implementing, but rather those of a faction of 'heretics' who were ruling in the boy-king's name, presumably kept their doubts to themselves.) Second, they had concluded that, if the rebels were admitted, then 'the safetie of the cittie' might well be threatened by a general collapse in law and order – with all of the grim consequences for the property and persons of the leading citizens which that would entail. Third, and conceivably most important of all, they had concluded that, in this same scenario, they 'themselves', as the chief local governors, might well be in danger of being apprehended and imprisoned by the rebels if they dared to gainsay them – just as many of the country gentlemen had been when they left Exeter and tried to return to their homes a few days before.

These were probably the key factors in persuading Exeter's town governors to reject the protestors' overtures, just as Hooker suggests, but they may have been swayed by other considerations as well. As we saw in Chapter 2, the Chamber had recently received powerful support from the centre in its continuing battle to clip the wings of the Chapter. There was every reason for the town councillors to hope that they might secure further help from Somerset's evangelising regime against the cathedral men in the future, moreover, and therefore for them to remain studiedly loyal. The good relationship that the town councillors had enjoyed with Lord Russell ever since he had first visited the West in 1539 and taken up temporary residence in his house at the former Black Friars may also have been significant. Russell was a powerful friend and advocate from the town governors' point of view. It made good sense for them to stay on his side and on that of the regime in which he was a key figure.[3] Nor should we overlook the fact that, just a month before, the

Chamber had at last succeeded in purchasing a mass of small properties formerly owned by religious houses in the city and suburbs of Exeter for the enormous sum of £1,497.[4] Some of these properties were quickly sold off to wealthy citizens; Hooker himself bought two of them.[5] The rebels would shortly demand that half of all the 'Abbey lands and Chauntrye landes' which had been seized and either sold or given away by the Crown should be confiscated from their new lay owners and restored to 'devout persons'.[6] It is hard not to suspect that the town governors would have regarded the prospect of having to disgorge any of their newly acquired ex-monastic properties as anathema – and that this alone may well have confirmed some of them in their decision to rebuff the protestors and to denounce them as 'enemies to God and the Kinge'.[7]

Most of the town governors favoured the old ways in religion and clearly took the decision to resist the rebels either out of a sense of abstract loyalty to the Crown, or for the more practical and frankly self-interested reasons outlined above. But these pragmatic loyalists were supported by a band of around a hundred reformists, who were the rebels' most determined and active opponents in the city.[8] Included in their number were probably the handful of local gentlemen whom Hooker records as having elected to remain behind in Exeter on 24 June: among them, Sir Roger Blewet, who was the nephew of the Cornish JP Sir Richard Grenville; John Beauchamp, who was Grenville's brother-in-law; and John Courtenay, who was the half-brother of Piers Courtenay, the reformist sheriff, who had recently been apprehended by the rebels.[9] Contemporary financial accounts confirm that several of these men played a prominent role in the subsequent defence of the city, as did Bernard Duffield, who was the steward of Lord Russell's house of the Black Friars.[10]

There were many good reasons for the town governors to set their faces against the protestors in June 1549, therefore. Rather more surprising, perhaps, is the fact that the cathedral canons followed suit. As we have seen, the Close had long been regarded by evangelicals as a key centre of local resistance to the new learning and, during the opening stages of the commotion, the privy councillors clearly suspected that one of Veysey's most senior administrators had himself been partly responsible for causing the stirs. Writing to Russell on 29 June, they noted that they had been informed that 'one Mr Blakston, an Ecclesiastical Commisarie', had been 'sedusing the ... people by dysparsying amongst them false and sedycyous advertisements of th'alteracion of relygyon'. The man whom the councillors had in their sights was John Blaxton, Veysey's commissary: then acting, in effect, as the bishop's deputy. They ordered Russell 'earnestly [to] treat' with Blaxton, and to command him publicly to renounce the views which he had previously expressed.[11] Fortunately for Blaxton, he appears to have been in Exeter as the rebels closed in upon the city and would therefore have been out of Russell's reach when the latter finally arrived in East Devon a few days later. On 26 June, the bishop's registrar noted that Blaxton – presumably sitting at the bishop's palace – had formally admitted a new incumbent to a benefice on that day, but this was the last entry to be made in the register for six weeks. Under the heading 'July', the following terse statement appears instead: '*hoc toto mense et usq ad septem diem sequentis mens Augusti civitatis Exon Rebellione obsessa est*' (i.e., 'all this month and up until the seventh day of August following, the city of Exeter was besieged by a rebellion'): words that provide independent confirmation of Hooker's statement that the city had been cut off by the rebels by the end of June.[12]

Blaxton disappears from view after 26 June, but it seems likely that he remained in the Close throughout the ensuing siege. We can be certain that a number of the canons did, for, despite his own distaste for their conservative religious views, Hooker was later to acknowledge that

> the chanons of the cathedral church which at that time were resident in their houses within the close there, namelie archdeacon [John] Pollard, Treasurer [Thomas] Southron, Chancellor [William] Luson and Master [John] Holwell, with others of the said church ... joined with the ... citizens in this service for the safeguard of the citie, and did kepe both watches and wards and their men readie at all times to serve in everie alarum and skirmish.[13]

The canons' possession of what was, in effect, an independent enclave within the city walls meant that, if they had decided to hold out a hand to the rebels, it would have been extremely difficult for the town governors to mount an effective defence. That the churchmen chose not to assist the insurgents, but to join hands with the city loyalists instead, suggests that, at this moment of supreme crisis, the senior clerics in the Close – like the conservative members of the Council of Twenty-Four – had concluded that to join the rebels would be to put their own persons and possessions in danger, and had therefore decided to place pragmatic self-interest before religious principle. The choices made by these two small groups of men in the Guildhall and the Chapter House in late June were of critical importance, because they ensured that – rather than becoming subsumed within the insurgency, as the rebel captains had initially hoped – Exeter would now become the storm centre of the rebellion instead: the glittering prize upon whose capture the insurgents' energies would henceforth be chiefly bent.

Hooker tells us that the siege of Exeter proper began on Tuesday, 2 July when the rebel forces appeared before the town walls. The insurgents were then about 2,000 strong, he notes, 'but afterwards they were manie more'. Hooker goes on to imply that the prospect of plunder had played a key role in motivating many of the attackers and that they were 'hopeinge to have the spoyle [of Exeter] and to measure velvetts and silks (as their terme was) by the bowe': a phrase that reminds us that many of the men in the rebel host were armed with longbows.[14] To this end, Hooker continues, 'they had caused manie of their wives with horses and panyers to come to the cittie, promising them that they would enter into the same and send them home laden with all kinde of silkes, velvetts and other housholde stuff'.[15] Possibly such tantalising prospects were indeed held out by some of the insurgents to their wives, but the women whom Hooker had plainly glimpsed from the city walls as they led their pannier-laden horses along in the rebel ranks are unlikely to have been there primarily for plunder. It was common practice at this time for large numbers of women to accompany armies on the march, so that they could forage for their menfolk and provide them with all sorts of other personal services while they were in the field.[16] Hooker's comment alerts us to the fact that the rebel forces included many women, therefore: women who – like those who had rioted at St Nicholas Priory in 1536 – are likely to have felt just as committed to the defence of the old ways in religion as their menfolk were, even if there is no evidence to suggest that the female rebels who took part in the Western Rising ever engaged in physical combat.[17]

Fortunately for the town governors, a great deal of work had recently been carried out on the city walls in order to strengthen them against any potential foreign attack, and in 1545 the citizens had purchased a suite of artillery pieces for the same purpose.[18] This meant that Exeter was already in a better position to resist the insurgents than it would otherwise have been and, as the rebels closed in, more work had been feverishly carried out in order to strengthen the defences still further. Thus the city had been 'viewed for armour', Hooker notes, 'men . . . mustered; souldiers . . . reteyned; captaines . . . appointed; warders for the daye and watchmen for the night assigned; ordinances att the gates & upon the walls placed; mounts [i.e., earthen mounds] in convenient places erected and all things else done as that present . . . necessities required'.[19] In addition, the citizens appear to have had the foresight to demolish at least the upper levels of the church towers of St Sidwell's and St Edmund's, in the suburbs, so that they could not be used to overspy the city walls.[20] According to the Welsh chronicler Ellis Gruffydd, the town governors were also fortunate enough to be able to call upon the services of two military experts from Calais, who had happened to be in Exeter in late June. One of these men, Robert Dillon, was 'servant to the master of the king's ordinance', Gruffydd notes, 'where he had learnt how to make gunpowder, of which there was great need in the town', and he had therefore been able to manufacture a sufficient quantity to meet the citizens' needs.[21]

Once the rebels had arrived before Exeter and found that the town governors were determined to oppose them, they took up their positions around the city and occupied the houses in the suburbs. From here, and from the open fields nearby, they loosed off hails of arrows upon the defenders, interspersed with harquebus fire. It was not long before the insurgents brought up ordnance to bombard the city gates as well, and – since these artillery pieces can scarcely have come from the countryside around Sampford Courtenay – their appearance on the scene indicates that the original protestors from mid-Devon had now been joined by contingents from elsewhere in the county, who would have been able to procure great guns from the ships that lay at harbour in the ports of North, South and East Devon.[22] Hooker records that, after they had first arrived before the city, the rebels' numbers 'did dailie more and more increase', and this burgeoning strength must surely have reflected the fact that – with the local gentry governors scattered, and Exeter itself under siege – the rebels seemed to be entirely in the ascendant.[23]

Thanks to the splendid historical detective work of Eamon Duffy, we now know that the insurgents established their main camp at St David's Down, just to the north of Exeter.[24] The suburb of St David's stands on a broad hill, or 'down', which overlooks the city and which is traversed by the main road leading from Exeter to Crediton.[25] St David's Hill would have been the first point from which the 'Sampford Courtney men' would have glimpsed Exeter when they initially advanced upon the city, then, and – as the hill affords a panoramic view of the buildings behind the town wall, just a few hundred yards away, on the other side of the steep defile formed by the Longbrooke Valley – it would have been the obvious place for the insurgents to establish their headquarters.[26] St David's Down offered other advantages, too. There were houses and a church here, which could provide the besiegers with shelter, for example. There was also a Norman ringwork – then known as 'New Castle' – standing a quarter of a mile away from the church, which commanded fine views over Rougemont Castle and the adjacent part of the city defences; the rebels would surely have occupied this ancient earthwork, as they are later said to have occupied others elsewhere.[27] Finally, it is worth noting that 'Saynte Davyes Downe' was – with nearby Southernhay – the site of Exeter's celebrated Lammas Fair, held annually on 1 August.[28] Many of the people who lived in the countryside around Exeter would already have been extremely familiar with St David's Down, therefore. And indeed – as hundreds of men and women from all over the county streamed into the rebel camp there during the heady days of July 1549, driving cattle before them, carrying in all sorts of other provisions and, it seems fair to assume, bearing crosses and banners as well – it would have been easy for them to feel as if they were participating in a kind of alternative fair: in a midsummer carnival, in which the world – for the time being at least – seemed in the process of being genuinely turned upside down.[29]

## II

While physical battle had been joined at Exeter on 2 July, a paper battle between the rebel leaders and the privy councillors in London was already well under way. Some days before the insurgents advanced on Exeter, and probably before they left Sampford Courtenay, their leaders had drawn up one of the formal 'supplications', or petitions for redress, that were frequently composed by groups of protestors in late medieval and early modern England, and which provide us with our best – and sometimes, indeed, our only – insights into their outlook and motivation. Between 10 and 29 June, Somerset and his fellow councillors appear to have picked up only scraps of information about the rebels' grievances. They knew, above all, that those who had risen up in the mid-Devon countryside were hostile to the new service book. They knew that the protestors resented the relief on sheep and cloth; that they anticipated other swingeing new taxes; and that they feared that it would no longer be possible for their children to be baptised on weekdays. Yet, when Somerset and his colleagues wrote to Russell on 29 June, this appears to have been the sum of their knowledge. Four days later, the situation had clearly changed, for, on 3 July, the imperial ambassador in London wrote to inform his master that the rebels were 'proposing certain articles concerning religion, and asking to have the mass restored, and to invalidate the last Parliament as unlawfully held during the king's minority'.[30] These 'articles' have not survived, but are surely identifiable with the list of 'grievances and complaints' that an anonymous French writer later noted was presented to the king, and to which someone at the heart of government – probably Somerset himself – wrote a long reply in the king's name: a reply that was published as a pamphlet, under the title of *A Message Sent by the Kynges Maiestie, to Certain of his People Assembled in Devonshire*, soon after the original letter had been completed at Richmond Palace on 8 July.[31]

Couched in the form of an – almost entirely negative – royal response to the document that had been presented to Edward a few days before, the *Message* allows us to reconstruct the broad thrust of the protestors' original supplication. Clearly, their petition had contained at least seven main requests: that they should be assured that the baptism of children would not hereafter be restricted to Sundays and holy days (as the rubric in the new prayer book seemed to imply); that the new service book should be withdrawn; that the doctrine of transubstantiation should be officially reaffirmed; that the use of English in church services should cease; that the ban on infant confirmation which the prayer book appeared effectively to institute should be rescinded; that the Act of Six Articles – with its harsh penalties for 'heretics' – should be restored; and, finally, that all of the Acts of Parliament passed since the death of Henry VIII should be repealed, and that no new ones should be passed until Edward came of age.[32] The debt which the Devon protestors' supplication owed to the demands made by the Cornish rebels in 1548, and to the ideas of other conservative thinkers like Gardiner, was made very clear in this last request. The fact that all of the grievances to which the author of the *Message* responds are religious ones is also significant, moreover. Had the protestors mentioned the relief in their original supplication, he would surely have discussed the new tax: all the more so as this was one of the few contested matters on which the regime was prepared to give any ground. It is also worth noting that, while all of the complaints that are addressed are religious ones, none of them focuses on complex doctrinal matters. A close reading of the *Message* therefore suggests that the original supplication of the Devon protestors – probably drawn up by the 'especiall man' at Sampford Courtenay and his 'referendaries' – was, above all, an attempt by a group of rural layfolk to defend the old ways in religion.[33]

The *Message* has more to tell us, too, for at one point the anonymous author – still speaking in the king's name – complains to the protestors that 'ye use our name in your writings, & abuse the same against our self', adding piteously, 'what injury herein dooe you us, to call those which love us to your evill purposes, by the authoritie of our name'.[34] These words provide a fascinating glimpse of the tactics that the mid-Devon protestors were by now using to reach out to others around them and underscore the fact that – far from being illiterate rustics as Hooker was later to imply – the rebel 'captains' at Sampford Courtenay were men who were perfectly capable of exploiting written communications: first, to set the existing machinery of local defence in motion; and then to operate it for themselves. The 'writings' referred to here were clearly warrants, sent out in the king's name, in order to summon men to join the insurgents. Similar documents are known to have been composed and circulated by Kett's followers in Norfolk later in the year.[35] None of the warrants sent out by the Devon rebels appear to have survived; such documents would have constituted evidence of treason after the rebellion had been suppressed, of course, and would therefore have been hastily destroyed by their recipients. Yet the mere fact that the protestors had claimed to be acting on the monarch's behalf is significant. It was a claim that reflected their conviction that the boy-king was not in charge of his own government but was being duped and misrepresented by his heretical advisers: those whom the protestors doubtless regarded as the true 'rebels'. And that the senior government figure who was himself ventriloquising the voice of the king as he wrote the *Message* should have spluttered with indignation as he condemned the rebel captains for doing much the same thing in their warrants can only be regarded as one of the minor ironies of history.

On the same day that the author of *A Message Sent by the Kynges Maiestie* laid down his pen, Lord Russell – who had arrived, perhaps a few days before, on the eastern fringes of Devon with a small force of men – sent several letters to the privy councillors informing them of his 'contynuall travaill for the staye of the Rabells in those parts'.[36] Unfortunately, these missives – like most of those that the lord privy seal wrote to the Council during the turbulent summer of 1549 – have been lost, but it is possible to reconstruct at least some of their content from the councillors' replies, which have survived (because copies of outgoing correspondence were routinely kept). Russell's letters were probably sent from Honiton, the market town in which Hooker tells us that the lord privy seal had established himself after he had left Hinton St George and advanced gingerly across the Somerset–Devon border.[37] That Russell should have been forced to halt his westward progress at Honiton, of course – and to remain there, as Hooker feelingly puts it, 'for a longe time' – speaks volumes in itself, because it demonstrates that, by early July, the countryside to the west of that town was securely in rebel hands, and Russell did not feel strong enough to venture any further.[38] The councillors' reply to his letter of 8 July, indeed, hints that the lord privy seal – feeling distinctly exposed in his present position – had given them to understand that he was now contemplating a backward move, rather than a forward one. 'As to the place of your own abode', the councillors wrote – in response to what was evidently a request from Russell for advice as to where he should himself reside – it was up to him 'to consyder which waie the rabells may be most annoyed, and the rest of the countres ajoyning well preserved in quiet, and [you] will, we doubt not, with all your possible delygence employe yourself'.[39] It is hard not to read this as a firm steer to Russell that he should stand his ground near Honiton, harass the rebels who occupied the villages in front of him, and continue to shield Somerset and Dorset to his rear. Elsewhere in their letter, the councillors responded to Russell's pleas for money and foot soldiers and promised to send him what they could.[40]

The suggestion that he should 'annoy' the rebels with the slender force that he had at his disposal can hardly have been received with enthusiasm by the lord privy seal. As Hooker notes, his position at Honiton was an unenviable one, for 'beinge forsaken of the commons and having but a slender guard and companie he lived more in feare than was feared, for the rebells in everie place increased, and his companie decreased, and he [was] not altogether assured of them which remained'.[41] As a result, Russell had little choice but to remain where he was, to raise what forces he could from the surrounding countryside, and to await reinforcements. His problems were almost certainly compounded by his close association with Sir Peter Carew – back at Russell's side by 10 July at the latest – who was widely hated in the region, both 'for his religion' and for his previous assault upon Crediton.[42] In a sense, Russell was forced to rely on the Carews and their reformist allies among the West Country gentry because they were the only ardent local supporters he had, but his decision to appoint Sir Peter and Sir Gawen to his advisory council – and, indeed, to spend part of his time living at Sir Peter's house at Mohun's Ottery – was unwise, because it tied him too closely to the Carews' faction and made it less likely that other, more moderate local gentlemen would come to his aid.[43] Tacitly recognising the difficulties that Russell faced, the councillors urged him to make good use of the time that he would inevitably be forced to spend in 'your abode nyhand [i.e., near] the sayd rebells' before his forces had been sufficiently built up to enable him to advance. Russell should cut off the insurgents' supply routes, the councillors urged, and should attempt to render them odious to the common people 'by spredinge abrode rumors of theyr develyshe behavours, crueltye, abhonmynable levings, robberies, murders and such lyke'.[44] Thus we see how the process of demonising the rebels had already begun: a process that was to intensify over the coming weeks and which would go on to define representations of them for the next five centuries.

## III

Lord Russell had good reason to feel anxious as he and his retinue hovered irresolutely in the countryside around Honiton in early July because, far away to the west, something was stirring: an unbowed spirit of popular resentment and defiance which was about to spring dramatically back into life and, within days, to conjure up a host still greater and more determined than that which already confronted the king's lieutenant in Devon. Sharp-eyed readers will have noted that, although Hooker entitled his original account of the rising 'The Beginning, Cause & Course of the . . . Rebellion in the Counties of Devon and Cornewall', nothing has so far been said about the events that occurred in the latter county during summer of 1549. This is partly because, despite the promise of his title, Hooker says nothing at all about how, when, why or even where the commotion in Cornwall started. In Hooker's later, printed narrative, we are simply told that 'the Cornish people' sympathised with the religious grievances of the Devonians and came in to join them – and matters are left at that. Hooker's reticence on this subject is perfectly understandable. He was not a native of Cornwall, he was not particularly well acquainted with affairs there and, as has already been stressed, the central aim of his narrative was to celebrate the loyalty of the citizens of Exeter in the face of 'popish' rebellion. From Hooker's perspective, all that needed to be said about the Cornish was that they had risen up in defence of the old faith, that they had tried and failed to take Exeter, and that they had at last been comprehensively defeated – and this, in effect, is what he does.

In the absence of much help from the most important contemporary chronicler of the Western Rising, then, historians have been left to rely on four main sources of information for their knowledge of the early stages of the 1549 rebellion in Cornwall. These are: first, the brief 'confessions' that were made by the Cornish rebel leaders in the Tower in October 1549 after the rebellion had been suppressed; second, the formal indictments that were drawn up against them soon afterwards in advance of their trials; third, a handful of retrospective anecdotes about the rising that are preserved in Richard Carew's *Survey of Cornwall*, first published in 1603; and fourth, a short narrative account of events compiled by the Cornish antiquarian William Hals a century later still, in *c.* 1680, and eventually published by Gilbert Davies in 1838.[45] Of these four sources, it is clearly that of Hals – written 150 years after the events that it purports to describe – that is the least reliable, but when Frances Rose-Troup came to compose her account of the initial stirs in Cornwall in her great history of the Western Rebellion, first published in 1913, she essentially followed the narrative that Hals had laid down.[46] And because Rose-Troup's book has remained the standard history of the rising ever since, Hals's ghost has continued to haunt accounts of the outbreak of the rebellion in Cornwall right up to the present day, even if his spectral presence has generally gone unrecognised.[47] To make matters more confusing still, the indictments that were drawn up against the Cornish rebel leaders in late 1549 appear to contain a crucial mistake, as I have argued in detail elsewhere, for they state that the rebellion in Cornwall broke out on 6 June, when, in point of fact, all of the other available evidence suggests that it broke out a month later: on or about 6 July.[48] So what really happened in Cornwall during the summer of 1549? In the absence of a Cornish equivalent of Hooker, we will probably never be able to provide a really satisfactory answer to this question, but the following pages tell the story as far as it is currently possible to reconstruct it: both from the four main sources set out above, and from other fragments of evidence that have emerged in the century since Rose-Troup's book was published.

The first piece of evidence to consider is a negative one: Hooker's insistence, at the very beginning of his narrative, that 'it is apparent & most certaine that this rebellion began and was first raised att a place in Devonshere named Sampford Courteney'.[49] These are emphatic words, and it seems unlikely that Hooker would have chosen to use them if he had had any suspicion that the rising had begun in Cornwall instead; the outbreak of rebellion in one's own native county was hardly something for an early modern gentleman to boast about, after all. And Hooker's implicit suggestion – that the Cornish rose after the Devonians did – is supported by an independent source that we have encountered once before: the accounts drawn up by John Killigrew the younger in 1551.[50] As we saw in Chapter 2, Killigrew was the son of John Killigrew senior, the captain of Pendennis Castle.[51] Killigrew himself was the 'paymaster' of the fortifications that Somerset's regime had begun to construct on the Isles of Scilly, 30 miles to the west of Land's End, to protect them from any sudden descent there by the French. The accounts that Killigrew submitted in 1551 detail the sums he had received from various Crown officials since his appointment as paymaster in 1548, and the sums he himself had laid out on fortifications and other related expenses during that same period. Among them is an entry which reveals that, on 23 June 1549 – the very same day that the Devon gentry rode out from Exeter to parley with the protestors at Clyst St Mary – Killigrew had received a payment of £100 'at Trewroe' from the deputy receiver of the Duchy of Cornwall.[52] That such a routine transaction could have taken place in the West Cornish town of Truro at this time strongly suggests that that district was not yet affected by any serious popular disorder.

But more revealing still is a subsequent entry which notes that, in late 1549, Killigrew had paid the commander of the garrison on the Isles of Scilly £325

> for the wages of one hundredthe soldyers ... sente by Sir Wylliam Godolphyn ... by thordre of his Majesties .... Counsaiell for the

> better defence of the said Isles during the Somer tyme ... which [soldiers] were shipped in ii barks at Pensance nigh the Mounte the xxvith of June anno eiusdm Regis iiicio [i.e., 26 June 1549].[53]

The significance of this payment is obvious. It seems inconceivable that Sir William Godolphin – who, as we have seen, had already put down one popular insurrection in West Cornwall and was fearful of further stirs there – would have calmly despatched 100 soldiers from Penzance to perform routine garrison duties on the Isles of Scilly if he had known, when he did so, that a full-scale rebellion was currently under way elsewhere in the county. The conclusion must surely be that, on 26 June, Cornwall had remained in at least 'a quavering quiet', and that trouble had only broken out in the county at some subsequent point, having presumably spread there from neighbouring Devon.

How this came about we do not know. It is possible that when word reached Cornwall, either on or shortly after 2 July, that Exeter, the regional capital of the West, was beset by forces that were determined to halt the recent religious innovations, this news had been enough in itself to inspire a spontaneous and celebratory uprising among the Cornish people as they glimpsed a fresh opportunity to turn back the evangelical tide. Alternatively, it is possible that the wave of popular anger that had begun to radiate outwards in every direction from Crediton after the Carews' attack upon that town on 22 June had simply rolled across the Tamar in early July, causing the inhabitants of Cornwall's eastern border parishes to rise up and join hands with their Devonian neighbours. In this context, it is interesting to note the fact that, in the surviving fragments of a ballad celebrating the rebels' eventual defeat, published in London towards the end of 1549, the loyalist author observed that 'The vicare of Ponwdstoke with his congeracion, / Commanded them to sticke to ther Idolatry'.[54] Poundstock is a parish in the north-eastern corner of Cornwall, just a few miles from the Devon border, and we know that the parish priest, Simon Moreton, was later executed for his part in the rebellion.[55] The balladeer's words clearly imply that Moreton had directed his flock to take up arms in defence of the old ways. Is it possible, then, that the balladeer had especially remarked upon this particular clergyman – the only priest who is mentioned by name in what survives of the original text – because it was at Poundstock, and at Moreton's instigation, that the protests in Cornwall had originally begun? For the moment, at least, we can only speculate.

What is clear, from a variety of different sources, is that – wherever the Cornish rebels initially rose – it was at Bodmin, Cornwall's most populous town, that they first began to gather in large numbers. In the brief account of Bodmin that he published in 1603, Carew noted that 'hither in the last commotion, flocked the Rebells, from all quarters of the shire, pitching their campe at the townes end, and here they imprisoned such Gentlemen, as they had plucked out of their holdes, and houses'.[56] From this we learn, not only that Bodmin had acted as the central rendezvous for the Cornish rebels, but also that, in Cornwall, just as in Devon, the insurgents had made a practice of imprisoning any gentlemen who refused to join them. Hals – writing a century later, and almost certainly drawing on Carew's text – provides much the same account, writing of Bodmin that 'here ... was the rendezvous of the Cornish rebels ... *anno* 3 Edward VI, who pitched their camp upon Castle Kynock ... and imprisoned such gentlemen as would not willingly ride with them'.[57] Hals's claim that the insurgents had pressed local gentlemen to 'ride with them' is probably anachronistic, as all the evidence we have suggests that the western rebels fought exclusively on foot. His reference to 'Castle Kynock' is intriguing, though. This structure – now known as Castle Canyke – is a large, multivallate Iron Age hillfort which still stands today on the outskirts of Bodmin. The earthwork could easily have housed and protected a temporary encampment of many hundreds of people, and while Hals's statement is not supported by any other contemporary source, it seems at least possible that it rests on an oral tradition that preserves genuine memories of the events of 1549.

The statements later made in the Tower by the two gentlemen who eventually emerged as the leaders of the rebellion in Cornwall similarly confirm that Bodmin was the place where the protestors had initially gathered. The first of these Cornish 'rebel captains' was Humphrey Arundell, esquire, who lived at Helland, just 3 miles from Bodmin. Humphrey, as we have seen, was the son of Roger Arundell, who had died in the 1530s, leaving Humphrey extensive estates in both Cornwall and Devon. Roger had been the brother of old Sir John Arundell of Lanherne; Humphrey was thus the cousin of Sir John Arundell the younger – the present master of Lanherne – and of the latter's brother, Sir Thomas.[58] Humphrey's character and outlook remain elusive. Although he was one of the wealthiest men in Cornwall, he was never selected as a JP, and it has been suggested that this was because he was a religious conservative.[59] That may well have been true – but there does not seem to be any hard evidence to prove it. An alternative theory that has sometimes been put forward to explain Arundell's exclusion from local power is that he was an especially quarrelsome individual: as is evinced by his involvement in a series of lawsuits before 1549.[60] On the other hand, as has been well observed, it was hardly unusual for a Cornish gentleman of Arundell's status to become involved in extensive litigation.[61] In 1570, the Protestant martyrologist John Foxe referred to Arundell, in his brief account of the rising, as the 'governour of the Mount', an appellation which suggests that Humphrey had, at one time, commanded the garrison there and which therefore implies that he had some military expertise.[62] So far, however, it has proved impossible to verify these points from other contemporary sources.[63]

After he had been captured at the end of the rising and imprisoned in the Tower, Arundell made a brief 'confession' of the part he had played in the rebellion, claiming that, during the opening stages in Cornwall,

> he and two others fled into a wood for feare of the rebells, and there remayned twoo dais, and after his wyfe, beinge great with child, desiered him this examinant to come to her, and so he dyd, and then a man of Bodman came to hym and procured hym to goo with hym to the rebells, and he refused, and then came mo[re] rebells and by force caried hym to Bodman, and on the morrowe he sent to Sir Hugh Trevanyon [a local JP] to know what he shuld do and he advysed hym to tarye with the rebells and to be in their favour to the intent to admyttygate [i.e., to restrain] their outragious doinges.[64]

Obviously, Arundell was doing all he could to suggest that he had been an unwilling participant in the rebellion, but when he states that the insurgents were already assembled in Bodmin when he himself first arrived upon the scene, we must surely believe him, for, if this had not been the case, his story would have stood no chance at all of being believed by his interrogators, because hundreds of eye-witnesses could have flatly refuted his words.

The testimony of Arundell's fellow rebel 'captain', John Winslade, esquire, of Tregarrick in Pelynt, similarly confirms that Bodmin had been the insurgents' initial rendezvous. Winslade, like Arundell, was among Cornwall's dozen wealthiest men, and, also like him, he had never been selected to sit on the county bench.[65] It seems probable that Winslade was a religious traditionalist, and that this had resulted in him being regarded as unreliable by the central authorities during the later 1530s and the 1540s.[66] Interestingly, he and Arundell are known to have been acquainted with each other before the rebellion began: in 1544, Arundell had leased land from Winslade.[67] In his own 'confession', Winslade alleged that he had been 'sent for by the rebells post, upon payne of burninge his howse, and thereupon he resorted to theym, and ther remayned with them four or fyve wekes, and was taken at Bodman'.[68] Once again, Winslade's claim that he had been intimidated into joining the rebels should probably be taken with a pinch of salt, but his claim that the rebels had threatened to burn down his house if he refused to join them is interesting, as this is exactly the same threat that the St Keverne men are said to have made against Hugh Mason the previous year.[69]

The confession of the third of the captured rebel leaders – Thomas Holmes, a yeoman from Blisland, 5 miles to the north-east of Bodmin – again confirms that it was in the latter town that the insurgents had originally foregathered. When he was interrogated in the Tower, Holmes admitted that he 'went foorthe with the parishioners of Blyston to Bodmin and contynued there amonge the rebells unto the end of the matter'.[70] The slight difference in tone between the statements of Arundell and Winslade, on the one hand, and that of Holmes, on the other, is worthy of note. Whereas the two gentlemen claimed to have been brought to Bodmin against their wills, Holmes freely admitted to having gone there of his own accord. That the yeoman should have declared that he 'went foorthe' with his fellow parishioners is interesting, moreover, as this particular form of words tends to suggest forward movement with a martial, even a spiritual, sense of resolve – and, as we shall see, it was precisely the same form of words that a Devon priest would subsequently choose to employ when he described how the young men of his own parish had set out on their journey to the rebel camp.

The indictment that was later drawn up against Arundell and Winslade alleged that they, together with many other 'traitors and rebels', 'did [on] 6 June' (*sic* – surely a mistake for 6 July, as we have already seen above)

> and for six weeks following, at Bodmyn and elsewhere in the county of Cornwall, by ringing of bells, hue and cry and otherwise, raise a multitude of malefactors to the amount of 1000 persons and upwards, with arms and banners displayed, and levy war against the king, and that they also dispersed writings and bills, to excite the lieges of Cornwall to levy war against the king.[71]

The reference to the rebels having dispersed 'writings' suggests that, in Cornwall, just as in Devon, the protestors had sent out warrants in the king's name ordering local communities to supply them with men, munitions and supplies. It would appear that the Cornish rebel leaders effectively hijacked the traditional machinery of local government in their county, in fact, in much the same way that their Devonian counterparts appear to have done in theirs: sending out their own orders to the parish constables and commanding these minor officials, in their turn, to communicate them to the people. Carew was later to remark that the Cornish constables' willingness to obey the rebel captains' precepts had been a vital factor in encouraging the protests to spread, noting that 'it was seene in the last Cornish rebellion, how the constables' command & example, drew many of the not worst meaning people, into that extremest breach of duty'.[72] Carew's claim that the rebels had brought many captured gentlemen to Bodmin is also supported by evidence of the indictment, which states that Arundell and Winslade had imprisoned 'many faithfull subjects of our . . . Lord the King, that is to say, knights, esquires and gentlemen' in the prison in that town.[73]

One of the central passages in the indictment alleges that, in addition to taking up arms and imprisoning members of the local elite, the Cornish insurgents had also cried and shouted out 'kyll the gentlemen and we wyll have the acte of sixe Articles uppe againe and ceremonies as were in King Henrye th'eights tyme'.[74] As I have argued at length elsewhere, and as we shall see in a subsequent chapter, there are good grounds for suspecting that the first three words of this alleged 'cry' may well have been fabricated by those who subsequently drew up the indictment.[75] The demand for the restoration of the Act of Six Articles, on the other hand – a demand that had also been made by the protestors who had risen up in West Cornwall in 1548, and in Mid-Devon just a few weeks earlier – and the demand for the retention of traditional religious ceremonies would appear to preserve the authentic voice of the Cornish rebels of 1549, for, as we shall see, these are both demands that the rebels made in their own articles.

## IV

Bodmin was Cornwall's administrative centre, and the few scraps of information we possess suggest that, with this key town in rebel hands, the revolt spread rapidly outwards in all directions, encountering only sporadic resistance from isolated bands of loyalist gentlemen. If the initial protests did indeed begin somewhere in the north-east Cornish countryside, then Sir Richard Grenville of Kilkhampton – one of the regime's most zealous local backers, and a man who had been prominent in the suppression of the West Cornish rebellion the previous year – would have been among the first of the Cornish JPs to come under threat. Grenville and his wife, Matilda, clearly fled from their home at this time in order to take refuge in a local stronghold where they hoped they would be safe.[76] Carew tells us that, 'at the last Cornish commotion, S[ir] Richard Greynvile . . . did, with his Ladie and followers, put themselves into . . . [Trematon] Castle', a twelfth-century fortress with an imposing central keep which stands on a hill overlooking the town of

Saltash, in the extreme south-east of the county. From here they bade defiance to the rebels, at least for a while. It was probably to Trematon that most of the East Cornish loyalists who had managed to escape the insurgents' clutches made their way, but a few may also have crossed over to St Nicholas Island – now known as Drake's Island – in the middle of Plymouth Sound. Carew notes that 'when the Cornish rebels, during Edw[ard] the 6['s] Raigne, turmoyled the quiet of those quarters . . . [the island] yielded a safe protection to divers dutiful subiects, who there shrowded themselves'.[77]

We know from another source that some of those who fled to St Nicholas Island took up their station in the fort that had been constructed there during the previous year in order to defend Plymouth against foreign attack.[78] Nor were these the only fugitives to find sanctuary from domestic insurrection in the fortifications that the Crown had recently built for the purposes of coastal defence, for it is clear that – in July 1549, just as in April 1548 – Pendennis Castle also became a place of refuge for local loyalists. In his retrospective account of his charges as paymaster of the western fortifications, John Killigrew the younger was later to note that he had laid out several sums of money 'for the defence of his highness castell of Pendenis . . . in the tyme of the Rebellion'. More specifically, Killigrew records that he had spent £40 'for the waiges of 160 soldiers retayned for the better defence of the saide Castell besydes th'ordenarye, serving ther by the space of x dayes endinge the xxth of Julye Anno RR p[re]d[i]c[to] iii [i.e., 1549]'.[79] This entry is particularly revealing, of course, because it indicates that John Killigrew senior, the captain of the castle, had first summoned men to defend it on 10 July, four days after what was probably the true date of the rebel gathering at Bodmin: which suggests, in its turn, that by this time the insurrection had spread to the countryside to the west of Truro.

Fortunately for the Killigrews, they were clearly able to gather more supplies, as well as more men, during the time that remained to them before the rebels closed in. In a petition submitted long afterwards, a certain Thomas Ennys of Gluvias, near Penryn, a few miles to the north of Pendennis, deposed that he had helped to victual 'the same castell to his power [i.e., as best he could] with mutton . . . & beer' at this time, and that he had then come into the castle himself and had been 'fullie determine[d] . . . to have remayned therein'. But because, at the age of seventy-two, he had been regarded as too elderly to withstand the rigours of a siege, Ennys complained, 'one John Kellygrewe . . . then Captain & keper of the sayd Castell, wylled your orator to dep[ar]te to his dwelling house'. As a result, Ennys went on, he was 'menasse[d]' by the rebels, who threatened to rob and imprison him unless he gave them money. Eventually, he was forced to hand over 40s. to 'one Coffen, then one of the Captens of the said Rebells' – nor was this to prove the end of his troubles, as we shall see in a subsequent chapter.[80] While the Killigrews were hastily preparing to repel an imminent rebel attack on Pendennis from the landward side, similar activity may well have been under way at Pendennis's sister castle of St Mawes. The chance survival of a document dated 19 July 1549, in which Thomas Treffry of Fowey – then describing himself as 'Captayne of the Kinges ma[jes]t[ie]s fortesse of Saynt Mowes' – acknowledged receipt of £57 from the hand of Reginald Mohun of Bodinnick, in repayment of certain monies that Treffry had previously laid out for the rigging of a ship, certainly hints that St Mawes may still have been in loyalist hands at this time.[81] And the fact that, during the 1930s, the great Cornish scholar Charles Henderson observed that Treffry 'almost alone [had] opposed the . . . Rebellion of 1549' makes this possibility more likely still – though, sadly, Henderson did not identify the original source on which his statement was, presumably, based.[82]

In the far west of Cornwall, it was St Michael's Mount that was to become the principal bolthole of the local gentry loyalists as the flood tide of rebellion surged westwards and caused them to abandon their homes in panic: presumably on or soon after 10 July. Carew was later to write of the Mount that, 'during the last Cornish commotion, divers Gent[lemen] with their wives and families, fled to the protection of this place'.[83] The loyalists may well have imagined that, once they had barricaded themselves within the great coastal fortress that had withstood so many sieges in the past, they would be safe from any threat that the rebellious countryfolk might conceivably be able to present. But if they did, they had underestimated both the determination and the military skill of their opponents. The rebels now began a full-scale siege of the Mount and quickly managed to discomfit the defenders: first by 'wynning the plaine at the hills foote, by assault, when the water was out', as Carew puts it, and then by capturing 'the even ground on the top, by carrying up great trusses of hay before them, to blench the defendants sight, and dead their shot'. Once the assailants had taken the high ground at the top of the hill on which the castle stands, the writing was on the wall for the beleaguered defenders. After this, Carew continues, 'they could make but slender resistance, for no sooner should anyone within peepe out his head, over those inflanked walls, but he became an open marke to a whole showre of arrows'. In the end, Carew concludes:

> this disadvantage, together with the womens dismay, & decrease of victuals, forced a surrender to those rakehel[l]s mercy, who, nothing guilty of that effeminate virtue, spoyled their goods, imprisoned their bodies, and were rather by God's gracious providence, then any want of will [or] purpose . . . restrayned from murdering the principall persons.[84]

Carew's description of the rebels as 'rakehells' – that is to say, as rascals or low-born persons – underscores his own distaste for them, and his concluding remark – that, had it not been for God's Providence, the insurgents would have murdered their gentry captives – must be regarded as tendentious, to say the least, and as more reflective of his own prejudices than of the rebels' true intentions. Yet, in its broad essentials, the story that Carew recounted in 1603 – that the local loyalist gentry had retired to the Mount, that the rebels had attacked them there, and that, after some fighting, they had succeeded in capturing the fortress – is fully confirmed by several depositions made in a legal case of 1565. The case related to the property of the late gentleman-lawyer and former MP William Trewynnard of Trewinnard, in St Erth, just a few miles from the Mount.[85] One of the local people who testified during the 1560s recalled that Trewynnard had died 'by reason of a great hurte and mortall wound which he receaved and cawght amongst the Rebelles in the Mo[u]nte at the late rebellion in the tyme of . . . King

Edward the Sixth'.[86] Another deponent, Margaret Newman, went into more detail, testifying that, 'yn the commosyon yere', Trewynnard had

> dyed Intestate beinge hurt with gowne powder at the assault by the rebells given upon the Castell of the Mownt; the same Wyllam with dvyers other gentellmen then there beinge of the kynges part[y] then defending & Resystinge the sayd Rebelles, and in sykinge of there apprehension, for which thereupon his house [i.e., Trewynnard's] was by the rebells afterwards spoyled.[87]

Newman's testimony confirms what Thomas Ennys's words have already suggested: that the rebels made a practice of robbing the houses of those whom they regarded as their principal enemies.

Local people will not have forgotten that Trewynnard was one of the gentlemen who had helped Sir William Godolphin to overawe the West Cornish countryside with a demonstration of armed might in July 1548.[88] But by July 1549, the boot was well and truly on the other foot. Now it was the rebellious commoners of Penwith and Kerrier who were the masters, while it was the loyalist gentlemen who found themselves powerless and overborne. What happened to Godolphin himself at this time is frustratingly unclear. It is possible that the man who had long been the regime's chief enforcer in West Cornwall was captured at St Michael's Mount and promptly imprisoned there, as a number of other loyalists are known to have been.[89] Yet it also possible that Godolphin – an experienced soldier, who would have been well aware of the Mount's military deficiencies – had chosen to seek refuge with the Killigrews instead.[90] Over the following weeks, Pendennis Castle was to be closely blockaded by the rebel forces, which were presumably composed largely of local men. It is hard to doubt that there would have been a strong contingent from St Keverne and the other parishes of the Lizard in their ranks: especially as we now know that the priest, John Wolcock – later to be described as one of the 'principal stirrers' of the revolt – was the vicar of Manaccan, in the heart of the Meneage.[91] In any case, it is clear that the inhabitants of West Cornwall had become fully involved in the rebellion within days of the gathering at Bodmin, while the fact that, as we shall see, the insurgents later appear to have demanded a liturgy in the Cornish tongue plainly indicates that a sense of Cornish cultural defensiveness had helped to fuel the rising.

The loyalists who had retreated into Trematon Castle may well have held out a little longer than their counterparts at the Mount. Carew was later to record that Sir Richard Grenville and his companions had 'endured the Rebels siege' at Trematon 'for a while'; that the insurgents had 'incamped in three places against it' – a statement which, again, suggests that the siege had lasted for some time – and that it had at first appeared that the insurgents, 'wanting great Ordinance [i.e., cannon], could have wrought the besieged small scathe [i.e., hurt]': in other words, that the rebels had been unable to distress the loyalists who were sheltering behind the castle's thick walls. Yet, in the end, Carew goes on, Grenville had been betrayed by 'his friends, or [rather] enemies', for 'some of those within' had slipped away 'by night over the wals'. With his garrison shrinking, Grenville now began to hearken to the siren voices of 'those without', who, Carew tells us, by 'mingling humble intreatings with rude menaces' persuaded Sir Richard 'to issue forth at a postern gate for parley'. As soon as he had done so, the insurgents 'laid hold on his aged unweyldie body [Grenville was fifty-five at this time], and threatened to leave it liveless, if the inclosed did not leave their resistance'. At this, the defenders had thrown down their arms and permitted the rebels to enter the castle. After they had come in, Carew avers, the insurgents had 'exercised the uttermost of their barbarous crueltie (death excepted)' on the captured defenders and 'the seely [i.e., innocent] gentlewomen, without regard of sexe or shame, were stripped from their apparel to their very smockes, and some of their fingers broken, to plucke away their rings'. Finally, Carew concludes, 'Sir Richard himself made an exchange from Trematon castle to that of Launceston, with the Gayle to boote [i.e. and was placed in the county prison there, too]'.[92]

Carew's outrage at the indignities that the rebels had heaped upon the captured gentry loyalists at Trematon is palpable, but, once again, he is honest enough to admit that none of the captives had been killed – or even, it would seem, very much harmed, beyond a few broken fingers.

The fact that Grenville himself – the man who, with Godolphin, had been most prominent in putting down the West Cornish rebellion of the previous year, and in condemning to death a number of the participants – should have escaped with his life is especially noteworthy, and again casts doubt on the picture that the later indictment was to paint of the Cornish rebels as murderous savages baying for gentle blood. Carew's statement that the rebels subsequently chose to imprison Grenville in the prison at Launceston Castle – a statement that is confirmed by another, contemporary source – is also interesting.[93] It made perfect sense to imprison Grenville here, of course: Launceston gaol was the most secure place of confinement in Cornwall. Yet the decision to incarcerate Sir Richard in this particular prison was also a deeply symbolic act. Grenville was one of the two most influential JPs on the new commission of the peace for Cornwall which had been issued after Somerset's regime came to power. By throwing him into 'the common Gayle of the shire for offendours', therefore, the rebel leaders were demonstrating to the world that they regarded this as an illegitimate commission, which had been issued by an illegitimate regime, and that they – the protestors who had risen up in the king's name – rather than the gentry who continued to back the protector, were now the true upholders of legitimate royal authority in Cornwall. More specifically, many local people would doubtless have regarded it as poetic justice that Grenville should now be immured in the very same gaol in which the rebels of 1548 had been imprisoned before they were dragged before him and the other judges of oyer and terminer at their trials.

Carew's retrospective account of events at Trematon Castle at the beginning of the rising – like his retrospective accounts of events at St Nicholas Island and the Mount at around the same time – is confirmed, in its broad essentials, by an independent and much earlier source. In a legal petition submitted in 1552–53, Robert Whetehyll, esquire – the husband of Grenville's daughter, Jane – was to complain that, during 'the tyme of the late rebellyon in . . . Cornewall', he had been 'in the Kynges highness servyce' and had been 'robbed and spoylled at the kynges maiestyes castell of Tramaton . . . by certeyn misruled persons, then being rebellious there, of certen hys goodes and c[h]attalles amounctying to the valew of 500 markes and more'.[94] Whetehyll's petition not only confirms that a clash had taken place between the rebels and Grenville's followers at Trematon, therefore, but also that the former had eventually robbed the latter of their goods, just as the rebels had robbed the captured gentry loyalists at the Mount. Whetehyll then went on to allege that a yeoman from Liskeard named John Daryette had been 'one, amongst others, that was a pryncypall offender, worker & procurer in & concerning the sayd spoyle and rob[be]ry'.[95] Liskeard is a market town some 11 miles from Trematon, so this statement tends to support the assumption on which we have been working so far: that those who attacked the various strongholds into which the gentry loyalists had fled were themselves local men.

The surrender of Trematon Castle brought loyalist resistance in East Cornwall to an end, at least as far as we can tell. It was probably soon after this, therefore, that the Cornish rebel leaders – having secured control of the whole of Cornwall, except for the isolated garrison at Pendennis (and, perhaps, St Mawes) – first assembled a powerful host, and then marched with it to the assistance of their fellow protestors in Devon. Almost nothing is known about how this force was recruited and organised – though Carew's comment about the crucial role played in the Cornish rising by the constables, noted above, hints that the men who served in the rebel army may well have been raised on a parochial basis: utilising precisely the same mechanisms that had customarily been used to raise men to serve the Crown.[96] Carew has only one brief remark to make on this subject, but it is a revealing one, nevertheless: he notes that the disturbances now 'grew to a general revolt, under the conduct of Arundel, Wydeslade, Rosogan and others, followed by 6,000 [men], with which power they marched into Devon'.[97] This comment is telling, first, because of what it reveals about the reputed strength of the Cornish host. If the rebels really did manage to raise 6,000 men, then this was a huge achievement, for, elsewhere in his *Survey*, Carew calculates that the total strength of the Cornish militia in 1599 was 6,030 men.[98] It is conceivable, of course, that having painstakingly worked out the latter figure, Carew had simply guessed that the rebels had been equally strong – but, even if one were to assume that this was so, it would still bear witness to his conviction that the insurgents had managed to raise Cornwall's entire military power in 1549.

The second telling point about Carew's comment is that it suggests that he believed the rebels to have possessed three chief captains: Humphrey Arundell, John Winslade and 'Rosogan'. Arundell and Winslade we have already met, but who was the third man? The work of John Foxe provides an important clue because, in his brief account of the Western Rising, the martyrologist noted that, among the rebels' 'chief Gentlemen Captains', had been included both 'James Rosogan' and 'John Rosogan'.[99] Carew would have been familiar with the *Acts and Monuments*, of course, so it is possible that he had simply picked up the name of Rosogan from there, but the fact that he chose to highlight it, when Foxe had included several more besides, suggests that Carew had his own reasons for regarding whichever of the two Rosogans he was alluding to as an especially significant figure. The Rosogans were a gentry family who came from the parish of St Columb, 16 miles to the west of Bodmin and 4 miles to the south of the Arundells' mansion house at Lanherne.[100] James is known to have been a co-defendant with Sir John Arundell in a legal suit at some point prior to 1547, so it seems reasonable to assume that the two men were acquainted with each other.[101] Beyond this, we know little more about the Rosogans and their connections, but Carew's evidence tends to reinforce that of Foxe, and to suggest that either one or both of these men was a key figure in the Cornish rebel host.

When did the central authorities first become aware of the gathering threat in Cornwall? The earliest official response to the disturbances there appears to have been a proclamation issued in London on 11 July, which authorised the forfeiture of the goods of all those who 'are at this present rebelliously . . . . assembled in . . . Devon and Cornwall'.[102] Clearly, then, the privy councillors now knew that Cornwall was up in arms and may also have suspected that the Cornish insurgents had entered into some sort of association with the Devonians. Yet the earliest surviving evidence of a physical conjunction between the Cornish and the Devon rebels only surfaces ten days later, in a letter sent on 22 July by the councillors to Lord Russell, who was still vainly trying to gather local men at Honiton in order to advance to Exeter's relief. In this letter – a response to an earlier missive of Russell's, now lost, which had been despatched on 18 July – the councillors advised him that, 'to the power gathered in Cornewall as joyne with the rebells, the proclamation [i.e., the proclamation made on 11 July] . . . shalbe some stay to them . . . [as it] maie peradventure withdrawe them back to save theyr owne'.[103]

This is an intriguing statement in several respects. First, it demonstrates that, by 18 July at the very latest, a substantial military force had emerged from Cornwall to join the insurgents in Devon. Second, it suggests that the arrival of the Cornish was a relatively new development – possibly one that the councillors had first learned of from Russell's letter of 18 July, or from 'the letters out of Cornewall conteyning the state of those countres' that he had enclosed with it (letters that Russell may well have received by sea, as any loyalists who were continuing to hold out in Cornwall were by now entirely cut off from the lord privy seal by land).[104] Third, it hints – through the councillors' proffering of advice as to how the Cornish 'power' might yet be 'stayed' – that, at this point, it was still hoped that the Cornishmen might not advance all that far. In this context, it is interesting to note that the letter of 22 July also contains the earliest surviving reference to the insurgency having spread to Plymouth, for the councillors expostulated against 'the treason wrought by the mayor of Plymouthe in the yelding upp of the towne to the rebells'.[105]

Previous histories of the Western Rising have assumed that the rebels occupied Plymouth in mid-June, but the councillors' rage, and the fact that, as a subsequent letter reveals, they were extremely confused about the true situation in the town, strongly suggests that its fall was a more recent occurrence. The contemporary Plymouth receivers' accounts shed a few more rays of precious light on the matter. These show that the mayor and his brethren had still been in full control of Plymouth on St John's Eve (i.e., 23–24 June), when they had held the annual Midsummer Watch at the town's high cross.[106] The entries in the accounts are undated, making it impossible to be sure exactly what happened when, but over the following days or weeks the town governors had organised a muster, taken part in a conference with two local gentlemen and held two extraordinary meetings at the Guildhall.[107] In the end, however, Plymouth's loyalist town councillors had evidently come to the conclusion that the town could not be defended against a determined attack because it contained no fortifications on its landward side, and had therefore taken the decision to retire with their most committed supporters into the relative security of the medieval 'castle quadrate', just to the south of the town, and the recently built fort on St Nicholas Island.[108] Having resolved upon this plan, it would appear that they sent a former mayor to Lord Russell by sea to inform him of what they had done.[109] The accounts do not reveal what it was that had prompted the town governors to fall back to these last-ditch positions; but, if their decision to abandon the town was indeed the result of Humphrey Arundell's sudden irruption into Devon with a formidable Cornish 'power' shortly before 18 July, then it is easy to understand why the privy councillors should have found Russell's letter of that date so particularly troubling, and why they should at once have set about arranging for him to be sent substantial reinforcements.[110] What had begun as an obscure village protest against the regime's religious policies just five weeks before had by now transformed itself into a genuine military challenge: a challenge that posed a threat to the very existence of Protector Somerset's regime, and thus to the progress of religious 'reformation' across the entire kingdom of England.

# 5

## Flood Tide
### 15–31 July 1549

The arrival of Humphrey Arundell with a powerful Cornish rebel host in Devon towards the middle of July, and the concurrent capture of Plymouth by the insurgents, caused huge consternation in the government camp – and during the next two weeks the Western Rising reached its zenith. As Arundell continued his march eastwards, as rebel forces continued to besiege Pendennis, Plymouth Castle and Exeter, and as Russell became increasingly convinced that he was about to face a determined assault on his small band at Honiton, it must have seemed to Protector Somerset that the whole of the West Country was on the brink of running up in flames, even as he was facing more and more serious popular unrest in other parts of the kingdom. Because so many important things were happening in so many different places at once during this crucial fortnight, it seems sensible to diverge here, for a time, from the purely chronological course that we have followed hitherto, and to consider simultaneous developments in several distinct geographical locations instead. To this end, the present chapter will be divided into five parts. The first part will consider the interactions that took place between Lord Russell and the Privy Council, as Russell grew ever more concerned about the rebels' growing strength. The second will discuss the various 'supplications' that the rebels produced in July and the government's response to them. The third will look at the sieges of the loyalist strongholds, while the fourth will analyse the few fragments of evidence that survive about conditions in rebel-held Devon and Cornwall. The fifth and last part will briefly consider the articles that were drawn up by the conjoined rebel forces around Exeter in late July – and will show how battle was finally joined between the rebels and Russell's forces in East Devon during the closing days of that month.

## I

From the moment the lord privy seal had first arrived in East Devon he had been extremely concerned about what he plainly regarded as the huge mismatch between the rebels' strength and his own. Most of Russell's letters to Somerset and the Privy Council have been lost, but his anxieties may be traced in their surviving letters to him. We have already seen that, as early as 10 July, the councillors had felt it necessary to provide Russell with what appears to have been a firm steer that he should dismiss any ideas of abandoning Honiton and re-establishing his headquarters further to the east instead. Two days later, Somerset wrote to Russell observing that, in 'your fyrst l[ett]res' from Devon, the latter had complained of 'the greatnes of theyr [i.e., the rebels'] nombers of footemen [i.e., soldiers] and your impossibilitie to have any [foot soldiers] to trust to'.[1] The refusal of local men – not only in East Devon, but in Somerset and Dorset, too – to come in to recruit his forces was a problem that was to continue to dog Russell throughout the following weeks, and one that underscored the fact that local opinion was firmly on the rebels' side. From the first, he had been forced to beg the Council to supply him with foot soldiers from outside the region to bolster his strength and, as there were no English foot soldiers ready to hand, the councillors had turned to 'strangers' instead – to the mercenary foreign soldiers who had recently been shipped over to England to fight in Somerset's forthcoming campaign against the Scots.[2] On 10 July, Somerset and his colleagues had written to Russell promising to send him 150 Italian soldiers armed with harquebuses, or portable firearms – 'hackbutters', in the contemporary phrase – as well as 300–400 horsemen led by the experienced military commander Lord Grey.[3] Some of Grey's men were clearly foreigners, too, for a London chronicler described them as 'certayne strangers, horsemen, in redd cottes'.[4] The councillors had also reassured Russell that they had a further 400 'horsemen strangers' standing by, together with 'one thousand alymanes fotmen' – that's to say, German infantrymen – should he require them.[5]

Russell's spirits may have been briefly lifted by this news, but, two days later, he received word from the protector that he had been forced to countermand Grey's orders and to redirect him and his forces – now consisting of 1,500 horse and foot, including 'a great number of ... foreign troops, such as Germans and Albanians' – to suppress a stir in Oxfordshire which had been caused 'by instigacion of sundry priests ... for these matyrs of religion'.[6] Grey and his men put down the Oxfordshire rising with savage slaughter around a week later, subsequently hanging at least one priest from his own church steeple.[7] Perhaps because of the diversion of Grey's forces, perhaps because the situation in the West was continuing to deteriorate, the regime now ordered another experienced commander to prepare to march to Russell's assistance. As early as 6 July, Somerset had written to Sir Anthony Kingston telling him 'to be ready with footmen and horsemen to depart as the ... council shall signify'.[8] Kingston, whose name would become inextricably linked with that of the Western Rising, was aged about forty at this time. He had led a contingent of men from Gloucestershire against the Pilgrims of Grace in 1536 and had later been knighted by Henry VIII.[9] His wife, Mary, had formerly been married to the late Sir William Courtenay of Powderham in Devon, so the sheriff of Devon, Sir Piers Courtenay – Sir William's son – was Kingston's stepson.[10] After his marriage, Sir Anthony appears to have divided his time between Devon and Gloucestershire. He was probably in the latter county when the protector first contacted him on 6 July 1549, and eight days later Somerset and his fellow councillors wrote to Kingston once again: this time in a letter that breathed a sense of extreme urgency.

The councillors began by noting that 'those most detestable Rebells and traytors to God, the kyngs Ma[jes]tie and the Commonwealth assembled in Devonshyre doe daylie increase their force & nombers in [such] sorte as it shalbe most requysit to mete & incontre with them in tyme before theyr power growes any further'. Accordingly, Kingston was ordered to make ready to depart, at an hour's warning, with all of the horsemen and footmen he could muster, for whatever destination the councillors should appoint. They went on to advise Sir Anthony that his 'mocion' should 'be so carefull, vigilant & circumspecte' that none of the rebels' 'spies, messengers, postes nor couriers' should be alerted to his actions. Should he happen to apprehend any such rebel emissaries, they stressed, he was 'to see them forthwith executed and hanged to the terror and example of th'others'.[11] We may assume that, soon after receiving these sanguinary instructions, Sir Anthony and his men set out for Devon.[12] Once he had arrived, Kingston was appointed as Russell's 'Provost marshal in the field': an appointment that, as we will see, was to have baleful consequences for West Country folk.[13]

Even as the councillors were ordering Kingston to prepare himself for his mission to the West, a new state of emergency was developing in East Anglia. Between 8 and 10 July, enclosures were destroyed by the countryfolk around Wymondham in Norfolk and over the following days these disorders escalated into a massive popular demonstration: a demonstration that is today known as Kett's Rebellion after its most famous leader, Robert Kett, a well-to-do yeoman.[14] Those who rose up in Norfolk and the surrounding counties during the summer of 1549 – and who were soon to capture the regional capital, Norwich – were motivated, at least on the face of things, by quite different grievances from those who had risen up at the same time in the West Country and Oxfordshire.[15] The articles that Kett's followers eventually drew up focused almost entirely on social and economic issues rather than on religious ones – and, indeed, the demonstrators were to make use of the new Book of Common Prayer in their open-air services.[16] The other groups of protestors who had risen up across much of the South-East of England at this time also appear to have been motivated primarily by economic grievances, and as the regime gradually managed to persuade these smaller bands to disperse – through promises of redress and pardon, liberally spiced with menaces – during the first two weeks of July, Protector Somerset took considerable comfort from this fact. Indeed, in a letter to Russell he went so far as to assure him that the protestors in Kent, Sussex, Essex, Hampshire and elsewhere had not only 'confessed their faults with very lowly submission', 'but also for [the reformed] rellygon declared themselves ... as, hearing of your rabells, thaye dessyre to dye against them [or, in other words, that they had expressed their willingness to die fighting in the field against the western rebels]'.[17]

While doubtless pleased to hear that many of the protestors in the South-East had been dispersed, Russell must have been extremely anxious to learn of the fresh stirs in Oxfordshire and East Anglia. Somerset's claim that the protestors who had recently submitted had not only expressed their enthusiastic support for the 'new learning', moreover, but had also evinced their willingness to fight and die against the traditionalist Western rebels can scarcely have left Russell feeling entirely reassured. While there were many differences between the Western rebels and those who had risen up elsewhere, there were many similarities, too. All of the different groups posed a threat to the established order, after all, and all of them were gathering in 'camps': hence the phrase that one man later used to denote that heady summer – 'the campyng tyme'.[18] While it may have suited some groups of demonstrators to present themselves as supportive of the Crown's religious policies in the hope that this would improve their chances of securing their economic and social goals, moreover, most of the rebel bands clearly included at least some traditionalists. Many contemporaries suspected – almost certainly wrongly – that even the East Anglian stirs were partly attributable to the machinations of 'popish priests', indeed, in mid-July, the councillors themselves wrote to the Lady Mary, alleging that her high-profile support for the old ways in religion had encouraged the risings in both Devon *and* Norfolk.[19] Bearing all of this in mind, Russell must have felt that he had good reason to fear that the rebel forces that were already ranged to his front might, at any moment, be joined by like-minded bands of protestors to his rear – he specifically told the Council at about this time that the rebels were boasting that they would shortly have 10,000 men to 'set on ... [our] backs' from Somerset and Dorset.[20]

On 17 July, the councillors wrote to Russell once again, this time apologising for the fact that, although he had requested that they send him the German foot soldiers whom they had assured him were standing by just a week ago, they were no longer able to do so. As they frankly admitted, this was partly because these foreign mercenary soldiers were so 'odyous to our people abrode . . . as we can hardly move them to receive them without quarrel here at hand'. Nevertheless, the councillors went on, 'the strangers horsemen, and Italyan hackbutters . . . shalbe with you as soon as they cane possabelye, being alredye in the waie thyther'. And while it was possible that the troops Sir William Herbert was then raising in Wiltshire and Gloucestershire – and to whom Russell had also previously been encouraged to look for aid – might be needed elsewhere, they cheerfully continued, he would presently 'be furnished of ayde of . . . the Lord Graie' – though, regrettably, Grey was still in Oxfordshire.[21] We do not know when this message reached the lord privy seal, but, when it did, it can only have reinforced his conviction that his desperate pleas for swift and substantial assistance were not being taken seriously enough by the Council.

Up to this point, Russell appears to have received no reinforcements at all. It is therefore easy to understand why, when he first heard of the advance of the Cornish rebel host into Devon – probably on 18 July – he should have been thrown into a state of near-panic. That this was indeed his reaction is suggested by several separate sources. The first and most of important of these is the letter that the Council sent to Russell on 22 July, responding to a letter, now sadly lost, that he himself had sent to them four days before. It is clear from this that, in his own missive, Russell – no longer content to ask for relatively minor reinforcements – had demanded that he should be assisted by 'a mayne force' instead: that is to say, by a powerful army. Significantly, the councillors repeated this phrase twice in the opening lines of their own letter, assuring Russell that they had taken cognisance of the passages in his previous communication in which 'you note the smallness of your owne power, the dayly increase of the rabells nombers, and the necessytie [for you] to have a mayne force', without which 'neythere can the cytie [i.e., Exeter] be relieved, ne the Rebells . . . resisted'.[22] Having observed that they had been sorry to have received a letter from him that smacked of 'desperation', and proffered a good deal of advice that was plainly designed to encourage Russell to hold his nerve, the councillors had then gone on to promise him that they would, indeed, send to his assistance the 'mayne force' that was, even then, being raised by John Dudley, earl of Warwick – though they noted that Warwick would need to pacify the ongoing stirs in East Anglia and Kent first.[23] This was a key concession, and one which suggests that – having received word of Arundell's advance – the Council was now inclined to take the threat from the West almost as seriously as Russell did himself.

The second piece of evidence that suggests that Russell was by now beginning to panic is an anecdote included by John Hooker in his *Life* of Sir Peter Carew. Having remained at Honiton 'for a long time', Hooker begins,

> still looking for the supply of men and money promised; and at length doubting to be assailed by the enemy, and having no power to withstand them, [Russell] was persuaded by the gentlemen of Dorsetshire to leave Honiton, and to go into Dorsetshire, and there to remain until he had some great force about him.[24]

Accordingly, the lord privy seal had evacuated his headquarters at Honiton and set off towards Chard.[25] But, 'as soon as he was thus departed', Hooker goes on:

> Sir Peter Carew, having knowledge thereof, took his horse at Mohun's Ottery, and rode up to the Blackdown and there met with ... [Russell], and having some speeches ... with him, declared what inconveniences were like to ensue to the encouraging of the enemy, the undoing of the country, and the great dishonour to himself, if he should now leave the country, and give the enemy scope and liberty to go forward. Which, when his lordship had well considered, he returned back again to Honiton, and never removed from thence until he gave the onset to his enemies.[26]

Hooker – who cannot have been present himself, and who presumably heard the story from Carew's own lips – does not provide a precise date for this incident. Previous historians have therefore tended to assume that Russell's temporary retreat occurred in early July.[27] Yet the fact that

Hooker notes, first, that the lord privy seal had already been in Honiton for 'a long time' when he decided to abandon it; second, that he was afraid that he would shortly be 'assailed' by the rebels – presumably because he believed they would be emboldened to attack him after they had been reinforced by the Cornish host now advancing under Arundell; and third, that he was planning to retire into Dorset in order to await reinforcement by 'some great force' – surely the 'mayne force' that Russell had demanded in his letter to the Council of 18 July – makes it hard to doubt that the abortive retreat to Chard had, in fact, occurred at some time after that date.

Finally, we should note that there survives an undated paper in Russell's own hand, in which he discusses the strategic position of Sherborne in Dorset.[28] In this paper – which was evidently written for the eyes of the privy councillors – Russell stresses that, in his opinion, Sherborne does not 'stand upon any such strayte, as the same, with any meane force, shall be a stay to the passage of the rebells eastward' – in other words, that the town cannot be regarded as a place of such natural strength that he and the small forces under his command might conceivably be able to occupy it in order to prevent the rebels from marching to the east. Instead, he presses, once again, for the despatch of what he terms 'an army abyll to withstand them in the face'. Russell then goes on to state that Sherborne is, nevertheless, 'a convenient place for a strength of men to lie in for the indifferent stay as well of Somersideshyre and Wyl[t]shire, as Dorsedshire, during the time that these rebels shall not pass the bo[u]nds of Devonshyre'. The thrust of the paper is obvious: if his forces were to retreat to Sherborne, Russell is suggesting, then they would be able to control Dorset, Somerset and Wiltshire from there while they waited for really substantial reinforcements to arrive. It has often been assumed that this paper was composed in either later June or early July, but the evidence discussed above makes it seem far more likely that it was written on or about 18 July – and that it therefore provides still further evidence of the lord privy seal's 'wobble' during these crucial mid- to late July days.[29]

Had Russell gone ahead with the strategic withdrawal that he was clearly envisaging at this time – and upon which, indeed, he seems to have briefly embarked, before swiftly changing his mind – its effects would almost certainly have been disastrous from the government's point of view. Such a retrograde movement would surely have encouraged the rebels to advance across the Devon border, and this in turn would have made it possible for them to raise many more men in the counties further to the east, where there was a great deal of covert support for their cause.[30] Hooker himself clearly believed that this is what would have happened if Carew had not intervened, for he remarked: 'and true it was, that if ... [Russell] had departed according to his first determination, there had grown thereby a greater fire than all the waters in five shires about would have been able to have quenched'.[31] Hooker's words – like the anecdote itself – are clearly intended to portray Carew in a highly positive light, of course. Nevertheless, there seems no reason to doubt that his account is accurate in the broad essentials: not only because it reflects what we know of the different characters of the two men – Russell, careful and cautious; Carew, bold and forceful – but also because it appears to be confirmed by the other pieces of circumstantial evidence we have already discussed above.[32] In any event, the councillors' next letter to Russell – written in response to one of his, dated 22 July – suggests that, by that date, his crisis of confidence was over, and he had adopted a more resolute posture, as the final part of this chapter will show.

## II

As Russell and his entourage had been bracing themselves for an imminent attack at Honiton throughout the first three weeks of July, a series of communications had been passing back and forth between the rebel captains in the West Country and the Privy Council in London, most of them connected with the insurgents' formal 'petitions' or lists of demands. Several such petitions were clearly sent up to the government between 10 June and 26 July, and, as none of the original documents has survived – though the texts of two of them were later printed in London – their history is complex and difficult to unravel.[33] As we have seen, the earliest of the rebel petitions appears to have been the one that was submitted to Edward by the mid-Devon protestors in late June, and to which a formal response had been made in the king's name in a letter – subsequently printed as *A Message Sent by the Kynges Majestie* – dated 8 July. The second petition was probably composed a few days after this date and incorporated the original grievances of the Cornish rebels. We only know of its existence because, in his subsequent 'confession', Humphrey Arundell admitted that, soon after they met at Bodmin, 'the [Cornish] commons and rebells made a supplication whereunto this examynate was pryvye'.[34] Arundell would hardly have admitted to this damning fact unless he had felt that he had no choice but to do so. It seems a fair assumption that he himself had signed the original supplication, therefore – and that he had later presumed that his interrogators were well aware of this fact.

Nothing is known about the contents of this 'supplication', but, as we shall see, elements of it may well have been incorporated within the two petitions that were later to be jointly composed by the rebels of Devon and Cornwall. It is just possible that the Cornish protestors' original manifesto had included a demand for changes in the composition of Edward's government, because, on 12 July, Somerset complained bitterly to Russell that the Western rebels 'speake to have to do in the governaunce of the kyng's Majestie', in other words, that they were demanding that their own nominees should be appointed to the king's Privy Council.[35] If the protestors really had made such a nakedly political demand, then this would have been a direct attack on Somerset's position as protector. It is hardly surprising, therefore, that, having relayed this news to Russell, Somerset went on to snarl that 'thaie shall knowe er[e] thay come anything nerer [to London] thay shall bothe be let of that porpose, and ... [as] rank Traytors receive there desertes on the waye'.[36] This comment – like the letter sent to Kingston two days later – shows that the gloves were now off as far as the lord protector was concerned.

The third document that is known to have been composed from the protestors' point of view at this time possesses a curious history. In 1550, a copy of what was almost certainly an original response to *A Message Sent by the Kynges Majestie* – a response written by an anonymous English author whose sympathies lay with the protestors, and who may, indeed, have been one of them – was published as a pamphlet in Paris. Entitled *La Responce du Peuple Anglois à leur Roy Edouard sur certains articles qui en som nom leurs ont este envoyez touchant le religion Chrestienne* – i.e., 'The response of the English people to their King Edward to certain articles that in his name have been sent to them touching the Christian religion' – this pamphlet provides a French translation of the original text, together with a short preface.[37] *La Responce* is a lengthy and sophisticated piece of work, and it has therefore been surmised that its author was a conservative cleric, and possibly – as the king's original message had been sent specifically to the mid-Devon protestors – a Devonian.[38] The fact that *La Responce* contains a reference to the 'barbaric' nature of the foreign mercenaries in the government's employ suggests that the original text on which the pamphlet was based may well have been written soon after news of Grey's savage onslaught upon the Oxfordshire rebels on 18 July had begun to spread, while the fact that its author writes as though a major confrontation between the western rebels and the Crown forces was imminently expected suggests a terminal date for its composition of around 29 July, as this is when the serious fighting between the two sides in East Devon began.[39]

*La Responce du Peuple* is not, despite its title, a text that embodies a collective popular response to the king's message of 8 July, but should instead be regarded as a personal response to that message: one that was composed by a single acute observer. There is no evidence to suggest that the original text on which it is based was ever presented to the king or, indeed, to suggest that it was ever read by anyone else at all until it was being prepared for publication in Paris. Nevertheless, it is a fascinating document. As well as providing a point-by-point rebuttal of the arguments made in *A Message Sent by the Kynges Majestie* – and in the process, of course, supporting all of the demands for a halt to religious innovation that the mid-Devon rebels had originally made – the author of *La Responce* makes a number of additional points of his own. He complains about the intimidation of conservative bishops, for example, alleges that the regency council has 'exceeded its authority by introducing religious reform' and argues – as so many traditionalists were to do at this time – that there should be no further legislative changes until Edward reached his majority.[40] He also castigates the councillors for their ruinously expensive wars and criticises them for calling in foreign mercenaries, suggesting that there is a danger that these armed strangers will, in time, overrun the entire kingdom. Finally, he makes it very clear that he believes that the message that had been sent in the king's name had, in fact, been written by Edward's 'governors' for their own self-serving purposes. One can well understand why the author of *La Responce* was so careful to preserve his anonymity; had the government been alerted to him and his outspoken text during the fervid time in which the tract was written, he would surely have been hanged.

The fourth rebel petition that we know of probably arrived in London around 22 July, by which time news of the two great risings in the East and West – together with a rash of lesser protests elsewhere – was beginning to cause real alarm among the privy councillors. On Sunday, 21 July, Cranmer preached a sermon in St Paul's in which he lamented 'the great plag[u]e of God now raigning among us ... which plag[u]e is the commotion of the people in most partes of this realm', adding, a trifle hysterically, that this 'plag[u]e of sedition and divicion amonge ourselves is the greatest plag[u]e ... heard of since the passion of Christ'.[41] Either on that day or the next, the councillors received the panicky letter from Russell, discussed above, in which he informed them of the advance of the Cornishmen and of the rebels' capture of Plymouth. In their response, written on 22 July, the councillors acknowledged that, as well as Russell's own letter, they had also received the other documents he had enclosed with it, including 'letters out of Cornewall conteynyng the state of those countres'.[42] The 'letters' referred to here may well have included communications sent up to Russell by sea from the besieged loyalists in Pendennis. As far as we know, these were the first detailed accounts which the councillors had received of the rising in Cornwall, and it is clear that – either within this package of documents, or within another similar one sent to them from the West shortly afterwards – they also received a copy of a petition to which the Cornish rebels had set their hands, because, in a letter to Russell written on 25 July, the Council observed that 'to the commons of Cornwalles supplicacion, yf thay be not soner repressed, answer shalbe made'.[43]

At first sight, it would seem that this can only be a reference to the 'supplication' which the Cornish protestors had drawn up after they first met at Bodmin. Yet independent evidence survives to suggest that the councillors were, in fact, referring to another lost petition: a petition that had been drawn up by the Cornish and Devon rebels together soon after Arundell and his forces had first advanced into Devon – perhaps at some point during the third week of July. This document clearly included elements of the original petition composed by the mid-Devon protestors at Sampford Courtenay in late June and probably included elements of the original petition composed by the Cornish rebels at Bodmin in early July as well. We know of its existence because, among the State Papers, there survives an undated document entitled 'The Kinges Ma[jes]ties Answer to the Supplication Made in the Name of his Highness Subiectes of Devon and Cornewall'.[44] This document can be dated on internal grounds to July 1549, and was almost certainly written between 25 and 27 July.[45] It may be regarded as a companion piece to the letter that the councillors had written in response to the original 'supplication' of the mid-Devon protestors on 8 July. The document is written in Somerset's own hand throughout and, in it, the protector once again sets out to confute the articles that the rebels had listed in their own 'bill of supplication'.[46]

From the text of the 'Answer', it is possible to deduce that the lost supplication with which it engages had repeated a number of the complaints about religious innovation that the mid-Devon protestors had previously made – including those which related to baptism, confirmation, the introduction of the new service book and the repeal of the Act of Six Articles – while introducing several new complaints along the same lines. Once again, therefore, one is left with the impression that the rebels' motives were primarily religious ones – but Somerset's 'Answer' shows that the authors of the latest rebel supplication had raised a number of other grievances as well. They had complained about the relief on sheep and cloth and about a general dearth of provisions, for example. They had indicated that they mistrusted the king's local 'officers and magistrates'. Perhaps more surprisingly, they had also bemoaned the failure of some local clergymen to conduct divine service, baptisms and burials at the appropriate times and adequately to explain the government's proceedings to the people. This last fact makes it hard to believe that the original supplication can have been scripted by conservative priests of the sort who are so often assumed to have been the true authors of the western rebels' articles, and suggests, on the contrary, that the supplication had genuinely embodied the view of the common people.[47]

Finally, and most intriguingly of all, the authors of this latest supplication had plainly requested – or, at the very least, had caused Somerset to believe they had requested – a liturgy in the Cornish tongue, for the protector observed at one point in his 'Answer' that 'ye saie certein Cornishmen be offended because they have not their service in Cornish, for so much as thei understand no English'. Needless to say, Somerset's response to this complaint was curt and unyielding: he retorted that, as Cornish-speakers had been unable to understand the old service in Latin, it scarcely mattered if they were unable to understand the new one in English.[48] This was a response that failed to address what was almost certainly the Cornish-speakers' principal concern, of course: that, if they accepted this liturgical switch, they would soon find themselves obliged to learn English. The inclusion of this particular complaint in the supplication is highly significant: first, because it suggests that, by now, there were many Cornish-speakers in the rebels' ranks; and second, because it makes it impossible to doubt that, by 1549, the attacks on the traditional religion that had always been so accommodating of Cornish culture were being construed by some Cornish people as attacks on the Cornish identity itself. It was probably the presence of a grievance specifically related to the Cornish language in the bill – coupled, perhaps, with the new salience that Cornwall had suddenly assumed in the councillors' minds after they learned of Arundell's advance – that caused them mentally to assign this supplication to the people of Cornwall alone, rather than to the people of Cornwall and Devon combined. And it seems fair to assume that, when the councillors informed Russell on 27 July that 'we have sent you the kyngs Ma[jes]ties answer to the rebells of Cornwalles supplicacion', they were, in fact, referring to the despatch of the text of Somerset's 'Answer' to the rebels of *both* counties.[49]

Further evidence of the councillors' growing concern about the threat posed by the Cornish rebels comes from a letter sent to Russell on 25 July, in which Somerset and his colleagues referred, with evident fury, to 'Humfrey Arundell's poyson sent a brod by his lettres'.[50] This was the first time that any of the rebel leaders had been referred to by name in the correspondence between Russell and the councillors: a fact which suggests that, in Arundell – a rebel captain who, by first raising a powerful host and then leading it, within days, into a neighbouring county, had demonstrated that he was capable of bold and aggressive military action – the councillors had recognised a formidable enemy. And that Arundell was now evidently engaged in sending out letters to proselytise for the rebel cause only made him more dangerous still. At their subsequent trials, both Arundell and Winslade were charged with having 'dispersed writings to excite the lieges of Cornwall against the king', and the fact that Arundell had a secretary – a man named Castell, who served him throughout the rising – hints at just how many letters, directives and warrants the rebel leader may well have sent out.[51]

Having been alerted to the dissemination of Arundell's epistolary 'poyson', the councillors at once ordered Russell to respond by causing it to be proclaimed 'that whosoever shall recevye, take, or he[ar], any such letter of wrtyting sent to incite, or move [people], either to favor, or take parte with them or ayde them with victuall or otherwise shalbe taken as rebells'. Anyone innocently coming across such 'letters' was to be ordered to deliver them to Russell at once, unread.[52] The fear – and rage – that the rebels' 'writings' inspired in the councillors' hearts is obvious from these comments, and it is hard not to suspect that their reaction partly reflected the fact that, through the simple act of scripting such documents, the rebels had undermined the regime's habitual attempts to present them as brutish and 'ignorant'. What made the insurgents' 'letters' all the more intolerable, from the councillors' point of view, was the fact that they were being delivered to parish priests with the instruction that they should be read out to their congregations, thus hijacking the most important conduit through which the government was accustomed to disseminate its own propaganda. This was an offence that the councillors considered worthy of the harshest punishment and they grimly signed off a letter to Russell on 27 July by noting that 'we do not doubt but ye have geven theyr espial [i.e., the rebels' spy, or messenger] that shuld carrie the letter to be publysshed in pulpets his dewe reward'.[53]

In addition to the two formal responses Somerset wrote in answer to the rebels' early supplications, and to the proclamations he and his colleagues instructed Russell to make on the ground, the councillors also drew up another proclamation in July in the hope of influencing the insurgents. Russell first received word of this in a letter of 10 July, in which the councillors assured him that they would 'send shortly unto you a proclamation which we think shall ... sett a terror and dvysyon amongst the rabells'.[54] The proclamation referred to here was evidently the one that was printed in London on the following day. Having begun by declaring the protestors to be 'rebels and traitors', it had then gone on to note that, as a result of their disloyalty, all of their 'goods, chattels ... [and] farms' had been forfeited to the Crown. Nor was this all, it concluded, for the king was now pleased to permit all loyal subjects who were able to take possession of any part of the rebels' forfeited property to enjoy it for themselves.[55] Russell had clearly received a batch of proclamations specifically relating to the rebels of Devon by 15 July – presumably a batch that had been prepared before news of the Cornish rising had reached London – and had then asked for further proclamations to be printed specifically in relation to the rebels of Cornwall, for, on 18 July, the councillors replied to his letter of three days before, noting that 'as to your devise to have lyke p[ro]clamacons to Cornewall as was lately sent to you for Devonshyre, we have taken ordre to have them out of hande, and do sende them downe unto you for satisfaccion of your desyre'.[56]

The councillors hoped that these proclamations would deter local people from joining the insurgents for fear that their neighbours – now officially licensed to help themselves to all rebels' goods – would seize their lands during their absence. And they were especially hopeful – as their letter of 22 July makes clear – that the proclamations might act as a check on the Cornish forces that had recently advanced into Devon and 'p[er]a[d]ventur withdrawe them back to save theyr owne'.[57] Somerset and his colleagues were still harping on this theme in a letter written to Russell five days later, which contains an intriguing passage. Responding to what was clearly an Eeyore-like remark from

Russell to the effect that the proclamations had so far 'wroght no great effect in Devonshyre', the councillors brightly responded that this was bound to be the case as long as the rebels remained in that county in force, for in such circumstances 'no man [would] dare medle to invade theyr possessions'. The situation would be just the same in Cornwall, the councillors went on, 'till the nomber be departed'. 'But when those campes and nombers . . . have removed and come forward,' they added, local men would be only too ready to seize 'theyr howses and lands. And they [the Cornish rebels] . . . [will be] glad to . . . return . . . to the defence of theyr owne.'[58] These words clearly testify to a perception on the councillors' part that, while there was already a substantial force of Cornish rebels in Devon, further 'nombers' were still preparing to 'come forward'. Despite the councillors' best intentions, then, their words simply underlined the intense vulnerability of Russell's position at Honiton in late July as he waited, apprehensively, for the swelling rebel host to advance.

## III

The speed with which Humphrey Arundell had first assembled a 'power' in Cornwall and then marched with it into Devon between 6 July and *c.* 16 July makes it clear that the Cornish rebel leader was all too aware of the need to strike quickly at Russell before he could be reinforced. Why, then, did so many of the Cornish rebel forces remain behind, as the councillors' words clearly indicate that they did? Distance must have been a factor. It would have taken a significant amount of time for bodies of fighting men to assemble in West Cornwall and march up to the Tamar, longer still for them to march on to Exeter. But even more important was probably the need to reduce – or at the very least to contain – the isolated loyalist strongholds that continued to hold out. We have seen that both the Mount and Trematon Castle were captured by the rebels during the opening stages of the rising, but it may well have taken some days for their garrisons to be overcome: holding up rebel forces that could otherwise have been deployed elsewhere. At Pendennis Castle this was definitely the case, moreover, and although we know little about the siege that took place there between 10 July and 20 August, it is hard not to suspect that it pinned down a sizeable number of Cornish rebel troops. In this section, we will briefly consider the three sieges of loyalist garrisons that are known to have taken place in rebel-held territory throughout the month of July and ask what their significance was to the history of the Western Rising as a whole.

Our knowledge of what happened at Pendennis rests almost entirely on John Killigrew's retrospective accounts. These suggest that, after having initially retired into the castle on 10 July with 160 'soldiers' – presumably a mixture of loyalist gentlemen's retainers and local countrymen in arms – the Killigrews had subsequently seen a diminution in their forces because, from 20 July onwards, only 100 soldiers had been paid. Conceivably, the missing soldiers had deserted to the rebels en masse, as some of Grenville's followers had done at Trematon. Alternatively, the Killigrews may have deliberately chosen to reduce the garrison in order to eke out their remaining supplies. If this was indeed the case, the surplus men could well have been evacuated by sea, because Killigrew's accounts show that two 'shippes of warre' were hired to assist the beleaguered loyalists. The first was 'a barke of Southampton of the burden of xxx ton' which was hired for two days at a cost of £1 per day. This could have been used to transport men, to bring in supplies or to send messages by sea. The second, larger ship belonged to one James Brankin of Southampton and was hired for eleven days. Killigrew later recorded that he had paid £14 to Brankin 'for the service of his shipe of the burden of clx ton well manned & furnesshed for the warres, which ship lay upon the sea beating suche groundes as were noysom to the said castell'.[59] These words suggest that Brankin's ship had acted in a close-support role: using its great guns repeatedly to rake the 'groundes' outside the fortification in order to drive off the insurgents and prevent them from firing on the defenders from there – in much the same way that, a century later, Parliamentarian warships were to harass Royalist soldiers investing the town of Plymouth.[60] Killigrew's words remind us that the regime controlled the seas around the south-western peninsula throughout the entire course of the rebellion – and that this was a powerful card in Somerset's hands.

We have no evidence at all to suggest how many insurgents maintained the siege of Pendennis – though, if they had to blockade the castle completely, their numbers must have been fairly substantial. And if a loyalist garrison did indeed continue to hold out in Pendennis's sister-fortress of St Mawes as well – as several pieces of evidence hint may have been the case – then even more rebel troops would have been required. The presence of the hired ships to which Killigrew's account attests – and, perhaps, of other ships in loyalist hands, too – would have made things extremely difficult for the besieging forces, because it would have enabled the garrison not only to communicate with the outside world, but also to bring in supplies and even, as we have seen, to harass the rebel forces with cannon fire from offshore. It is possible that among the rebel leaders who had to wrestle with these problems was the man named 'Coffen', who extracted £2 from Thomas Ennys after he had left Pendennis in July, and whom Ennys later described as 'one of the captens of the said rebels'.[61] We know from Hooker that a Devon gentleman named Coffin was one of the rebel captains – his first name is sadly unrecorded – and it has generally been assumed that this individual was one of the Coffins of Portledge, near Bideford.[62] Quite possibly it was this man whom Ennys encountered near Pendennis – though there were Cornish Coffins, too – and, if so, his presence would suggest that some Devonian rebels were active in Cornwall, just as we know that many Cornish rebels were active in Devon. Whoever the overall commander of the rebel forces at Pendennis may have been, he cannot have found blockading the castle an easy task and would certainly have needed to retain a sizeable body of men in order to maintain the siege.

Information about the siege of Plymouth Castle is almost as scant as information about the siege of Pendennis. As we have seen, the town governors had initially managed to ensure that Plymouth stood aloof from the rebellion, but, around the middle of July, the local loyalists – including, presumably, at least some of the town governors – had been forced to abandon the town and retire into last-ditch positions in the old castle and in the new fort on St Nicholas Island. That this was a reaction to the arrival of an outside force, rather than to an insurrection that had taken place within the town itself, is strongly suggested by a brief passage in the fragmentary loyalist ballad of late 1549, which notes of the rebels that 'they came to Plumowith the Kinges trusty towne': thus contrasting mobile insurgents with stationary loyalists.[63] A stray comment of Somerset's, which suggests that the town had been 'spoyled' by the insurgents, also hints at an initial assault from without.[64] Yet, once the rebels had taken control of the town, it is probable that many of the inhabitants joined them. The Plymouth receivers' accounts provide a straw in the wind here. In 1548, the individual who compiled these records had flatly termed the West Cornish protestors 'rebells' and the man who was later executed on Plymouth Hoe – and who was almost certainly one of them – 'the traytor of Cornewalle'. When listing the expenses the town had incurred during the troubles of 1549, however, the accountant did not use such pejorative terms to refer to the insurgents: indeed, he never specifically referred to them at all, despite listing a whole series of payments that had patently been made in an effort to resist them.[65] It is hard not to suspect that this reticence reflects the fact that, in 1549, many of the townsfolk – and perhaps even some of the town governors – had themselves been 'rebels', with the result that the entire episode was later airbrushed, as far as was possible, from the town accounts.

What conditions were like in rebel-held Plymouth over the following weeks it is impossible to say because the evidence is so slight. One, rather later source reports that the insurgents seized a number of cannon in the town, which they took away to reinforce the main rebel host, which was then besieging Exeter.[66] Another chance reference reveals that the protestors 'spoyled' certain victuals which had been gathered in Plymouth for the king's service at sea.[67] The author of Plymouth's 'Black Book', finally, later recorded that 'our stepell [was] burnt, [in 1549] with all the townes evydence in the same by rebelles': a statement that indicates that the insurgents had not only targeted written records while they were holding Plymouth, but that they had also carried out at least one act of deliberate arson.[68] We must not forget that this evidence comes from the pen of a loyalist writer, however, who would have had his own reasons for wishing to portray conditions in rebel-held Plymouth in the most anarchic of lights.

We know that the insurgents conducted a close blockade of the castle, and that the loyalists defended themselves with great guns, because an early seventeenth-century source records that a certain 'Thomas Cropp' – almost certainly the same man who had carried a letter from Plymouth to Sir Peter Carew in Cornwall in April 1548 – 'was slaine by the breakinge of a peece of ordinance in defence of the castle of Plymouth against the rebels at the Commocion in the West in the time of King Edward the 6'.[69] It seems probable, too, that – at Plymouth, just as at Pendennis – access to the sea and to shipping in loyalist hands was an important factor in helping the castle to hold out. As soon as the privy councillors heard of the loss of Plymouth, on 22 July, they ordered one 'Cotton' – clearly Thomas Cotton, who, just a few weeks before, had been appointed vice admiral of the Narrow Seas – 'to passe with certen of his shippes and gallyes that waie' in an attempt to win back the town, and while loyalist sea captains were unable to compass such a feat, in the short term at least, they probably were able to assist the defenders of the castle, just as they did at Pendennis.[70] As we have seen, moreover, the Plymouth loyalists were able to despatch eastwards by sea a former mayor, one Thomas Crowne, carrying 'the towns l[ette]res to my Lord Privy Seal', and it was probably thanks to the information contained in these letters that Russell was later able to reassure Somerset that the mayor of Plymouth had not acted treacherously 'in yelding upp of the towne to the rebells', as had originally been thought.[71] Of the rebel forces that conducted the siege, nothing is known. They may all have been townsfolk and Devonians, or they may have included some Cornishmen whom Arundell had despatched to help blockade the castle. Whoever they were, it would have suited the rebel captains far better to have been able to draw on all of the manpower of Devon's second most populous town in order to recruit their main host, rather than to have been forced to detach or reserve men from that force in order to neutralise the loyalists in Plymouth Castle.

While the sieges of Pendennis and Plymouth Castles remain shadowy affairs, miniature epics of courage and endurance, of which only the bare outlines can now be discerned, the siege of Exeter stands out in vivid colour – from the defenders' point of view, at least – thanks to Hooker's splendid eyewitness account of the affair. The story of how the citizens withstood the rebel forces throughout the month of July has been told many times before and will therefore be only relatively briefly rehearsed here: not least because we can be sure that, as Hooker was present throughout the siege, his narrative can be relied upon as an extremely well-informed – though necessarily biased – account of events.[72] As we have seen, the town governors had, for a variety of reasons, taken the decision to resist the rebels' overtures at the end of June, and throughout the ensuing weeks they were to be assisted in defending the city against them, not only by a band of around a hundred ardent reformists, but also by many more traditionalist townsfolk, who – like the Chamber men – were fearful of the potential consequences of permitting the insurgents to enter the city. Exeter stood in an eminently defensible position, its ancient walls were strong and had recently been repaired, and it was well supplied with arms and ammunition. As a result of these factors and of the defenders' own resolve, the rebels were successfully held at bay throughout the whole of July. During this time, indeed, the greatest threat to the city seemed to be posed by treachery from within, rather than by direct assault from without.

Hooker notes that many of the city's traditionalists – 'Papists', as he scornfully terms them – contrived to keep up communication with the besiegers throughout the siege: by holding 'open speeches over the Citties walles', by shooting arrows with messages bound to them to and fro, and even by attending physical 'parlyes' with the insurgents in the rebel-held suburbs. The tenor of these conversations, Hooker avers, was always 'to discover ... one to th'other their traitorous practises and devellish devises ... for the betrayinge of the Cittie and to wyn in religion'; yet, thanks to the resolution of the defenders, he adds, such plots were always foiled.[73] One of the moments of greatest peril for the Exeter loyalists, in fact, came when they appeared to be on the verge of falling out with each other. This dispute arose when John Courtenay – the imprisoned sheriff's brother and one of the gentlemen who had volunteered to remain behind in the city before the rebels arrived – attempted to discourage Bernard Duffield, Lord Russell's steward, from mounting sallies against the insurgents in the suburbs, arguing that such attacks were risky and served little military purpose. The mayor and his brethren agreed with Courtenay, summoned Duffield to appear before them and ordered him to halt his operations at once. But Duffield, feeling his honour to have been impugned, refused to obey and 'fell out in foule and disordered speaches', with the result that he was committed to prison.

Hearing of this, Duffield's daughter, Frances, 'came more hastilie than advisedlie unto the mayor, somewhat late in the evening', and demanded that her father be released. When her request was denied, Hooker goes on, 'she waxed so warme, that not onlie she used verie unseemlie tearmes and speeches unto the maior, but also, contrarie to the modestie and shamefacedness required in a woman, speciallye young and umarried, ran most violently upon him, and strake him in the face'. This sudden and unexpected assault on the mayor sparked a major panic in Exeter. The common bell, which was used to summon the citizens in times of emergency, was rung in alarm, while a rumour flew around the streets 'that the mayor was beaten or killed'. Now, Hooker continues,

> the whole commons immediatlie in great troops & the most part in arms, ran to the Guildhall, where the maior was, who, though he was safe, yet were they so greeved with this injurie, that they would in all hast have run to the Lord Russell's house, where she [i.e., Frances Duffield] was then gone, and have fetched her out.

This was a dangerous moment, for, if the citizens had gone in search of Duffield at the Black Friars and attempted to drag her out by force, a confrontation might well have ensued with the members of her father's household and, perhaps, with his other supporters among the city loyalists. This in turn would have provided the perfect opportunity for the rebel forces prowling just yards from the city walls to strike. In the end, crisis was averted. The mayor managed to prevail upon the citizens to leave Duffield where she was until tempers had cooled, while the cathedral canons – who the rebels might well have expected would, at last, at this moment of maximum opportunity, have somehow contrived to admit them – came to the mayor instead 'and then and there verie friendlie did comfort him, and offered to stand by him and to assist him in all the best service they were able to doo for his defense and the safetie of the cittie'.[74]

The canons' decision to stand by the mayor at this time was a critical reverse for the besiegers, and a clear sign that they were unlikely to be able to regain the city as a result of assistance from within – however sympathetic the majority of the inhabitants may have been to their cause. Why, then, did the rebels persist in maintaining their siege? Three main answers present themselves. First, and most obvious, the city simply was too tempting a prize for the insurgents to be able to resist it. Second, as the rebels' numbers continued to swell, and as they received news that they would soon be joined by powerful reinforcements from Cornwall, they may well have calculated that they would soon be able to overwhelm the defenders through sheer force of numbers. Third, and most important of all, they knew that food supplies within the city were running short. As Hooker notes, 'the store of victuals ... was verie slender and smale', and although the town governors did all they could to eke out what there was and to make sure that everyone was provided for, by late July there was no longer any bread to be had, many were reduced to eating 'horse-flesh', and the prospect of famine was beginning to stare the citizens in the face.[75] As the Devon rebel captains looked down on the beleaguered city from their camp on St David's Down at this time and waited impatiently for Arundell's Cornishmen to join them, they could well have been forgiven for believing that – within a week or two at most – either hunger or the application of overwhelming force would compel the citizens to give up the unequal fight and surrender. And, as we shall see, if Russell had delayed his advance for just a few days longer than he did, the city might well have fallen into the rebels' grasp.

## IV

What were conditions like in the districts of Devon and Cornwall that were controlled by the rebels between 10 June and 31 July 1549? This is a question we will probably never be able to answer in detail because so little relevant evidence has survived. This, in turn, is almost certainly a result of the fact that, after the rising had been crushed, both the defeated insurgents and the victorious loyalists would have had good reason to destroy any documents that had been composed by the rebels during 'the commotion time': the former, because of the highly incriminatory nature of such documents; the latter, because such writings stood as mute testament to a period of 'misrule' and social inversion in which the power of the local gentry governors had been utterly overthrown. In consequence, we are usually forced to rely on the words of the rebels' enemies when it comes to assessing what was happening in the districts that they controlled – and, as we have already seen from the councillors' instructions to Russell to spread rumours about the rebels' 'develyshe behavours', much of what the regime's apologists wrote on this subject was naked propaganda: material that was specifically designed to portray life in rebel-held territory in the worst possible light. Nevertheless, some of it is revealing, especially insofar as it relates to the experiences of those loyalists who were unfortunate enough to find themselves in the rebels' power. The anonymous composer of the ballad published in late 1549, for example, wrote of the western rebels that

> They did robe and spoile al the Kynges frendes
> They called them heritekes with spight & disdayne,
> They roffled a space lyke tirantes and Findes [i.e., fiends]
> They put sume in preson [i.e., prison] & sume to greate payne.[76]

While the claim that the rebels had 'ruffled' – that is to say, swaggered – like 'tyrants' or 'fiends' is clearly hyperbole, most of the specific charges that were made in these lines can be confirmed from other sources.

We have already seen that many local loyalists were, indeed, imprisoned and reviled as 'heretics' by the insurgents, and there is a good deal of independent evidence to show that the rebels also made a practice of breaking into the houses of those whom they considered to be their enemies and 'spoiling' – in other words, plundering or pillaging – them. At the height of the rebellion, for example, Sir Gawen Carew, who owned much property in Devon, observed bitterly that '[I] have ben spoyled of all such things as I had here by thes traytors'.[77] The Cornish loyalist gentleman Reginald Mohun of Bodinnick, who appears to have sought refuge in either Pendennis or St Mawes as the rebellion in Cornwall took fire, was likewise reported to have been 'spoiled' by the insurgents.[78] Once the rising was over, the Privy Council agreed to defer a debt owed by Thomas and John Harrys of Crediton 'by reason that they were spoiled in the last commotion by the rebells', while in 1550 two Cornish gentlemen, Sir Hugh Trevanion and John Trelawney, wrote to the lord chancellor to apologise for their inability to send him some documents he had requested, explaining that 'at the time of the last commotion in Cornwall, the one of our houses was so spoiled by the rebels that then among other writings they took and carried away the same'.[79] Similarly, a South Devon man named Richard Pomeroy later alleged that many documents had been stolen from him when one William Webber,

> being a great capteyne & rebell in the late commocion in the west parties ... [did] with diverse other rebells ...... break [into] the house of the said Richard ... & ... not only spoyled & tooke awaye muche of the goodes of the said Richard ... but also, as he verily supposyth, at the same tyme toke away certayne evydences, dedes, charters, mynements & writyngs.[80]

Some unfortunate loyalists had their houses pillaged on several occasions. This was true of Alexander Carvanell, for example, a yeoman of the guard and an ardent reformist, who lived at Bosavern in St Just in the far west of Penwith, and who had already suffered the indignity of being kidnapped by local traditionalists some years before, when he had attempted to prevent them from sailing on what he termed 'a pope-holy pilgrimage' to Brittany.[81] Carvanell later complained that, on 29 July 1549, a band of men led by John Esseball had broken into his house and stolen money and goods, while another group of men had come and pillaged the house again on 2 August. Carvanell went on to stress that he himself had been away from home at the time in the king's service in 'the retinue of the ... lord pryvye seale'; clearly, he was one of the few Cornish loyalists who had managed to escape imprisonment and join Russell's forces at Honiton.[82] The fact that several of those whose houses were 'spoyled' made specific reference to the seizure of writings is interesting, because other evidence also survives to suggest that – like those who had taken part in earlier rebellions – the western rebels had particularly targeted legal documents.[83]

We have already seen that, at Plymouth, a local chronicler recorded of 'the commotion time' that 'then was our stepell burnt, with all the townes evydence in the same by rebelles'. The 'stepell' referred to here was presumably the fine new steeple that had been constructed atop the parish church during the 1530s, and – as it seems unlikely that the rebels had set out to destroy the church itself – we must assume that they had fired the steeple with the deliberate intention of destroying the documents stored there. This assumption becomes a near-certainty when we learn from another source – a complaint lodged after the rebellion by two Devonians about a missing will and inventories – that 'yn the late commosion in the west partes the Regestrie of the ordinarie [i.e., the bishop] where the said will and inventories were proved and exhibited was distrayened and burnt by the rebells'.[84] There are other stray references to the rebels stealing or destroying documents, as well. One of the plaintiffs in a legal case relating to a piece of land in the mid-Devon parish of Hatherleigh, for example, was to note, in around 1551, that a lease relating to the property had been lost 'in the late rebellion'.[85] And in the market town of Okehampton, just down the road, a group of local people were to depose as late as 1611 that 'they have . . . heard that there were divers deeds and writings belonging to the said Towne whereof . . . some in the time of the rebellion in those parts, commonly called the "Comocion" . . . were lost, imbezzled or made away'.[86] From the evidence surveyed above, it would seem that the insurgents' motives for targeting such records were mixed: with some individuals appropriating specific documents in the hope of personal gain, and others destroying any records they could find as a matter of policy – perhaps in order to lash out at property owners as a class. There are hints here of the social tensions that were so evident in the contemporaneous stirs in East Anglia.

If official records were destroyed by the rebels, then so were 'heretical' religious texts; not surprisingly, the new service book proved a prime target. The German reformer Martin Bucer was later to inform a friend that the western rebels had 'gathered up all the copies of the Prayer Book which they could find and burnt them in their camp'.[87] In Morebath, the parishioners purchased a second service book in the wake of the commotion, almost certainly because what the vicar of Morebath, significantly, termed the 'furst communion boke' in the churchwardens' accounts had been destroyed during the rising.[88] The work of destruction is far quicker and easier to effect than the work of re-construction, but it would appear that – during the few brief weeks of grace that the rebellion afforded them – the inhabitants of at least one local community also began to restore the physical appurtenances of the old faith. The churchwardens' accounts of Stratton in north-east Cornwall record that 'ye ro[o]de . . . yn ye rodeloft' in the church there, previously taken down in accordance with the royal injunctions of 1547, was 'set up . . . agen' at some point during 1549.[89] Clearly, the parishioners had taken advantage of 'the commotion time' in order to return the great crucifix to its former place of honour in the rood loft.[90] It was an action that spoke volumes about the commitment the people of Stratton felt to their traditional faith – and about the confidence with which they were now looking forward to the imminent restoration of the old world.

In part, this confidence probably stemmed from the fact that, as Eamon Duffy has rightly observed, most of those who supported the insurgency are 'unlikely to have considered themselves to be rebels at all', but rather good Christian men and women, who were defending both their king and their faith against a wicked cabal of heretics in London whom they believed to have taken advantage of Edward's youth in order unlawfully to seize power.[91] As we have seen, the rebel captains sent out their warrants in the king's name and made use of customary mechanisms to raise troops and communicate information. These things tend to suggest that – far from descending into anarchy, as the regime's apologists repeatedly averred – rebel-held Devon and Cornwall had continued to be administered much as usual throughout late June and July. The crucial difference, of course, was that 'orders from above' were now coming from the rebel leaders rather than from the regime in

London, and that the implementation of these orders was now being overseen by local rebel captains rather than by the JPs. The fact that, at some point between *c.* 15 and 25 July, the vicar of Morebath, Sir Christopher Trychay, was able calmly to record in the churchwardens' accounts that a series of payments had been made for supplying five young men of the parish with money, swords and bows 'at their going forth to Sent Davys Down ys Camppe' – in other words, at their setting out to join the rebel host – and that these costs had subsequently been covered via a formal rate levied on the parishioners makes the sense of order and legitimacy that had prevailed in many local communities at this time very clear.[92] It is likely that both the band of young men who marched into the field from Morebath in July 1549 and the neighbours who supplied them with arms and money were responding to a formal summons that had been sent to the parish by the rebels in the king's name – and that bands of men had been similarly raised from scores, if not hundreds, of other West Country parishes at the same time. What makes Morebath exceptional is the fact that – thanks to the ineffectual way in which Trychay later tried to disguise the true nature of the payments – the evidence that it sent men to recruit the rebel host has survived.[93]

While the Crown's apologists liked to claim that law and order had completely broken down in the rebel-held territories, moreover, other scraps of evidence tend to suggest that – with access to the normal royal courts having been curtailed – the task of administering justice in those districts was simply assumed by the rebel captains instead. To illustrate this point, we may turn to a case from Launceston. During the mid-1540s, the bailiffs of Launceston had been engaged in a legal dispute with a certain John Andrews of the North Devon town of Torrington, and had pursued this case through the royal courts in London. But, 'shortly after the commotion began in ... Devonshire and Cornewall', the bailiffs were later to complain, Andrews had 'accompanied himselfe with the rebells of the same commotion and made complaint by byll to the captaynes of the same rebells of thys holle matter against your ... oratours [i.e. your petitioners, or supplicants]'. As a result, the bailiffs concluded, the case had been decided in Andrews' favour 'as by divers wrytinges of . . . [W]indislande and other rebells of the sayd Commocion, ready to be showed, more at large doth and may appear'.[94] The bailiffs' words reveal that, just as the 'especiall man' at Sampford Courtenay had taken on the role of an arbiter of 'causes' in Devon, and just as Robert Kett had dispensed justice from beneath 'the tree of reformation' in Norfolk, so John Winslade had set himself up as a quasi-magistrate in Cornwall. We know from Winslade's later 'confession' that he had remained 'contynually at Bodman' during the rebellion, so the testimony given in this case raises the intriguing possibility that the two main Cornish rebel leaders may have agreed among themselves that Winslade would stay behind in the county town to oversee the civil administration of rebel-held Cornwall, while Arundell led the Cornish rebel forces off to the east.[95] However this may be, the bailiffs' casual reference to their possession of 'divers wrytinges' composed by the rebels is tantalising and reminds us, once again, that the insurgents almost certainly generated a substantial corpus of letters, warrants, bills and other documents of which not a single original example now appears to be extant. In the absence of these documents, detailed knowledge of what day-to-day life was like in rebel-held Devon and Cornwall will forever elude us.

## V

The final ten days of July 1549 were a breathless time for the commanders of the opposing forces: a time in which fortunes seesawed wildly, and in which both Lord Russell and the rebel captains before Exeter waited desperately for the arrival of the reinforcements which, they hoped, would enable them to prevail. We left Russell in Honiton, to which town he had been persuaded to return by Sir Peter Carew after he had briefly started to withdraw towards the east: probably on either 19 or 20 July. Hooker implies that Carew had succeeded in convincing Russell that he must adopt a more assertive stance if he were to stand a chance of holding back the rebels until Lord Grey arrived, and it would appear that Russell did indeed move into action soon after his return. On 22 July, he sent a (now lost) letter to the councillors in which he evidently informed them of a recent military feat because, in their reply – which was a good deal more cheerful than most of their previous letters to the lord privy seal – they observed that '[we] be right glad of your good begyning ... and trust of as good successe to follow'.[96] What this 'successe' was we do not know for sure, but Hooker's comment that, after returning to Honiton, Russell had then remained there, 'savinge one night [spent] att Otterie where as it fell out he was more in feare than in p[er]ill', provides a clue.[97] These words show that Russell had advanced to Ottery St Mary – a town 6 miles to the east of his headquarters – and had occupied it overnight, before falling back to Honiton again on the following day.

Hooker's testimony is supported, moreover, by an entry that the boy-king in London made in his private chronicle: an entry that was presumably based on information he himself had received from the West. Having heard that the rebels were on the point of taking Exeter, Edward recorded, Russell had 'thought to have gone to [relieve]' the city by 'a by-way' – not via the direct route along the Fosse Way, in other words, presumably because the insurgents had barricaded it, but via another, more circuitous route – 'of which the rebels having espial, [they] cut [down] all the trees betwixt Ottery St Mary and Exeter. For which cause the Lord Privy Seal burned that town and ... returned home.'[98] These words suggest that, having realised that Russell was planning to advance upon Exeter by way of Ottery St Mary, the insurgents had promptly cut down many trees and laid them across the roads leading from that town towards the city, thus foiling his plans. In revenge, Russell had fired Ottery St Mary before returning to Honiton. There is no other evidence to suggest that Russell had burned down houses at Ottery St Mary – an action that, in the light of what had happened at Crediton in June, would surely have been most unwise – but, as the basic story of an advance to Ottery St Mary followed by a swift withdrawal appears in both Hooker's account and Edward's chronicle, it seems safe to assume that such a manoeuvre did indeed take place. Further evidence that a minor action had occurred at this time emerges from a letter that the councillors sent to Russell in response to one of his dated 25 July, in which they observed that 'ye did encounter a skirmishe with them [i.e., the rebels] in the streights': possibly a reference to a clash in which

Russell's troops had tried, and failed, to advance along the line of the Fosse Way, barricaded as it was by the rebels, before diverting instead to Ottery St Mary.[99]

Meanwhile, Arundell and the Cornish rebel forces under his command were hastening eastwards. We do not know what route they took, but it is possible that they advanced from Plymouth through the South Hams to Totnes and from there to the vicinity of Exeter. What we can say for certain is that, by 27 July at the latest, the Cornishmen had completed their long march to the east, for on that day a gentleman serving with Russell's forces, signing himself only as 'R.L.', sent up a copy of yet another set of rebel articles to London: one that was proudly headed 'The Articles of Us the Commoners of Devonshyre and Cornewall in Divers Camps by East and West of Excettor'.[100] This document – the so-called 'Fifteen Articles' – was the final manifesto of the western rebels.[101] The demands it contains have been studied in depth by many previous historians and, this being the case, they will not be interrogated in detail here.[102] The crucial point to stress is that almost all of the rebels' demands were religious ones – and that they were phrased in the most intransigent and uncompromising way.

The very first article, for example, declared that 'We wyll have all the ... holy decrees of our forefathers observed ... and who so ever shal agayne saye them, we holde them as Heretikes'.[103] A number of the new articles – like the demand for the new service book to be withdrawn, for example, and the demand for the Act of Six Articles to be reinstated – were familiar from previous rebel petitions. Others – like the demand that Moreman and Crispin, the two cathedral canons who had been imprisoned for their 'seditious preaching' in the West in 1547, should be freed from the Tower of London and sent home again – were entirely new. In Article 12 – which avers that 'we think it very mete, because the Lord Cardinal Pole is of the king's bloode, [that he] shuld ... [be] sent for to Rome and promoted to be first or second of the kings counsayl' – we perhaps see a later formulation of the lost rebel demand that had caused Somerset to rage against the insurgents that 'they speake to have to do in the governaunce of the Kyng' earlier in July.[104] There were no articles that reflected specifically economic grievances, and only one that might be said to reflect a 'social' grievance: the demand that a limit should be set on the number of servants that individual gentlemen were permitted to retain – though even this may have been an attempt to blunt the potential military muscle of specifically 'reformist' gentlemen like the Carews.

Like the earlier supplication, the Fifteen Articles were drawn up in the names of the commoners of both counties but included several clauses that related to Cornwall alone. The most striking of these was the final part of Article 8, which declared that 'we wyl not receive the newe service because it is but lyke a Christmas game, but we wyll have our old service . . . in Latten, not in Englysh, as it was before. *And so we the Cornyshe men (whereof certen of us understand no Englysh) utterly refuse thys new Englysh*'.[105] Here, the sense of Cornish cultural defensiveness to which Somerset had adverted in his answer to the previous supplication was again made explicit – though in the Fifteen Articles, we may note, there was no specific demand for a Cornish liturgy. The articles did, however, include the statement that 'for the particular grieffes of our Countreye, we wyll have them so ordered, as Humfreye Arundell & Henry Braye the Kynges Maior of Bodman, shall enforme the Kynges Maiestye': a statement which shows that there were a number of specifically Cornish grievances which the insurgents were determined to have redressed.[106] Sadly, there is no indication of what these 'particular grieffes' may have been – though the pointed reference to Braye as '*the Kynges*' mayor of Bodmin provides still further evidence of the rebels' self-image as loyal subjects protesting against the misrule of 'evil councillors'.

Immediately beneath the text of the Fifteen Articles appear the names of the five men who proudly described themselves as the 'Chiefe Captaynes' of the rebels: 'Humphrey Arundell, [John] Berry, Thomas Underhill, John Sloeman and William Segar'. Two of these individuals – Underhill and Seagar – were 'the first captaines' of the protestors at Sampford Courtenay, while Sloeman was probably a Sampford Courtenay man too, as this was a common surname in the parish during the sixteenth century.[107] The fact that Underhill, in particular, continued to enjoy a pre-eminent position among the rebels was clearly acknowledged by 'R.L.'. In the covering letter he had composed to accompany the Articles – a letter that was later published alongside them, evidently at the regime's behest, in London – 'R.L.' wrote that 'a greate part of ... [the rebels] continueth with their fyrst Captain called Underhyl, a taylour of Sampforde Courteny'. 'I thinke they kepe him styl, because they can not fynde his match,' 'R.L.' went on, adding, sarcastically, that Underhill was 'a Captaine wel chosen by the devil at the first'. (It is worth noting, incidentally, that, in all of Hooker's accounts of the rising, Underhill's first name is given as William, rather than as Thomas. Which name was the correct one unfortunately remains unclear.) Beneath the names of the captains appear the names of 'the foure Governours of the Campes': 'John Tompson, pryeste'; 'Henry Bray, mayor of Bodman'; 'Henry Lee, maior of Torri[ng]ton'; and 'Roger Barret, Prieste'.[108] Little is known about these men, but the fact that Bray and Lee were the mayors of large towns indicates that both were individuals of comparatively high social status, while the 'camps' they governed may well have been composed of East Cornish and North Devon men, respectively. That Arundell's name appears at the head of the list makes it clear that he was now before Exeter in person and indicates that – perhaps because of his high social rank, perhaps because of the strength of the forces under his command – he was now accepted as the rebels' overall leader.

All of the evidence suggests that the Fifteen Articles were drawn up soon after Arundell and his men had arrived before Exeter and were thus the product of a particular moment when the insurgents' confidence must have been reaching new heights. This was certainly the opinion of the early twentieth-century historian W.J. Blake, who, in a neglected passage, suggested that 'the remarkably extravagant demands and hostile tone of the articles' – on which so many writers have commented – had perhaps reflected the fact that 'the Devon rebels had been reinforced by their Cornish allies, who were ... eager to take the offensive against the royal forces'.[109] Blake's insight is important because it helps to refute the view that the defeat of the western rebels was largely the result of their own limited horizons: of their supposed decision to concentrate on the prosecution of the siege of Exeter to the exclusion of all other objectives, and of their alleged inability to grasp that their one realistic hope of achieving their aims was to march swiftly eastwards, to gather up support from the neighbouring counties and to tackle the government's forces head-on.[110] It is clear from their letters that neither Russell nor Somerset took such a view. Both men plainly believed that the rebels were doing all they could to reach out to supporters elsewhere, with the aim of marching eastwards as soon as it was feasible to do so. Intriguingly, this is a view that appears to have been shared, many years later, by a descendant of one of the rebel leaders. During the 1590s, John Winslade's grandson Tristram – then a Catholic exile at the Spanish Court – observed, in the course of a lengthy discourse in Latin on 'the present condition of Cornwall and Devon', that, when 'messengers' had been sent by the western rebels to Somerset, Dorset, Wiltshire and Hampshire in 1549, the inhabitants of those counties had 'urged vehemently that . . . they should hurry to London by forced marches in order to attack the enemy with joined strengths'. Moreover, the people of Wales had sent a similar message to the insurgents, 'binding their faith to them in a holy manner, that if they [i.e., the rebels] hastened their journey to them, they would meet them with all their troops on Salisbury plain'.[111] Such a conjunction, had it been achieved, would have set Edward's very throne in hazard.

It is hard to be sure how accurate Tristram Winslade's information was, of course, and one could well retort that the rebels did not, in the end, respond to these alleged urgings. But, as we have seen, Arundell's remarkably swift march from Cornwall to Exeter demonstrates that he was well aware of the need for the insurgents to move fast, and it seems unlikely to be a coincidence that, within a day or two of 'R.L.' sending off the articles that revealed that Arundell was now present before Exeter with his Cornishmen, the rebel leaders – who had hitherto seemed perfectly content to maintain a defensive posture in the countryside between Exeter and Ottery St Mary – suddenly went over to the offensive. Hooker reports that, towards the end of July, Lord Russell was advised 'that the rebells were cominge towards Honyton to assaile him and were come as farr foorth as Fenyngton Bridges'. Full of alarm, Russell assembled his forces and marched out to Feniton, 3 miles from Honiton, to do battle with the advancing rebel troops, whose numbers are unspecified but were clearly substantial.[112]

Russell was in an extremely vulnerable position at this time. A few days before, he had informed the Council that he possessed just 600 or 700 horsemen and, while he had also stated that he 'look[ed] to have' up to 1,000 foot soldiers from Dorset and Somerset to reinforce them, it is not clear how many of these infantrymen had arrived by 29 July, the day on which he probably rode out to Feniton.[113] Contrary to the standard account of the rebellion, at this point Russell appears to have possessed only a 'small band' – consisting largely of loyalist gentlemen and their retinues – rather than anything that could be termed an 'army'.[114] The rebels' overall numbers, by contrast, were estimated at anything between 7,000 and 10,000 – though several thousand of these men would have been engaged in the sieges of the three loyalist strongholds, of course, while many of the Cornish contingents may still have been in the process of marching eastwards.[115] The battle that took place at Fenny Bridges was a crucial encounter, therefore, for Russell had to defeat the rebel advance forces which had already moved against him before any more of their comrades could arrive to reinforce them and overwhelm him through sheer force of numbers – and in the end it proved a very close-run thing. Having taken counsel with the Carews, Russell advanced to the east bank of the River Otter. Here, he found some of the insurgents posted upon the bridge itself and 'the greatest companie' drawn up on the other side of the river; 'as soone as they perceived the Lord Russell and the gentlemen with all their troope to be come,' Hooker reports, 'they make themselves readie to the fight'.[116] The loyalist forces now charged the rebels on the bridge and drove them back – Sir Gawen Carew being shot through the arm with an arrow in the process – 'and then,' Hooker goes on, 'being over the water, they gave the onset uppon the rebells . . . and so ferclie they followed uppon them that they gave them the overthrowe and slew verie manie of them'.[117]

Judging the battle to be over, 'the souldiers and serving men' in Russell's company now fell to pillaging the rebel dead, but were interrupted in the midst of this ghoulish task by the sudden appearance of what Hooker terms 'a new supplie of 800 Cornish men' under the command of Robert Smyth, a gentleman from St Germans.[118] This is the first specific reference that Hooker makes to the presence of

Cornishmen among the insurgents, which again suggests that the arrival of the Cornish forces was a relatively recent development. That these troops were led by a man from the extreme south-eastern corner of Cornwall, moreover, tempts one to suggest that Smyth's men may have been the first of the Cornish contingents to have arrived before Exeter: they having had the least far to travel. Russell's troops now closed with Smyth's, and the ensuing conflict was 'verie sharpe and cruell', Hooker reports, 'for the Cornish-men were verie lustie and freshe and fullie bent to fight out the matter'. But in the end they, too, were worsted and forced to retire.[119] Hooker later claimed that 'about 300 rebells' had been killed, but this was probably an overestimate, for the Devon gentleman John Fry – who was serving in Russell's forces – noted just a few days later that 'ye second fyght was at a place callyd Vynyton, aboute a brydge theare, wheare were slayne of the rebelles as I suppose above one hundreth, & of our men but three'.[120] Whatever the precise death toll may have been, the battle of Fenny Bridges was a disaster for the insurgents, because, although Russell – fearful of further attacks – did not press home his advantage and retired to Honiton that night, he had done enough to save himself. Either later that night or the following day, Lord Grey finally joined him, with a force of highly experienced foreign soldiers – and further powerful reinforcements were on the way.[121] Although the rebels may not have realised it yet, the scales had tipped decisively in the government's favour.

**1.** Portrait of Edward VI, possibly by William Scrots. This portrait of Henry VIII's only surviving son, which was probably completed not long before Edward acceded to the throne in January 1547, poignantly captures the brittle majesty of the boy-king.

**2.** Portrait of Edward Seymour, Duke of Somerset, by an unknown artist. Seymour was Edward VI's uncle, and quickly established himself as Lord Protector of the realm following the accession of his nine-year-old nephew. The policies of the regime he led were subsequently to prove disastrous for the people of England.

¶ The order of the Communion.

**3.** Title page of *The Order of the Communion* (1548). The regime's decision to impose this new order of communion in English on parishes across the realm at Easter 1548 may well have helped to fuel the insurrection that took place in Cornish-speaking West Cornwall a few days later.

**4.** St Keverne Church, Lizard Peninsula, West Cornwall. It was in the perennially rebellious parish of St Keverne that the 'Cornish Commotion' of 1548 began – and the vicar of St Keverne was subsequently to be hanged as a 'rebellyer' in the aftermath of the much greater insurrection of 1549.

5. Launceston Castle, site of Cornwall's county gaol. It was here that many of the Cornish 'commotioners' were imprisoned before their trials in 1548 – and here, too, that many loyalist Cornish gentlemen were to be immured by the Western rebels during the following year.

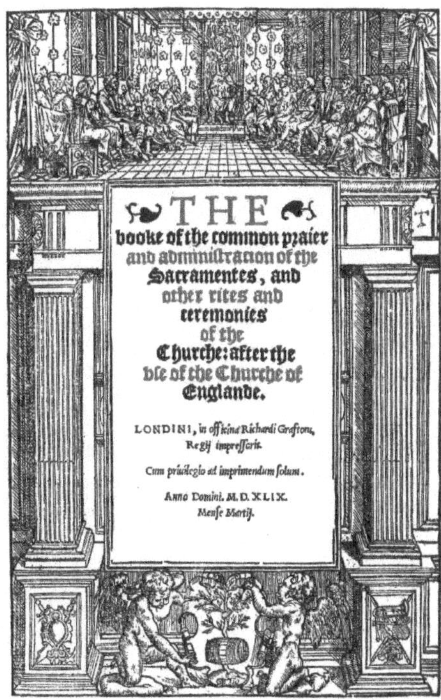

THE
booke of the common praier
and administracion of the
Sacramentes, and
other rites and
ceremonies
of the
Churche: after the
vse of the Churche of
Englande.

LONDINI, in officina Richardi Graftoni,
Regij impressoris.

Cum priuilegio ad imprimendum solum.

Anno Domini. M.D.XLIX.
Mense Martij.

6. Title page of *The Book of Common Prayer* (1549). When the central regime ordered that this new prayer book, in English, should be employed in church services across the kingdom from June 1549 onwards, the fuse was lit that would lead to an explosion of popular anger in the West Country.

**7.** Sampford Courtenay Church, Devon. It was at this church that the fateful confrontation between William Underhill, William Seager and the vicar of Sampford Courtenay took place on 10 June 1549: a confrontation which would, within days, result in a multitude of protestors against the new service-book gathering nearby.

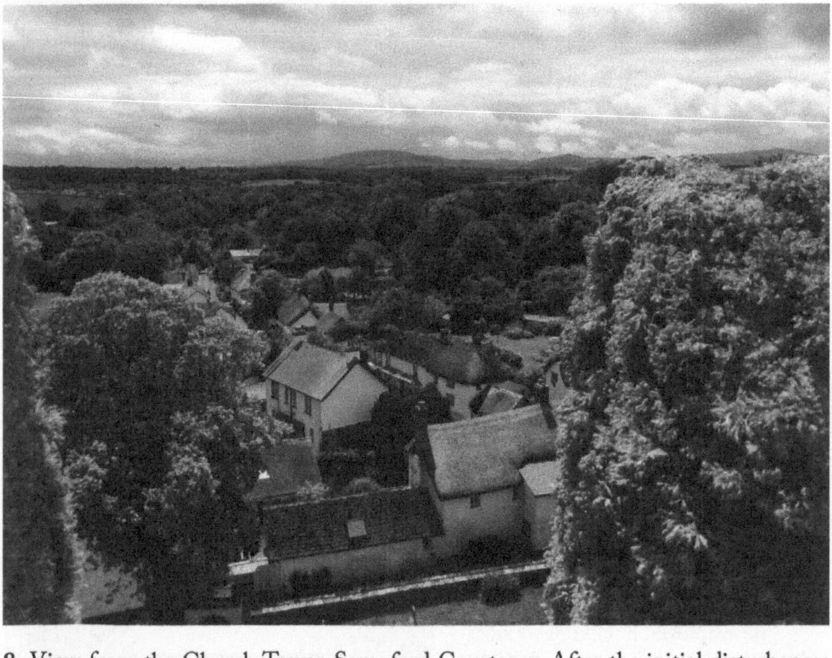

**8.** View from the Church Tower, Sampford Courtenay. After the initial disturbances at Sampford had occurred, the 'especial man' who now put himself at the head of the protestors established his headquarters in the church tower, where, so the privy councillors sneered, he kept his 'fond office'. This photo shows the view from the tower, looking to the south-east.

**9.** Portrait of Sir Peter Carew, after Gerlach Flicke. Sir Peter – together with his uncle, Sir Gawen – led the first attack by loyalist forces upon the Devon protestors in 1549, and he was one of the rebels' most implacable local adversaries thereafter.

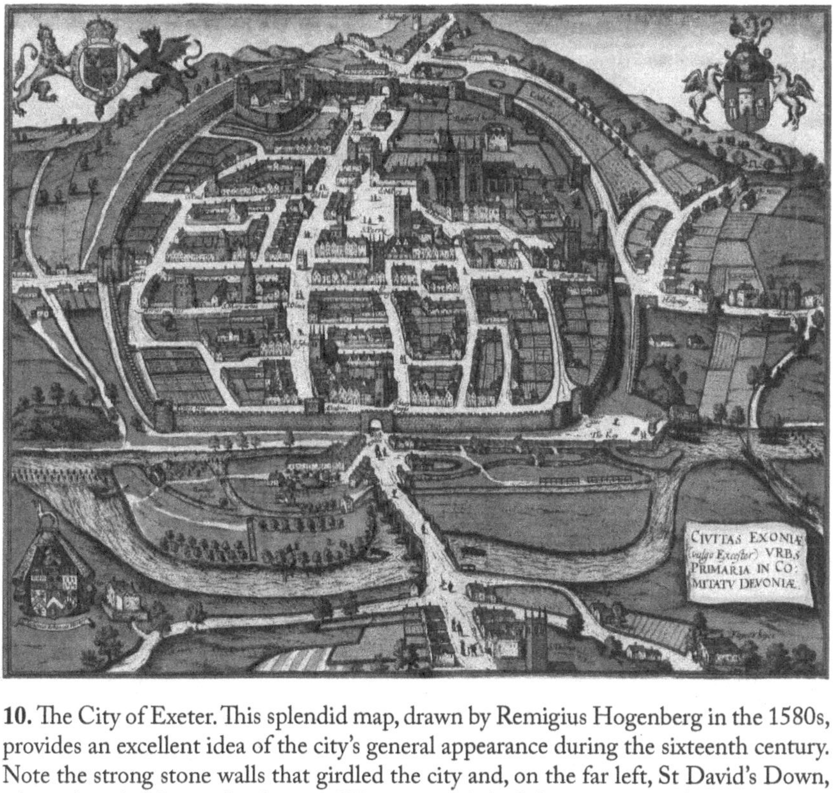

**10.** The City of Exeter. This splendid map, drawn by Remigius Hogenberg in the 1580s, provides an excellent idea of the city's general appearance during the sixteenth century. Note the strong stone walls that girdled the city and, on the far left, St David's Down, where the rebel forces that besieged Exeter established their camp in 1549.

**11.** Pendennis Castle, Cornwall. Originally constructed on the orders of Henry VIII in order to protect the Carrick Roads from foreign attack, Pendennis was to prove a key place of refuge for local loyalists during the Cornish risings of both 1548 and 1549.

**12.** Portrait drawing of John, Lord Russell, by Hans Holbein, *c.* 1532–43. Russell was the most powerful nobleman in the far South-West of England. Appointed as the King's Lieutenant in the West in 1549, he led the royal army that eventually crushed the rebel forces.

**13.** Portrait of the Lady Mary, by Master John, 1544. Henry VIII's eldest daughter, Mary – depicted here at the age of around 28 – was a devout adherent of the old faith. As the Duke of Somerset's evangelising regime began to crumble in 1549, many religious traditionalists nursed the hope that Mary would soon be installed as regent.

**14.** Portrait drawing of Sir Gawen Carew, by Hans Holbein, *c.* 1532–43. The uncle of Sir Peter Carew, and, like him, an ardent evangelical, Sir Gawen took part in the initial attack on the Devon protestors at Crediton in June 1549, and was subsequently wounded in the arm with an arrow at the battle of Fenny Bridges.

**15.** Portrait drawing of 'the Lady Ratclif' by Hans Holbein, *c.* 1532–43. The identity of the sitter is not known for sure, but some authorities have suggested that she is Mary Arundell, the half-sister of Sir Thomas Arundell. Mary Arundell was one of the Lady Mary's ladies-in-waiting, and could conceivably have facilitated contacts between her mistress and her half-brother in 1549.

**16.** Gravestone in Sampford Courtenay churchyard. This early twentieth-century gravestone bears witness to the fact that, although the rebel captain John Sloman was defeated, and presumably killed, in 1549, his family – like those of several of the other rebel leaders – continued to thrive in their home-parish for centuries to come.

# 6

# Defeat
## August 1549

The arrival of Lord Grey of Wilton and his forces transformed the military situation in the South-West. Grey himself was a ruthless and experienced fighting man, described by one contemporary as 'the best soldier in England', while the troops under his command were largely made up of foreign mercenaries who had recently been shipped across the Channel by the government in order to fight against the Scots.[1] These men were hardened professional soldiers who had spent much of their lives under arms, and it is telling of their attitude that, after having arrived at Honiton and been informed of the fight that had just taken place at Fenny Bridges, they 'much bewailed their evil lucke that they had not come sooner to have byn partakers of this service'.[2] The journey that Grey and his men had taken into the West had been a circuitous one. As we have seen, the Privy Council had originally intended to send Grey to Russell's assistance 'with a band of horsemen and some hagbuters footmen' during the second week of July.[3] Yet no sooner had this decision been taken than the rising in Oxfordshire had forced the councillors to change their plans, and to despatch Grey with a hastily assembled battle group – including what one contemporary observer described as 'foreign troops, such as Germans and Albanians' – to deal with the new threat instead.[4] Edward VI had noted in his journal at this time that Grey had departed with '1,500 horsemen and footmen', and it seems probable that this force included the 200–400 'horssemen' led by Grey himself, a party of 300 Italian 'hagbutters', or arquebusiers, under the command of the Genoese Captain Paulo Baptist Spinola, and around 1,000 'almaynes fotmen', or German *Landsknechte*.[5] All of these units, it will be remembered, had been dangled in front of Russell as potential reinforcements on 10 July and, in the standard history of the Western Rising, it is implied that all of these units did indeed eventually arrive in Russell's camp, after having marched there directly from the Midlands.[6] Yet the true picture appears to have been more complicated than this.

Following the defeat of the insurgents in Oxfordshire, Grey had not set off to join the lord privy seal straight away. Instead, he and Spinola had directed their steps to Bristol – the second city of the kingdom, and another place in which serious disturbances had recently occurred – in order to pre-empt any further outbreaks of trouble there.[7] A local chronicler recorded that, towards the end of July, 'the Lord Gray' came to Bristol 'with a band of men intended against Scotland, having in pay one Captain Spinosa [*sic*] with 300 soldiers [and] billeted in this city, from whence they marched to Honiton'.[8] It seems probable that Grey had ridden to Bristol with the cavalrymen whom he had led into Oxfordshire, as well as with Spinola's arquebusiers, and that these troopers had been quartered in the countryside around Bristol while Spinola's infantrymen had been billeted within the city itself. If this was not the case, then the troopers clearly rejoined Grey during the course of his march from Bristol to Devon because Hooker records that, when Grey arrived at Honiton, it was with 'a crue of horssemen, and one Spinola, an Italian, with three hundred shott'.[9] There is no evidence that the German infantrymen who had formed part of the taskforce sent against the Oxfordshire rebels had accompanied Grey to Honiton, though, so we must presume that these troops had been left behind in the Midlands: the councillors having reverted to their original plan of sending Grey into the West Country with his horsemen and the hackbutters alone.[10]

Who were the 'horssemen' who accompanied Lord Grey? Hooker does not say, but other contemporary and near-contemporary sources permit us to answer this question with a fair degree of confidence. To begin with, it is clear that most, if not all, of the troopers were foreigners, for a London chronicler stated that Grey came to Honiton 'with certayne strayngers, horsemen in red cottes'.[11] Second, we may be sure that Grey's force included the band of 210 Burgundian cavalrymen who had recently been shipped over from Calais to Dover under the command of the mercenary Captain Jacques de Germiny, because Raphael Holinshed, writing in 1577, observed that 'there were certeine strangers that came [into Devon] with my lord Greie, as Captaine Germane ... with a band of horsemen, most part Albanoises and Italians'.[12] Holinshed's claim that de Germiny's own troopers were mainly Albanian and Italian can be disproved from other sources – but is significant nevertheless.[13] The Italians to whom Holinshed refers were evidently Spinola's men, while the Albanians were members of yet another mercenary band. As we have seen, Albanian troops are definitely known to have accompanied Grey when he set out against the Oxfordshire rebels and these can only have been the 140 Albanian cavalrymen who had recently been brought over to England under the command of Captain Petro Zanga.[14] Holinshed's words strongly suggest that both de Germiny's *and* Zanga's bands had accompanied Grey on his march to Devon, therefore, and that these two units of mercenary soldiers had made up the bulk of Grey's cavalry force. Certainly, both captains are known to have been with Russell by early August.[15] In addition, we know from the king's journal that a further band of 200 soldiers from Reading led by William Grey – whom the Council had informed Russell to expect in a letter of 22 July – also joined the lord privy seal at around this time.[16]

The reinforcements brought into Lord Russell's camp by Lord Grey of Wilton and William Grey at the end of July therefore appear to have amounted to around 900 fighting men in all. To these, Russell could add the force of 600–700 horsemen that he had already managed to raise by combining his own retinue with the retinues of other loyalist gentlemen and the foot soldiers whom he had been busily engaged in raising in Dorset and Somerset over the preceding weeks. In a letter written on 18 July, Russell had told the councillors that he was hoping to recruit 1,000 infantrymen from these two counties, and we know from another source that he succeeded in raising at least 500.[17] By the beginning of August, therefore, it would appear that Russell had managed to assemble an army of at least 2,500 men, rather than an army 'which was not then above a thousand' strong, as Hooker was later to claim (see Table 1).[18] Russell was still hugely outnumbered by the insurgents, of course, who may well have been able to call on more than 10,000 men, but the rebel forces were scattered all over the West Country, while the lord privy seal's troops were concentrated in one place. Not only this, Russell was now well supplied with money, with ordnance, with horsemen and, perhaps most important of all, with soldiers who were well versed in the use of the most up-to-date firearms. These advantages were to prove crucial in the bloody battles that were soon to come.

**Table 1: Estimated composition of Lord Russell's army on 1 August 1549**

| | |
|---|---|
| Russell's English horse | 650 men |
| De Germiny's Burgundian horse | 210 men |
| Zanga's Albanian horse | 140 men |
| William Grey's force | 200 men |
| Spinola's Italian foot | 300 men |
| Russell's English foot | approximately 1,000 men |
| Total | 2,500 men |

## II

As Russell marshalled his forces at Honiton, the most recent set of rebel articles was being pored over by the privy councillors in London. This time, it was not Somerset who composed a formal response to the insurgents' demands – as he struggled to cope with the sea of troubles the regime was by now facing, both at home and abroad, he probably had his hands too full – but rather Archbishop Cranmer, to whom the protector may well have delegated the task. As one would expect, Cranmer, the chief architect of the religious settlement against which the rebels were protesting, was determined to give the insurgents both barrels, and he responded to each of their articles in turn in a lengthy diatribe which – as the archbishop's most recent biographer has well observed – was 'from the moment of its opening address to "the ignorant men of Devonshire and Cornwall" . . . monotonous and unattractive in its shrill hostility'.[19] While the first draft of Cranmer's response was probably written in August, the text does not appear to have been completed until the end of the year, by which time it was no longer terribly relevant.[20] More interesting in many ways is the still-lengthier 'Answer to the Articles of the Commoners of Devonshire and Cornwall', the authorship of which remains uncertain, but which now seems likely to have been composed by the evangelical schoolmaster and dramatist Nicholas Udall.[21] Udall's 'Answer' to the Fifteen Articles was clearly written before battle had been fully joined in Devon, because, in addressing the insurgents, he spoke repeatedly of the merciful nature of the king, 'whom I see so slack to use his royal sword in avenging himself on you', and urged them to seek pardon while there was still time.[22] Udall's text provides us with a detailed picture of how one loyalist writer regarded the insurgents at the moment when the insurrection reached its zenith, in other words, and is therefore worth considering at some length.

Is it possible that Udall was quartered in the field alongside the royal forces as he wrote his 'Answer'? Sadly, there is nothing in the text to support such an assumption, and it seems altogether more likely that he was safely ensconced somewhere well away from the seat of the action as he settled down to compose his text: probably in the capital. Udall had clearly read the printed *Message* which had been sent to the rebels in the king's name on 8 July and, while he could well have got hold of a copy of this in Devon, there are several passages in the 'Answer' that demonstrate that he had also read the letter by 'R.L.' which was published as a pamphlet alongside the Fifteen Articles at some unknown date after 27 July.[23] If Udall had been in Devon, there would scarcely have been time for him to have received a copy of this tract before Russell moved out against the rebel forces on 3 August. Yet, if he had been in London, he could easily have read it during the first week of August and then composed the 'Answer' immediately afterwards. The fact that, at one point in his text, Udall taxes the rebels with having committed such 'wilful ... rebellion ... as the like ... hath never ... been ... known since the beginning of the world', moreover – words that strongly recall those Cranmer had used in his sermon against the insurgents at St Paul's on 21 July – hints that Udall himself may have been present on that occasion: again indicating that, when he wrote the 'Answer', he was residing in the capital.[24]

If this was indeed the case, then Udall cannot have been nearly as au fait with the situation on the ground as were those who were actually serving in Russell's army. Nevertheless, we must presume that – wherever he was when he wrote his riposte – he had been able to keep relatively well abreast of the developing situation in the West. And although Udall's text – like Cranmer's – is essentially a point-by-point rebuttal of the rebels' demands for an end to religious innovation, interlarded with relentless sideswipes against the 'Popish priests' and 'rank Papists' whom the regime and its supporters blamed for instigating the protests, it does contain some more personal sidelights on the rising, too.[25] Udall appears to have been well versed in the various arguments that the rebels had put forward to justify their actions, for example, noting that 'some wranglers allege that the proceedings came not from the king, but from his Council', while 'another sort allege for their defence that the King is not yet of age'.[26] He also plainly recognised that many – perhaps most – of the protestors perceived themselves as dutiful subjects: because he not only observed that 'some perchance will say, We resist not our King. We mean nothing against his Majesty's royal Crown, person or dignity', but also frankly acknowledged that 'forsooth, I can full well believe that a great part of you are good simple people, and are persuaded that ye do well, and that ye have not directly meant any harm against the King'.[27] Here, Udall showed himself a good deal more sympathetic than Cranmer – although, of course, his words were clearly written in the hope of persuading the ordinary rebels to submit themselves to the Crown's mercy.

Udall was just as affronted as Cranmer by the high tone of the rebel articles, however – and he was especially infuriated by Article 8. The concluding words of this famous article appear to have reflected the rebels' perception that the directive in the new service book that congregations should divide into men and women on either side of the chancel before taking communion had resulted in mid-service peregrinations which bore an unseemly resemblance to the opening stages of a traditional feast-day dance; as a result, they had roundly declared that 'we will not receive the new service because it is but like a Christmas game'.[28] Udall was outraged by this statement. 'Call ye the word of God but a Christmas game?' he asked incredulously; 'Call ye the Holy Bible a Christmas game? Call ye the holy sacraments of the body and blood of Christ, and the sincere administration thereof a Christmas game?' Udall then went on furiously to deny that there was any sense at all in which the new service could be compared to a Yuletide pastime. 'All the days of your life after ye will curse, abhor, detest and defy all such pernicious ringleaders of mischief as will attempt or entice you to make any more such midsummer games as ye have now at this present time played,' he raged, 'and doubt ye not but ye shall find the right using of the new service a better Christmas game than this is a midsomer game.'[29]

Udall's characterisation of the Western Rising itself as a midsummer game is fascinating. It chimes with – and, indeed, may conceivably have helped to inspire – Hooker's later characterisation of the insurrection as an 'enterlude', or play, in which the rebel captains had been 'the chiefe players', and highlights once again the widespread contemporary perception that there was a 'carnivalesque' element to the rebellion, as to so many other popular protests in early modern England.[30] Udall may well have been influenced in his choice of phraseology by recent events in London, moreover, for, on 27 May, the city aldermen – anxious to forestall any gatherings that might lead to outbreaks of disorder in the capital – had ordered that young people were not to be permitted 'to make any May Games or to resort to any ... gatherings of people together at any interludes'. As disorder had begun to flare up across the whole of southern England in early July, this order had been reissued and the aldermen had sought the lord chancellor's approval 'for the staying of all common interludes and plays within the city'.[31] The privy councillors had not only approved of this local initiative, but had subsequently decided to extend the ban across the entire kingdom. On

6 August, a proclamation had therefore been issued prohibiting all plays and interludes in England, lest they encourage 'division, tumults and uproars in this realm'.[32] Udall was almost certainly composing his 'Answer' during the very week in which this proclamation was published – and its implicit association of rebellion with festivity may well have been in his mind as he drafted his vitriolic response to Article 8. Despite his repeated warnings to the insurgents of the 'plague of mortality which (unless ye call for mercy in season) must needs light upon you by the severe rod of princely justice', however, even Udall cannot have guessed that the rising which he derided as a midsummer game would shortly result in such a tragic denouement for so many of the players.

There are two further respects in which Udall's 'Answer' is worthy of note. First, it is interesting to observe that – perhaps because he himself had spent some time in Cornwall – Udall appears to have been far more sympathetic to the Cornish rebels' complaint about the imposition of the new prayer book in English than Cranmer had been. Whereas the archbishop had effectively given Cornish-speakers to understand that, if they did not understand the new service book, then they must either lump it or learn English, Udall took a very different tack.[33] This was made apparent in a passage that strongly suggests that Udall knew of the demand that had apparently been made by the Cornish rebels, in an earlier set of articles, for a liturgy in their own tongue – and which at least opens the possibility that he had seen a connection between the 1548 rebellion in West Cornwall and the contemporaneous imposition of the 'Order of Communion' in English, too. 'Good neighbours, ye Cornishmen,' Udall began,

> If ye . . . understand no English and for that consideration had by the way of petition made humble request to the King's Majesty . . . that 'We the Cornishmen, being a portion of your most loving . . . subiects . . . most humbly beseech your Majesty that . . . we may by your graces provision have the same fourme of divine service and communion . . . turned into our Cornish speech' . . . I doubt not but that the King . . . would have tendered your request and provided for the accomplishment of your desires.

But, Udall continued, '"We Cornishmen utterly refuse this English", is an high word and a full: unfit to proceed from subjects to their prince and sovereign liege lord'.[34] By suggesting that it was not the Cornish people's preference for their own tongue that was unreasonable, but merely the way in which that preference had been expressed, Udall was portraying himself here as one who respected the Cornish sense of cultural difference and saw no reason why provision should not be made to accommodate it within the parameters of reformed church practice: perhaps because he was shrewd enough to recognise that, if the perceived connection between the defence of the old faith and the defence of 'Cornishness' could be broken, then the strength of religious conservatism in Cornwall would almost certainly be significantly reduced.

The second respect in which Udall's answer to the Fifteen Articles differs quite markedly from that of Cranmer is in its frequent use of the language of camping. As we have seen, the fact that large groups of protestors began to establish semi-permanent camps at traditional open-air meeting places during the summer of 1549 was regarded by local governors as a phenomenon that was both novel and highly disturbing. The earliest documented instance of such a camp being formed is during the major enclosure riot that occurred at Northaw in Hertfordshire in May 1548, and it is possible that the practice had originated there before going on to become widely emulated during the following year.[35] It is sometimes suggested that camping was a distinctively South-Eastern practice, and that there was a clear divide between the rebels of East Anglia and the Home Counties with their static camps and the more mobile rebels of the West, but this contrast may well be overdrawn. The first action of the Cornish protestors in July 1549 had been to 'pitch . . . their campe at the townes end' near Bodmin, after all; the Cornish rebels had then gone on to 'incamp . . . in three places' against Trematon Castle soon afterwards, and it was to 'sent davys down ys camppe' that the young men of Morebath had set off towards the middle of that same month.[36] In the Fifteen Articles, moreover, the western rebels had proudly proclaimed themselves to be assembled 'in divers Campes by East and West of Excettor'. Cranmer, rather surprisingly, did not pick up on this verbal cue; indeed, he never once mentioned the word 'camp' in his reply to the insurgents: perhaps because, by the time his response was finished and the rebellions had been crushed, the term was considered simply too subversive for use in a public document.

Udall, by contrast, made repeated allusions to camps and camping throughout his 'Answer'. At one point, for example, he expressed his profound sense of shock that the protestors should have 'encamped yourselves (as ye call it)' against the king's 'towns and cities'.[37] This reference is particularly interesting because it shows that Udall, too, regarded the word 'encamping' as an entirely new coinage, at least as far as it applied to episodes of popular protest. Elsewhere in his text, Udall lamented the fact that the protestors had been so bold as to seek redress 'not by complaint, as is the part of subjects, but by encamping themselves and rebelling against their natural prince'.[38] Here, his phraseology suggests that he regarded 'encamping' as a form of petitioning carried out by more forceful means. On several occasions, Udall observed that none of the rebels' grievances warranted such an extreme response as 'encamping': noting on one occasion that 'this is a very fond . . . article to be made a matter for subjects to encamp themselves against their king's proceedings', for example, and on another that 'neither this article nor any of the others is such whereof ye should encamp yourselves and ask a peticion of your sovereign with naked sword in hand'.[39] The sense of pride with which the rebels spoke of their newly formed camps clearly angered Udall. It was abhorrent that 'subjects' should rebel 'against their prince, and by plain words profess encamping of themselves', he wrote at one point, while at another he declared that the sin of rebellion was all the more unpardonable for 'being bolstered and bragged out with open encamping in the field'.[40] So closely did Udall associate the rebels with the physical camps they had formed, indeed, that on one occasion he elided the two, referring to 'ye Devonsheir and Cornish men, both captains and *campers*'.[41] Elsewhere, he used the word 'camping' as a simple synonym for 'rebelling', begging his 'countrymen' to 'leave off . . . your camping at your own doors'.[42]

Udall's repeated references to camps and camping in his 'Answer' to the Fifteen Articles demonstrate that he did not regard the formation of rebel camps as an exclusively south-eastern phenomenon. His text appears, at first sight, to provide further important evidence to show that, in this respect, the contrast between the eastern and western rebels has been greatly exaggerated, therefore. Yet it should also be noted that, if Udall was indeed in London when he wrote the 'Answer', then his perception of the western rebels and their activities would have been heavily coloured by the reports that were pouring into the capital about the doings of the protestors in East Anglia, the Thames Valley and Kent. It may well be that although Udall had the text of the western rebels' demands in front of him as he wrote, his mind was also full of the reports that any well-informed person in London would have heard about the doings of the eastern protestors – and that, as a result, his text gave the practice of 'camping' a higher profile than it would have done had he been composing his 'Answer' on the spot in East Devon. Be this as it may, Udall's warnings to the western rebels to seek pardon from the king while they still could were almost certainly out of date by the time he wrote them, for, on Saturday, 3 August, Lord Russell and the 2,000–3,000 troops whom he had assembled in the vicinity of Honiton at last set out to do battle with the protestors.

## III

According to Hooker, Russell's decision 'nowe to loose no more time, but to give the adventure upon the enemie' was prompted, first, by the arrival of the long-awaited reinforcements under Lord Grey, and second, by the fact that the lord privy seal had recently been 'advertised' from Exeter that the city was in desperate straits and could not hope to hold out for much longer.[43] Both of these factors were surely critical in prompting Russell finally to seek a conclusion with the rebels, but it is possible that the king's lieutenant in the West was swayed by a third consideration, too. Ellis Gruffydd, a Welsh soldier serving in the English garrison of Calais, later recorded that 'the Lord Privy Seal saw his opportunity to attack the besiegers *before the Cornishmen arrived*'. This statement suggests that, while some of the Cornish rebel forces had arrived before Exeter in time to take part in the action at Fenny Bridges on 27 July, many of their fellow countrymen were still in the process of marching up from the west: meaning that Russell – having received his own reinforcements – now had a precious window of time in which to act before the rebels could concentrate all of their own forces.[44]

The events of the next three days may be reconstructed from Hooker's later accounts and from a letter sent by John Fry – one of the loyalist gentlemen who was serving in the king's army – to John Thynne just two weeks afterwards. On Saturday, 3 August, Russell's forces set out from Honiton and, after having diverted from the line of the main road – perhaps because it had been barricaded by the rebels – they marched 'over the downs' to Woodbury, some 9 miles to the south-east of Exeter. Here, the king's army halted beside a windmill that formed a prominent feature in the local landscape. Four miles north-west of Woodbury lies Clyst St Mary, the village that had been a key rebel centre since the risings first began to escalate, and which now stood directly in the line of march between Russell's forces and Exeter. According to Hooker, when 'the rebels of saint Marie Clist' heard of the royal army's advance, they at once

> with all their force and power came forth, and marched onwards, untill they came to the foresaid mill, where they offer[ed] the fight, and notwithstanding they were of verie stout stomachs, & also verie valiantlie did stand to their tackles [i.e., kept up the struggle], yet in the end they were overthrown, and the most parte of them slaine.[45]

Fry later estimated there were 'slayne of the rebelles' in this engagement 'les than one hundredth, as I thykne', but 'of our men none slayne . . . yt I hard of' – though he conceded that 'after ye end of ye fight were iii or iiii of our men slayne yt folyshely went abrode to spoyle': that is to say, to take goods by force from the local people, a practice that would henceforth be indulged in at every opportunity by the Crown's forces in the South-West.[46] It is clear from Fry's words that the grossly asymmetrical casualty figures that had been reported in the wake of the engagement at Fenny Bridges had again been apparent in the wake of the fight at Woodbury, and – as no contemporary writer was to fault the rebels' courage or commitment – it can only be assumed that this grim disparity reflected the insurgents' lack of horsemen and modern handguns.

Having either killed or driven off their attackers, Russell's troops now encamped themselves in the fields around the windmill, and later that day Miles Coverdale – a leading evangelical preacher, who was accompanying the royal army and who would two years later be appointed bishop of Exeter – gave a sermon to the assembled soldiers 'and caused a generall thanksgiving to bee made unto God' for their recent victory.[47] As Russell and his troops bedded down at Woodbury that night, the rebels made determined preparations to resist the royal army's renewed advance towards Exeter on the following day. According to Hooker, 'the rebels which remained in . . . Clyst St Mary, hearing of the evill successe befallen to their neighbours, and they doubting [i.e., fearing] that their turne would be next to receive the like, did [now] spread abroad the newes and request to be aided and assisted'. Accordingly, Hooker goes on, 'forthwith in great troopes resorted unto them a number of their companions out of everie quarter, to the number . . . . of six thousand men, and in all hast they make themselves and all things in a readiness to abide the brunt' of the royal army's attack.[48] It will be noted that Hooker presents the rebels' decision to concentrate at Clyst St Mary as, in effect, an accident: as a simple consequence of the fact that the inhabitants of the village had called for help. Yet it seems far more likely that the rebel captains before Exeter had deliberately chosen Clyst St Mary as the site at which they would offer battle to the royal forces because the village stood beside the bridge that then formed the lowest crossing point of the Clyst, the little river which Russell's army would have to cross before it could break through to relieve Exeter.

Early on Sunday, 4 August, Russell and his army advanced upon Clyst St Mary, arriving before the village at around 9 a.m. The rebels had erected great earthen barricades, or 'rampires', on three sides of the village – presumably to the north, south and east, as on the west their position was protected by the River Clyst – and it was against these fortifications that the royal forces initially threw themselves. After some 'bickering', Russell's troops managed to capture the barricades, driving the defenders back into Clyst St Mary itself, and, as the king's soldiers eagerly pursued the chase, it began to look as if the day was already theirs.[49] Yet events were about to take an unexpected turn. At some point over the preceding weeks, the rebels had been joined – for reasons that remain unclear – by Sir Thomas Pomeroy, of Berry Pomeroy in South Devon, who had promptly become 'one of the[ir] chief captaines'.[50] Pomeroy was the most socially elevated of all the rebel commanders, and he was also, according to a later source, a man who had fought in Henry VIII's French wars and who thus possessed considerable military experience.[51] As the rebels fell back from the barricades, with Russell's forces hot on their heels, Pomeroy broke away from the main rebel force and concealed himself 'in a furze close' just outside the village, accompanied only by a trumpeter and a boy with a drum. Then, once Russell's troops had rushed past and were between him and the village, Pomeroy 'commanded the trumpet to be sounded, and the drumme to be stricken up'. Startled, and fearing that this martial music betokened an imminent attack on their rear, Russell's troops now panicked and fled, leaving their wagons and, still more important, all of their artillery pieces abandoned on the highway just outside the village. The triumphant rebels at once sallied out, seized both the wagons and the 'ordinances', and hauled them back into Clyst St Mary. Here, they swiftly redeployed the captured weapons and made ready to use them against their former owners.[52]

It was an astonishing turnaround, and even as the insurgents at Clyst St Mary were rejoicing at their success in humiliating the royal army, rebel sympathisers in Exeter were making their most determined effort yet to seize control of the city from within. Hooker records that, at 8 o'clock that same morning, a companie of 'malecontents' rose up 'in everie quarter of the citie' and 'g[o]t into the streets, walking with their weapons and in their armour, as [if] to fight with their enimies'. As they strode defiantly through the city, the demonstrators taunted the local evangelists, shouting: 'Come out these heretikes and twopennie bookemen! Where be they? By God's wounds & bloud we will not be pinned in to serve their turne. We will go out and have in our neighbors [i.e., the rebels]; [for] they be honest, good and godlie men'. Had these railing words provoked a physical confrontation between the two religious factions in Exeter – as the demonstrators clearly hoped they might – or had the protestors managed to seize control of the South

Gate – where Hooker concedes that there was indeed 'a little stur' – the rebels might yet have been admitted to the city at the eleventh hour. But, in the end, the town governors succeeded in facing down the demonstrators, and in confining those whom Hooker terms 'the bel[l] we[th]ers of this flock' to their own houses.[53] By the end of that morning, then, the hopes of the rebel sympathisers in Exeter had been dashed – while, at Clyst St Mary, farce was about to be succeeded by bloody tragedy.

Russell's men may have abandoned their initial attack on the village and fled in disorder, but they quickly regrouped and, in Hooker's words, 'recovered the hill': by which he presumably means that they reoccupied the low eminence that stands immediately to the east of Clyst St Mary and is today breasted by the A3052. Having surveyed the surrounding countryside from here, seen that there were no further rebel forces approaching and realised that they had, in fact, been deceived by Pomeroy's ruse, Russell and his commanders now resolved to launch a second attack on the village and ordered their troops to move forwards once again. Yet before they set off, Hooker observes,

> it was advertised unto my lord, that ... everie house ... [in Clyst St Mary] was fortified and full of men, and that it was not possible for anie to passe that waie without great perill ... Whereuppon order was given, that as they passed and entered into the towne ... they should set the houses on fire.[54]

Firing the village made good sense in military terms, of course, as it was the quickest and easiest way of driving the insurgents out of the buildings that they had fortified, but it is hard not to suspect that the order to burn Clyst St Mary to the ground also sprang, at least in part, from the royal commanders' desire to avenge themselves upon the rebellious commoners who had humiliated them during the earlier attack.

Russell's forces now moved in to mount a second assault upon the 'bulwarks' on the outskirts of the village, which the rebels had clearly reoccupied in the wake of the royal army's flight earlier that day. It would appear, from Edward VI's later brief description of the battle, that Russell ordered Captain Spinola and his Italian harquebusiers to pin down the defenders of one of the rebel bulwarks with a withering hail of fire, while a certain Captain Travers assailed a second barricade with a strong party of horsemen. Meanwhile, the bulk of Russell's army – consisting of both the vanguard and the main 'battle' – charged down the hill to assault the rebel bulwark on the east side of Clyst St Mary.[55] Hooker tells us that the Somerset gentleman Sir William Francis led the vanguard and that, 'leaving the waie which he tooke before' – presumably the main road into the village from the east – Francis 'tooke now another waie [instead], which waie was both deepe and narrow'.[56] It seems almost certain that this 'waie' was the present-day Frog Lane/ Bishop's Court Lane, a typical deep Devon lane with high banks and hedges on either side, which runs parallel to the A3052 for a time before diverting sharply to enter Clyst St Mary from the north. Francis may well have adopted this alternative approach to the village in order to bypass the rebel bulwark athwart the main road, but, if so, it proved a costly error, for, as Hooker notes, 'the enemie being upon the bankes upon everie side of the waie, with their stones so beat him, that they stroke his headpiece [i.e., his helmet] fast to his head . . . whereof he died'.[57] Nor was Sir William the only one to suffer from this barrage of stones and other missiles, for Sir Hugh Paulet of Hinton St George – who had also joined Russell's army by this time – later noted that 'of one hundred archers in his [i.e., Francis's] company', no fewer than seventy-nine later 'departed hurte from the place'.[58]

The decisive encounter between the royal forces and the rebels appears to have occurred at some point along this same deep lane: perhaps towards the lower end of the roadway, where the lane emerges into the village. During the early 1600s, a descendant of Henry Ley, a gentleman from Plymouth, recorded that 'in the time of E[dward] the 6 . . . he with his two men, served on horseback in the West Contrey against the rebels which made the great commotion' and went on to give a dramatic account of Ley's experiences at the battle of Clyst St Mary: an account that was clearly based on Ley's own reminiscences. 'Being in the third ranck of those horsemen that gave the charge upon the enemy, at the lane called Clist Lane,' Ley's descendant later recorded,

> he was received with two pikes, th'one bent against his horse which was hurte therewith, and th'other bent against himself, with which he was unhorst, and two of his short rybbs broken, and had bene presentlie ... slaine by a [rebel] billman, yf John Smith of Kingston, who served in the iiiith ranck, had not charged his staffe at the byllman and slaine him.[59]

In Ley's view, the struggle between Russell's horsemen and the rebels in 'Clist Lane' had clearly been the engagement that decided the battle, for he concluded his tale by noting that 'by this onset of the horsemen the rebels were discomfeited and manie of them slaine'.[60] Yet, despite the success of the royal army in routing their enemies in the lane and in breaking through to the village itself, the rebels still refused to give up the fight. Hooker notes that, as Russell's soldiers pressed into Clyst St Mary, they 'set fire on everie house as they passed by', in accordance with the orders they had previously been given. Nevertheless, he goes on, 'the rebelles, conjoining themselves in the middle of the towne, did stand at their defence, where the fight was very fierce and cruell'. Hooker concludes this part of his narrative by stressing the horror of the ensuing struggle: 'for some [of the rebels] were slaine with the sword', he notes, 'some burned in the houses, some, shifting for themselves were taken prisoners, and manie thinking to escape over the water were drowned [in the River Clyst] so that there were dead that daie, one with another, about a thousand men'.[61] John Fry put the rebel dead at about half that number, but was similarly awed by the ferocity of the fighting, noting that the royal army's 'fourth & greatyst fight' with the insurgents had been 'on Sonday ye iiiith of Aygust ... at a place callyd ... Clyst'.[62] There, 'we had suche a great & long fight as ... I have not seine nor heard of the like', Fry wrote, and although he estimated that only twenty of Russell's men had been killed, Sir Hugh Paulet was later to claim that many hundreds of loyalists had been wounded, and that no fewer than 500 of the soldiers who had been raised in Somerset and Dorset had 'caryed away the smartes with them yn one day from Clyst'.[63]

Having captured – and destroyed – Clyst St Mary itself, Russell's troops now pressed on to take their next objective: the long, low bridge over the River Clyst which lies at the foot of the village. The rebels had fortified this 'with great trees and timber' and had placed a piece of ordnance behind the barricade, but some of Russell's horsemen managed to ford the river some way above the village and to attack the rebel position from the rear. As a result, it was not long before the bridge was secured and Russell's entire army was able to march over the Clyst and to draw itself up on 'the great heath, named Clist Heath' on the other side.[64] At this point, another terrible slaughter ensued. No sooner had Russell's forces crossed the river than Lord Grey, scouting ahead with his cavalry, had ridden up 'to the top of the hill which is in the middle of the Heath' to view the surrounding countryside. From here, Grey descried – or thought he descried – 'a great companie' of men assembled upon Woodbury Hill, to the rear of the army, who appeared to be marching towards Clyst St Mary. Assuming these men to be rebel reinforcements – whereas, in fact, they may simply have been a group of local countryfolk who had gathered at this elevated point in order to watch the battle from afar – Grey at once rode back to inform Russell of what he had seen. 'Whereupon,' Hooker nonchalantly observes,

> it was concluded [by the king's commanders] that the prisoners whom they had before taken at the windmill, and in the towne [i.e., in Clyst St Mary], who were a great number, and which if they were newlie set upon, might be a detriment and a perill unto them, should be all killed, which forthwith was done, everie man making a dispatch of his prisoners.[65]

If Hooker were our only source for this dreadful massacre, then we might well be tempted to doubt his word, but, in fact, his testimony is supported by that of Henry Ley, who was later to recall that, in the wake of the battle at Clyst St Mary, 'manie' of the rebels had been 'slaine *and executed*'.[66] It seems certain that the killings took place, therefore, but we will probably never know just how many of the captured men were cut down in cold blood upon the heath. The Jacobean historian John Hayward was subsequently to write that, after the battle was over, Russell's soldiers, thirsting for 'revenge and blood', had killed more than

900 of the insurgents – and these words have sometimes been taken to provide a reliable indication of the total number of prisoners who were killed.[67] Yet Hayward was writing many years after the events he purports to describe, and his statement was clearly based partly on Hooker's narrative and partly on a comment made by Edward VI in his journal to the effect that, after Russell's forces had driven the rebels from the bridge, 'there were in a plain about 900 of them slain'.[68] It is conceivable that the figure cited by the king related only to the prisoners who had been killed in the aftermath of the battle, but it seems more reasonable to assume that it related to the total number of insurgents who had been killed during the course of the day's fighting, especially as Hooker estimated the overall number of rebel dead at a similar figure. Hayward's account almost certainly exaggerated the extent of the killings, then. Even so, the incident may well have been the worst recorded massacre in the West Country's early modern history – and it provided a grim foretaste of the terrible revenge that the king's commanders and the county's local governors were now preparing to unleash on all those who had dared to challenge the accepted social and religious order.

Having sheathed their bloody swords, Russell's men now encamped themselves on Clyst Heath for the night and prepared to renew their advance on Exeter on the following day. The king's commanders may well have assumed that, after the dreadful punishment they had suffered over the previous forty-eight hours, the rebels would offer little further resistance. If so, they were to be disappointed, for no sooner was news of the defeat brought to the rebel captains before Exeter than they despatched another large body of men to Clyst Heath to block the royal army's path. During the night of 4–5 August, these fresh rebel forces – said to have been about 2,000 strong – positioned themselves 'in the lower side' of the heath, next to the highway running between Clyst St Mary bridge and Heavitree, where, according to Hooker, 'they did intrench and fortifie a place fast by a hedge, and secretlie there ... did place their ordinance, & make themselves in readiness'.[69] It was perhaps on this occasion that, as John Foxe was later scornfully to record, the rebels, 'to make their part more sure by the helpe and presence of their consecrated God and maker, brought with them unto the battaile the pyxe under his canaby [i.e., canopy], and instead of an altar where he was hangyng before, set him now ryding in a carte'.[70] By bringing a pyx – that is to say, one of the ornate containers in which the consecrated bread was traditionally elevated above the altar in a church – into the field with them, the insurgents were making the most public statement possible of their commitment to the old faith and they doubtless believed that they were marching, in a sense, under the conduct of God himself. 'Neither was there lackyng masses, crosses, banners, candlesticks, with holy bread ... [and] holy water,' Foxe sneered, 'to defend them from devils and all adversarye power, which in the end neither could help their frendes, nor yet could save themselves from the hands of their enemies.'[71]

As dawn rose on Monday, 5 August, the rebels – clearly still full of offensive spirit – shot off their guns at the royal forces as they lay encamped on the hill at the centre of the heath. Russell responded to this challenge by drawing his army out into the field once more, dividing it up into three parts and unleashing an all-out assault on the bulwark that the insurgents had thrown up across the road leading to Exeter during the night. The lord privy seal had a number of pioneers among his troops and, as the battle raged in front of the rebel rampart, these military engineers methodically cut a passage through several of the hedge banks that the insurgents had relied upon to flank their position. As a result, a party of royal troops was able to coast around the rebels' fortifications and to attack the insurgents from the rear. A scene of terrible carnage now took place in the roadway behind the rebel bulwark, for, as Hooker records, the insurgents were 'intrapped on either part: the hedges of the high waye beinge on the sides, and the King's armie [both] before and behinde them, whereof ensued a verie greate murder, verie few of the rebells escaping but that they were ... [either slaine] or taken'.[72] In a later account of this same engagement, Hooker observed that 'great was the slaughter, and cruell was the fight', and was scrupulous enough to acknowledge that 'such was the valour and stoutnesse of these men [i.e., the insurgents], that the Lord Greie reported himselfe, that he never, in all the wars that he had been in, did know the like'.[73]

Once again, the rebels' desperate courage had proved of little avail against the superior training and equipment of the royal forces and, once again, the contrast between the casualties that had been suffered on either side was stark. Fry later recorded that at 'ye fyft fight ... on Monday ye Vth of August ... were slayne of the rebelles as I suppose above one hundredth, & of our men, yt I could percevye not above iii or iiii'.[74] Yet, despite winning his third major victory in as many days, Russell still did not feel strong enough to force his way through to the relief of Exeter and, in the wake of the battle of Clyst Heath, he marched to the little port of Topsham, 4 miles to the south of the city, where his army spent that night. Russell may well have taken this decision because he was aware that further powerful reinforcements were about to join him from the east under the command of Sir William Herbert and that, with this addition of strength, his final push on Exeter would be all but irresistible. It may well have been this news, too, that finally persuaded the rebel captains that they had no choice but to abandon the siege. Fry later observed that, after the slaughter at Clyst Heath, 'all ye rest of ye rebells yt were on the Est & South p[ar]ts of Excester fledd', while Hooker concurs, recording that the rebels abandoned their positions in the city suburbs under cover of darkness that evening: a fact that only dawned on the citizens when 'the gentlemen which were kept prisoners in the churches and in other places about the citie, being now at libertie, came straight to the walles at about midnight, & gave knowledge thereof to the watch'.[75]

In the early hours of Tuesday, 6 August, Herbert joined Russell at Topsham with what Fry admiringly described as 'a ryght fine band of menne, well appoynted'.[76] At the core of Herbert's force were 1,000 foot soldiers from South Wales, and it seems probable that these infantrymen were escorted by bands of horsemen under the command of Herbert himself and of other loyalist gentlemen from Wales and Gloucestershire, perhaps including Sir Anthony Kingston.[77] Having been reinforced by Herbert, Russell now possessed an army of approximately 5,000 men, and with this powerful force at his back he finally set off for Exeter. The king's army arrived before the walls of the city at 8 a.m. that morning 'to the great joy and comfort of the long-captivated citizens', as Hooker later wrote, 'who were no more glad of their deliverie, than was his lordship and all good subiects joyfull of his victorie'.[78] Delighted as the city's loyalists were, the rigours of the siege had left both them and their traditionalist neighbours half-starved, and Russell accordingly directed that none of his troops should enter the city until the citizens had been supplied with food. He himself, meanwhile, set up his camp in St John's Fields in Southernhay, just outside the city walls, and it was here that he received the mayor and his brethren, shortly after his arrival, and congratulated them on their brave defence of the city.[79]

## IV

Throughout the following week, the royal army remained quartered in the vicinity of Exeter, where Russell, in Hooker's words, busied himself in 'setting all things in good order, rewarding the good & punishing the evill'.[80] One of Russell's first acts was to inform the Privy Council of his success in relieving the city and dispersing the besiegers, and within days this news was being trumpeted to the skies in the capital.[81] On Saturday, 10 August, a London chronicler recorded that 'the Archbishop of Canterbury made a colation in Pawles quire for the victory that the ... Lord Privie Seale had on Monday last past against the rebells in Devonshire', going on to note that Cranmer had informed the congregation that Russell had not only relieved Exeter, but had also 'slew, hurte and tooke prisoners of the sayd rebells above iiii M [i.e., 4,000], and [had] after hanged divers of them in the towne and about the countrye'.[82] Needless to say, Somerset and his colleagues were delighted by the glad tidings from the West, but they were also anxious to ensure that there should be no jostling for precedence among the most influential figures in Russell's camp. On 9 August, Somerset therefore wrote to Sir Peter and Sir Gawen Carew, advising them to absent themselves from Russell's advisory council in order to avoid any 'contestation' with the newly arrived, and more senior, gentlemen in the royal army.[83] The next day, the Privy Council wrote to Russell himself, ordering him to admit only six named individuals – including Lord Grey, Sir William Herbert and Sir Hugh Paulet – to serve among his official advisors.[84] Needless to say, the Carews were aggrieved by this demotion – which hinted at a perception on Somerset's part that they wielded an undue influence over the lord privy seal – but Russell at once went out of his way to demonstrate that Sir Peter and Sir Gawen nevertheless continued to enjoy his special favour.[85]

As we have seen, the property of the Devon and Cornish rebels had already been declared to be forfeit to the Crown, and Russell, as the king's lieutenant in the West, now exploited this fact in order to award the lands of three of the wealthiest rebel leaders – all of whom were still in arms – to the Carews and their sidekick, William Gibbs. Thus Sir Peter was promised the lands of John Winslade, Sir Gawen was promised the lands of Humphrey Arundell, and Gibbs was promised the lands of John Bury of Silverton. Russell could scarcely have done more to emphasise his continued sense of allegiance and gratitude to the Carews. And while the Carews and Gibbs reaped the richest rewards, many other loyalists who had done 'good service' against the insurgents also received the 'gift' of rebel prisoners, who were handed over to them, in Hooker's words, 'both bodies, goods and lands'.[86] These luckless individuals were subsequently forced to 'ransom', or to buy back, both their own persons and their property from their new 'owners' for exorbitant sums. Nor was it only those former rebels whom Russell and his chief commanders specifically chose to 'gift' to their followers who suffered in this way, for the king's soldiers had been given licence to treat the countryside around Exeter as occupied enemy territory and they took full advantage of this. According to Ellis Gruffyd, Herbert and 'his Welshmen . . . ravage[d] the land as . . . [did] the foreign horsemen from Calais under Captain Dgermayn, who . . . did great destruction in the country . . . [by taking] goods as well as by capturing people and forcing them to pay ransom like soldiers'.[87]

With the royal forces firmly back in control of the countryside around Exeter, local people had no choice but to submit. Writing to Thynne on 16 August, Fry reported that 'above tenne thousand persons have sued for theyre pardons to my Lord Prevey Seale & to wothers by hem appointed for the same', which suggests that in the wake of the rebel defeats in East Devon in 1549 – just as in the wake of other rebel defeats elsewhere during the Tudor period – elaborate spectacles of public repentance were staged, with huge crowds of former insurgents abasing themselves before the victorious royal commanders in order to signify their submission.[88] While mercy was extended to the rebel rank and file, summary justice was meted out to the perceived stirrers of the insurrection. As the king's lieutenant in the West, Russell possessed the power to impose martial law – and to direct his provost martial to execute any rebels who had been captured in arms after the most perfunctory of trials. It is evident that, by mid-August, he was already making selective use of this sanguinary power, for Fry laconically observed that there had been 'put to execucion of the rebelles all redy xvi'.[89] Among these unfortunates was Robert Welsh, the vicar of St Thomas near Exeter, who was hanged in chains from his own church tower.[90] Priests appear to have been even better represented among the western rebels than they were among the rebel groups who rose elsewhere in England during 1549, and Fry informed Thynne that 'in every of the fyghtes' between the insurgents and the government forces 'there were dyvers prystes in the fyld fyghtying ayenst us, & some of them slayne at every fyghte'.[91] Welsh was by no means the only local priest to be singled out for exemplary punishment, moreover, for the evidence of a later law suit shows that, on 14 August, the curate of Pilton in North Devon was likewise 'hanged in chains' by local loyalists for participating in the rebellion, while the parson of nearby Bittadon only just escaped a similar fate.[92] It is evident from these cases that, by the middle of August, supporters of the Crown had managed to regain control of the countryside around Barnstaple, and that here, just as in East Devon, clerics who were regarded as local ringleaders of the rebellion were being generally hunted down.

The insurgents may have been forced to relinquish their grip on Exeter and Barnstaple, but they still held the whole of Cornwall and much of West Devon, and within days they had regrouped at Sampford Courtenay, the village that had, for more than two months, been the Devon rebels' chief headquarters. News of the insurgents' continued defiance was already current in London by 15 August, when the imperial ambassador in England, François van der Delft, reported from there that 'the Cornishmen' were 'not so badly beaten' as had first been claimed, and that they had 'assembled again ... in order to guard the road to their country'.[93] In a letter written from Exeter on 14 August, Sir Gawen Carew provided Thynne with a more detailed picture of the situation, informing him that while 'the most part of thys shere ys com in & resevys ther pardon', the inhabitants of the northern parts of the county remained defiant. Not only this, rebel forces were continuing to besiege Plymouth Castle, while, most threateningly of all, Sir Gawen reported, 'Arondell gethers hes pore [i.e., power] stell in Cornewalle & determenes to geve us the battell by anything yt we can perseve to the contrary'. The Cornish rebel leader remained very strong, Sir Gawen went on, and 'has a goodly bande of men, I thinke to the number of vii M [i.e., 7,000] & upward'. This was a highly impressive figure, especially as the rebels had already lost many men in the battles around Exeter. Nevertheless, Carew concluded, 'God holding of his hand over us, as he has hitherto, we ar strong inought for him'.[94]

Sir Gawen's reference to Humphrey Arundell 'gathering his power' in Cornwall is a fascinating – and deeply revealing – one, and makes it clear that, following the shattering defeats which the insurgents had suffered in East Devon between 3 and 6 August, the Cornish rebel commander had hastened back across the Tamar with the aim of recruiting his forces there and putting a substantial army back into the field. In order to do this, and to concentrate as large a force as possible at Sampford Courtenay, Arundell would have had no choice but to draw off some of the rebel troops that were besieging Pendennis and Plymouth Castles – and this in turn may well help to explain why, just a day after Carew wrote to Thynne, the town of Plymouth was recaptured by loyalist forces. We know that this was the case because, in the register of St Budeaux, a little parish that lies just to the north of the town, the following entry appears immediately beneath a reference to the christening of one 'Tamsine Pope' on 15 August 1549: 'The same daye were the Rebells driven out of Plymouthe, & lxxx of them taken prisoners'.[95] In the margin beside these words, the single word 'Commotion' is written in large letters.[96] Thanks to this brief comment, it is now possible to pinpoint, for the first time, the day on which the protestors lost control of Plymouth, while the fact that no fewer than eighty 'rebells' are noted to have been 'taken prisoners' suggests that there must still have been a sizeable insurgent force in the town at the time of its recapture.

Many questions about how the rebel occupation of Plymouth came to an end remain tantalisingly unanswered. Were the rebels who were captured all strangers to the town, for example, or did they include many local men in their ranks? And where did the loyalist forces who are recorded to have 'driven out' the insurgents come from? Had the defenders of the castle decided to launch a sudden sally, after having learned that most of the forces that had previously been blockading them had been drawn away in order to bolster the rebel host at Sampford Courtenay? Had Russell despatched a party of horsemen from Exeter to scatter the rebels in the South Hams, relieve Plymouth Castle and recapture the town itself?[97] Or had loyalist sea captains somehow contrived 'to land [men] at the backs of the rebells' from ships cruising off the Devon coast: a tactic which Russell had definitely urged the government to adopt in a letter written just four days before?[98] We will probably never know – but it is hard to doubt that, for many of the luckless individuals who were captured at Plymouth in August 1549, retribution was swift in coming. Soon after recording a payment of 3s.4d. which he had made as '[a] Reward to my lord privye sealls trompeter' – presumably at the time of the castle's deliverance – the loyalist keeper of the receivers' accounts went on to note an altogether less celebratory series of payments which he had made for the construction of certain 'gallowes' in the town, including one payment made to seven carpenters 'for workyng all nyght, & for makyng the gallowes', together with further sums laid out for the provision of food, drink and candles for them while they worked.[99] At Plymouth, just as in the countryside around Exeter and Barnstaple, therefore, the re-establishment of loyalist control had clearly been accompanied by the imposition of martial law – and by a wave of executions.

Meanwhile, at Exeter, Russell was becoming increasingly alarmed by reports of the rebels' growing strength at Sampford Courtenay, and on Friday, 16 August, he ordered his forces to move out against the insurgents.[100] Concerned as he clearly was by the rebels' remarkable resilience and by their dogged refusal to abandon their cause, Russell can scarcely have doubted that the military advantage now lay overwhelmingly with him, for by this time he possessed an army of between 7,000 and 8,000 men: having been reinforced, as Hooker puts it, not only by '[Sir] William Herbert w[i]th his Welshmen', but also by 'the gentlemen which from out of all parts of the Countrie did [now] resorte to him, as alsoe of the Commoners which had yielded & gotten pardon'.[101] Russell must have regarded many of the local gentlemen who had suddenly come in to assist him following the arrival of Lord Grey with a distinctly jaundiced eye, of course, nor can he have placed much reliance upon the former rebel footmen who had been dragooned into serving in his army after having opposed it in the field just days before. But by this time he possessed more than enough military muscle to be confident of keeping any waverers in his own ranks in line. Just before the royal army left Exeter, Fry wrote another letter to Thynne, updating him on the situation. 'At thys present,' Fry observed, 'the people in all Devonshhyer & Somsersetshyer be metely well in quiet, except the parties abowte Samford Courtenay & Okeyngton, xvi or xxty myles beewast Exeter, wheare (as wee be advertised) be a great number of Rebells, & the most part of them Cornyshe menne.' 'Thys present daye we shall marche furth out of Exceter towards Samford,' Fry continued, 'and so from thens (yf God wyll) into Cornewall, where I pray God geve us the leke victory yt he hath geven us heretofore.'[102] It is evident from this letter that Fry, like Carew before him, regarded the Cornish as the most formidable opponents that the royal army now faced.

Although most of Russell's own despatches from the West have been lost, his letter to the Privy Council describing how his army first approached and then assaulted the rebel position at Sampford Courtenay has fortunately survived, and this missive provides us with a vivid, blow-by-blow account of the events of the next few days. On Friday, 16 August, Russell later wrote, his army marched the 7 miles from Exeter to Crediton and, finding the narrow Devon lanes 'very comberous', rested in the town that night. On Saturday, the army marched out once again in the direction of the rebels' 'campe at Sampford', and on Sunday, 18 August – by which time the royal forces were presumably quite close to the village – a skirmish took place between the rival 'scouts', during the course of which the loyalists were lucky enough to capture 'one Maundere', who 'was one of . . . [the rebels'] cheefe captaynes'. Buoyed up by this initial success, Russell now ordered Herbert to advance with 'a good parte of our Army' to the vicinity of the rebel 'campe' in order 'to viewe [it] and see what service ... [m]ight be done for the invasion thearof'. Accordingly, Herbert and his troops moved still closer to Sampford Courtenay, where, in Russell's words, they found 'the Enemyes strongly encamped, as well by the seat of the grounde as by the entrenchinge of the same': a turn of phrase which suggests that the rebels had taken up their station on the prominent hill that lies a mile or so to the east of the village, above Green Hill Cross, and which is now traversed by the road to Winkleigh.[103]

Sir William Herbert at once ordered the 'great ordenaunce' of the royal army to be deployed against the rebel camp and, while the loyalist gunners held their enemies 'in play', Russell's pioneers again set about hacking through the hedges that the insurgents had relied upon to flank their position, so that the king's soldiers would be able to pass through these obstacles and move into the attack. Once this work had been completed, Russell continues, the rebels 'were assaulted with good courage, on ... the one syd with our footmen, and on ... the other syde with ye Itallyane Harquebutieres'. Yet, even as Herbert's troops were pursuing their attack against the rebel camp on the hill, Russell goes on, 'Humfrey Arundell with his whoall powere came out [presumably from the village itself] on ... the backs of our forwarde, being thus bussyed with the Assault of the campe'. This is the first time that the Cornish rebel leader is definitely known to have fought in the field in person against the king's army, and Russell acknowledges that 'the suddene shewe' of Arundell and his troops 'wrought such feare in the harts of our men as we wished our poure [i.e., power, or strength] a great dealle more, not without good cause'. But, despite the shock caused by Arundell's unexpected onslaught, the Crown's forces quickly rallied. Lord Grey – who had been assisting Herbert in the attack upon the hill – now left Sir William to continue 'the enterprise agaynste the campe', while he himself returned to the main body of the royal army, put himself at the head of the troops who were following on behind the vanguard and ordered them 'to turne their faces to the Enemyes in the shewe of Battell'. A stand-off between Grey's forces and Arundell's forces then ensued, with 'nothinge for an ower but shotynge of ordinance', while, on the hill, Herbert continued to pursue his desperate assault upon the rebel camp. Eventually, he overcame the resistance of the stubborn defenders and put them to flight. Fresh loyalist horsemen now came up to assist Herbert's forces in 'the chase', the lord privy seal later recalled, during the course of which some 'v or vi C [i.e., 500 or 600] of the rebelles' were killed. And 'amongst them', Russell added, was 'slayne one Underhill, who had the charge of that Campe'.[104] Clearly, then, Underhill had continued to command the Sampford Courtenay rebels until the very last.

By now it was becoming late, and Russell was determined to crush the rebels completely and to drive them out of Sampford Courtenay before nightfall. Accordingly, he decided that he himself with his own 'company' would assault the village from one side, that Herbert and Sir Anthony Kingston would assault it from the other 'with their footemene & horsemene', respectively, and that Lord Grey and the main 'battle' would advance to engage Arundell's troops face to face. According to Russell, at the sight of the entire royal army advancing, 'the Rebelles stomackes so fell from them as without any blowe they flede' – but there was clearly some fighting at the barricades on the edge of the village, for Hooker records that 'one ap Owen a Welsh gentleman ... giving the adventure to enter the rampier at the town's ende, was there slaine by the rebels'.[105] Yet, even if they managed to hold off their attackers for a while, the insurgents – exhausted, outnumbered and, as always, heavily outgunned – were eventually overwhelmed and they took to their heels, leaving sixteen pieces of ordnance behind them. Hundreds of men were killed in the ensuing rout, with the king's cavalry cutting down the defeated rebels in their droves as they fled along the moorland roads towards Cornwall. In his letter informing the Privy Council of his victory, Russell estimated that some 700 rebels had been killed in this pursuit and 'a far greater number' captured. Only the onset of darkness ended the slaughter.[106]

We now know that the battle of Sampford Courtenay marked the end of the Cornish rebels as a coherent fighting force, but at the time matters did not seem so clear cut. Throughout the preceding weeks, after all, the rebel bands had repeatedly regrouped after suffering even the most crushing military defeats – and Russell clearly feared that they would now do so again. In the immediate aftermath of the battle, he therefore ordered his troops 'to repair with all . . . speed into . . . Cornwall to apprehend . . . [the] captains and stirrers of the . . . rebels lest peradventure they . . . might make any farther busyness . . . in raising of the people . . . of Cornwall to make farther rebellion'.[107] Following the repeated bloodlettings of the past few weeks, however, the Cornish people no longer possessed the capacity to resist. Next morning, Russell received news that Arundell himself – who had fled westwards the night before – had been apprehended in Launceston after he had, allegedly, begun 'to practys with the townesmene' for the murder of the loyalist gentlemen who were imprisoned in the castle there. Russell promptly despatched the Carews to Launceston with 'a good band to keepe the towne in a staye' and set off in their footsteps with the rest of his army later that day.[108]

Meanwhile, Russell sent further troops under Sir William Herbert into south-west Devon, presumably in order to ensure that the rebel forces which had, until very recently, been besieging Plymouth Castle were also entirely dispersed.[109] It must have been at around this time that Herbert gave 'the ransominge of a parish' near Bere Ferrers to Henry Ley as a reward for his good service against the insurgents. Herbert's grant meant that Ley was now entitled to demand that each of the inhabitants of Bere – which the royal commander clearly regarded as a rebel parish – should pay him a substantial sum of money as a 'ransom', or fine, for their supposed role in the commotion. Yet in the end – as Ley's early Stuart descendant was later to record, with evident familial pride in Henry's moderation and charitable attitude towards his neighbours – he chose 'onlie' to 'ransome . . . the parson for xl li (i.e. £40)', 'and pardoned the rest without ransom, whose posteritie do at this present remember him for the same'.[110] That Ley should have taken the decision to mulct the parish priest while sparing the members of his flock, of course, almost certainly reflected the fact that he, like so many other loyalists, blamed the rising primarily on the influence of traditionalist churchmen. Ley is not the only South Devon gentleman who is known to have been rewarded for rallying to Russell's banner at this time. The Stuart antiquarian John Prince was later to record that, during 'the western rebellion', Richard Reynell of East Ogwell near Newton Abbot,

> having charge of a troop of horsemen, did special good services; when in suppressing and confounding those traytors, he being sorely wounded, and hurt, it pleased the king's majesty ... to grant his warrant to ... [Russell] then general of those wars, for the rewarding the said Richard Reynell with the demesnes of Weston-Peverell and house called Pennicross ... near Plymouth.[111]

Reynell may well have been hurt during the course of a fight in the South Hams: conceivably when Plymouth was recaptured from the rebels.

Even as Herbert was stamping down the last embers of rebellion in South Devon, Russell was advancing across the Tamar – and by Tuesday, 20 August, he and his army were at Launceston, which the Carews had evidently taken possession of the day before.[112] Writing to Thynne from Launceston on that day, Sir Hugh Paulet triumphantly informed him that 'I trust thys busyness now resteth yn good staye for ... the viiith conflycte with the rebellys ended on Saterday last [*sic*], yn which byckerynge I dare affyrme there hath ben ii M [i.e. 2000] trayters slayne'.[113] 'Humfrey Arundell and all the chief rebels ... being left yn lyff are [now] yn warde,' Paulet went on, 'and the ... Mount is repossessed, so as I hope the weight of theys rebellion ys overpassed, with such a skowrge that the memoryall wyll not be lightly forgotten.' The implication of these final words, of course, was that the slaughter of the insurgents had been so great that it would serve as a brutal object lesson to anyone who might be tempted to rebel again in future. Even so, Paulet was forced to acknowledge that

> yt semyth requsyst that the countrey be kept in staye by a good power for a tyme, because the people shew themselfes to be very tyckell and redy to ryse again yn sundry places yf they might receve ... any convenient ayde to their purpose, being skarsely well qualyfyed [i.e., subdued] at this present yn the North partes of Devon and the borders of Somerset ioyninge apon the same.[114]

This is a remarkable statement, because it demonstrates that – despite the bloody slaughter of the previous weeks – West Country folk were still looking for any possible opportunity to resume the fight. Paulet was quite right to see North Devon and West Somerset as a continuing focus of resistance, moreover, for while the privy councillors were able to boast on 24 August that, in Devon, 'the contrie commethe in daly . . . by . . . thousands to crave their pardon', and that three of the Devon 'capitaynes' who had previously remained at large – including Sir Thomas Pomeroy – had now come in to give themselves up, they were also forced to admit that John Bury and several of the other rebel leaders who had 'escaped from the sword have attempted in the meane seson to stirr up Somersetshire, and have gotten them a band or camp'.[115] It has tended to be assumed that the group of insurgents who marched into Somerset from Devon at this time had done so after having retreated up the Exe Valley from the siege of Exeter. Yet this was clearly not the case, for Hooker's unpublished narrative specifically states that it was after the battle fought at Sampford Courtenay that 'sundrie of the Cornishemen & other [rebels] dwelling in the parts not farr from thence . . . hopeinge . . . to finde some better fortune . . . [fled] to the number of a Thousand persons . . . into Somersettshere'.[116] This statement not only makes it clear that the rebels who revived the flame of insurrection in Somerset had made their way there from Sampford Courtenay, therefore, it also shows that among these die-hards were many Cornishmen. The fact that Hooker goes on to state that 'one Coffin a gentleman' was the rebels' chief captain is also intriguing, because – if this was the same 'Captain Coffen' who is known to have been active near Pendennis some weeks before – his presence would tend to confirm that Arundell had, indeed, brought up reinforcements from West Cornwall in order to stiffen his forces immediately before the battle of Sampford Courtenay. However this may be, Russell was determined to ensure that Bury, Coffin and their followers were crushed as quickly as possible, and he therefore ordered Paulet and Sir Peter Carew to ride eastwards from Launceston 'with a great companie' to hunt them down.[117]

Meanwhile, royal control was being re-established across the whole of Cornwall. Russell himself appears to have advanced as far west as Bodmin over the next day or two.[118] John Winslade was captured here and was subsequently interrogated by Russell himself, while 'the servants of the Lord Grey' rode as far south as Pelynt near Looe, on the

South Cornish coast, in order to rifle Winslade's house at Tregarrick.[119] Another of the Cornish rebel leaders, James Rosogan, is known to have been buried in his home parish of St Columb Major on 25 August: having perhaps fallen victim to summary justice.[120] In the far west of the county, too, all resistance was by now at an end. As Paulet's letter shows, the Mount had already been recaptured by 20 August, while the fact that Killigrew ceased paying the additional soldiers whom he had retained on that same day strongly suggests that the siege of Pendennis came to an end at around the same time.[121] We may be sure that royal authority was swiftly reasserted over the whole of the Meneage, moreover, for, on 24 August, two more local priests, John Wolcock, vicar of Manaccan, and 'Robert Raffe', vicar of St Keverne, were led out to be hanged at St Keverne as 'Rebellyers'.[122] The document that records their fate – an inventory of the two men's goods, which, like the goods of all 'traitors' taken in arms, were forfeit to the Crown – does not state why it had been decided to execute Wolcock alongside Raffe at St Keverne, but it is surely possible to guess. It was at St Keverne, after all, that the 'Cornish commotion' – the rising that contemporaries viewed as the prelude to the Western Rebellion – had begun in April 1548, so, by staging the public execution of Wolcock and Raffe here in August 1549, the local gentry governors were demonstrating that the wheel had come full circle, and that those who had sowed the storm had reaped the whirlwind.[123] Were Wolcock and Raffe hanged from the tower of St Keverne church? The record is silent, but the fate of Robert Welsh of St Thomas and of the rebel cleric from Oxfordshire who had been hanged from the steeple of his own church in July makes it seem all too probable that they were.

By the time that Wolcock and Raffe were led out to their execution, only one group of rebels remained in arms: the thousand or so men who had fled eastwards to Somerset in the wake of the battle of Sampford Courtenay under the conduct of Bury and Coffin.[124] It seems possible that, as they hastened through Somerset in the general direction of Frome during the final week of August, the members of this last rebel band were still hoping against hope that they might somehow be able to rekindle the flames of rebellion in the district in which the popular protests against enclosure in the West Country had first broken out some four months before. Yet time was running out for Bury and Coffin, for the horsemen whom Russell had sent from Launceston to pursue them were by now closing in fast and, on 27 August, Paulet and his company finally 'overtooke' the rebel band at the little hilltop village of Kingweston, 3 miles north-east of Somerton.[125] Little is known about the engagement that followed, but many years later Henry Lyte, a local gentleman, was to recall that his father had often told him that, when he was a boy, 'at the commotion tyme', he had been 'holpen . . . upp' into a tree by one of his father's servants in order to 'see the skurmyshe in Kingwestons lease'.[126] Lyte's description of the fight between the king's troops and the rebels as a 'skirmish' suggests that it had not lasted all that long, while his statement that the encounter had taken place 'in Kingwestons lease' permits us to identify the probable site of the engagement as an area of grassland named 'Bushy Leaze', which is shown lying adjacent to the 'Great Common' to the south of Kingweston church in a map of 1839.[127] Beyond this, all that can be said for sure is that the insurgents were 'overthrown', that many of them – including Bury and Coffin – were captured, and that Coffin was carried as a prisoner into Exeter.[128]

A list of expenses drawn up at this time at the direction of Sir John Thynne, then serving as the sheriff of both Somerset and Dorset, sheds a gruesome light on the fate of the ordinary rebels who were captured at Kingweston. Initially, the captives appear to have been dragged to the nearby market town of Bruton. Then, on 29 August, 104 men were brought from Bruton to the cathedral city of Wells, where they were tied up with cords and imprisoned for eight days. Two other captives were conveyed directly to Bath, where, the list recorded, 'they suffered as was appointed' and were hanged in irons. It may well be that the rest of the prisoners had already been sentenced to death, for, over the following days, a series of executions took place at ten more Somerset towns and villages, while three batches of prisoners were pardoned and released.[129] That so many executions took place in Somerset indicates that a number of local men had joined the rebels who had escaped from Sampford Courtenay – and, indeed, the indictment against John Bury was later to state that, not only at Kingweston, but at several other places in Somerset besides, he had 'by proclamation and hue and cry raise[d] a great multitude, to the amount of 1500 persons'.[130] The local gentry governors had had every reason to be alarmed by this final, flaming comet of rebellion, therefore, and this undoubtedly helps to explain the savagery with which they now treated the captured insurgents. It comes as little surprise to find that several executions were staged in Frome, where the disturbances in the West of England had first broken out in May, or to find that those who suffered here were hanged, drawn and quartered. Thynne made payments at Frome not only for wood for a fire to burn the executed men's 'entrails', but also for 'a pan and trivet' to 'seeth' the victims' severed limbs: presumably before these ghastly memorials were coated with tar and placed on public display.[131] And as the executioner and his assistants went about their grisly work in Frome, a similar reckoning was being exacted across the length and breadth of Devon and Cornwall.

# *Part III*
## *The Aftermath*

# 7

## Retribution
### September 1549

As August passed away into September, the black tide of repression that had already swept from one end of the West Country to the other in the wake of the royal army continued to overflood the land: with hundreds, if not thousands, of local people being punished for the parts which they had played in the rebellion. The most high-profile victims, of course, were the surviving rebel leaders, whom the privy councillors had been determined to apprehend, to interrogate and to make a terrible example of from the moment that the first stirs in Devon began.[1] The protector himself had pointedly reminded Russell of his expectations in this regard three days after the relief of Exeter, when he had told the king's lieutenant in the West that 'we wold gladlye here of Humfray Arondells doyyngs and demeanour, and how ye shall demeane yourself with hyme [i.e., when Russell had at length interrogated him], whome we trust shortyle ye shall have in yo[ur] hands'. Somerset had then gone on to stress that it was crucial 'for the Kyng's Ma[jes]ties honor' that Arundell, Winslade and Underhill – whom he clearly regarded as the three key rebel leaders – should not 'escape due ponyshment; but [rather] that the[i]r example shuld be [a] terror this great while to all the countrey', and serve as a warning to local people 'not to attempt such kynd of rebellion agayne'.[2] Russell can have been left in no doubt whatsoever that Somerset expected him to capture the chief rebel leaders alive if possible, therefore, and to question them closely about the origins of the insurrection before consigning them to their inevitable fate. Over the following weeks he strained every nerve to bring about the successful apprehension of these men.

## I

The first of the rebel 'captains' to fall into Russell's hands had been Sir Thomas Pomeroy, who had been captured in the wake of the battle at Clyst St Mary and, presumably, interrogated by the lord privy seal or by one of his senior commanders soon afterwards. Rather surprisingly, Russell appears to have concluded, from these initial investigations, that it would be politic to treat Sir Thomas with kid gloves, for, in a lost letter sent to the Council, he had asked for their permission to grant Pomeroy a pardon. Writing back to him on 10 August, the councillors had readily agreed to this request, merely stipulating that the pardon should be granted to Pomeroy 'secretlie', and that he should be 'traveled with', or worked upon, 'all that tyme of the promise thereof, for sp[ec]iall service to be fyrst done by hym ... in the apprehendyng of Humfray Arandell, Underhill, or some other of the most notable'.[3] The councillors were content that a pardon should be offered to Pomeroy, in other words, but only on condition that he first provide Russell with information that would lead to the capture of the key rebel leaders. The fact that Pomeroy was later described as 'a symple gente' makes it seem probable that, after having captured Sir Thomas, the lord privy seal had concluded that the rebel knight was a man of limited intellect, rather than one of those who had actually directed the insurrection, and that it would therefore make sense to offer this gullible – and potentially malleable – individual a pardon, in the hope that he would subsequently help Russell to reel in the bigger fish.[4]

'Symple' Pomeroy may have been, but he was clearly not without guile, for within days of his initial apprehension, he had somehow succeeded in making his escape, prompting the Council to write to Russell, in a subsequent letter, that 'ye do well to make the most diligent serche ye maie for Sir Thomas Pomeraie'.[5] Meanwhile, Russell had succeeded in apprehending a second rebel leader, Robert Paget, who appears – rather remarkably – to have been the brother of Somerset's close ally and fellow privy councillor, Sir William Paget.[6] The lord privy seal, understandably enough, had been uncertain as to how he should proceed in such a ticklish case and, in one of his lost letters, he had evidently asked the Council for their guidance on the matter. Russell's query had elicited a brusque response from Somerset, however, who had promptly written back to stress that, if it could be demonstrated that Paget had indeed been a 'Captyon of rebellion', then he should receive 'indyfferent justice', whatever his family connections. Somerset's clear implication was that Paget should be executed at once – as a number of the other subaltern rebel leaders had already been – rather than sent up to London for further examination.[7] This seems puzzling, for one might well have expected the protector to have regarded a rebel captain who possessed a sibling on the Council as someone whose activities cried out for the most thorough and searching investigation. That Somerset should have chosen to indicate to Russell that Robert Paget should be hanged with all speed instead, therefore, suggests, either that the protector had possessed complete trust in Sir William Paget's loyalty and had thus been anxious to spare him the public embarrassment that the incarceration of his rebel brother in the Tower would inevitably cause, or else that he had feared that, if Paget were closely interrogated, facts might emerge that would cause dissension to erupt among the privy councillors and would therefore destabilise the regime. Whatever the truth may have been, Russell clearly disregarded Somerset's instructions and continued to hold this disconcertingly well-connected rebel captain as a prisoner instead, for, a month later, the protector sent Russell a curt letter noting that he could not but 'marvel' that Paget was still alive and ordering that he be executed at once. Paget's eventual fate is unknown.[8]

As the royal army had advanced westwards during mid-August, several other rebel leaders had been swept up in the dragnet. Thus Maunder, the shoemaker, had been captured on the eve of the battle of Sampford Courtenay, as we have already seen, while Humphrey Arundell had been apprehended at Launceston on 19 August.[9] It seems probable that Henry Bray, the mayor of Bodmin – who had evidently marched into Devon with the main body of the Cornish host in mid-July – had been captured at around the same time, for, on 21 August, the Council had written to Russell directing him '[to] send up hither as [soon as] ye can conveniently Humfray Arundell; Maunder; the mayor of Bodmin, and ii or iii of the most rankest Traytors and ringleders of them here to be examined, and after to be determined of as shall apperteyne'.[10] There is no evidence to show that Maunder and Bray were ever sent up to the capital, so it may well be that – after Russell had gone on to capture a number of the rebels' gentlemen-leaders over the following days – he had decided that the shoemaker and the mayor, both of whom were commoners, were second-rank captains and might therefore be either executed or imprisoned locally. Another leading rebel, Thomas Holmes of Blisland – who was later alleged to have raised '1,000 persons' in Bodmin on 1 August, whence they had presumably advanced into Devon – may also have been captured on or around 18 August, for he later deposed that he had 'contynued amonge the rebells unto th'end of the matter ... and was in the fyld when the fray was'; probably a reference to the battle of Sampford Courtenay.[11]

John Winslade – together, perhaps, with his son, William, who was later to be listed among the chief rebel captives – had been apprehended at Bodmin a day or two after the royal army had marched into Launceston, while the elusive Pomeroy had evidently been recaptured at about the same time, for, on 24 August, the Council had written to the English ambassador at the imperial court, Sir Philip Hoby, informing him that 'the Devonshire men are well chastised & appeased' and adding that 'three ... of their capitaynes have voluntarily come in and ... submitted them self: Sir Thomas Pomeroy, knight, Wies and Harries, who before were fled and could not be found'.[12] As we shall see in a moment, independent evidence now permits us to identify the other two rebel 'captains' who had 'come in' at the same time as Pomeroy. One of them was William Harris, the eldest son of John Harris of Hayne in West Devon, who was himself a serjeant at law and the former recorder, or retained legal adviser, of the city of Exeter.[13] The other was John Wise of Sydenham in Marystow, again in West Devon, who had married Alice Harris, John Harris's daughter, and was therefore William Harris's brother-in-law.[14] These were both substantial men, and it therefore comes as little surprise to find that, after having learned of the capture of the Devon rebel captains, the councillors had issued a new instruction to Russell on 27 August, directing him 'to geve order for the sure sendying upp . . . hither unto us, not only of Humfrey Arundell, but also of Pomery, Wyse and young Harrys, whome we intend to examyne here to pyke out of them further matter'.[15] (Conceivably, it was after receiving this new directive to convey Arundell and the three Devon gentlemen to London that Russell had decided not to send up Maunder and Bray as the Council had originally requested.) On the same day that this letter was written, John Bury and the gentleman known only as 'Coffin' had been captured at Kingweston, whence they had subsequently been taken to Exeter, meaning that, by now, the king's forces in the West had at last succeeded in securing 'all of the cheefe & princypall [rebel] Capitaynes' who remained alive.[16]

In late August, Russell returned from Bodmin to Exeter, bringing his most important captives with him.[17] He had already 'examined', or interrogated, John Winslade in person, as had Lord Grey, while – presumably soon after his arrival in the city – Russell is stated to have questioned Bury, too. Sir Hugh Paulet had interrogated Arundell, meanwhile, and 'Mr Herbert' – probably Sir William Herbert – had interrogated Holmes.[18] The precise nature of these 'examinations' is left unspecified, but it seems fair to assume that they were of a sufficiently robust nature. Even so, Russell and his senior commanders were not experienced interrogators, they did not know precisely what information Somerset and his fellow councillors were most anxious to wring from those whom they termed the 'arch-traytors' – and they did not have access to the grim and uniquely persuasive engines of torture which were housed in the Tower.[19] In early September, therefore, Russell despatched his principal captives to London under the conduct of Lord Grey and Zanga's band of Albanian horse, whose services were now desperately needed elsewhere.[20] Russell's decision to provide Arundell and his fellows with such a formidable escort may also have been partly influenced by the careful instructions that the councillors had sent him on this subject just a few days before. 'When ye send upp the prysoners, we do not doubt but that ye will send them upp strongly [guarded] enough', they had begun, adding that Russell should instruct those who were given the task of escorting the prisoners that, if any attempt should be made to rescue them, they should be killed at once, that their guards 'may geve accompt of them to us, quik or dead'.[21]

Grey and his reluctant travelling companions clearly made good time. On 9 September, Sir Richard Scudamore – a gentleman of evangelical leanings, who acted as Sir Philip Hoby's financial agent in London – wrote to Hoby from his house at the Black Friars, in order to provide his friend with the latest news from the capital.[22] 'It may please yow to be advertesyed,' Scudamore began, 'that yesterday my Lord Grey arrived at the courte and brought with hym certeyn of the captaynez of the traytours of the West contry.' Among their number, Scudamore continued, were

> Humfrey Arrundell; [John] Wynslade and his sonne; [John] Bery; Coffyn; Sergeant Harryes eldyst sonne [i.e., William Harris]; [John] Wyes, Sergeant Harryes sonne yn lawe; [William] Fortescue [an individual whose identity remains obscure, but who probably belonged to a branch of the Devon gentry family of that name] and [Thomas] Holmes.[23]

Intriguingly, Scudamore paused to note, in passing, that 'thes last two weare Sir Thomas Arondelles men', before remarking that the nine 'traytours' whom he had already listed had been accompanied by 'one other, who was theyr clerk, whos name I knowe nott'.[24] (This was a reference to the man referred to only as 'Castell', who, as we shall see, was later said to have served as Humphrey Arundell's secretary during the commotion.) That Scudamore should have gone out of his way to note a connection between Fortescue and Holmes and Sir Thomas Arundell – himself the brother of that same Sir John Arundell of Lanherne who was already immured in the Tower on suspicion of having encouraged the rebellion – strongly suggests that whispers were by this time circulating in the capital that both Sir Thomas *and* Sir John Arundell had been complicit in the insurrection that had been led by their cousin, Humphrey. Independent evidence that at least two of the captured rebels were believed to possess a direct link with the Arundells of Lanherne is provided by the comment made many years later by John Hooker, in his printed narrative of the rebellion, that 'Coffin and Holmes' had been 'servants to Sir John Arundell, knight'.[25]

The fact that Scudamore, writing in the immediate aftermath of the insurrection, stated that Fortescue and Holmes had been servants of Sir Thomas Arundell, whereas Hooker, writing at some time before 1587, stated that *Coffin* and Holmes had been servants of Sir *John* Arundell, is a little confusing, of course, and, in the absence of further evidence, we cannot know which of these two statements most closely approximates to the truth. Nevertheless, that Hooker should have chosen – in the concluding paragraph of the last, the most detailed and the most frankly worded of all of his narratives of the Western Rising – to make a direct and unambiguous link between two of the leading rebel captains and Sir John Arundell – an individual who features nowhere else in Hooker's text – seems highly significant, and surely hints at a settled conviction, on the Exeter chronicler's part, that the Western Rebellion had received strong encouragement from Lanherne. Nor were Scudamore and Hooker the only contemporaries to nurse such suspicions, as Chapter 8 will make clear.

It is perhaps worth noting here that, although Scudamore and Hooker described Fortescue, Coffin and Holmes as 'servants' of the Arundells, this should not be taken to imply that the three rebel captains were individuals of low social status. On the contrary, as we have already seen, all nine of the captives who were brought up to London in September 1549 appear to have been gentlemen, apart from Holmes – and even he was a prosperous yeoman. The fact that, a year later, the printer and translator Walter Lynne – himself a Londoner and therefore someone who might conceivably have watched the prisoners being brought into the capital with his own eyes – recorded that 'the Cornysh and Devonshyre men' had been defeated and 'many of their gentilmen taken' tends to underscore this point – and reminds us just how socially elevated the leaders of the Western Rebellion appear to have been in comparison with the leaders of the other risings that had taken place elsewhere in the country in 1549.[26]

Following their arrival at the court at Westminster, Scudamore went on to inform Hoby, the captured rebel leaders 'were brought to stand all togeather [so] that the kynges maiestye (standing upon the leades) might see them'.[27] The picture of the boy-king gazing down impassively from the roof of his palace upon the bedraggled group of men who, just a few weeks before, had been marching at the head of an army that was determined to reverse his government's religious policies is a poignant one, and it is impossible not to suspect that – as Edward's eye roved over the dejected 'arch-traitors' who had been assembled for his delectation far below – he must have wondered what his own fate might have been, had Russell's army failed to defeat the insurgents. After the king had viewed the rebel leaders, Scudamore went on, 'they weare brought before the counsel, and, after examynacyon . . . weare conducted by my Lord Greyes men furth, and soe on horseback without saddelles . . . were conveyed towardes London with the band of Albaneyses attending upon them'.[28] Scudamore's observation that the western rebels had been compelled to ride to the capital without saddles reveals that they had shared in the humiliation of the East Anglian rebel leader Robert Kett and his brother William, who – after having been captured and carried up to London following the defeat of their own forces in Norfolk in late August, and brought to the court 'pynned by th'armes in penny halters' – had been forced to undertake a similar journey just two days before.[29] In a letter written to Hoby on 7 September, Scudamore had crowed that the Londoners had 'suffycent[ly] wondry[d]' at Kett as he had passed through the streets of the capital on his way to prison, and that the rebel leader had ridden 'not lyke no stoute captain, for his saddell was but a shyp skynne'.[30] We may presume that the same thing could have been said of Arundell and his fellows as they were conveyed by Zanga's men through those same streets just two days later.

Once the members of this tragicomic parade had arrived at Fleet Bridge – which straddled the Fleet ditch, just outside the city's Lud gate – William Winslade, Harris, Wise and Fortescue, together with Castell, were detached from the rest of the company and confined in the Fleet prison, in present-day Farringdon Street. Arundell, John Winslade, Coffin, Bury and Holmes, meanwhile – who were clearly regarded as the most important of the captives – 'weare caryed throwgh London to the Towre'. By the end of that day, only a single, straggling member of the unhappy band of men whom Grey had brought up to London remained unconfined: Scudamore concluded his account of the western rebels' arrival in the capital by observing that 'I had almost forgotten one traytor, Sir Thomas Pomeroy, who remayneth at Hownslowe very syke, or ells he had borne companye with the rest'.[31] It is clear that, at some subsequent point, the ailing Pomeroy was brought up to the capital from Hounslow – then a village, lying some 12 miles to the west of Westminster – and incarcerated with the first group of rebel leaders in the Fleet.[32]

After the doors of their respective prisons had clanged shut behind them, nothing further was heard of the rebel leaders for almost two months. We must presume that all nine men underwent intensive interrogation – and that the information which Castell provided against his former comrades proved especially damning. In a note that they had earlier appended to the list of individuals whom they were sending up to the Council 'from the Weste p[ar]tes', Russell, Grey and Herbert had been at pains to stress that Castell – who, they observed, had acted as 'Secretary to Arundell *by compulsyon*' during the rebellion – was not being despatched to London as a prisoner, but rather as 'th'accuser of Arundell and Coffyne'.[33] This conjunction is interesting in itself, and suggests that Russell and the others saw Coffin as one of the most important of the rebel leaders. Having commended Castell to Somerset and urged the protector to act as 'good Lorde' to him, Russell and his colleagues had then gone on to note, not only that Castell had 'come in' to them voluntarily, but also that 'in the myddes of the hottest sturre he [had] sent his secret advertisement to Mr Godolphin and other [loyalist] gentilmen of so much as he knewe of Arundell his procedinge': words that perhaps provide still further support for the theory that Godolphin had managed to remain at liberty – presumably in Pendennis Castle – throughout the course of the rebellion.[34] Who Castell was remains unclear. It has been suggested that he might well have been a relative of that John Kestell of Kestell, in Egloshaye in Cornwall, who had married Jackett, the daughter of John Coffin of Portledge in North Devon – perhaps himself a relative of the rebel leader of the same surname – during the reign of Henry VIII.[35] This is an attractive theory, though for the moment it remains impossible to prove. What is hard to doubt is that Castell, as Arundell's former secretary, would have possessed a mass of incriminating evidence at his fingertips and would therefore have proved extremely useful to those who interrogated the rebel leaders.

Arundell, Bury, John Winslade and Holmes were later to inform the king's attorney that, after having first been questioned by Russell and his commanders in the West, they had subsequently gone on to be 'examined' by the lord chancellor, Sir Richard Rich (in Bury's case), and by 'Mr Smyth', 'Mr North' and 'Mr Mason'. These three individuals were probably Sir Thomas Smith and Sir Edward North – both, like Rich, members of the Privy Council – and Sir John Mason, who was the king's secretary for the French tongue, and was also later to be appointed to the Council.[36] Rich was notorious as the man who, in 1546, had himself turned the wheels of the rack on the heretic Anne Askew – the only woman who is known to have been tortured in the Tower – and while there is no hard evidence to show that Arundell and his fellows were subject to similar treatment, it seems all too probable that they were. Certainly, Somerset had been stressing to Russell from as early as 29 June that, if those who had been behind the initial stirs in Devon should refuse to reveal 'the fyrst and orgynall begynnyngs hereof' after they had, at length, been captured, then they should be 'sent hether upp to us' so that they 'wold upon the rack or terror confesse'.[37] The fact that 'Coffin' was never referred to again after his confinement in the Tower on 9 September seems ominous, and raises the possibility that he may have died there at some point over the succeeding weeks: perhaps as a result of torture or some other form of deliberate mistreatment, perhaps as a result of simple illness.

## II

As the men who had been identified as 'the arch-traitors' did their best to adjust themselves to conditions in the Fleet and the Tower, fate had already caught up with many of the individuals whom the regime and its apologists had consistently portrayed as the second-rank stirrers of sedition during the summer of 1549: traditionalist priests. Ever since the break with Rome, conservative clerics had found themselves squarely in Henry VIII's sights, with the old king periodically subjecting such individuals to threats and occasional harsh punishments, as well as to public mockery and abuse. As early as June 1535, for example, Henry – in holiday mood following the execution just the day before of John Fisher, bishop of Rochester, for opposing his divorce – had attended an outdoor pageant, based on the Book of Revelation, which had treated its audience to a graphic representation of several ecclesiastical figures being decapitated. It was noted at the time that the king had made a special point of showing himself at this spectacle, 'in order to laugh at his ease, and encourage the people' – and that he had sent a letter to Anne Boleyn advising her not to miss the repeat performance, which was planned for a few days' time.[38]

Two years later, Henry had been driven to paroxysms of fury by the participation of many monks and priests in the Pilgrimage of Grace, and had personally directed that the most fearful punishments should be inflicted upon the offenders, ordering the earl of Derby to apprehend 'the late abbot and monks' of Sawley, for example, 'and, without any manner of delay, in their monks' apparel, [to] cause them to be hanged up as most errant traitors'. A few days later, Henry had reiterated this bloodthirsty order, and had provided still more precise instructions about how the monks were to be punished, telling Derby that, if he found that they had encouraged the protests in any way, he should 'cause the said abbot and ... the chief of the monks to be hanged upon long pieces of timber ... out of the steeple, and the rest to be put to execution in sundry places as you shall think meet for the example of others'.[39] In the end, the disturbed state of the country had made it impossible for Derby to put these savage orders into effect, but, after the pilgrims had been dispersed and the duke of Norfolk had been sent into the North as the king's lieutenant there – in which capacity he possessed the power to impose martial law and to pass summary judgement upon offenders – a number of clerics had been executed.[40] Two canons of Warter Priory had been 'hanged in chains' at York, for example, while the subprior of

Watton had suffered the same grisly fate at his own priory.[41] Further executions had followed during the later 1530s and, throughout the rest of Henry's reign, clerics accused of remaining loyal to the pope had continued to be executed from time to time as traitors.[42]

The regime of Protector Somerset had maintained an equally hostile attitude towards 'popish priests'. As we have seen, Somerset himself had ordered that 'a lewd priest' from West Cornwall should be brought up to London for questioning in 1547, while, during the following year, the evangelical establishment had chosen to single out the priest Martin Geffrey as the most important leader of the 'Cornish commotion', and had ensured that, after his trial at Westminster, he had been hanged, drawn and quartered at Tyburn. It is striking, too, that, from the moment that they had been informed of the major rebellion in the West during the following year, the privy councillors had laid the blame for the rising squarely at the door of conservative priests – and that Somerset had initially been convinced that the vicar of Sampford Courtenay was one of the chief rebel captains. The outbreak of the disturbances in Oxfordshire soon afterwards, moreover – disturbances in which a number of priests had been involved – had only confirmed the councillors in their belief that the widespread popular unrest that they were then facing across the south of the kingdom had been, in large part, clerically inspired. After he had crushed the Oxfordshire rebels in July, Lord Grey had gone on to take advantage of several recent proclamations directing that those who participated in unlawful assemblies should be proceeded against according to martial law.[43] On 19 July, he had ordered the local gentry governors to execute a dozen of the captured rebels – including, significantly, four priests – at various places in the county and, perhaps drawing inspiration from Henry VIII's orders of 1536, had given specific instruction that the vicar of Chipping Norton should be hanged from his own church steeple.[44] Henry Joyes had been duly executed soon afterwards, as had at least one other local cleric.[45] Grey's actions had set a grim precedent, therefore – and within days he and his troops had set off to join Russell's forces in Devon.

As Grey had hastened westwards, damning new evidence linking priests with the much bigger insurrection that was then raging in Devon and Cornwall had emerged. In late July, as we have seen, the western rebels had composed a fresh list of 'articles' and had sent them up to London. Among these was one which had not only demanded that John Moreman and Richard Crispin – the two conservative cathedral canons who had been imprisoned for their doctrine during the previous year – should be released from the Tower, but which had also stipulated that the king himself should provide these men with 'certain livyinges' in the West Country, so that they might 'preache amonges us our Catholycke fayth'.[46] It is easy to imagine the privy councillors grinding their teeth in fury as they read these defiant words, which plainly demonstrated the inspiration the protestors had drawn from the example of the incarcerated canons. Nor was this all, for the new set of articles had also supplied irrefutable proof that priests were playing an active role in the rebellion itself. The document had been signed by a number of the leading protestors, including four men who had proudly, if unwisely, described themselves as 'the Governours of the [rebel] Campes'; among these last had been 'John Tompson Pryeste' and 'Roger Barret Prieste'.[47] By late July, therefore, the regime and its allies had been given good reason to conclude that their suspicions that conservative priests had played a crucial role in stirring up the protests in the West had been fully justified – and this in its turn had plainly encouraged them to adopt an increasingly harsh attitude towards clergymen who were known, or suspected, to hold traditionalist views.

Soon after the final set of rebel articles had appeared, they had been printed in London alongside a copy of a letter from an anonymous Devon gentleman serving in Russell's forces, who had signed himself only as 'R.L.'. What makes this missive especially interesting from the point of view of the present discussion is the violent antipathy that it breathes towards priests. R.L. had made it clear, from the start of his letter, that he blamed conservative clerics just as much as the rebels' lay leaders for causing the stirs in the first place, and that he believed there to be many 'priestes' in the rebels' ranks.[48] R.L. had then turned to comment on the Crown's recent suppression of other risings elsewhere, and had praised the Council for having tempered justice with mercy when it came to punishing the ordinary 'offendours'. Nevertheless, he had gone on, 'to say my mynde . . . yf the Kynges sworde light[ed] shorte upon any [during the suppression of these stirs] it was upon . . . ranke Popish priestes, repining against the kynges . . . doctrine'. Having made it clear that he believed that 'rebel' priests had got away far too lightly in the wake of the other risings, R.L. had declared that, if martial law were imposed 'in every shire', then the current disturbances would soon be brought to an end.[49] R.L.'s letter provides us with one of the few glimpses we have of attitudes towards priests among the West Country gentlemen who had come in to join the royal army in East Devon in July 1549. His lapidary words make it clear that, even before Russell had been joined by Grey and his men – who had shown no compunction about making a brutal example of rebel clerics in Oxfordshire – there had been some in Russell's camp who had been advocating similarly radical measures. And after battle had finally been joined in East Devon a few days later, and the royal forces had encountered a number of rebel priests fighting in the field, clerical fatalities had swiftly begun to mount: partly as a result of deaths in action, partly as a result of the operation of summary justice.

Writing to Sir John Thynne on 16 August, the loyalist gentleman John Fry had first informed his correspondent of the many captives whom Russell had taken during the recent fighting around Exeter, and had then gone on to observe that

> the most part of them, & of such other as were taken prisoners, have confessyd that the prestes have ben the great occasion of thys comociọn [and that] further in every of the said fyghtes ther were dyvers prystes in the fyld fighting ayenst us, & some of them slayne at every fyghte.[50]

Fry's words not only provide further evidence of the fact that local loyalists had believed priests to be playing a crucial role in the rebel host, they also demonstrate that a number of rebel priests had already been killed in the fighting. By this time, moreover, Russell had clearly begun to exercise the brutal punitive powers he had been afforded as the king's lieutenant in the West. Hooker specifically notes that Robert Welsh –

the vicar of St Thomas, who was hanged from his own church tower soon after the relief of Exeter – 'was *by order of the marshall law* condemned to death'.[51]

Once Devonian loyalists had started to emerge from the woodwork in the wake of Russell's victories around Exeter, priests who were either known or believed to have supported the insurrection had clearly been targeted for bloody revenge. On 14 August, for example, one of the servants of the earl of Bath – whose family seat lay in North Devon, but who appears to have been either absent or lying low over the previous three months – had ordered a number of men from the countryside around Barnstaple to help him to arrest the parson of Bittadon and the curate of Pilton, both of whom were alleged to have been rebels. The parson had managed to escape, but the luckless curate had been apprehended and subsequently hanged in chains at Pilton, it was later recalled, 'to the example of all others' by virtue of a warrant from Russell '& by the marcyall lawes'.[52] Following the defeat of the rebels at Sampford Courtenay, and the advance of Russell's forces over the Tamar, similar executions of 'rebel' priests had occurred in Cornwall. As we have seen, an inventory preserved in the National Archives reveals that, on 24 August, Robert Raffe, the vicar of St Keverne, and John Wolcock, the vicar of the nearby parish of Manaccan, had been hanged by local loyalists as 'rebellyers' and their goods confiscated by the Crown.[53]

We can be certain that Raffe and Wolcock had not been the only Cornish priests to have suffered upon the gallows, moreover. Writing many years later, the Protestant historian and martyrologist John Foxe was to observe that 'of Priestes, which were principall sturrers [of the rising], and some of them Governours of the [rebel] campes and after executed, were to the number of VIII, whose names were Rob[ert] Bochim, John Tompson, Rog[er] Barret, John Wolcocke, Will[iam] Alsa, James Mourton, John Barow [and] Rich[ard] Benet'.[54] Wolcock we have already met, while Alsa and Bennet were the incumbents of the Cornish parishes of Gulval and St Veep, respectively.[55] Bochim was perhaps a relative of John Bochym, of Bochym in Cury parish in the Lizard: another reputed rebel.[56] The benefices, if any, of the other four priests referred to by Foxe are unknown, but these individuals may well have been Cornishmen, too, for it seems probable that Foxe took his information from a contemporary list of clerical executions that had been carried out specifically in Cornwall (none of the priests to whom Foxe refers is known to have been a Devon man). Nor does this exhaust the tally of known Cornish clerical casualties, moreover, for Robert Royse – the incumbent of St Cleer, who was later noted to have been 'attainted' at some time prior to March 1550 – surely met his end in the aftermath of the Western Rising, too.[57]

It seems fair to assume that most of the priests who fell victim to summary justice in Devon and Cornwall were executed soon after the royal forces had regained control: that is to say, during late August and early September. Nor was it in the West Country alone that supporters of the regime were believed to be taking a violent revenge on traditionalist clergymen at this time, for, on 5 September, Hoby's evangelical correspondent, Sir Richard Scudamore, wrote from London to inform him that the earl of Warwick was then in Norfolk 'mynystreng justyce upon dyvers of the ryngleders' of the recent rebellion there, 'amongst whom', Scudamore noted with grim satisfaction, 'ther goeth many preestes to wrake [i.e., there are many priests who suffer]'.[58] Only one priest is definitely known to have played a leading role in Kett's rebellion and, as neither he nor any other local cleric can be shown for certain to have been executed after the risings in East Anglia had been suppressed, it is possible that Scudamore was misinformed.[59] Quite conceivably, he was conflating reports from the West – where, as we have seen, a string of clerical executions undoubtedly did take place in the immediate aftermath of the 'commotion' – with reports from East Anglia, where, as far as we know, all of those who were executed by the loyalists after Kett's eventual defeat were laymen. Whatever the truth may be, Scudamore's words provide further evidence of the pitiless attitude towards conservative clerics that had become so commonplace among regime loyalists by the autumn of 1549. It is clear that, in the West Country at least, public executions of those who were regarded as 'rebel priests' had continued until as late as October.[60]

Writing in 1753 – and almost certainly drawing on the parish registers of Stratton, now sadly lost – a local antiquary observed that 'one

Simon Mourton, vicar ... of Poundstock, was hanged at the market house of Stratton for high treason' in the aftermath of the rebellion. 'He was hanged upon the 13th day of October 1549', the antiquary went on, 'and buried the 18th day of the same month', adding piquantly that 'the cross or pedestal whereon he hung is wanting, but the stone in which it was fixed is still to be seen'.[61] We have already encountered Simon Moreton once before and have seen that – according to a loyalist ballad published soon after the rising – he had been responsible for leading his parishioners into the field to join the rebel host. Why it should have taken more than six weeks for Moreton to be executed after the rebellion had been suppressed we will probably never know, but the fact that his body was not buried until five days after he had been hanged strongly suggests that his corpse had been left suspended from the market cross for some time in order to overawe the inhabitants of the town and the surrounding countryside. Moreton may not have suffered alone, moreover. The Stratton parish accounts, drawn up in the wake of the rising, record payments made not only for the purchase of a 'pardon' for the parishioners, but also for the erection of a gallows in the town and 'for helpyng them upe'.[62]

On the basis of the fragmentary evidence that still survives, it is clear that at least fourteen priests in Devon and Cornwall met their deaths at the hands of loyalists during the rebellion and its immediate aftermath: the thirteen executed men who have already been discussed above, and John Brown, the parson of Langtree, in North Devon, who was later noted to have been 'slayne' during 'the late commocyon'.[63] It is vital to stress that the figure for the total number of clerical fatalities that has been arrived at here is a minimum rather than a maximum one, moreover. Fry's highly revealing letter – a letter that specifically refers to rebel priests having been slain in each of the bloody engagements that took place between Russell and the insurrectionists – strongly suggests that the true number of dead priests was higher still. And, indeed, close examination of Bishop Veysey's register – a volume in which the bishop's scribe recorded the admission of new incumbents to parishes in the diocese – suggests that a significant number of the presentations made to local parishes after 1 September 1549 had been occasioned by the killing or removal of the previous incumbents. During the seven months between 1 September 1549 and 28 March 1550, the register refers to the appointment of new incumbents in six local parishes whose priests are definitely known to have been either executed or slain during the rebellion. In each case, the scribe who compiled the register simply noted that the previous incumbent had died, without specifically stating that the vacancy had occurred as the result either of 'the natural death' or the resignation of the previous incumbent – as had generally been the case when admissions had been recorded in the register before. It seems probable that these terse allusions to vacancies having arisen 'through death' were coded references to the fact that the previous incumbents had been killed during the insurrection, therefore. If this is the case, the fact that four more Devon parishes – including Marystow, John Wise's home parish – were likewise noted to have become vacant 'through death' during this same period strongly suggests that their incumbents had also died during the commotion.[64]

On 15 March 1550, the bishop's scribe made an explicit reference to the punishment of a 'rebel' priest when he recorded that the living of St Cleer had become vacant as a result of the 'attainder' of the previous incumbent.[65] But immediately after this entry, a new scribe began to compile the register: a scribe who, on 29 March, recorded the admission of a new incumbent to a living that was simply described as 'now ... vacant'.[66] This conveniently neutral formulation had not been used in the register before, but, over the following year, it was to be deployed again on no fewer than fifteen occasions.[67] It is tempting to suggest that the new scribe had resorted to this phrase in order to avoid the embarrassment of having to make further explicit references to 'rebel priests' – and that the former incumbents of at least some of the parishes whose vacant status was referred to had also died as a result of their involvement in the commotion. The register permits us to identify the priests who had previously been appointed to the benefices described as 'vacant' by the new scribe; of these sixteen men, nine disappear from the historical record after 1549.[68] Were these 'missing parsons' all priests who had been slain during the rising? It is unlikely that we will ever know, but if we conclude, first, that the benefices which the original scribe had noted as vacant 'through death' before 28 March 1550 were definitely those of men who had died during the commotion, and second, that the studiedly neutral phraseology which the new scribe began to deploy thereafter was, in some cases, intended to cloak a highly inconvenient truth, then the total number of clerical fatalities that can be either shown or strongly suspected to have occurred as a result of the rising at once goes up to between nineteen and twenty-seven. This is a substantial figure by any estimation, representing between 3 and 5 per cent of the total number of parochial clergy in the diocese, and suggesting that the Western Rebellion probably resulted in the deaths of more clerics than any other sixteenth-century popular protest, apart from the Pilgrimage of Grace.[69]

In addition to the substantial number of traditionalist clerics who were killed or executed during the rising and its immediate aftermath, there were clearly many more who were terrorised, fined or otherwise punished. The experiences of John Curtes, the parson of North Lew in West Devon, may well have been typical in this respect. In a petition for redress that he submitted some years later, during the reign of the Catholic Queen Mary, Curtes was to recall that, at the time of the 'grevous sturre, tummulte & comocyon' that had 'risen and happened amongst the ... people ... of Devon' in 1549, he had taken no part in the disturbances, 'but [had] continually kept his house & his ... parishe churche'. The form of words hints that Curtes was carefully distinguishing himself from those other local priests who had, indeed, left their homes and churches behind them in order to march into the field with the rebel host. While he had not gone so far as to join the insurgents in person, however, Curtes had clearly sympathised with their cause, for he went on to note that, throughout the course of the insurrection, he had continually 'sayd masse and other devyne service' at North Lew, 'as in the Church of this realme is now ... used & celebrated': in other words, once the rebellion had begun, he had reverted to the old – and by then officially proscribed – church service.[70] It is tempting to suggest that many other parish priests whose hearts were with the protestors – even if they were too old, too frail or too circumspect to join them in person – may have similarly continued to celebrate the old service for as long as the rebels remained in control.[71]

Once the rebellion had been crushed, however, priests who had conspicuously continued to celebrate the mass would have found themselves an obvious target for vengeful loyalists, and Curtes lamented that, as a direct result of his 'celebracion of the blessed masse ... according to the auncient and laudable use of the catholic churche', he had been 'apprehended as a traytour by one Philip Denys ... Gentilman, and by him at that tyme menaced and thretned to be hanged as a traytour for doing the same'. In words that vividly convey the atmosphere of terror which had descended across the region in the immediate aftermath of the rising, Curtes then went on to relate that, although he had known himself to be 'faultless of the said ... rebellion', yet, 'considering the perilous estate and daunger of that tyme, and perceiving diverse ... to be putt to grievous execucion that were then taken to be manyfesst and greate offenders', and 'greatly fearing the ... peril of death through greate threatenynges and menaces', he had eventually consented, 'for the saveguard of his life', to be 'bounde to such order as the said ... Denys would then take with him'. Having terrified Curtes into submission, Denys had next forced him to sign a legal document, by the terms of which the wretched cleric had promised to pay Denys £4 per annum for the rest of his life, or a fine of £60 should he ever fail to stump up. Curtes had accordingly paid £4 each year to Denys throughout the rest of Edward's reign, only daring to withhold this extorted annual payment after the young king had died and his Catholic half-sister had succeeded him. And even then, Curtes complained, Denys had had the effrontery to pursue him through the local courts for debt.[72]

Other West Country clergymen are known to have undergone similar travails in late August and September 1549. Thus, the parson of a parish near Plymouth was 'given' by Herbert to the Devon gentleman Henry Ley as a reward for the latter's service in the royal army, as we have seen, and was subsequently forced to 'ransom' himself – or buy back his freedom – at a cost of £40.[73] A similar fate befell Gabriel Morton, the vicar of Lelant, near St Ives. During the reign of Elizabeth I, it was noted that, 'in the tyme of the late wicked commosyon and rebellyon ... in Cornwall', Morton had been 'notyd to be a rebell, and was therefore, as an offender, geven by ... [Russell] unto Sir Anthonye Kyngeston, knight. By reason whereoff the saide Sir Anthonye ... gave the ... [profits of] the same benefice ... unto one John Tewennecke of Botreux Castell'.[74] This reference to Kingston and to his disposal of the property of a 'rebel' cleric is significant, for it tends to support the claim, made in other Elizabethan sources, that Sir Anthony had served as Russell's 'Provost-marshall in the field' in Cornwall in the immediate aftermath of the rebellion and that, in that capacity, he had overseen the punishment of a number of the insurgents: a point to which we will shortly return.[75] Another Cornish clergyman, Edward Man, the vicar of Tregony, near Truro, appears to have been threatened, like John Curtes, with denunciation as a rebel unless he agreed to accede to the wishes of a local gentleman. In 1583, it was deposed in an Exchequer case that, many years before, a certain John Trevanion had forced Man to allow him to erect some new mills on his glebe, 'the rather to acquit [the vicar] from some danger and trouble he was in about the time of the insurrection in Cornwall'.[76]

In the light of these pieces of evidence, it is hard to doubt that local priests would have been even more anxious than were local laymen to secure one of the pardons that Russell, as the king's lieutenant, had been authorised to grant – usually, it would appear, in return for a cash payment – to those repentant rebels who made 'speciall su[i]t' for them and whom he regarded as deserving of mercy.[77] In a Chancery petition submitted a year or two later, a certain 'Robert Tothill ... [of] the countie of Devon' recalled that, 'about the first day of September ... [1549] in the tyme of the late Commosyon', he had been approached by one 'John Stowell, clarke, of ... [that] county', who 'had chaunced to be an offender in the said commosyon and ... was lyke to have suffered deth for his said offences'. Stowell had begged Tothill to procure a 'pardon' for him and for another man, William Salter, from 'the ... Lord ... [Russell] then Lewetenant to ... the King for the repressing of the said Rebells'. Stowell had assured Tothill that he would pay him the substantial sum of 4 nobles (i.e., £1.6s.2d.) in exchange 'for his paynes ... taken in that behalf'. Tothill had agreed to this arrangement, had duly obtained the pardon and had handed it over to Stowell soon afterwards. But, so Tothill later claimed, Stowell and Salter had subsequently failed to pay him the money he was owed and 'so to do they have always refused, and yet doth, against all right and conscience'.[78] It is hard to be sure whether Tothill was the true victim here, or whether we should regard him instead as yet another vulture who had been seeking to exploit the extreme vulnerability of local priests in the immediate aftermath of the commotion: in this case, by attempting to extort extra sums of money from Stowell in addition to the cost of the pardon itself.

While lesser clergymen right across the diocese of Exeter were suffering the most extreme punishments, the senior clerics at the top of the ecclesiastical hierarchy – the cathedral canons – appear to have ridden out the storm relatively unscathed. This doubtless reflected the canons' politic decision to join hands with the city authorities, rather than with the advancing rebels, in the critical days before the siege of Exeter began. Even Veysey's commissary, John Blaxton – the man who had been accused, back in June, of helping to incite the rebellion in the first place, by spreading 'false and sedycyous advertisements of th'alterac[i]on of Relygyon' among the people – appears to have somehow succeeded in worming his way out of trouble. On 8 August, just two days after the siege of Exeter had been raised, Blaxton had presented George Carew – the archdeacon of Totnes, who also happened to be the brother of Sir Gawen Carew and the uncle of Sir Peter – to the position of cathedral precentor.[79] It is hard not to suspect that Blaxton had been strong-armed into doing this, but the fact that he had been able to oblige the Carews in this way – and to continue making presentations to other benefices over the succeeding months – demonstrates that the commissary had contrived to remain a free man, despite his settled hostility to 'the new learning'.[80]

While none of the cathedral canons found themselves joining Crispin and Moreman in the Tower in the wake of 'the commotion time', the rebellion nevertheless resulted in a further downward lurch in the power and authority of the dean and Chapter. On 14 September 1549, the cathedral clergymen agreed to surrender control of no fewer than fourteen of their local manors to a succession of named individuals. Of these manors, one was leased to Russell, three to Herbert, one to Paulet, three more to other local gentlemen, and one to George Carew.[81]

It seems overwhelmingly probable that these leases were made as a means of rewarding the men concerned for their leading roles in suppressing the insurgents, and that the canons had either been coerced into making the grants, or had felt it prudent to do so voluntarily while they still could. The Chapter's decision to lease the remaining five manors to four senior men from among their own ranks is harder to explain, but – as at least two of these individuals are known to have been prominent in the defence of Exeter – the grants made to them may well have been further rewards for loyal service which were at the same time intended to pre-empt any attempt by the regime to appropriate these manors, too, for its lay supporters.[82] If the position of the Chapter was weakened by the events of the rebellion, this was even more true of the man who stood at the very apex of the local church hierarchy: Bishop Veysey himself. Veysey had remained quietly at his house in the Midlands throughout the years 1546–49, but this fact was clearly held against him by some regime loyalists, who believed that he might have done more to prevent the rebellion had he been present in Exeter.[83] Writing long afterwards, Hooker was to aver that the 'commotion in this diocese . . . was in some part . . . imputed to this bishop, because he lay far from it, and dwelled in his own country'. As a result of such muttering, Hooker goes on, Veysey eventually decided to 'resign . . . the bishopric'.[84] Whether Veysey really jumped or was in fact pushed remains unclear, but, in 1551, the bishopric was transferred by the Crown to Miles Coverdale: an ardent reformer and a man who had both accompanied, and preached to, the royal army during its campaign in the West two years before.[85]

## III

A good deal of information has survived about the ways in which the rebels' lay and clerical leaders were treated in the immediate aftermath of the rising – and about the ways in which clergymen who were either known or suspected to have favoured the insurgents' cause were mulcted and harried – but our knowledge of what befell the rebel rank and file at this time is much more patchy and impressionistic. That hundreds of ordinary rebels had already been killed during the series of military encounters that had taken place in Devon during the preceding weeks can scarcely be doubted. In a brief account of the siege of Exeter penned in 1559, an account that has been overlooked by all previous historians of the rising, Hooker was to claim that 100 rebels had been killed during the course of that episode alone, noting that 'many men' had been 'slayn on both partes ... [there], whereof were xxii [i.e., 22] of the Citie and 1c [i.e., 100] of the Commons'.[86] The casualties the rebels had suffered during the course of the intermittent skirmishing around the walls of Exeter had clearly been dwarfed by the casualties they had gone on to sustain while fighting in the field against Lord Russell's army, moreover.

As early as 10 August, a Londoner had recorded in his private 'chronicle' that, in the process of breaking the insurgents' grip upon Exeter, Russell had 'sl[ain], hurte and tooke prisoners of the sayd rebells above iiii M [i.e., 4,000], and after hanged divers of them in the towne and about the countrye'.[87] This estimate of the insurgents' casualties was almost certainly exaggerated, but three days later, the imperial ambassador had reported that 'over 2,000 peasants ... [had been] killed, and about 300 taken prisoners' during the recent fighting around Exeter, a figure that sounds a good deal more plausible, while John Fry, who had himself been a participant in these savage battles, put the number of rebel dead at around 1,000.[88] The names of the vast majority of these men will never be known, but among them was probably one John Turpyn, of Littleham near Exmouth. No less a figure than Sir Thomas Denys was later to depose of him and a close relative, William Turpyn, that they '[did] as trayterous and rebellious p[er]sons in the late commosion in the west parties ... beare armure and levye warre agaynste our soveraigne Lord the king ... in which commosion the said John Turpyn was slayne and ... [William] dryven to sue for his p[ar]don'.[89] From these words, it seems overwhelmingly likely that John was one of the hundreds of slaughtered insurgents who had been consigned to mass graves on the battlefield after the fighting of 3–8 August, while William had been one of the thousands of local men who had flocked to receive Russell's pardon during the succeeding days.[90]

The rebels had suffered further heavy casualties during the fighting in mid-Devon later that month. In a letter written the day after the battle of Sampford Courtenay, Russell had informed the Council that more than 1,300 of the insurgents had been killed during the fight itself and the subsequent pursuit, while 'a far greater number' had been taken prisoner.[91] All of the surviving sources agree that, taken as a whole, the rebel casualties had been enormous. Thus the contemporary Welsh chronicler Ellis Gruffyd referred, graphically, to 'the slaughter of the commons in Devon', while the Elizabethan chronicler John Stow was to observe that Lord Grey's foreign soldiers 'slewe many people' during their sojourn in the West.[92] One of the few contemporaries to hazard a guess at the total number of rebel dead was Sir Hugh Paulet. Writing to Thynne from Launceston on 20 August, Paulet observed that, during the course of the 'byckerynge' that had taken place over the last two months, 'I dare affyrme there hath ben ii M [i.e., 2,000] trayters slayne'.[93] Bearing in mind Fry's statement that 1,000 rebels had been killed in the fighting in East Devon alone, and Russell's statement that 1,300 had been killed at Sampford Courtenay, Paulet's figure seems distinctly on the low side, but it is the only strictly contemporary estimate we have. The final word on the total number of rebel dead should go to Hooker, who was probably as well informed about this subject as anyone else. Writing in 1587, he observed that 'of the number of them [i.e., the rebels] who were slaine, there is no certaintie knowne . . . howbeit it was accounted by such as continued in the whole service of this commotion to be about foure thousand men'.[94] This figure was echoed by Stow in 1592 and has been accepted as accurate by most subsequent historians: the true death toll may well have lain somewhere between 3,000 and 4,000 people.[95]

Included among the rebel dead were an unknown number of laymen who, like their clerical confrères, had been taken and executed by the royal forces and the regime's local supporters, either during the campaign itself or in its immediate aftermath. The privy councillors had for some time been making it clear to Russell that they expected him to proceed in the most brutal fashion against captured rebel 'ringleaders' – and, indeed, against captured rebel sympathisers of all sorts. On 17 July, for example, they had sent a letter to the king's lieutenant in which they had urged him to 'hang two or three' of those who were reported to be speaking in favour of the insurgents. Turning to the case of a rebel 'spy' whom Russell had recently apprehended, the councillors had then added, in grimly sarcastic tones, 'we do not doubt but ye have geven . . . [him] his due reward'.[96] Having been informed by Russell that he had already executed a number of subaltern rebel leaders whom he had captured during the initial encounters in East Devon, moreover, the councillors had hastened to make it clear that they wholly approved of his actions. 'We do like well yoor ordering of the ring leaders,' they had assured him, 'and recon no less than you do that sharp justice must be executed upon those sondrie traytors which will learne nothing but by the sword.'[97] Following the crushing defeat of the rebels in East Devon, the councillors' apprehension about an imminent rebel advance on London – and thus their lust for blood – had begun to cool, prompting them to inform Russell, in a letter of 11 August, that he should spare 'the common and mean men' among the captured rebels. Nevertheless, they had gone on, he was to continue to 'execute the heads and cheyf styrrors of the rebellion . . . in so diverse places as ye maie to the more terror of the unrulie'.[98] As we have seen, Russell appears to have obeyed these instructions with alacrity, and multiple executions are known to have been staged at several places in Devon after the rebel forces had eventually been put to flight.

Following Russell's return from Cornwall to Devon in late August, the task of 'pacifying' the former county appears to have been left in the hands of Sir Anthony Kingston, who, as provost marshal of the royal army, was responsible for executing those who had been condemned under martial law. The anecdotes that the Elizabethan chronicler Richard Grafton was later to tell about Kingston's activities in Cornwall are so graphic, and so peculiarly indicative of the atmosphere of terror which then pervaded the county, that they are worth quoting at length. After having noted that 'many of the people of that Countrey that were doers or mainteiners of this rebellion . . . were executed among themselves . . . as they had right well deserved', Grafton went on to observe that 'among other the offendors in this rebellion I thought it well to note twaine [i.e., two], for the maner of their execution seemed strange'.[99] The first of these unfortunates was a man named Bowyer, whom Grafton describes as the 'Maior of . . . Bodmyn', and who had, presumably, succeeded to this office after the capture of the previous mayor, Henry Bray, in the wake of the battle of Sampford Courtenay.[100] According to Grafton:

> This Maior had been busie among the rebelles, but some that loved hym sayd that he was forced thereunto, and that if he had not consented to them, they would have destroyed him and his house. But howsoever it was, this was his ende. On a certaine day Sir Anthony Kingstone, being Provost-marshall in the field, wrote his letter unto the sayde Maior declaring that he . . . would come and dine with him [on] such a day. The Maior seemed to be very joyous thereof and made for him very good preparation. And at the time appointed, Sir Anthony . . . with his company came and were right hartely welcomed . . . And before they sate down to dinner, Sir Anthony, calling the Maior a syde, shewed him that there must be execution [of former rebels] done in that towne [and that, to that end, a pair of gallows must be erected, and] that the same . . . [must] be redy by the ende of dinner. The Maior went diligently about it, and caused the same to be done. When dinner was ended Sir Anthony called the Maior unto him and asked him if that were redy that he spake to him of, and he aunswered it was redy. Then he tooke the Maior by the hand and prayed him to bring him to the place where the . . . [gallows] was, and he so did. And when Sir Anthony saw them, he sayde to the Maior, 'Thinke you they be strong enough?' 'Yea Sir', sayd he, 'that they are'. 'Well then', sayd Sir Anthony, 'get you even up to them for they are provided for you'. The Mayor cried 'I trust you meane no such thing to me?'. 'Sir' sayth he, 'there is no remedy; you have bene a busie Rebell, and therefore this is appointed for your reward', so that without longer respite or tarrying, there was the Maior hanged.[101]

There is no way of knowing how accurate this account is, for Grafton was writing nearly two decades after the events he described. But, if we are to credit another, much later source, it would appear that Kingston possessed a peculiar animus against 'rebels' and that, after having returned to Gloucestershire following the campaign in the West, he went so far as to make careful provision for the perpetual maintenance of a gallows, two ladders and halters in his home parish of Painswick for the execution of any local men who should dare to rebel against the Crown in future.[102] During the 1590s, moreover, Grafton's anecdote about the mayor of Bodmin was to be repeated by Richard Carew, who observed in his own short description of the town that 'Sir Anthony Kingston, then Provost-marshall of the Kings armie, hath left his name more memorable, then commendable among the townsemen, for causing their maior to erect a gallowes before his owne doore, upon which (after having feasted Sir Anthony) himselfe was hanged'.[103] It is conceivable that Carew simply lifted this tale from Grafton's text, of course, but the specific detail about the gallows being erected before the mayor's door does not appear in the latter account, while Carew's phraseology certainly seems to suggest that the episode was still both remembered and resented in Bodmin at the time he was writing.

The second anecdote told by Grafton to illustrate Kingston's gallows humour relates to a miller living near Bodmin, who had, so the chronicler observes, 'bene a very busy Verlet in that Rebellion, [and] whom . . . Syr Anthony . . . [also] sought for'. The miller had been warned of his impending arrest, Grafton goes on, and accordingly:

> he having a good tall fellow to his servaunt called him unto him and sayd, 'I must go foorth, if their come any to aske for me, say that thou art the owner of the Myll . . . and in no wise not me'. The servant promised his Maister so to do. Afterwards came Syr Anthony . . . to the Myllers house and called for the Miller, the servant answered that he was the Miller. Then sayd Maister Kinston, 'How long hast thou kept this Mill', and he aunswered 'three yeares'. 'Well then', sayde he, 'come on thou must go with me', and caused his servants to lay handes on hym, and brought him to the next tree, saing 'you have bene a rebellious knave, and therefore here shall you hang'. Then cryed he & sayd that he was not the Miller, but the Miller's servant.

> 'Wel then', sayd he [i.e., Kingston], 'you are a false knave to be in two tales [i.e., to tell me two different stories], therefore hang him up', sayd he, and so he was hanged. After he was hanged, one beying by, sayd to Syr Anthony . . . 'surely this was but the Miller's man'. 'What then', sayd he, 'could he ever have done his Maister better service than to hang for him?'[104]

Once again, it is impossible to establish the veracity of Grafton's anecdote, but the story of the luckless miller's man does not seem implausible in the light of the evidence that we have already surveyed about the execution of the rebels' clerical leaders. Some idea of the impression that Kingston's cruelty made upon local people is provided by the fact that his exploits apparently continued to be remembered in Cornwall, not only during the 1590s, when Carew was writing, but even a century later, when the Cornish antiquarian William Hals claimed to have come across several oral traditions relating to the provost marshal's depredations. The first of these stories concerned one 'Mayow of Glevyan' in St Columb Major, who had apparently been hanged by Kingston 'at the Taverne signe post in that Towne'.[105] According to Hals, the tradition related that Mayow's offence had not been a 'Capital' one, and that his wife had therefore been 'advized by her friends to hasten to the town after the marshal and his men, who had him in his custody, and beg his life'. Unfortunately, Hals goes on to relate, in her efforts to 'render herself a more amiable petitioner before the Marshal's eyes, this dame spent so much time in attiring herself and putting on her French hood, then in fashion, that her husband was put to death before her arrival'. To modern ears, this tale has an unpleasantly chauvinistic ring to it, but it may well preserve genuine folk memories of a time in which distraught local women had indeed arrayed themselves in their best clothes in a desperate attempt to make a good impression on their rebel husbands' captors as they begged them to spare their lives. In a similar vein, Hals recorded a second grim anecdote about Kingston, again gleaned, in all probability, from oral tradition: that he had 'hanged one John Payne, the mayor or portreeve of St Ives, on a Gallows Erected in the midle of that Town'.[106] Hals has been well described as the 'most inaccurate of Cornish historians', and we should view his testimony with caution, but contemporary documents make it clear that both Mayow and Payne were genuine historical figures, and it seems all too likely that they were indeed executed in the wake of the rebellion: if not by the dreaded Kingston himself, then by some other vengeful loyalist whose name was later forgotten.[107]

That dreadful things happened in Cornwall in late August and early September 1549 is made hard to doubt by a petition for redress which was submitted during the reign of Queen Mary by Thomas Ennys, the elderly man from Gluvias whose claim to have sent in provisions to Pendennis Castle at the start of the commotion we have already discussed. After the insurrection had been crushed, Ennys went on to relate, he had been apprehended by a loyalist named Stephen Playsted and accused of helping the rebels. Playsted had then demanded that Ennys give him the enormous sum of £400 in order 'to compound' for his alleged offences. When Ennys had refused to pay what was, in effect, a ransom, Playsted had directed that his unfortunate victim should be bound about the hands with a rope, and that the rope should then be tightened 'wyth a styck' until the blood spurted out at Ennys's fingernails. Not content with this, Playsted had subsequently ordered that ropes should be similarly bound and tightened about Ennys's head, ears and worse still, genitals, with similarly excruciating effects. Not surprisingly, having been subjected to this barbarous 'torment', Ennys piteously concluded his story, he had agreed to give Playsted everything he possessed.[108]

The general context within which these sorts of outrageous practices took place in Cornwall is well set out in the testimony of William Lower, a loyalist Cornish gentleman, who, as he was later to recall, 'dyd . . . s[er]ve . . . under the leading of the . . . lord Russell . . . generall unto the . . . kyng for the supp[re]ssing of the rebelles . . . wythyn the Countyes of Cornwall & Devonshere'. Following Russell's victory over the rebels 'at Saundford att the laste conflicte', Lower deposed, the lord privy seal had sent him and many others 'whyche then dyd s[er]ve the . . . kyng . . . ynto . . . Cornwall' with orders to apprehend 'the . . . [messengers], captaynes and styrreres of the rebelles' and to prevent them from encouraging the Cornish people to make further resistance. At the same time that he issued these orders, Lower went on, Russell had

> farther made gen[er]all p[ro]clamac[i]on for the co[m]forte of the seyde Sowdyeres, that after the ... Sowdyeres had taken the seyd ... [rebels] or any of them, that they ... shold take ther goodes and cattalles as goodes forfeyted and co[n]fyscate to their awen p[ro]per use and behoffe, aswell by v[e]rtue of the seyd commaundement as also by v[er]tue of a p[ro]clamtion by the seyd ... kyng.[109]

This, of course, was a reference to the proclamation which the government had issued in July, declaring that, as the western men were 'rebels and traitors', their property was forfeit to the Crown and might therefore be lawfully seized by all loyal subjects.[110] No sooner had he arrived back in Cornwall, Lower went on, than he himself had taken advantage of Russell's 'commaundement' in order to seize silver plate worth £8 from one John Bealburye of Liskeard, 'a notable rebell'.[111]

Lower was unable to enjoy his loot for long, however, because other jackals were hot on his heels, and as soon as the main body of the royal army had moved into Cornwall, local laymen who were suspected of having taken part in the rebellion were 'given, body and goods', to individual loyalists in order to reward them for their service during the commotion, just as several rebel priests are known to have been. As a result, Lower subsequently testified, 'the seyd Bealburye and hys goodes were then yeaven by warrant ... unto one William Spenser, then likewise a Sawdyour ... ayents the said rebels' – and Lower was forced to pay Spenser the cash value of the plate, as it had originally formed part of Bealbury's goods.[112] Another Cornish layman who is known to have been 'gifted' by Lord Russell to one of his followers at this time was 'Thomas Bossins': perhaps a member of the Boson family of West Penwith. It was later recalled that 'for serten offences by him then perpetrated and done with [the] rebels there', Bossins had been 'given unto Mr Roger Kympe by the ... Lord Russell ... then generall and, so being given, compounded ... [i.e., ransomed himself] for the summe of £20'.[113]

The same treatment was accorded to many suspected lay rebels in Devon, a point that is well illustrated in the writings of Robert Furse, a yeoman of Dean Prior, who penned a family memoir during the 1590s. In this valuable and unusually candid work, Furse recorded that his forebear John Furse of Swimbridge in North Devon – a former servant of Sir Thomas Denys – had been gifted to an unknown loyalist in the aftermath of the rising, despite the fact that he had been wholly uninvolved in it. According to Robert, 'thys John was . . . gretelye spoyled in the comosyon . . . for he was then geven bodye and goods leke a rebel and y[e]t durynge all the time of that Rebellyon he was continuallye in his bedde sycke and not abell to travell'. This 'trouble' had cost John Furse more than £140, Robert went on, though after his death his wife, Margaret, had been able to prove that her husband had been 'a good subject' before the magistrates at Exeter Castle, 'and by that meanes she was released of some charges which otherwise she had paid'.[114] Elsewhere, Furse refers in passing to one Edmond Rowland, of Bow in mid-Devon, who 'yn the commosyon tyme yn Kynge Edward the Sextes tyme . . . was then undershryfe of Devon and was by that menes in grett donger of his lyfe and all his goodes'.[115] Finally, in his short biography of John Morshead of Dean Prior, a former hundred constable, Furse pauses to record that 'in the commosyon by procurement his goods was geven wrongefullye but y[e]t hit coste hym £26 13s 2d [to compound]'.[116] Robert Furse's sense of injustice at the arbitrary proceedings that had taken place in the wake of the insurrection was plainly very strong, even forty years on, and contemporary legal records provide further evidence of alleged lay rebels being ransomed in Devon. Thus a badly damaged petition in an undated chancery case refers to a gentleman who had been presented with 'the body and goods of one Thomas Wannell [of Devon] beinge then a Rebell' as 'a gift' by Russell, following 'the late Commocion and Rebellyon in the West parties'.[117]

In addition to the many individuals who were specifically charged with having been rebels, and were therefore forced to pay fines or ransoms, there can be no doubt that there were many hundreds, if not thousands, of local people who were robbed of their goods by the royal forces simply because they were living in what was now deemed to be enemy territory. Hooker records that, after Russell's army had relieved Exeter, 'the whole countrie [round about] was then put to the spoile, and everie soldier sought for his best profit', adding that Herbert's Welsh soldiers in particular had, 'by their special industries and travells', extracted huge quantities of 'corne, cattles and vittels' from the people of the surrounding parishes in order to supply the half-famished citizens of Exeter.[118] Hooker's testimony is confirmed by that of Gruffyd, who notes that Herbert's Welshmen had been 'given permission to ravage the land, as . . . [were] the foreign horsemen . . . under Captain Dgermayn who . . . did great destruction to the country . . . [by stealing] goods as well as by capturing people and forcing them to pay ransom like soldiers'.[119] A London chronicler similarly noted that the West Country had been 'very sore wasted' in the wake of the rebellion, 'for all the company of ye lords [i.e., Russell and Grey]', and particularly 'ye straung[ers]' among them, had 'had leave to spoyle'.[120] Occasional scraps of evidence concerning these episodes of plundering survive in later court records. One of John Winslade's servants later deposed, for example, that, in the wake of the commotion, 'the servants of the Lord Grey' had come to Winslade's house at Tregarrick and rifled it, in the process breaking up a chest in which documents had been kept.[121] Similarly, in a legal case of 1564, an East Devon woman named Joan Pyne deposed that various items which her deceased husband had left her had been 'spoyled and stolled . . . at the last commotion there was now in Devonshire'.[122] It is possible that it was the insurgents who had taken Pyne's goods, of course, but it seems altogether more likely that Russell's soldiers were to blame.

The worst excesses of the royal forces and their local supporters had presumably taken place during mid-to-late August, while the rebellion was still in the process of being suppressed, but even after the fighting was over, it had taken a surprisingly long time for the vengeful loyalists to be reined in. On 27 August, the privy councillors had written to Russell ordering him not to publish 'the generall pardon' to the inhabitants of Devon and Cornwall that had already been drawn up, but instead to grant clemency only to those individual supplicants whom he considered to be deserving of mercy. By proceeding in this fashion, they had observed, it would be possible to ensure that 'by that tyme we shall think good to put furth the pardon, the persons most culpable' would all have been dealt with: either 'by execution or detention'.[123] Yet the councillors' decision to delay the publication of the general pardon can only have encouraged Russell's local supporters to believe that they continued to enjoy carte blanche when it came to punishing former rebels, and it would appear that, soon after this, Somerset and his colleagues had become alarmed by the reports that were by now starting to reach them of continued arbitrary proceedings in the West. In particular, they were disturbed to learn that, as we have seen, Russell had been freely distributing 'the lands and goods of the rebells' to his own soldiers, citing, as his authority for doing so, the proclamation declaring the insurgents to be traitors that had been issued in July. On 10 September, the councillors wrote to Russell informing him that he was misinterpreting the proclamation; that it had only been intended to authorise the confiscation of the property of rebels who were still in arms, not of former rebels; and that public opinion was bound to be repelled by 'this example of men's goods to be thus taken away without any order of any law'. They made it clear to Russell that they expected him to desist from making any further such grants, therefore, before concluding with the stern admonition that

> we consider, besides all this, that your men, being in the kings wages and under your government, might have been well stayed from going to the spoyle, and that by these gifts the multitude of the common people, seinge ther lands and goods geven from them, wer thereby made the more desperate.[124]

Russell may well have been offended and aggrieved by this letter, which – in its suggestion that he had exceeded his authority by 'gifting' the former rebels' lands and goods to his supporters, and in its blunt criticism of his soldiers' treatment of the civilian population – appeared to indicate a remarkably abrupt change of tack on the part of the privy councillors and, more particularly, on the part of the lord protector himself, who continued both to lead and to dominate the Council. Nevertheless, it seems safe to assume that, once he had received these very explicit instructions, Russell would have ordered the seizure of the former rebels' possessions to cease – and we know for certain that, by 25 September at the very latest, the general pardon had been published.[125] It was one thing for Somerset to order Russell to temper the severity of his proceedings against the inhabitants of the West Country, however, and quite another thing for Russell to ensure that such orders were promptly obeyed by local loyalists on the ground. In a letter sent to Sir William Godolphin and the rest of the Cornish JPs on 30 September, Russell himself angrily denounced the orgy of repression that was still clearly under way in Cornwall. 'You shall understand', he fulminated,

> that sythe your departure from me [presumably when Russell had been in Bodmin in late August] ther hath passed no daye in the whych I have not hard sondry grevonces and horryble complayntes from . . . Cornewall: some pore men oppressed withe extreame and unreasonable composicions; some greved withe unjust exactions by ther land lordes; some spoyled by one gentylman; som utterly undone and impoverished by another; some forced to entre in to bondes; some emprysoned and threatened with deathe for their goodes; some boren in hand [i.e., made to believe] that ther goodes and landes ar gyven [away], where noo warrant is to be showed; some persecuted withe one crueltye; som withe another; and the hole Comyns universally vested withe such extreamitye, wronge and oppressyon as (I assure you) no sclaunder or reproche was ever hard or reportyd lyke unto this; whych at the present to the great dysworshippe and discredyt of all the gentylmen of the shyre is generally spred and brutyd in every honest mans mowthe.[126]

Russell conceded that 'a great part of this faulte . . . procedyth of the meanor sorte of gentylmen, their servants and others', yet he warned the JPs that the 'infamye' of the manifold injustices that were now being perpetrated in Cornwall reflected upon them, too, and ordered them to bring the situation back under control with all possible speed.[127] That Russell – who had himself been so recently castigated by Somerset for his own harshness in punishing the rebels – should now have felt it necessary to upbraid the JPs and loyalist gentlemen of Cornwall in such extravagant terms makes it hard to doubt that a Tudor form of 'White Terror' had by this time been raging in that unhappy county for over a month. Outraged – and surely terrified – by the fact that the ordinary people of Cornwall had risen up in rebellion twice in the past two years, loyalist local governors there were clearly continuing to act with brutal vindictiveness, as they sought simultaneously to punish and to cow a population that they by now regarded as almost entirely composed of 'rebels and traitors'. The situation in Devon may not have been quite as polarised as it was in Cornwall, and the level of repression in that county may therefore not have been quite as harsh, but we may be confident that similar outrages against alleged former 'rebels' continued to occur on both sides of the Tamar throughout the month of September. Nor could the brutalised local people count on Lord Russell to exercise a moderating influence over affairs in the region for very much longer, because – even as he wrote to the Cornish JPs on 30 September – the lord privy seal was preparing to return to the East with the core of the army that he had assembled to confront the western rebels in order to intervene in the political crisis that was by then fast developing in the capital. And, as we shall see in the following chapter, it was in London, rather than in the West Country itself, that what may be regarded as the final remarkable twists in the story of the Western Rebellion were to be played out.

# 8

## Aftershocks
### October 1549 to January 1550

When Humphrey Arundell and his fellow captives had first been dragged before the Privy Council for questioning in early September, it would have been easy for the dejected rebel leaders to believe that the duke of Somerset was now the undisputed master of all that he surveyed. With the royal armies led by Russell and Dudley having bloodily suppressed the major insurrections that had taken place in the West Country and East Anglia, and with loyalist nobles and gentlemen having either put down or pacified the many smaller stirs that had broken out among the common people elsewhere, it did indeed briefly appear that the protector had managed both to restore order in the kingdom and to secure the long-term future of his regime. Yet in truth the shattering events of the preceding summer had fatally undermined Somerset's government and – even as the duke was savouring the military victories that had been won by the king's lieutenants in Devon and Norfolk – currents of opposition were swirling and eddying beneath the surface: currents that would swiftly gather strength and combine, and which would, within a few short weeks, lead to the protector being ignominiously toppled from his place at the king's right hand. Historians have long recognised that the Western Rising played a crucial role in precipitating the series of bitter factional struggles that occurred in and around London between October 1549, when Somerset's enemies first moved against him, and January 1550, when the politico-religious complexion of the regime which would from now on govern England in the boy-king's name at last became clear. But what has hitherto been overlooked is the fact that the imprisoned captains of the western rebels were themselves caught up in this complex power struggle, and that the eventual fates of Arundell, Winslade, Bury and Holmes – far from having been sealed from the moment they were consigned to the Tower, as has generally been assumed – may well have been dependent upon that struggle's eventual outcome. For, as we shall see in this chapter, within a month of Arundell and his fellows having arrived in London, with their hopes apparently in ruins, the prospect was at least fleetingly to arise that the cause of traditional religion in which they and so many others had ventured their lives might still triumph: that, as a result of the social and political aftershocks which the 'commotion time' had set off, religious victory might yet be snatched from the jaws of military defeat.

## I

The roots of Somerset's fall may be traced as far back as February 1547, when Thomas Wriothesley, earl of Southampton – one of the last remaining religious conservatives on the Privy Council – had been dismissed from both his position on the Council board and his office as lord chancellor.[1] Wriothesley, who was charged with having misused his office and spoken 'unfitting words' about the protector himself, had blamed Somerset for his disgrace and, although he had subsequently been readmitted to the Council, he had clearly continued to nourish a secret animus against him.[2] According to several later sources, Somerset's old ally Dudley had also been jealous of his power, and had long been plotting against him.[3] More generally, Somerset's imperious and overweening manner appears to have gradually succeeded in alienating many of his fellow councillors during the first two years of Edward's reign. It was the dramatic events of spring and summer 1549, however, that had caused criticism of the protector and his policies to grow ever louder and more insistent among England's ruling class – and which had thus given Somerset's political rivals their opportunity. Many English gentlemen believed that the rhetoric of 'commonwealth', much favoured by some of

Somerset's most ardent supporters, encouraged radical, socially levelling ideas among the common people.[4] They believed that the protector's attempts to ensure that the acts against enclosure were enforced through the use of government commissions were dangerous and promoted popular disorder. More particularly, as we have already seen, they believed that the proclamations which Somerset had issued, vigorously restating his government's determination to tackle the problem of enclosure, had themselves been largely to blame for the disturbances that had broken out across much of England soon afterwards.[5]

Nor was this all, for, once these widespread popular disorders had begun to occur, Somerset had been accused, not only of treating the protestors with kid gloves and of sympathising with many of their grievances, but even of deliberately encouraging the stirs.[6] From the point of view of Humphrey Arundell and the other imprisoned captains of the western rebels, such allegations, when they first came to hear of them, may well have seemed hard to credit. Admittedly, Somerset had held out the offer of pardon to the Devon protestors during the early stages of the Western Rising, in return for their agreement to disperse and go back to their homes. But this was standard practice for early modern rulers faced with manifestations of civil unrest and, as we have seen, from late June onwards the protector had remained implacable in his hostility to the western rebels and more than willing to sanction the harshest measures against them. Only after he had received word that the rebel army had been put to flight had Somerset begun to urge Russell to show a measure of restraint towards the defeated insurgents. Yet it is important to stress that the harsh stance which Somerset had maintained towards the western rebels had reflected the fact that he regarded them as 'papists' and 'traitors': as men who were utterly opposed to the evangelical regime that he himself led, and who posed a mortal threat to it.

Somerset's attitude towards the bands of common folk who had risen up in protest across much of South-East England during the commotion time, by contrast, had been a good deal more ambivalent. These groups of demonstrators had stressed social grievances, rather than religious ones, and indeed their public pronouncements had frequently given the impression that they were seeking to work *with* the protector's government – both in propagating the message of evangelical reformation and in tackling the corruption and greed of local governors – rather than setting out to challenge or subvert the central regime itself.[7] The fact that Kett's followers made pointed use of the new prayer book in the services that they conducted in their camp has already been touched upon, while a group of protestors from Essex had clearly couched a (lost) set of articles which they sent up to the government in July 1549 in strongly evangelical terms, stressing their 'hunger' to receive the word of 'the Gospell'.[8] The fact that the uprisings in the South-East were later collectively remembered as 'the Rebellion of Commonwealth', moreover, and that some of the leaders in Kent were referred to by contemporaries as 'commonwealths', again underlines the point that the disturbances which had occurred in this part of the kingdom were very different from those which had simultaneously taken place in the South-West.[9]

Bearing all of this in mind, it is hardly surprising that Somerset had chosen to adopt a more conciliatory approach towards the south-eastern protestors: making repeated offers of pardons if they would agree to go home, for example, agreeing to grant a number of their requests and even authorising payments to be made to some of the ringleaders in return for their agreement to bring the protests to an end. At first, this policy had been remarkably successful and, as we have seen, in early July, the Privy Council had been able to assure Russell that the protestors in five south-eastern counties had not only been 'appeased and thoroughly quieted', but that they had declared themselves to be fully behind the regime's religious policies, and ready to fight and die against the 'popish' rebels of the West.[10] Unfortunately for Somerset, his attempts to defuse all the south-eastern commotions through the use of a similar combination of negotiation and appeasement had broken down in East Anglia – and, as a result, the Crown had only been able to quell the protests in Norfolk through the application of overwhelming military force. By that time, moreover, many local governors in the South-East had become extremely alarmed by the way in which Somerset had persisted, so they felt, in holding out a hand to the protestors in that part of the kingdom over the past three months – and had even come to suspect that, 'itching after popularity', the protector was acting more in the interests of the common folk than of the traditional ruling class. This suspicion had been well summed up by the Kentish gentleman Sir Anthony Aucher in a letter written to Somerset's personal secretary, William Cecil, in early September. After having bemoaned the activities of 'these men called Common Welthes and their adherents' in Kent, Aucher had gone on to complain that the local gentry scarcely 'dared' to proceed against the protestors, because some of those whom they had already apprehended and sent up to London had procured pardons. This had caused some of Kent's local governors 'to be ingellocy [i.e., jealous] of ... [Somerset's] friendship', Aucher had gone on to warn Cecil, 'yea, and to be playne, [to] thinke my Lord's Grace rather to will the decaye of the gentilmen than otherwyse'.[11]

By August 1549, then, a combination of dismay at the popular anger that Somerset's religious and economic policies had unleashed and growing unease at his apparent social radicalism had served to alienate a wide swathe of gentry opinion – and had thus created a window of opportunity for the protector's political rivals. Nor is it any surprise to find that, as Somerset's enemies had begun to move surreptitiously against him and to cast about for an alternative figure to take his place at Edward's right hand, their thoughts should first have turned to the king's half-sister the Lady Mary. As we have seen, Somerset himself had long suspected that the protests possessed a political dimension, and in July he had despatched a letter to Mary – who was then residing at Kenninghall in Norfolk – complaining that her servants had been among 'the chief stirrers' of the protests in both Devon and East Anglia.[12] Mary had indignantly denied these charges and, as far as we can tell, her protestations of innocence had been genuine. But, even if no emissaries had passed between the rebel camps and Kenninghall, at some point during the following month Mary had definitely been approached by a group of malcontents from within the Council itself. In mid-August, John Dudley, earl of Warwick, had advanced to Cambridge at the head of a powerful army, with orders from Somerset to disperse the rebels in Norfolk, who had recently inflicted a humiliating military defeat on a smaller body of loyalists led by the marquis of Northampton. At around the same time, the imperial ambassador, François van der Delft, had ridden north from the capital to visit Mary, who – as he was later to inform the emperor – had travelled down to her mansion house at New Hall in Essex 'in order to communicate some things to him'. The tidings that Mary bore, Van der Delft went on, had been of crucial political significance, for, during the course of his stay, the princess had told him that she 'had received trustworthy information that there was much rivalry and division in the Council for . . . Warwick, Southampton, [the earl of] Arundel and the Great Master [i.e., William Paulet, Lord St John] were working against the protector . . . and sending to sound her to see if she would lend her favour to an attack on the protector, whom they wished to impeach'.[13] To these approaches, Mary told the ambassador, she had returned a studiedly noncommittal answer.

The conversation that Van der Delft describes clearly took place at some time during late August, and is the earliest piece of evidence to show that Dudley, who was a long-standing evangelical, Wriothesley, who was a firm traditionalist, and Arundel and Paulet, who were essentially religious *politiques* – men who were ready to adopt whichever path seemed most likely to serve their own interests – were by now making common cause behind the scenes in order to oust Somerset from power.[14] But who can have brought these strange bedfellows together? Intriguingly enough, the marriage broker appears to have been none other than Sir Thomas Arundell, the brother of Sir John Arundell, then confined to the capital on suspicion of complicity in the Western Rising, and the cousin of Humphrey, the leader of the western rebels.

The name of Sir Thomas Arundell has cropped up on a number of occasions already during the course of this book, and it is worth pausing for a moment in order to remind ourselves of who he was, and of the position he enjoyed, not only in the West Country, but also on the national stage. Having grown up at Lanherne, Thomas Arundell – like many of the other young men who would later go on to serve as Henry VIII's key administrators – had begun his career in the household of Cardinal Wolsey. Here, he had met and befriended Stephen Gardiner, the future bishop of Winchester, with whom he was subsequently to remain close.[15] In 1530, at the age of about thirty, Thomas had married Margaret Howard, one of the granddaughters of the duke of Norfolk: the nobleman who would later come to be regarded, with Gardiner, as one of the two key defenders of traditional religion in England. Having been knighted by the king and served in a number of government offices – including that of receiver of the Court of Augmentations in the South-West – Thomas had subsequently become rich through the acquisition of former monastic lands, but he himself was evidently no religious reformer.[16] In 1536–37, as we have seen, there had been hints that he had played down the seriousness of the anti-iconoclastic riot that had taken place in Exeter, while in 1538 Henry VIII himself had written a thunderous letter to Arundell in which he had accused him and the other Cornish JPs of being too soft on those whom the king termed 'the papisticall faction'. Sir Thomas had managed to scramble back into Henry's favour after this unnerving experience, and had not only survived, but thrived at the royal court during the 1540s – by which time, of course, the 'king's reformation' had juddered to a halt, resulting in a church settlement that was tolerable, if scarcely congenial, from the point of view of most religious traditionalists. Having been appointed as chancellor to Henry's last queen, Catherine Parr, Arundell had busied himself in consolidating the landed estate that he had already built up near Shaftesbury in Dorset, and by late 1546 the king had clearly been planning to advance Sir Thomas to a barony.[17] Henry's death in January 1547, however, had led to both Arundell and his brother, Sir John, suffering a series of reverses.

First, Sir Thomas – despite his wealth of experience in Crown office – had found himself left out in the cold at the formation of Edward VI's government. Second, while many of the other leading figures at court had been showered with honours within days of the boy-king acceding to the throne – rewards that, so it was claimed, the old king had promised them towards the end of his life – Sir Thomas's putative barony had failed to materialise. Third, as we have already seen, both Sir Thomas and Sir John had been removed from their accustomed place on the Cornish commission of the peace, a demotion they can only have regarded as a mortal affront. It is hard not to suspect that these reverses had reflected the more general *bouleversement* that had occurred at court during late 1546 and early 1547, as religious conservatives – among whom the Arundells were certainly numbered – had fallen into disfavour and 'gospellers' had begun to exert an increasingly firm grip on the levers of power. Even before the death of Henry VIII, Gardiner had been banished from the king's presence, for example, while – as a result of the folly of his erratic son – Norfolk had been attainted of high treason. Henry's death had resulted in the duke narrowly escaping the block, but Norfolk had remained a prisoner and had subsequently been joined in the Tower by Gardiner, when the latter's dogged resistance to the new regime's religious policies had eventually proved too much for Somerset and his colleagues to tolerate. By this time Wriothesley had already been humbled and Mary effectively sidelined, leaving the defenders of the Henrician religious settlement with no apparent leaders – or at least with none who had much power to act. Like so many others who found themselves out of sympathy with the religious policies of the Edwardine regime, Sir Thomas Arundell may well have retired into private life and politic silence throughout the first two years of the boy-king's reign: certainly, there is little evidence of his activities during this period. But, in July 1549, he had suddenly resurfaced.

During that month, as we have already seen, Sir Thomas's brother, Sir John, had been accused by Russell of refusing to assist him against the western rebels. Within days, he had been apprehended, brought up to London and interrogated by the Council. Unsurprisingly, Sir John had entirely rejected the allegations, but the councillors had plainly remained convinced that he had something to hide, for, on 27 July, they had written to Russell, summarising Arundell's answers and directing him 'to examine the full trough hereof, and ... to send us a playne discourse of all ... Sir John Arendells doings that he may be charged'.[18] On that same day, moreover, Sir John had been bound in a formal recognisance, first, not to leave London without express permission, and second, to stand ready to appear before the Council again whenever he should be summoned in order 'to aunswer to such matters as shall or may be to him objected'. Significantly, one of the two other men who had signed the recognisance – and who had therefore rendered themselves collectively liable to a fine of £4,000 if Sir John should fail to abide by its terms – was his brother, Sir Thomas, upon whose estates Sir John may well have been staying at the time he was apprehended.[19] Sir Thomas had clearly rushed to his brother's side, then, and during these late July days he must have become all too well aware of the fact that – having aroused the suspicions of a regime that believed itself to be facing an existential threat – Sir John was now in a highly parlous position. Was it concern for his brother's safety that first prompted Sir Thomas to become involved in plotting against Somerset? Or is it possible that the Arundells had *already* been covertly encouraging the western rebels – as some clearly believed at the time – and that, with his brother now firmly in the regime's sights, Sir Thomas took the high-risk decision to escalate his oppositionist activities and to set about engineering a political coup that would topple the government from within?

We will never know precisely what prompted Sir Thomas Arundell to act as he did – or, indeed, whether he first began to conspire against Somerset of his own volition or at the request of some other, more powerful figure. That he did play a central role in bringing about the alliance that was forged between Dudley, Wriothesley and the other disaffected lords at some point in August is hard to doubt, however, because that fact is attested to by no fewer than three contemporary commentators. The first is Van der Delft, a man who, as we have seen, was well informed about the plot. Some weeks after the coup that eventually ousted Somerset had taken place, the imperial ambassador was to inform his master that 'Mr Thomas Arundell' – whom he described as 'a good catholic man' – had been '[the] prime instrument in uniting the lords against the Protector'.[20] The second contemporary to comment on Arundell's role in the affair was the poet George Cavendish, another old servant of Wolsey's, incidentally, and someone who may well have known Sir Thomas in person. In a series of rather macabre poems entitled *Metrical Visions* which he finished writing in the 1550s, and in which individuals who had been executed during the reign of Henry VIII and his son were depicted reflecting mournfully on their fate in verse, Cavendish put the following words into the mouth of Sir Thomas Arundell:

With the Duke of Northumberland I was in consultacion,
Who bare the Duke of Somerset high indignacion,
I was cheafe councellor in the first overthrowe,
of the Duke of Somerset, which few men dyd know.[21]

Here again, Arundell was presented as having been a key figure in the protector's fall. The third contemporary to suggest that this had been the case was the evangelical firebrand – and ardent supporter of Somerset – John Ponet. In his bitingly satirical work *A Shorte Treatise of Politike Power*, first published in 1556, Ponet was to write, with seething resentment, of the dark days in 1549 'whan Wriothesley, [Sir Thomas] Arundell and [Sir Richard] Southwell conspired with th'ambicious and subtil Alicibiades of England, the Erle of Warwike . . . to pull the good duke of Somerset . . . out of his authoritie'.[22] Ponet had a good deal more to say about this subject, as we shall see, and his identification of Southwell, another religious traditionalist, as a key figure in the plot, is especially intriguing, but for the moment it is enough to note that three contemporaries, all with quite different politico-religious viewpoints, believed Sir Thomas Arundell to have been intimately involved in the conspiracy against Somerset.

Why might Arundell have been particularly well qualified to 'unite the lords against the Protector', in Van der Delft's striking phrase? As we have seen, Sir Thomas possessed long-standing links with both Gardiner and Norfolk – who, despite their imprisonment in the Tower, were still regarded as the leading champions of the traditionalist cause – and they in turn were commonly regarded as allies of Wriothesley. It may also be significant that Sir Thomas's half-sister, Mary – his father's only child by his second wife – had, in 1545, married Henry Fitzalan, earl of Arundel: the man whom Van der Delft was later to identify as one of the four privy councillors who had initially conspired against Somerset.[23] Mary Arundell had served in the Lady Mary's household, moreover, and it is clear that Sir Thomas, too, had either been close to the princess before this time, or had hoped to become so in the future. Van der Delft was later to remark that, at some point after the old king's death, Sir Thomas had asked to be admitted to Mary's service, but that

Somerset had refused to allow it; could this have been because he already regarded Arundell as potentially dangerous?[24] Sir Thomas enjoyed many powerful connections among those who favoured the 'old learning', then, and this was also true of Sir Richard Southwell, the fourth man whom Ponet was later to accuse – along with Dudley, Wriothesley and Sir Thomas himself – of having orchestrated the conspiracy against the protector. Like Sir Thomas, Southwell was a religious conservative and an ally of the Howards, and, like him, he possessed links with Mary; indeed, Southwell was the keeper of her palace at Kenninghall.[25] Crucially, Southwell was also an old friend of Dudley's, having served with him against the Scots in 1542.[26] It does not seem implausible to suggest that Sir Thomas Arundell and Southwell might have been the middlemen who helped to bring Dudley and Wriothesley together, therefore – and, even, perhaps, to convince Dudley that, if he threw in his lot with Wriothesley, they would be able to persuade Mary to come out on the conspirators' side.

Ponet's subsequent charge that Dudley, Wriothesley, Sir Thomas Arundell and Southwell had been the prime movers in the plot against Somerset is doubly intriguing, moreover, because, just as the Arundell brothers were later to be accused of having been secretly hand in glove with the 'commotioners' of the West, and of having counted several of their 'servants' among the rebel captains, so Southwell was later to be accused of having been one of the original 'authors' of the rebellion in Norfolk, and of having been secretly hand in glove with its leader, Robert Kett.[27] Some dizzying possibilities open up here. Could it be that, at the beginning of August 1549, Wriothesley and other traditionalist plotters in the capital had briefly envisaged a scenario in which both the Western Rising and 'Kett's rebellion' might be turned – thanks to the machinations of the Arundells and Southwell – to their own ends, and then – in conjunction with an aristocratic coup d'état – harnessed in order to bring about, first, the downfall of Somerset and the evangelical regime that he led, and second, the triumphant installation of the Catholic Mary as regent? Was this the prospectus that was initially outlined to Dudley – perhaps by Sir Thomas Arundell? And did Dudley himself initially give the impression that he might be prepared to abandon his own reformist views in order to go along with such a scheme? Speculation along these lines is almost certainly unprofitable and, even if some leading religious traditionalists had hoped that they might be able to harness the rebel armies in their own cause, those hopes would quickly have been dashed after the western rebels had been crushed at Sampford Courtenay on 18 August, and Kett's followers – who had remained resolutely unmoved by traditionalist blandishments throughout – had been slaughtered by Dudley's troops at Dussindale ten days later. Though there was no longer any possibility of a traditionalist coup taking place with the assistance of the rebels, however, there was still the possibility of a traditionalist coup taking place without them and, to many contemporary observers, this is precisely what seemed to be happening during the fractious autumn of 1549.

## II

Following the blood bath at Dussindale, Dudley – now at the head of a large and victorious army – found himself in a far more powerful position than he had been just a few weeks before, and it appears to have been at this point that he crossed the Rubicon that divides the contemplation of conspiracy from outright conspiratorial action. According to a document entitled 'Certayne Brife Notes of the Controversy between the Duke of Somerset and [Dudley]', which was later to be compiled by an anonymous former servant of Somerset, Dudley had been particularly angered when, in the wake of his victory, the protector had refused his requests to grant rewards to his supporters.[28] As a result, the anonymous writer goes on, Dudley had begun to 'undermine' Somerset and to confer 'with all the Dukes enemyes, as well those that was for religion as other ways; and so brought by his policy the hole faction [i.e., the religiously conservative faction] upon his [i.e., Somerset's] necke upon a pretence that Quene Mary should be requent [i.e., regent]'.[29] It will be noted here that the author of the 'Notes' – who clearly regarded Dudley as a villain of the deepest die – claims that it was Dudley who first made overtures to the traditionalists, in late September, whereas the evidence of Van der Delft not only suggests that this conjunction may have already occurred by mid-August, but also – when read alongside the testimony of Ponet and Cavendish – raises the possibility that it may have been the traditionalists, through the good offices of Sir Thomas Arundell, who had first made overtures to Dudley. However this may be, the conspiracy now rapidly took shape and, in early October, Somerset – who was then with Edward at Hampton Court – received the alarming news that Dudley, Wriothesley and most of the other privy councillors were assembled in London, whence they were now preparing to advance upon the royal court with their retainers in order to take possession of the king's person by force.

The story of what happened next has been told many times before. In brief, Somerset initially sought to resist the dissident councillors – 'the London lords', as the author of the 'Notes' was later to term them – by summoning both the forces under Russell and Herbert, which were then returning from the West, and the inhabitants of the surrounding countryside to his assistance. Russell and Herbert were plainly alarmed by the fact that the protector now appeared to be actively encouraging the common people to interfere in affairs of state, though, and on 8 October they sent him a letter in which they not only observed that 'your graces proclamations . . . put a brode for the rasyng of the Commons we mislike very much', but also made it clear that they were not prepared to take Somerset's part in what they significantly described as the quarrel 'betwene your grace and the nobilitye'.[30] Two days later, printed copies of a proclamation containing a series of accusations that the London lords had drawn up against the protector – in which he was accused, among other things, of having 'laboured to sowe division in the Realme among the Nobles, Gentlemen and Commons' – were dispersed among those who had previously rallied to Somerset at Hampton Court; many of these individuals, seeing how the tide was running, now decided to slip away.[31] As a result, the beleaguered protector was left with little choice but to surrender both himself and the king into the hands of his former colleagues, and by the end of the day on 11 October, political power had passed from the protector to the London lords – that is to say, the rest of the Privy Council. At some point during that same day, the victorious councillors drafted a letter to England's ambassadors abroad, in which they informed them that the country was now under new management, and took the opportunity to reiterate their key charges against Somerset: that he had favoured and countenanced the leaders of 'the rebellious commons' during the previous summer, and that he was, indeed, 'the very occasions of the said tumults himself, as sithens have manifestly appeared, meaning thereby . . . to have destroyed the nobilitie and other honest personages of the realm' and in the process to have cleared his own way to the crown.[32]

Here, as in most of the other public pronouncements that they made during the course of the October coup, the councillors took good care to present themselves as men who were motivated by purely secular concerns: by their determination to preserve both the king and the traditional social hierarchy from imminent destruction at the hands of a Machiavellian schemer. Yet few at the time believed this to be the whole story. With Somerset having been arrested and proclaimed as a traitor, and the bewildered boy-king having been removed from the care of his evangelical uncle, England now appeared, to many contemporaries, to be on the brink of a doctrinal about-face: of a return to a 'merry world' from which the 'gospellers' would be extirpated, leaving the kingdom safe for those who had held true to the old faith. Rumours that the London lords meant to install Mary as regent and to bring back the mass were flying around the capital from the moment that the plot took fire. From the point of view of the religious conservatives who lay imprisoned in the Tower, including, we may surely suspect, Humphrey Arundell and his comrades – who had risen, after all, primarily in defence of the Henrician religious settlement – October 1549 must have seemed pregnant with hope.[33] Certainly, the auguries looked immensely promising for them.

The author of the 'Certayne Brife Notes' was later to recall that, at the moment the conspirators had swung into action, 'there was divers catholickes called into counsel . . . for the Lady Maryes sake, she hoping to have bine Regent' – the individuals to whom he was referring were almost certainly Nicholas Wotton, Sir Edmund Peckham and Sir Richard Southwell, all of whom had taken up their places on the Privy Council by 6 October at the latest.[34] Southwell's elevation surely reflected his role in orchestrating the plot, while Peckham was an old friend of Wriothesley's.[35] Nor were these personnel changes of purely academic interest as far as the prisoners in the Tower were concerned, because Southwell, with Paulet, now seized control of the fortress in the name of the dissident councillors, who promptly ordered its lieutenant 'to suffer certain others to enter ... [the complex] for the good keeping thereof to his Majesties use'.[36] Immediately afterwards, 'Sir Edmund Peckham ... and Leonard Chamberlain, esquire, with their servauntes', were directed by the lords 'to enter into the Tower as associates to the ... Lieutenant for the better ... guard of the same'.[37] Peckham we have already met; Chamberlain was another stout religious conservative.[38] As a result, Arundell and his comrades would have suddenly found that their previous guards had been replaced – or, at the very least, reinforced – by the retainers of two prominent traditionalists. The arrival of Somerset himself, together with a dozen of his closest adherents, as dejected prisoners in the Tower just a week later, can only have encouraged the existing inmates to believe that the world was in the process of being turned upside down. Meanwhile, at the centre of power, the former conspirators were riding high, with Wriothesley, Southwell and Sir Thomas Arundell now widely viewed as the coming men.

John Ponet was later to remember the political climate that had prevailed in the immediate aftermath of the coup with evident distaste, posing the rhetorical question 'who then for a while [bore sway] but they three?' (i.e., Wriothesley, Arundell and Southwell). He went on to recall that Wriothesley, 'that before was banished the Court, is [now] lodged with his wife and sonne next to the king', adding, with his trademark scorn: '[Now] every man repaireth unto Wriothesley, honoureth Wriothesley, sueth unto Wriothesley ... and all things be done by his advise, and who but Wriothesley?' Meanwhile, Ponet continued, '[Sir Thomas] Arundell ... [was] promised to be next to the king: grome of his stole, or Comptrollour of his house at the least'.[39] This is a highly significant statement, because the groom of the stool was the king's closest personal body servant during the sixteenth century and therefore enjoyed unique access to the monarch, while the post of comptroller of the household was a major office of state. Ever since Somerset had assumed the role of protector, the office of comptroller had been held by his closest political ally, Sir William Paget – so the fact that Sir Thomas

Arundell was considered to have a realistic chance of being appointed as comptroller in Paget's place in October 1549 is a clear sign of just how far in the ascendant his political star then was. Finally, Ponet added with still deeper disgust, 'Southwell (for his whisking and double diligence) must be a great Counsaillour in any wise'.[40] This is a curious turn of phrase. The term 'double diligence' carried connotations of deceit during the Tudor period, and was a forerunner of the modern term 'double-dealing', while the word 'whisking' appears to have conveyed a broadly similar meaning.[41] It is conceivable that Ponet was making a cryptic reference to Southwell's alleged collusion with Kett here: more probable, perhaps, that he was simply accusing Sir Robert of betraying Somerset's trust by conspiring against him. In any case, Ponet's central point – that Southwell, like Wriothesley and Arundell, had been expected to assume a leading role in the boy-king's government in the immediate aftermath of the coup – is perfectly clear.

As Ponet's retrospective comments well illustrate, an atmosphere of fevered expectation reigned among religious conservatives in the capital throughout the first half of October 1549. On the 8th of that month, Van der Delft wrote joyously to the emperor, informing him that he was assured on every hand that Mary would soon be made regent; that Gardiner would shortly be released from the Tower; and that Dudley was preparing to align himself firmly alongside 'the foremost councillors', who are all 'catholics'.[42] Gardiner himself clearly hoped that his deliverance was imminent, for, on 18 October, he sent an effusive letter to Dudley, offering up his thanks to God for 'giv[ing] your Lordship the honour to be . . . a meane[s] for the reliefe . . . of this realme from the tyrannous government of the Duke of Somerset', and imploring the earl to bring about his own speedy release.[43] Norfolk must have entertained similar hopes, as must Moreman and Crispin, the two conservative canons of Exeter Cathedral who had been imprisoned in the Tower since 1547, and whose release the western rebels had demanded just months before. And while the position of Humphrey Arundell and his comrades – all of whom stood accused of being traitors who had levied actual war against the Crown – was obviously very different from that of the other traditionalist captives – most of whom were accused merely of having spoken out against the Crown's religious policies – the western rebel captains may well have shared in the general sense of expectation that, with the old regime having been toppled, its religious opponents would now be freed, especially as Sir Thomas Arundell was widely expected to be a leading figure in the new government.

There is no evidence of any direct communication between Sir Thomas and the imprisoned men, but, while suspected traitors were supposed to be kept incommunicado in the Tower, they often found means of passing messages back and forth to those in the outside world.[44] We should note, too, that Sir Thomas's traditionalist ally, Sir Richard Southwell, was not only one of those who had initially seized control of the Tower for the 'London lords', but was also one of the three privy councillors who was later noted to have interrogated the rebel captains there.[45] More intriguing still is the fact that, as has already been observed, some contemporaries believed Southwell to possess a suspiciously close relationship with at least one of those men. According to an anonymous Elizabethan writer, in the immediate aftermath of the coup, Southwell had ransacked the chamber of Somerset's secretary and had carried away a formal 'deposition' – previously made by the East Anglian gentleman Sir Thomas Knyvett – which had alleged that Southwell himself had been one of 'the authors' of the Norfolk rebellion and that he had been in secret collusion with Kett. Over the following weeks, moreover, the same writer had noted darkly, 'none of the counsell [had] resorted to Kethe in the Tower but only Southwell'.[46] The picture that is being painted here is clearly that of a former conspirator, now on the cusp of power, who was nevertheless keeping surreptitiously in touch with his former rebel protégé, and it does not seem implausible to suggest that a similar sort of relationship might well have existed between Sir Thomas Arundell and his imprisoned cousin, Humphrey – and, indeed, his 'man', Thomas Holmes – or that Sir Thomas might have cherished genuine hopes that, with the old faith on the brink of being restored, the men who had risen in its defence just months before might still be saved. Yet there is many a slip between cup and lip, and, despite the traditionalists' great expectations, they had not yet secured their ascendancy.

While it was an alliance between Dudley and those of 'the old sort' that had brought Somerset down, his own religious inclinations were quite contrary to theirs – and this was not the only reason for Dudley to have decided, within days of the protector's fall, to begin distancing himself from his former allies. Evangelical sentiment was much stronger in London and the South-East than it was in the rest of the kingdom, for example, meaning that there might well have been significant popular opposition here, if an attempt had been made to return the country to the old faith. In addition, there were still a number of evangelicals on the Council itself – including that supremely adroit politician Archbishop Thomas Cranmer – some of whom would have been certain to resist any dramatic reversal in religious policy. Perhaps most important of all, the king himself was a fervent evangelical, who – as Dudley must soon have come to realise – would never have willingly accepted a return to the religious settlement of his father. Mary herself, meanwhile – ever-hesitant – showed few signs of thrusting herself forward as regent; had she decided to assume this role, of course, Dudley's hopes of becoming the power behind the throne would at once have evaporated. As a result of such considerations, we may assume, Dudley now turned against his erstwhile co-conspirators, if he had not been plotting to do so all along, and aligned himself with the evangelical faction on the Council instead. This volte-face, in its turn, marked the beginning of a bitter factional struggle which would continue to rage at the heart of English politics throughout the last three months of 1549: a struggle between the adherents of the old faith and the adherents of the new as they strained every nerve to wrest power away from their rivals. And – as always in Tudor court politics – upon the success of the chief contestants in this battle for power would hang the ultimate fate of their friends and followers.

## III

The first signs that Wriothesley and his traditionalist allies had a fight on their hands were not long in coming, for, as early as 8 October, the dissident lords had assured the mayor, aldermen and common councillors of London that, despite the widespread rumours to the contrary, they had no intention of 'goe[ing] about to alter and reduce mattiers of religion to the state they were in afore'.[47] This might well have been regarded by the conservative privy councillors as a convenient fiction: as a sop to evangelical sentiment in a city in which such sentiment was precociously deep-rooted and strong. Yet, seven days later, a number of new men were appointed to the king's privy chamber, that is to say, to his group of intimate household servants, in order to replace Somerset's disgraced adherents and it is interesting to note that, although the previous groom of the stool had been one of those consigned to the Tower just a few days before, Sir Thomas Arundell was not chosen to replace him – despite the fact that, according to Ponet, he had been widely tipped as the next holder of this crucial office.[48] Instead, most of the places in the king's immediate entourage went to convinced evangelicals and allies of Dudley: a serious reverse for the traditionalists.[49] A few days after this, moreover, a letter was sent in Edward's name to the stoutly evangelical city of Zurich in Switzerland which strongly suggested that those who were now at the helm in England were determined to ensure that their country did not deviate from its previous religious course.[50] Wriothesley and his allies can only have been infuriated by this letter and by a subsequent royal proclamation, issued on 30 October, which made it a punishable offence to spread rumours that, as a result of Somerset's fall, 'the good laws made for religion should be now altered and abolished, and the old Romish service, mass and ceremonies . . . renewed and revived'.[51] Wriothesley himself fell ill at around this time, and it has been plausibly suggested that his health may have been weakened by his chagrin at the unexpected turn of political events.[52] Yet, if the traditionalists were down, they were not yet out, and several pieces of evidence suggest that, at around the time the proclamation was issued, they staged a spirited fightback.

On 1 November 1549, a meeting of the Privy Council was held. The list of attendees in the register – with which the formal record of the proceedings at each meeting begins – simply reads 'present as before', referring back to a previous meeting of 28 October at which fourteen councillors – not including Wriothesley – had been listed as present.[53]

But, as historians have long been aware, the record of attendance at these meetings is unreliable, and this may well explain why a marginal note made elsewhere in the register states that, on 1 November, ten named councillors – this time including Wriothesley – had agreed to discharge the recognisance of £4,000 under which Sir John Arundell had been bound in July, meaning that he was now at liberty to come and go once more.[54] This note strongly suggests that Wriothesley *had* been at the meeting held on 1 November, therefore – and it is hard not to suspect that he had had a hand in ensuring that the restrictions which had previously been placed on Sir Thomas Arundell's brother were lifted. Nor may this have been his only significant intervention at this time, for, on 2 November, it was recorded in the same register that '[on] this day Sir Thomas Pomeroy, William Wynslade, William Fortescue, John Wise & William Harrys were discharged out of the Flete by the Lordes commaundement'.[55] These five individuals had never been regarded by the Council as being as culpable as the western rebel captains who had been immured in the Tower. Pomeroy, as we have seen, had been offered a pardon if he would agree to inform on his fellows, while Wise and Harris had surrendered themselves voluntarily to Russell's forces after the rising had been crushed. Nevertheless, it is hard to see why these five men – all of whom had been in actual rebellion against the Crown just three months before – should have been released without punishment at this time, unless they had found an able advocate on the Council. Wriothesley seems the most likely person to have argued for their release: egged on, perhaps, by Sir Thomas Arundell, whose 'man' William Fortescue is alleged to have been.[56]

We do not know if news of the release of the prisoners in the Fleet reached the western rebel captains held in the Tower, but, if it did, it can only have encouraged them to believe that the balance of power on the Council was now shifting in a favourable direction as far as they were concerned. Certainly, as MPs took their seats in the new Parliament, which opened on 4 November, rumours of a traditionalist resurgence again seem to have been rife in the capital. On 7 November, the evangelical John Hooper wrote to a friend on the continent from there, confiding that he was 'greatly apprehensive of a change in religion' in

England, although 'as yet no alteration has taken place'.[57] On that same day, Van der Delft sent off his latest despatch to the emperor, in which he informed him that he had recently heard that 'Paget is to give up his post as controller and it is said that Mr Thomas Arundell, a good man and of the old faith, is to have it'. Rumours of Sir Thomas's imminent elevation were plainly circulating once again, therefore – and it is crucial to note that, if Arundell had, indeed, been appointed as comptroller at this time, he would not only have secured a key position close to the king, but would also have been made a privy councillor by virtue of his new office, thus permitting him to offer powerful support to Wriothesley, Southwell and the other religious conservatives on the Council.[58] To make matters more threatening still from Dudley's perspective, Sir Thomas remained in close communication with Mary and had indeed been to see her, the ambassador reported, just days before, in order to renew his offer to enter her service – and also, we may suspect, to renew the conspirators' previous entreaties to her to put herself forward as regent.[59]

It was clearly in response to this looming threat that, at some time between 2 and 6 November, Dudley took decisive steps to head off his rivals' challenge and to secure his own dominance on the Council. If plans really had been afoot to compel Paget to step down as comptroller at this time, then they were hastily either shelved or scuppered, while on 6 November, Bishop John Goodrich of Ely, an old friend of Cranmer's, appeared at a meeting of the Council for the first time, having been summoned by Dudley and Cranmer, so an anonymous Elizabethan writer would later recall, specifically in order 'to encounter the other syde' on the Council.[60] Goodrich was later to be joined by Henry Grey, marquess of Dorset, another 'protestant', the same writer would record, whom Dudley and Cranmer had called into the Council for precisely the same purpose.[61] In consequence, Arundell's hopes of becoming a privy councillor were dashed, and the balance of power on the Council tilted decisively towards the evangelicals.[62]

It is probably no coincidence that it was soon after this – with the conservative faction on the Council now firmly on the back foot – that preparations began to be made for the trial of the rebel captains held in the Tower. Already, on 22 October, a detailed list had been drawn up of all of the prisoners who were incarcerated in the great royal fortress: now including Somerset's adherents, of course, as well as the western rebels, the two Ketts, sundry religious conservatives and other assorted malefactors.[63] And although there is no hard evidence to show when the Crown's lawyers first began to draft the formal indictments against the rebels, it seems reasonable to assume that this process got under way at some time in mid-November, as the earliest surviving reference to the impending trial appears in a letter written on the 22nd of that month. If the indictments were indeed drafted in mid-November, then it is important to stress that those legal documents were the products of a specific political moment: a moment in which Dudley and his evangelical allies were seeking to harness the mood of black reaction that had set in among the English ruling class in the aftermath of the 1549 rebellions in order to tighten their own grip on power. Dudley faced two main groups of enemies at this time: the traditionalist faction, on the one hand, whose ambitions he had so far managed to thwart but who remained a potent threat; and Somerset and his imprisoned followers, on the other, to whom Dudley was then probably planning to administer the coup de grâce. It has not been sufficiently emphasised by historians, perhaps, that the trial of the rebel leaders, which eventually took place in late November, was played out against this complex political backdrop – and that at least some of the charges which were drawn up against the accused men may therefore have been carefully crafted in order to further the ruling junta's political ends, rather than being mere uncomplicated recitations of what the rebel captains had actually said and done during 'the commotion time' itself.

The first sign that a trial – or at least the simulacrum of a trial – was in the offing came on 22 November, when Richard Scudamore wrote to Hoby informing him that '[Robert] Keytt shall shortely goo to Norfolke to execucyon'.[64] These words make it brutally clear that, even before Kett's trial had begun, both his guilt and his ultimate punishment had already been decided upon by the men in power, and this may also have been true of the western rebel captains, whose stories were about to become intimately entwined with that of Kett. On 23 November, a commission of oyer and terminer was issued to Sir Richard Lyster, the chief justice of the King's Bench, and to five other judges, ordering them to conduct 'the trial ... of all High Treason[s] ... committed by Humphrey Arundell, John Bury, John Wynchlade, Thomas Holmes, William Kette ... and Robert Kette'.[65] The Crown's decision to put the leaders of the Western Rebellion and the Norfolk Rebellion on trial together was both a highly deliberate and a highly political one, of course, because it at once created the impression that the six men had been engaged in a common enterprise: an impression that, as we shall see, Dudley and his allies on the Council had good reason to wish to foster. Two days later, a precept was issued by Lyster to the constable of the Tower, ordering him to convey 'the bodies' of the four western rebels and of the Kett brothers to Westminster for trial.[66] The trial itself then took place at Westminster Hall – the customary venue for English treason trials – on 26 November 1549.

No eyewitness account of the trial appears to exist, but the proceedings can be reconstructed, in outline at least, from the surviving indictments. These show that Bury and Holmes were both charged with having levied war against the king and with having killed 'divers of the king's lieges', while William Kett was charged 'with having consorted with ... [his brother] and other traitors in arms against the king'.[67] There is nothing particularly surprising about these charges, which do, indeed, seem to have faithfully reflected the three men's actions. The charges made against Robert Kett, Humphrey Arundell and John Winslade, however – the three men who were evidently regarded by the Crown's lawyers as the 'arch-rebels' – were longer, more detailed and, perhaps, more tendentious. For, as well as being charged with having levied war against the king and with having facilitated the imprisonment of many 'knights, esquires and gentlemen', Kett was also charged with having led 'a multitude of malefactors' who had been heard 'crying out and vociferating in English "Kill the gentlemen"'.[68] It is possible that some of Kett's followers really had used these incendiary words; social tensions in East Anglia ran deep during the mid-1500s, and there is general agreement in contemporary sources that the rebellion in Norfolk had been a genuine 'rising of the people', in which there had been few, if any, gentry participants.[69] Nevertheless, that the Norfolk rebels should have, allegedly, called for the killing of gentlemen was remarkably convenient from Dudley's point of view.

This particular passage in the indictment against Robert Kett, when read out in open court, can scarcely have helped but remind the spectators – of whom there would have been some hundreds, if not thousands, gathered in Westminster Hall on that late November day – of the terrifying rumours that had been circulating among the social elite during 'the commotion time' of the preceding summer: that Somerset was deliberately stirring up the poor to 'destroy' the rich in order to pursue 'some greater enterprise' of his own.[70] The allegation that Kett's followers had cried out 'kill the gentlemen' would not only have served to damn the Norfolk rebel captain forever in the eyes of England's ruling class, it would also have served to persuade many members of that class – albeit, perhaps, subconsciously – that those who had engineered the duke's downfall had, in the process, succeeded in narrowly averting the destruction of the entire social order. Is it possible that these three murderous words had never been uttered by Kett's followers at all, therefore? Had they, rather, been plucked out of the air by the Crown's legal advisers – the men who would have drawn up the indictment – and then cynically embedded within that document for political purposes: perhaps in consultation with Dudley himself, or with one of his allies on the Council? Cromwell is certainly known to have worked alongside Henry VIII's 'learned counsel' in drafting indictments against suspected traitors during the 1530s, so there is no particular reason to doubt that a similar collaboration could have occurred a decade later.[71] In the end, the jury must remain out on the question of whether Kett's men had really cried 'kill the gentlemen!' But when we turn to examine the indictment that was presented against Arundel and Winslade on that same day and find that it contains precisely the same incendiary phrase, then there are surely good grounds for suspecting the veracity of the words that the Crown's lawyers had placed, retrospectively, in the mouths of the western rebels.

Like Kett, Arundell and Winslade were charged with having levied war against the king, and with having imprisoned 'divers knights, esquires and gentlemen'. These things they – or, at least, the Cornish rebels collectively – had certainly done. But, like Kett, Arundell and Winslade were also charged with having led 'a multitude of malefactors' who had expressed themselves in violent language: this time by 'crying out "Kill the gentlemen, and we will have the Act of Six Articles up again, and ceremonies as were in King Henry the Eighths time"'.[72] The claim that the Cornish rebels had called for the restoration of both the Act of Six Articles and the Henrician religious settlement is wholly convincing, for it is borne out by the public pronouncements that they themselves had made in June and July. As I have argued in detail elsewhere, however, there is not a shred of evidence to suggest that the West Country insurgents had called for the killing of gentlemen.[73] On the contrary, as we have already seen, all but one of the eleven 'captaynez of the traytours of the West Contrey' who had been brought up to London as prisoners in September had themselves been gentlemen, while further rebel gentlemen from the South-West had continued to be dragged before the Council over the succeeding weeks: including Thomas Dowriche of Sandford in Devon and Richard Roscarrock of Cornwall.[74] The very day after the rebel captains were tried, indeed, Scudamore was to inform Hoby that 'withyn these ii dayes ther was brought furth of the West contrey [to London] ii gentlemen being of the rebellyons ther . . . for speaking of sedycyous words myndyng to stere up a nue comocyon'.[75] The western rebels appear to have included many gentlemen in their ranks, therefore – so why should the indictment against Arundell and Winslade have claimed that their followers had been thirsting for gentle blood?

It is hard to avoid the conclusion that the answer to this question is a nakedly political one. By yoking together an – invented? – popular call for the killing of gentlemen with what had clearly been a genuine popular call for a return to the old faith in the indictment against Arundell and Winslade, the framers of that document can only have been seeking to convey the impression that the western rebels, just as much as the eastern rebels, had been more than willing to participate in what the dissident lords had previously claimed to be Somerset's murderous scheme to eliminate the ruling elite. In this way, the statement in the indictment – when read out before the assembled spectators at the trial – would have served still further to denigrate the reputation of the imprisoned duke. Yet, at the same time, by alleging that the Cornish rebels had been determined both to murder gentlemen and to restore the old faith, the framers of the indictment were able neatly to rebut the claim that evangelical religion was inextricably associated with social radicalism – a favourite theme of conservative political thinkers – and to turn that claim on its head by implying that it was, in fact, 'popery' that was innately inimical to hierarchy. The inclusion of this one sentence in the indictment against Arundell and Winslade was therefore beautifully calculated to convince upper-class Englishmen, not only that the two former rebels were richly deserving of a traitor's death, but also that both the duke of Somerset and his adherents *and* those who wished to return to the Henrician religious settlement posed a clear and present danger to their own property, their own liberty and ultimately their own lives. It need hardly be emphasised that, from Dudley's point of view, this was the very set of conclusions that it would have been most convenient for the members of the political nation to have drawn from the treason trial which had been staged – in large part for their benefit – at Westminster Hall on 26 November.

## IV

Whether or not the wording of the indictments had been twisted for political purposes, the result of the trial itself was a foregone conclusion. The six men all pleaded guilty when they were brought before the bar – as was usually the case in Tudor treason trials – and all were sentenced to the customary traitor's death. Writing to Hoby on 27 November, Scudamore cheerfully reported that 'yesterday ther was arrayngned at Westminster hall Arundell, Wynslade, Bery, and Holmes, rebellyonns of the West contrey, and the two Keyttes, who, confessing theyr fawltes, weare all condemned to be hanged, drawn and qwarteryd'.[76] Meanwhile, the conservative faction on the Privy Council – whose potential resurgence now represented the last hope of the condemned western men – were in disarray. Van der Delft had written to the emperor on the day of the trial itself to inform him that Wriothesley was 'very ill and in danger of death', adding despondently that 'if he were to fail us now, I should fear matters might never be righted'. The councillors, the ambassador went on, had begun to hold their meetings at the house of Dudley, who was a follower of 'the new religion . . . and wishes to maintain it'. If Wriothesley did not shortly recover, therefore, and resume his leadership of the conservative faction, Van der Delft implied, the cause of the old faith would be irretrievably lost.[77] Scudamore, writing from the opposite religious standpoint, saw things very much the same way. Writing to Hoby on 27 November, he noted that Wriothesley was not only lying 'syke at his howse', but was also, 'as some saye, verye wilde': presumably as a result of the general drift of political affairs.[78] In a subsequent letter, Scudamore reported to Hoby in triumphal tones that, on 27 November, Goodrich and Grey had been formerly sworn in as members of the Privy Council, which, he declared, 'putteth all honest hartes yn good coumfort for the good hope that they have of the perseveraunce of Goddes woord'.[79] The evangelicals' grip on power was tightening, then – and clear evidence that this was so appeared on 1 December, when Sir Ralph Hopton, the knight marshal, was sent with forty men to act as assistant to the lieutenant of the Tower, in place of Chamberlain and his retinue, who were promptly paid off.[80] An evangelical ally of Dudley had now replaced a conservative ally of Southwell as the commander of the additional forces that had been sent to guard the fortress, therefore – and this must have sent an ominous signal to the condemned western men, who had been returned to their former lodgings after their trial.[81]

Nevertheless, Humphrey Arundell and his comrades may still have been able to discern the faintest glimmers of hope amid the darkness that now enveloped them in the Tower. They were still alive, for one thing, unlike the Ketts, who had received extremely short shrift in the wake of their trial, as was usually the case with condemned traitors. Robert and William Kett had been placed in the hands of the sheriff of Norfolk on 29 November, carried by him to Norwich and then – just as Scudamore had predicted – executed in the heart of the county over which they had so briefly held sway: Robert by being hanged in chains from the walls of Norwich Castle and William by being similarly suspended from the steeple of Wymondham church.[82] The fact that the western rebels had not yet suffered a similar fate hints that powerful friends were continuing to do what they could to stave off their executions. Certainly, attempts are known to have been made to restore the fortunes of other traditionalist prisoners held in the Tower at this time. On 5 December, Scudamore informed Hoby, with evident relief, that a recent attempt to have the duke of Norfolk released had been foiled, adding, 'I trust this be the working of God for it can be judged non otherwyse, but the begynnyng of this suytt [i.e., for the duke's release] was prvyely procured by some of the old sort to the entent to make theyre part [on the Council] the stronger'.[83] There had also been a rumour, Scudamore went on, 'that master Courtney shold come at lybertye'. This was a reference to the young earl of Devonshire – another religious traditionalist – who had been held as a prisoner in the Tower since the execution of his father, Henry Courtenay, marquess of Exeter, for treason almost ten years before.[84] The release of either of these great noblemen, as Scudamore fully appreciated, could well have caused Dudley and his allies serious problems.

It is intriguing, too, to note that – either on, or shortly before, 14 December – a serious quarrel took place in London between Sir John Arundell and Sir William Godolphin. We know about this dispute because it was recorded in the Council register on that day that the two men had been bound over to keep the peace, 'and neyther by theymslefes, frendes, nor servants or others [to] procure displeasure th'one to th'other, and [to] appeare from day to day before the Lordes untill such tyme as their Lordships shall have h[e]ard and decided the causes being in variaunce betwext them'.[85] Sadly, no further evidence about the quarrel has survived, but this clash between Arundell – the Cornish gentleman who was believed, by some, to have secretly encouraged the rebels – and Godolphin – the Cornish gentleman who had been most unbending in his opposition to them – was surely related to the events of the previous summer. Godolphin had been pricked by the king as the new sheriff of Cornwall during the preceding month, and this may well help to explain his presence in the capital in late 1549: conceivably, he had been expecting that, like the sheriff of Norfolk, he would shortly be given the congenial task of escorting 'his' traitors back to his own county and overseeing their executions there.[86] Whatever had brought Godolphin to London in the first place, it seems probable – as several historians have suggested – that, once he was there, he had openly accused Sir John of favouring the rebels, leading to an angry confrontation between the two men.[87] Yet one of the most interesting things about the minute in the register, from the point of view of the present discussion, is that it reveals that, as late as this, the councillors did not simply take Godolphin's side, despite his trenchant hostility to 'the old sort', but declared themselves ready to mediate between the two men instead. This strongly suggests that, although the evangelicals were by now in the ascendant on the Council, traditionalists like Arundell still possessed powerful backers there, too.

All this was to change towards the middle of December, when the Machiavellian Dudley pulled off his most dramatic political manoeuvre yet. At that time, Wriothesley – by now restored to some measure of health – was, together with the earl of Arundel and Lord St John, engaged in interrogating the duke of Somerset in the Tower. Most contemporary observers were confidently expecting that Somerset would shortly be tried and executed, and this is clearly what Wriothesley was anticipating, too. But he was also secretly intent on pulling down Dudley, along with the duke, so that the way would at last be clear for the traditionalist faction which he led to assume control of the Privy Council. According to the author of the 'Certayne Brife Notes' – which provide such a crucial insight into the vicious factional struggles of late 1549 – while Wriothesley and his colleagues had been interrogating Somerset on 'sertayne articles concerning his treasons', the duke had repeatedly parried their questions by affirming that everything he had done as lord protector had been 'by the advice, consent and counsel of the earle of Warwicke [i.e., Dudley]'. This had appeared to give Wriothesley his opportunity and, after the duke's examination, he had turned to his colleagues and declared that it was now plain that Somerset and Dudley were *both* traitors, and that both should therefore die. The earl of Arundel had apparently given his 'consent' to this 'advyce', suggesting that, on the day appointed for Somerset's execution, Dudley, too, should be seized 'and have as he had deserved'. Paulet had appeared to concur with his fellows, but that evening he had rushed to Dudley's house to inform him of what was afoot. Forewarned, Dudley had responded in the most audacious way: by abandoning his plans to execute Somerset and by preparing to rehabilitate the fallen duke instead – thus opening the way for the resurrection of the original evangelical alliance which had been fractured by the October coup.[88]

By 19 December, rumours were circulating that Somerset's life would be spared and, within days, the duke – no doubt amazed and relieved in equal measure – was enjoying the freedom of the Tower.[89] On Christmas Day, moreover – in a move that was designed to send the clearest possible message to the world that the process of religious 'reformation' in England was not about to stall, but was rather on the point of intensifying still further – the Council despatched a letter to the bishops in which they reiterated the regime's continued support for the Book of Common Prayer, and once again stressed that those 'evil disposed persons' who had claimed, ever 'since the apprehension of the duke of Somerset', that they would shortly 'have again their old Laten service' were sorely mistaken.[90] It was the end of the line for the conservative faction, and their fall came just days later. On 29 December, Southwell's name appeared for the last time on the list of councillors.[91] Two days later, Wriothesley and the earl of Arundel were ordered to depart from the court and remain in their houses, while – as a delighted Scudamore subsequently reported to Hoby – 'Sir Thomas Arundell and Mr Rogers of the prvyey chamber weare likewise comaundyd to keep [to] theyr howse without further lybertye'. What had led to the sudden disgrace of these powerful figures, Scudamore went on, 'is not openlye known, but some imagyneth that they went about the subvercyon of [the reformed] relygyon'.[92] Van der Delft, looking on from the other side of the doctrinal divide, agreed with this analysis. Writing to the emperor on 14 January, he lamented that Dudley and his allies were now preparing 'to persecute and crush' their traditionalist rivals completely 'out of existence'; that Wriothesley and the earl of Arundel had been driven from the court; and that 'Sir Thomas Arundell, who openly belonged to the good faith ... [had] been cast into prison'.[93] Soon afterwards, both Southwell and Sir John Arundell were confined to the Fleet and – with those who had once had the power to succour them now joining them in durance – the fate of Humphrey Arundell and his comrades was finally sealed.[94]

We catch what may well be one of our final glimpses of the Cornish rebel leader in a letter that William Reskymer – the brother of one of the gentlemen who had assisted Godolphin in his attempts to overawe the common people of West Cornwall in 1548 – wrote to that same brother from London on 20 January 1550. This missive, which is both damaged and written in an especially villainous hand, is largely concerned with a murder that had recently taken place in the capital, but it also contains a couple of lines that appear to read as follows: 'as to [the?] pryseners of ou[r]? countye, the wond [i.e., the one?] them ys yn the Flete for his labour, that ys Sir John Arrendell, an[d] hys pretty captyne ys yn the marshels howeys since ys confess[i]o[n]'.[95] If my transcription of this passage is accurate – and honesty compels me to admit that I cannot be certain that this is the case – then Reskymer's words are fascinating, for they clearly hint, first, that he believed Sir John Arundell to have been the *éminence grise* behind the Western Rising, and second, that he believed the man whom he scathingly termed Sir John's 'pretty captyne' – surely Humphrey Arundell – to have been acting, in effect, as his cousin's military surrogate.[96] Reskymer may have been quite wrong to think this, of course, but at the very least his comment provides further evidence to suggest that Sir John Arundell was believed by his own fellow countrymen, as well as by many in London, to have been up to his neck in the Western Rebellion.

By the time Reskymer penned this letter, preparations for the condemned men's execution were getting under way. Scudamore later informed Hoby that the original plan had been for Humphrey Arundell and Thomas Holmes to be 'drawn' from the Tower to Tyburn and despatched there on 24 January. The wicker hurdles on which it was customary for traitors to be dragged to the gallows at a horse's tail had duly been brought to Tower Hill on that day, Scudamore reported, 'and yet the prisoners did not die'. The reason for the delay, he explained, was that, when the two men 'perceavyd that ther was no way but deth, they dessyred to have some respyte for the dischardge of theyr conscience . . . both for the preservacyon of the kynges majestye and the sauffegarde of . . . the realme, but what is theyr confession I knowe not'.[97] The fact that it was only now that Arundell and Holmes – the two rebel leaders who possessed the closest links with the Arundells of Lanherne – had, apparently, realised that their executions were inevitable is interesting, and again hints that, up until this point, the two men may have been hoping against hope that powerful sympathisers might somehow intervene to save them: the one way that a convicted traitor in this era might hope to escape death.[98] What their last-minute confession may have been we will never know, but it seems probable that their words threw still further suspicion upon Sir John Arundell, for, on the very next day, he was 'removed' from the Fleet 'and brought to the Towre'.[99] Five days later, he was joined there by his brother, Sir Thomas, prompting the king to note in his journal that 'Sir Thomas Arundel and Sir John [were] committed to the Tower for conspiracies in the west parts'.[100]

The other two captains of the western rebels, Winslade and Bury, had originally been expected to be sent back to the West Country and executed there, but this plan, too, was subsequently altered: the authorities evidently having decided that a multiple execution in the capital would send out a more powerful message.[101] On the morning of Monday, 27 January, all four of the western rebel leaders were therefore taken from the Tower, tied to the hurdles that had been made ready for them and dragged through the streets of London to Tyburn.[102] As the doomed men set out on their final journey, they were watched by crowds of spectators: among them, two of Winslade's own servants, who were later to testify that they had seen the rebel captains pass by 'when they went to Execucion'.[103] According to the much later 'memoir' of the Devon yeoman Robert Furse, William Gibbs – the close associate of Sir Peter Carew, to whom Bury's lands and goods had been granted by Russell as a reward for his services against the rebels – was also present among the spectators: perhaps exulting in the fact that, with Bury's death, there was no longer any possibility of the grant being reversed. If we are to credit Furse's testimony, Bury first 'callede' out to Gibbs 'as he went to his execuyson' that he had acquired one of his former manors through dishonest means, then added that 'I thynke God in the revenge thereof hathe layed this plage justely upon me', and finally begged Gibbs to ensure that the manor was restored to its rightful owners. It comes as little surprise to find that, according to Furse, Gibbs was entirely unmoved by this plea and subsequently sold the manor to someone else; especially as we know, from another source, that Gibbs had already compelled Bury's wretched wife, Margery, to borrow money in order to buy back some of the household goods that he had seized from her imprisoned husband.[104]

Several contemporary chroniclers recorded the names of those who had been taken out to suffer at Tyburn on that day, and the fact that each of these writers placed Arundell's name at the head of the list provides further confirmation that he was generally regarded as the leader of the insurrection.[105] One of them observed in passing that Arundell was 'a gentleman borne': an observation that rather tended to undercut the official line that the western rebels had been bent on subverting the established social order.[106] And it is worth noting that another, rather later chronicler, writing in 1560, stated that it was 'Sir John Arundell' who had been conveyed to Tyburn on that fatal day: this confusion is another hint, perhaps, of the intimate ties that had been rumoured to exist between Humphrey and his more socially exalted cousin at the time that the executions were carried out.[107]

Of the condemned men's final minutes nothing is known, beyond the dreadful sanguinary outcome. Were Arundell, Winslade, Bury and Holmes permitted to make short speeches to those who had assembled to watch them die, as was then the custom, after they had mounted the ladders that led up to the gibbet? Or were they simply 'turned off' straight away by the executioners, in order to ensure that there was no chance of their uttering any 'seditious' words to the spectators? All that can be said for certain is that each of the victims would have been, first, cast off the ladder and suspended from a rope, then cut down while he was still alive, next castrated and disembowelled, and, finally, cut into quarters and beheaded. It was at Tyburn that the terrible closing scene of the 'midsummer game' was enacted, then, and once the principal players had made their bloody exits, their severed heads were taken away and 'set upon' London Bridge, in what may be said to have constituted the most grisly of final bows.[108] Here, the pitiful relics long remained to serve their minatory purpose, and later that year, an anonymous evangelical rhymester gleefully cautioned religious conservatives in the capital to beware of what they said lest, 'like . . . the last yere's Traitors', they should 'be taken, and quartered like a baken [i.e., a butchered pig]'.[109] 'God save the Kinges majestie, long for to reigne', the poet jubilantly concluded, 'To suppresse al rebells and truthe to maynteyne!'[110] His exultation was justified, for, with the defeat of the western rebels, the execution of their leaders and the routing of 'the old sort' both at the court and on the Council the triumph of the evangelical cause in England could at last be said to be complete.

# Conclusion

During the early 1600s, the antiquary John Norden completed his 'topographical and historical description of Cornwall', a work that drew very heavily on Richard Carew's *Survey of Cornwall*, published just a few years before, in 1603. Upon arriving at St Keverne, in the course of his virtual perambulation of the shire, Norden paused, just as Carew had done before him, to remark that it was in this far western parish that 'the Cornish commotion' of 1548 had begun. Yet having presumably digested Carew's observation that, during the following year, the perturbations which had first manifested themselves at St Keverne had 'grown' into 'a general revolt', Norden then departed from his predecessor's script in order to pronounce his own brief epitaph on those who had risen up in protest in the West Country in 1549. 'Though throwgh their multitude and mightie favourites [they] aspired high, and went farr,' Norden remarked, 'yet came they shorte of their purpose, and fell as rebells.'[1] His words nicely encapsulate the way in which many late sixteenth- and early seventeenth-century English Protestants viewed the Western Rising in retrospect: as an extremely formidable and ambitious challenge to Edward VI's government, which had come close to achieving its aims, but which had, fortunately and no doubt providentially, been defeated, transforming its leading participants at a stroke from potential king-makers – or perhaps one should say queen-makers – into doomed 'rebels'. Other writers, both at the time of the rising itself and ever since, have been far more scathing, both about the protestors and about their aims. For John Hooker, the mid-Devon countryfolk who had initially set off from Sampford Courtenay for Crediton in June 1549 were not just posturing players taking part in a self-penned 'enterlude', but literal lunatics, 'for the sun being in cancer, & the midsummer moone at full, their minds were imbrued in follies', while for A.L. Rowse, writing nearly 400 years later, the insurgents had been 'poor fools', whose programme had been 'a complete, a pathetic manifesto of Catholic reaction', and whose blood had been spilt in a vain attempt to turn back the tide of history and to 'fight . . . against the future'.[2] Many other historians – while eschewing such pejorative language – have tended to agree that the Western Rising was a quixotic enterprise that was bound to end in failure.

Other scholars have argued, conversely, that the rising posed a serious threat, not just to Somerset's government, but to the progress of the English Reformation as a whole, and it is the latter view that has been taken here. As we have seen, the initial stir at Sampford Courtenay had been led by a group of *coqs du village*, or parish worthies, and it is clear that commoners had continued to take the lead in the tumults that had ensued in Devon, right up until the start of the siege of Exeter, when, as a disdainful Elizabethan writer was later to sniff, the protestors had 'encamped them selfes round about the walles in great nombers, every Hick and Tom making himself a capitan'.[3] After the siege had got under way, however – and after the protests had spread to Cornwall, a few days later – individuals of a more elevated social status had clearly begun to join the rebels. Hooker was later to recall that, from around this time onwards, 'certein gentlemen and yeomen . . . both in Devon and Cornewall' had been 'contented, not onelie to be associates of this rebellion, but also to carrie the crosse before the processyon, and to be captains and guiders of this wicked enterprise'.[4] The decision of Humphrey Arundell and John Winslade, two of Cornwall's wealthiest men, to place themselves at the head of the rebels at Bodmin, either on or around 6 July, had been especially important: partly because it had conferred a greater air of legitimacy upon the protests; partly because it had brought in a small knot of other gentlemen who were allied to

Arundell and Winslade; and partly because – through Humphrey Arundell's close kinship with his cousins, Sir John and Sir Thomas – it had forged a potential link between the protestors and two figures of genuine regional and national importance.

From the first week of July onwards, the western rebels had exhibited a growing sense of purpose. By 12 July, Somerset had evidently come to fear that they not only possessed a political programme – that 'thay speake to have to do in the governaunce of the kyng's Ma[jes]tie', as he put it in a letter written to Russell on that day – but also that they were preparing to march on London in order to put that programme into effect: a point that was made clear by the protector's subsequent grim remark that 'thaie shall know, ere thay come any thing nerer, [that] they shall bothe be let of that purpose, and ... [as] rank Traytors receyve their desertes on the way'.[5] And although later historians have tended to castigate the rebels for having failed to appreciate that their one real hope of achieving their aims was to venture out of their own 'country' and to march upon the seat of power, this seems an unjust criticism, at least as far as the Cornishmen are concerned. A loyalist source retrospectively observed of the Cornish rebels that they 'cam[e] very fast', adding that 'they sayde thay woulde [march] thorow [the country] without any pause': comments that clearly imply that they had declared their intention of marching upon London as swiftly as possible.[6] And, as we have seen, the evidence suggests that they had been as good as their word, for, by 27 July, Cornish rebel forces had been encamped before Exeter, 40 miles to the east of the Tamar, while, by 29 July, Cornish rebel forces had been among those that had set out to attack Russell at Honiton, 20 miles still further east. If Russell had retreated to Dorset in mid-July, as he very nearly did, or if the battle of Fenny Bridges had gone the other way, it seems hard to doubt that Humphrey Arundell and his followers would have pursued their eastward march into the neighbouring counties, where there were many who looked eagerly to their coming.

Nor was it only from 'the common sort' that the western rebels might have hoped to receive assistance, had they penetrated into Somerset, Dorset, Wiltshire and the counties beyond, for – as Norden's cryptic allusion to the protestors' 'mightie favourites' reminds us – from mid-July onwards, as the insurrection reached its height, it had begun to be whispered that the insurgents possessed powerful backers among the English political elite: up to, and possibly including, the Lady Mary herself. Whether Mary had really gone so far as to hold out a tentative hand to the western rebels at this time we will probably never know. But the fact that Sir Thomas Arundell – a man who possessed close links with both the princess and with the insurgents, and whose brother was apprehended on suspicion of colluding with the rebels in mid-July – is known to have been engaged, just a few weeks later, in engineering a conspiracy that was designed to pull down the protector and install Mary as regent is intriguing in itself, and hints that, by the second half of July, the Western Rising had transcended its origins in a remote Devon churchyard to become a movement of truly national political significance.

What are the most important new insights to have emerged from this study, and how do they enable us to refine and extend the traditional narrative of the rising which was originally laid down by Frances Rose-Troup more than a century ago? There are eight specific changes of interpretation, or at least shifts of emphasis, that I would like to highlight here. First, this book has suggested that the doctrinal dispute that took place between Nicolles and Crispin in Devon in 1547 was a good deal more important than has hitherto been realised, that their very public quarrel served both to illustrate and to exacerbate the religious divisions which already existed in West Country society, and that that same quarrel may conceivably have fed into the popular disturbances that occurred at Exeter towards the end of that year.

Second, this book has shed new light on the 'Cornish commotion' of 1548 – and has raised the possibility that, just as the introduction of the new prayer book in English served as the trigger for the rising at Sampford Courtenay in 1549, so the introduction of the new communion service in English may have helped to trigger the rising in the Lizard Peninsula, a wholly Cornish-speaking district, in 1548. More generally, it has been argued here that, because the Cornish people retained their own distinctive identity during the early sixteenth century – an identity that the religious and social changes which were being brought about by the Reformation tended to undermine – a sense of Cornish cultural defensiveness may well have been a contributory factor to the popular risings that occurred in Cornwall in both 1548 *and* in 1549.

The third, and perhaps the most important, way in which the present study has challenged the traditional narrative of the rising is by suggesting that the initial gathering of the Cornish rebels did not take place at Bodmin on 6 June – as the later indictment of Arundell and Winslade states – but rather on 6 July. If this argument is correct, then it at once helps us to see, first, that Protector Somerset was by no means as hopelessly out of touch with what was going on in the far South-West during the initial stages of the rising as has often been claimed, and second – and much more significant – that, far from having taken seven weeks to raise a Cornish host and march with it to Exeter, as used to be thought, Humphrey Arundell and his lieutenants had in fact managed to achieve both of these feats – and at the same time to capture and besiege various loyalist strongholds within Cornwall itself – in just three weeks. This shortened timeframe reinforces the point that has already been made above: that, from the regime's point of view, the western rebels' movements must have looked far more purposeful and menacing, in July 1549, than traditional accounts of the rising would suggest.

The fourth way in which my research has challenged the accepted narrative is by demonstrating that, throughout that same month of July, Lord Russell's forces were much weaker than has hitherto been appreciated. Previous claims that the 'pusillanimous' Russell had been 'idling in camp', when any general worth his salt would have been engaged in vigorous action against the rebels, are patently unfair, therefore.[7] In fact, it is clear that, right up until 29 July, Russell had remained extremely short of men – and this underscores the point that the battle of Fenny Bridges was a desperately near thing and that, if Arundell had been able to bring up more Cornishmen to East Devon just a day or two earlier, he might well have been able to force the king's lieutenant in the West into headlong flight.

The fifth new insight to emerge from this book is that the number of traditionalist priests who were slain or executed during the course of the revolt was a good deal higher than was previously thought, and that more priests probably died as a result of the Western Rising in 1549, indeed, than as a result of any other Tudor rebellion apart from the Pilgrimage of Grace. This finding can only be said to reinforce Rose-Troup's central thesis, that religion lay at the very heart of the Western Rising: an argument that was powerfully restated by Aubrey Greenwood some thirty years ago, and with which, having re-examined all of the available evidence, I would strongly concur.

The sixth way in which the present study may be said to have shifted existing perspectives on the rebellion is through its demonstration of the fact that, although the rebels were defeated in battle in August, their aims came tantalisingly close to being achieved during the factional struggle that raged in London thereafter: a struggle that they themselves had helped to precipitate. This, of course, helps to reinforce the argument that the insurgents should not be written off as hopeless reactionaries who were engaged in a futile struggle to hold on to a lost (Catholic) past and to stave off an inevitable (Protestant) future.

The seventh new insight to emerge from this book – and again, I would argue, a particularly important one – is the fact that the trial of the rebel leaders can only be properly understood within its precise political context, and that, once that context has been examined, it becomes possible to see that the indictment that was drawn up against Arundell and Winslade in advance of their arraignment – a document that suggested that their followers had been blood-crazed class warriors – was almost certainly crafted with political ends in mind. If I am right to argue this, and to suggest that the western rebels' supposed cry of 'kill the gentlemen' was a cynical fabrication by Crown lawyers allied with Dudley and his faction, then the chief evidential prop of the notion that the Western Rising, just as much as 'Kett's rebellion', was primarily 'a social conflict' – a notion that had already taken root among the ruling elite in London by late 1549 and which has continued to circulate among historians ever since – promptly collapses in a cloud of dust. No one would deny that there were tensions between commoners and gentlemen in the sixteenth-century West Country, of course, and – as I have argued elsewhere – after the rising was over, those tensions seem to have become more evident, in Cornwall at least, as local gentlemen rushed simultaneously to punish the insurgents and to distance themselves from their cause. But to suggest that the rising had begun as a social protest seems to fly in the face of the surviving evidence, and it is tempting to suggest that the government only succeeded in persuading the ruling class that this had been the case because the West Country was so remote from the political centre that it was relatively easy for the regime to control the narrative about what had taken place there during the summer of 1549.

Finally, it should be noted that this book has both supported and, in some ways, expanded upon the thesis that Helen Speight was the first to advance in detail, during the 1990s: that the influence of the Arundell family of Lanherne had been far more important in the history of the Western Rising than scholars had hitherto realised. Speight argued that Sir John and Sir Thomas Arundell, already disaffected from the Edwardine regime as a result of its religious policies, had adopted an attitude of 'benign passivity towards the rebels' in June–July 1549, and that this had allowed the disturbances to spread.[8] The present study has fully supported the first part of Speight's argument, while opening up the possibility that the second part may not go far enough – and that the brothers may, in fact, have been hand in glove with the rebels – or, at the very least, in active communication with them – from early July onwards, if not before. Sir Richard Scudamore's testimony, discussed above, now makes it seem almost certain that Sir John and Sir Thomas Arundell were arrested and thrown into the Tower in February 1550, not as a result of Sir John's previous dispute with Godolphin, as has often been claimed, but instead as a result of what Humphrey Arundell and Thomas Holmes had revealed about their dealings with the two brothers in their last desperate confessions: confessions that they had made in the vain hope of averting their own imminent executions. William Reskymer's comments, meanwhile, hint at a contemporary perception that, when he placed himself at the head of the Cornish rebels, Humphrey Arundell had been acting as Sir John Arundell's surrogate. That this may well have been the case is further suggested by the fact that, as Cheryl Hayden has recently pointed out, it seems probable that the two infant sons of Humphrey Arundell were subsequently taken into the Arundells' household at Lanherne as gentleman-servants, as William Winslade's son is definitely known to have been.[9] Had Sir John been outraged by the previous accusations that he had been colluding with the rebel captains, it is unthinkable that either he or his eldest son would have taken in the arch-rebels' fatherless progeny in this way, after Sir John himself had finally been released from the Tower in 1552. (Sir Thomas was not so lucky, having been beheaded earlier that year for allegedly plotting against Dudley.) There is nothing to suggest that the Arundell brothers had deliberately engineered the rising; in Cornwall, just as in Devon, the stirs appear to have begun as genuinely popular affairs. But, as this book has shown, there is a good deal of fragmentary evidence to suggest that – once Humphrey Arundell had placed himself at the head of the Cornish host – Sir John and Sir Thomas may have attempted to guide, to channel and otherwise to exploit the Western Rising as part of a game played for the highest politico-religious stakes.

What of the ordinary men who led the original stir at Sampford Courtenay: the yeoman farmers who were the 'true begetters' of the Western Rising, and who remained central figures within it until the last desperate battle was fought out on their own fields? William (or Thomas) Underhill was slain in that battle, as we have seen, but his name clearly remained one to conjure with in Devon for years to come. In 1560, an Exeter tailor named Hugh Southey was summoned to appear before the city magistrates about a minor misdemeanour. Southey evidently lost his temper during the interview that followed, because he subsequently told the justices that 'it will come to pass as some have said: that they hoped to see some of the tailors hanged and that a report have been that a new Underhill would rise up among them again'.[10] Southey's words both outraged and terrified the JPs, and obscure as they are, they clearly imply that, just as Robert Kett was long remembered as the champion of the downtrodden in East Anglia, so William Underhill was long remembered in much the same way in Devon.

Of the other three 'Sampford men' who are recorded to have played a prominent part in the rising, William Seagar and John Sloman – both of whom served as rebel captains – and the individual known only as 'Lethbridge', who is said to have struck the first blow at William Hellions, nothing is known for sure; we may surely suspect that they, too, perished on the battlefield or were executed in the immediate aftermath of the rebellion. But in Sampford Courtenay, just as at Lanherne, some of the rebel leaders' descendants – or, at least, some of their relatives – clearly survived and flourished. A survey of the manor of Sampford Courtenay, drawn up in the 1560s, shows that several tenements in the parish were still held by Underhills, Slomans and Lethbridges at that time.[11] The Sampford Courtenay 'protestation returns', compiled in 1641, include the names of eight adult male Underhills, three adult male Slomans and one adult male Lethbridge, all of whom took an oath, or protestation, in that year, to remain true to the king, to the Parliament and, in a sign of how times had changed, even in remote mid-Devon, to 'the true reformed Protestant Religion'.[12] A petition that was sent up to the House of Commons in the names of the parishioners of Sampford Courtenay six years later, moreover, in midsummer 1647 – a petition that lamented, irony of ironies, the killing of 'protestant Englishmen' by the Catholic rebels in Ireland – was signed by both 'Thomas Lethbridge' and 'Henery Underhill', who, from the prominent position of their signatures on the page, were evidently then among the leading parishioners.[13] And if one visits Sampford Courtenay today, one may still see the names of more recently departed Lethbridges and Slomans inscribed on the slanting gravestones that stand scattered about the churchyard. The village remains a beautiful, unspoilt place: unscarred by the 'development' that has recently spilled out from Exeter to engulf much of the East Devon countryside over which the battle of Clyst Heath was fought. And as I lay down my pen today, it is my earnest hope that both the village and its surrounding countryside will be protected and preserved forever, so that they may always stand as living memorials to the brave men and women who gathered there to defend both their faith and their accustomed way of life on that fateful Whitsun Monday, almost 500 years ago.

# ENDNOTES

## Introduction

1. Bod., Rawlinson MS, C.792, 'The Beginninge, Cause & Course of the Comotion . . . in . . . Devon and Cornewall . . . collected by John . . . Hooker', f. 1.
2. B. Cresswell, *The Edwardian Inventories for the City and County of Exeter* (London and Oxford, 1916), p. xii.
3. Carew, p. 124v.
4. A. Fletcher and D. MacCulloch, *Tudor Rebellions* (4th edn, Harlow, 1997), p. 63.

## Chapter 1: Presages: The West Country under Henry VIII

1. L. Toulmin-Smith (ed.), *The Itinerary of John Leland, in or about the Years 1535–43: Parts I to III* (London, 1907), p. 240.
2. W.T. MacCaffrey, *Exeter, 1540–1640: The Growth of an English County Town* (Cambridge, Massachusetts and London, 1958; 1978 edn), p. 11.
3. D.H. Pill, 'The Diocese of Exeter under Bishop Veysey' (unpublished MA dissertation, University of Exeter, 1963), pp. 2–7.
4. Toulmin-Smith, *Itinerary*, p. 239.
5. T. Greeves, 'Four Devon Stannaries: A Comparative Study of Tin-Working in the Sixteenth Century', in T. Gray (ed.), *Tudor and Stuart Devon: The Common Estate and Government* (Exeter, 1992), pp. 39–74.
6. Toulmin-Smith, *Itinerary*, p. 174.
7. Pill, 'Veysey', p. 270.
8. Toulmin-Smith, *Itinerary*, pp. 212–13.
9. J.A. Giles (ed.), *William of Malmesbury's Chronicle of the Kings of England* (London, 1847), p. 134.
10. Toulmin-Smith, *Itinerary*, pp. 174–5.
11. Carew, pp. 86r, 89v–90r.
12. See A.L. Rowse, *Tudor Cornwall: Portrait of a Society* (New York, 1941; 1969 edn), p. 88; J. Cornwall, *Revolt of the Peasantry 1549* (London, 1977), p. 41.
13. Toulmin-Smith, *Itinerary*, p. 180.
14. E. Duffy, *The Stripping of the Altars: Traditional Religion in England, 1400–1580* (New Haven and London, 1992; 2005 edn), pp. 142, 146.

15. Carew, pp. 86r, 123v.
16. Toulmin-Smith, *Itinerary*, p. 179.
17. Rowse, *Tudor Cornwall*, pp. 95–6.
18. M. Stoyle, *West Britons: Cornish Identities and the Early Modern British State* (Exeter, 2002), pp. 14–15; for the most authoritative discussion of this subject, see M. Spriggs, 'Where Cornish Was Spoken and When: A Provisional Synthesis', *Cornish Studies*, 11 (2003), pp. 228–69.
19. F.J. Furnivall (ed.), *The Fyrst Boke of the Introduction of Knowledge, Made by Andrew Boorde* (London, EETS, Extra Series, 10, 1870), pp. 122–5.
20. Carew, pp. 66v–67r.
21. C.D. Yonge (ed.), *The Flours of History . . . Collected by Matthew of Westminster* (2 vols, London, 1853), vol. 1, p. 272.
22. Carew, p. 67r.
23. J. Norden, *Speculi Britanniae Pars: A Topographical and Historical Description of Cornwall* (London, 1728), p. 28. Norden's text was originally composed in *c.* 1610.
24. Toulmin-Smith, *Itinerary*, p. 185; Carew, p. 144r.
25. For Sir John Arundell and the power his family wielded in Cornwall, see Speight, pp. 25, 60, 77.
26. Toulmin-Smith, *Itinerary*, p. 185.
27. Speight, p. 27.
28. For the cost of the two forts, see D. Linzey, *The Castles of Pendennis and St Mawes* (London, 1999), p. 25.
29. D&C, 3551 (Chapter Act Book, 1521–1536), ff. 124r–125r. I am most grateful to John Draisey for permitting me to consult his transcriptions and translations of this volume.
30. Toulmin-Smith, *Itinerary*, p. 196.
31. Ibid.; D&C, 3551, ff. 124r–125r.
32. Toulmin-Smith, *Itinerary*, pp. 196–7.
33. For the Godolphins of Godolphin, see J.P.D. Cooper, 'Godolphin, Sir William, b. in or before 1518, d. 1570', in *ODNB*.
34. Carew, p. 159v.
35. Rowse, *Tudor Cornwall*, p. 97; Speight, p. 15.
36. DHC, ECA, Book 51 (John Hooker's Commonplace Book), f. 351.
37. Pill, 'Veysey', p. 317.
38. R. Whiting, *The Blind Devotion of the People: Popular Religion and the English Reformation* (Cambridge, 1989; 1991 edn), p. 118.
39. For a penetrating recent discussion of Lollardy, see P. Marshall, *Heretics and Believers: A History of the English Reformation* (New Haven and London, 2017), pp. 104–19.
40. Whiting, *Blind Devotion*, p. 23.
41. G.W. Bernard, *The King's Reformation: Henry VIII and the Remaking of the English Church* (New Haven and London, 2005), pp. 40–1.
42. For the use of the term 'evangelical' by early sixteenth-century reformers to describe themselves, see D. MacCulloch, *Tudor Church Militant: Edward VI and the Protestant Reformation* (London, 1999), pp. 2–4; Marshall, *Heretics and Believers*, p. 159.
43. J. Foxe, *The First Volume of the Ecclesiastical History, Contayning the Actes & Monumentes of Things Passed in Every Kinges Time* (London, 1576), pp. 1009–12.
44. Bernard, *King's Reformation*, p. 89.
45. Ibid., p. 155; *L&P*, *VI*, 1468 (1), (7).
46. *TRP*, No. 158, pp. 229–32.
47. Whiting, *Blind Devotion*, p. 245.
48. DHC, ECA, Book 51, f. 342v.
49. G.R. Elton (ed.), *The Tudor Constitution: Documents and Commentary* (Cambridge, 1960; 1972 edn), p. 355.

50. Ibid., p. 370.
51. *L&P, VIII*, 359.
52. Speight, p. 144.
53. Ibid., p. 146.
54. E. Duffy, *The Voices of Morebath: Reformation and Rebellion in an English Village* (New Haven and London, 2001), p. 91; Duffy, *Stripping of the Altars*, pp. 394–5.
55. W.H. Frere and W.P.M. Kennedy (eds), *Visitation Articles and Injunctions: Volume II, 1536–1558* (London, 1910), pp. 1–11.
56. On Tregonwell, see Rowse, *Tudor Cornwall*, pp. 176, 187–9; J. Youings, *The Dissolution of the Monasteries* (London, 1971), pp. 67, 74, 78, 88, 180–3.
57. TNA, SP 1/106, f. 159.
58. Ibid.
59. DHC, ECA, Book 51, f. 343. For the best previous account of the riot at St Nicholas Priory, see Speight, pp. 149–50.
60. DHC, ECA, Book 51, f.343.
61. TNA, SP 1/102, f. 33. This document is calendared under 1536 in *L&P, X*, 296, but clearly dates to the following year.
62. Ibid.
63. Ibid.
64. M.H. and R. Dodds, *The Pilgrimage of Grace, 1536–37, and the Exeter Conspiracy, 1538* (2 vols, Cambridge, 1915), I, pp. 355–57.
65. Ibid., pp. 243, 245–7, 249, 257, 259–60, 269, 329–30; DHC, ECA, Book 51, f. 343v.
66. Rose-Troup, p. 174, citing D&C, letter 75.
67. On Haynes, see C.S. Knighton, 'Haynes [Heynes], Simon (d.1552)', in *ODNB*; D. MacCulloch, *Thomas Cranmer: A Life* (New Haven and London, 1996), pp. 193, 301.
68. *L&P, XII*, 2, No. 182.
69. TNA, SP 1/118, f. 248. For previous accounts of the Carpyssacke affair, see Rose-Troup, pp. 29–31; G.R. Elton, *Policy and Police: The Enforcement of the Reformation in the Age of Thomas Cromwell* (Cambridge, 1972; 1985 edn), pp. 295–96; Speight, pp. 151–2; J.P.D. Cooper, *Propaganda and the Tudor State: Political Culture in the West Country* (Oxford, 2003), pp. 118–21.
70. TNA, SP 1/118, f. 248; E. Hall, *The Union of the Two Noble and Illustre Famelies of Lancastre & Yorke* (London, 1548; 1809 edn), p. 477.
71. TNA, SP 1/118, f. 248.
72. On the use of the banner of the five wounds by the Pilgrims, see Dodds and Dodds, *Pilgrimage of Grace*, I, pp. 139, 238, 261, 344; II, p. 300.
73. TNA, SP 1/118, f. 248.
74. See Jules Breton's painting *Le Pardon de Kergoat en Quéménéven en 1891* (1891).
75. Cooper, *Propaganda*, pp. 119–20.
76. TNA, SP 1/118, f. 248.
77. TNA, SP 1/119, f. 143
78. *L&P, XII, 1*, 1127; Speight, p. 152.
79. See *L&P, XII, 1*, p. 204; J. Bellamy, *The Tudor Law of Treason* (London, 1979; Abingdon, 2013 edn), p. 207.
80. See *L&P, XII, 2*, 595; Speight, p. 152.
81. Rose-Troup, p. 174.
82. D&C, 3552 (Dean and Chapter Act Book, 1537–1556), ff. 1r–v. I am most grateful to John Draisey for permitting me to consult his transcriptions and translations of this volume.
83. *L&P, XII, 2*, no. 557, p. 211.
84. DHC, Chanter, 15 (Bishop Veysey's Register, Volume 2, 1519–51), ff. 74–6 (my italics).
85. Ibid., f. 76.
86. Ibid., f. 83.

87. DHC, ECA, Book 51, f. 344.
88. Frere and Kennedy, *Visitation Articles*, pp. 34–43 (quotations pp. 37–8).
89. Whiting, *Blind Devotion*, p. 66; Duffy, *Voices of Morebath*, pp. 96–7.
90. Dodds and Dodds, *Pilgrimage of Grace*, II, pp. 310–25.
91. On the Council of the West, see C.A.J. Skeel, 'The Council of the West', *TRHS*, 4th series, 4 (1921), pp. 62–80; J.A. Youings, 'The Council of the West', *TRHS*, 5th series, 10 (1960), pp. 41–59.
92. D. Willen, *John Russell, Earl of Bedford: One of the King's Men* (RHS Studies in History, no. 23, London, 1981), p. 30; Youings, 'Council of the West', p. 43.
93. See H.M. Speight, 'Local Government and the South Western Rebellion of 1549', *Southern History*, 18 (1996), p. 4; Speight, pp. 1–3.
94. *L&P, XII, 2*, p. 595.
95. W.J. Blake, 'The Rebellion of Cornwall and Devon in 1549', *JRIC*, vol. 18, part 1 (1910), p. 152; Speight, pp. 153–4.
96. Speight, p. 80.
97. For Grenville, and the tension between him and the Arundells, see Speight, pp. 56, 68.
98. Elton, *Tudor Constitution*, pp. 389–92.
99. MacCulloch, *Cranmer*, pp. 237–56.
100. Bernard, *King's Reformation*, pp. 542–79.
101. On Blaxton, see Pill, 'Veysey', pp. 14–15, 38; T.F. Mayer and C.B. Walter, *The Correspondence of Reginald Pole, Volume 4, A Biographical Companion: The British Isles* (Aldershot, 2008), pp. 61–6; DHC, Chanter, 14 (Bishop Veysey's Register, Volume I, 1519–51), passim.
102. D&C, 3552, ff. 14v–15v.
103. Ibid., ff. 15v, 20r.
104. Rose-Troup, p. 177.
105. On Carew, see J. Wagner, *The Devon Gentleman: A Life of Sir Peter Carew* (Hull, 1998); J.P.D. Cooper, 'Carew, Sir Peter (1514?–1575)', in *ODNB*.
106. J. Maclean (ed.), *The Life and Times of Sir Peter Carew Knight* (London, 1857), pp. 1–12.
107. Ibid., pp. 22–38, 36–7.
108. On Dudley's religious views, see B.L. Beer, *Northumberland: The Political Career of John Dudley, Earl of Warwick and Duke of Northumberland* (Kent, Ohio and London, 1973), pp. 66, 68–9, 98; on Carew and the heretical book, see *L&P, XX, 2*, no. 995, p. 490.
109. *L&P, XX, 2*, no. 995, p. 490; Cooper, 'Carew'.
110. See Speight, p. 112.

**Chapter 2: Foreshocks: The Disturbances of 1547–48**

1. D.E. Hoak, *The King's Council in the Reign of Edward VI* (Cambridge, 1976), p. 34.
2. S. Alford, *Edward VI: The Last Boy King* (London, 2014), p. 24 (quotation).
3. J. Loach, *Edward VI* (1999), pp. 25–7.
4. Hoak, *King's Council*, pp. 43–4.
5. M.L. Bush, *The Government Policy of Protector Somerset* (London, 1975), pp. 1–2.
6. On Somerset's religious beliefs, see Bush, *Protector Somerset*, pp. 102–12; D. MacCulloch, *Tudor Church Militant: Edward VI and the Protestant Reformation* (London, 1999), pp. 42–51.
7. On Edward's religious beliefs, see MacCulloch, *Tudor Church Militant*, pp. 20–41.
8. *APC, II (1547–50)*, p. 11.
9. For Paulet's subsequent attempts to 'enforce the Reformation' in the Channel Islands during the early 1550s, see C.S.L. Davies, 'Paulet, Sir Hugh, *b.* before 1510, *d.* 1573', in *ODNB*.

10. P.E. Barnes (ed.), *Memorials of the Most Reverend Father in God Thomas Cranmer . . . by John Strype* (2 vols, London, 1853), I, pp. 207–9; D. MacCulloch, *Thomas Cranmer: A Life* (New Haven and London, 1996), pp. 369–70.
11. Speight, p. 91.
12. H. Speight, 'Local Government and the South-Western Rebellion of 1549', *Southern History*, 18 (1996), p. 4. It is interesting to note that, on 22 July, Sir John Arundell received a royal pardon for an unspecified offence: see *CPR, Edward VI, II*, p. 140. Whether or not this offence was connected with Sir John's removal from the Cornish bench two months before must remain a matter for conjecture.
13. Speight, pp. 88, 94.
14. P. Nicolles, *The Copie of a Letter Sente to One Maister Chrispyne* (London, 1547).
15. J.P. Collier (ed.), *Trevelyan Papers prior to AD 1558* (Camden Society, Old Series, 67, 1856), p. 194.
16. J.P.D. Cooper, 'Godolphin, Sir William, *b.* in or before 1518, *d.* 1570', in *ODNB*.
17. *APC, II*, p. 100.
18. W.H. Frere and W.P.M. Kennedy (eds), *Visitation Articles and Injunctions: Volume II, 1536–57* (London, 1910), p. 114.
19. E. Duffy, *The Voices of Morebath: Reformation and Rebellion in an English Village* (New Haven and London, 2001), p. 118.
20. Frere and Kennedy, *Visitation Articles, II*, pp. 115–26.
21. Ibid., pp. 115–26, 61–4.
22. MacCulloch, *Cranmer*, pp. 375–6.
23. Duffy, *Morebath*, p. 119.
24. Nicolles, *Copie of a Letter*, dedication.
25. Ibid.
26. Ibid.
27. Frances Rose-Troup suggested that Crispin and Moreman were imprisoned 'early in 1547': see Rose-Troup, p. 108. Yet, as both men are known to have been present at a meeting of the Exeter Cathedral Chapter held on 29 October 1547, but their names do not appear on the list of attendees thereafter, it seems reasonable to assume that they had, in fact, been arrested shortly after the latter date: see D&C, 3552 (Dean and Chapter Act Book, 1537–56), f. 47v. In a recent article, it has been noted that Crispin and Moreman were both absent as canons at Exeter between 1547 and 1551: see W.H. Campbell, 'The Canons Resident of Exeter Cathedral, 1506–1561', *RTDA*, 146 (June 2014), p. 130.
28. *CSPD, Edward VI*, p. 48.
29. Barnes, *Memorials of . . . Thomas Cranmer*, I, p. 208; MacCulloch, *Cranmer*, p. 369.
30. Nicolles, *Copie of a Letter*, title-page and dedication.
31. *L&P, XII*, 2, no. 557, p. 211.
32. Nicolles, *Copie of a Letter*, dedication.
33. DHC, ECA, Mayor's Court Book, 81 (1545–47), f. 106.
34. J.A. Muller, *Stephen Gardiner and the Tudor Reaction* (London, 1926), pp. 164–7.
35. J. Wagner, *The Devon Gentleman: A Life of Sir Peter Carew* (Hull, 1998), p. 103.
36. D. Pickering, *The Statutes at Large, from the Thirty-Second Year of K. Hen. VIII to the Seventh Year of K. Edw. VI* (London, 1763), pp. 260–1; D. MacCulloch, 'Parliament and the Reformation of Edward VI', *Parliamentary History*, vol. 34, part 3 (2015), pp. 389–90.
37. G.W. Bernard, *The King's Reformation: Henry VIII and the Re-making of the English Church* (New Haven and London, 2005), pp. 500–5 (quotation p. 502).
38. MacCulloch, *Tudor Church Militant*, p. 63.
39. Pickering, *Statutes at Large*, pp. 267–86.
40. DHC, ECA, Exeter Chamber Act Book, 2 (1509–60), f. 89r.

41. The letter was addressed to 'the Dean and cannons', but Exeter's radical dean, Simon Haynes, was almost certainly attending the convocation in London when the letter was sent.
42. *APC, II*, p. 534.
43. Ibid.
44. *APC, II*, pp. 538–9. For 'sedicious letters' similarly 'cast about the city' at Canterbury in 1548–49, see Canterbury Cathedral Archives, Canterbury, F/A/14, 1546–53, f. 113. I owe this reference to Daniel Spencer.
45. *APC, II*, pp. 538–9.
46. As Diarmaid MacCulloch has observed, 'seditious' was a term that members of the evangelical establishment regularly used as a label for traditionalist views: *Tudor Church Militant*, pp. 84–5.
47. *APC, II*, p. 534 (my italics).
48. The 'Bill for the enlarging of the Liberties of the City of Exeter' was passed in the Commons in February 1548, and in the Lords in February 1549: see Anon., *Journal of the House of Commons, Volume I, 1547–1629* (London, 1802), p. 8; Anon., *Journal of the House of Lords, Volume II, 1509–1577* (London, 1767), p. 342.
49. Speight, p. 113; *CPR, Edward VI, V*, p. 317.
50. W. Page (ed.), *The Inventories of Church Goods for the Counties of York, Durham and Northumberland* (Surtees Society, 97, 1896), p. xi.
51. DHC, Chanter, 15 (Bishop Veysey's Register, Volume 2, 1519–51), f. 115r.
52. I. Arthurson, 'Fear and Loathing in West Cornwall: Seven New Letters on the 1548 Rising', *JRIC*, new series, II, vol. 3, parts 3–4 (2000), p. 70; Rose-Troup, pp. 57–8.
53. E. Duffy, *The Stripping of the Altars: Traditional Religion in England, 1400–1580* (New Haven and London, 1992; 2005 edn), p. 456; *APC, II*, p. 536.
54. *APC, II*, pp. 535–6.
55. Ibid.
56. Ibid., p. 536.
57. R. Whiting, *The Blind Devotion of the People: Popular Religion and the English Reformation* (Cambridge, 1991), p. 110, citing TNA, STAC 3/2/14.
58. J.E. Cox (ed.), *The Works of Thomas Cranmer: Archbishop of Canterbury, Martyr, 1556* (2 vols, Cambridge, 1846), II, p. 510 (author's italics).
59. Ibid.
60. Muller, *Gardiner*, p. 171.
61. MacCulloch, *Cranmer*, p. 384.
62. Cox, *Works of Cranmer*, II, p. 511. See also *TRP*, I, no. 300, pp. 417–18.
63. J. Ketley (ed.), *The Two Liturgies, AD 1549 and AD 1552, Set Forth by Authority in the Reign of King Edward VI* (1844), pp. 4–5; MacCulloch, *Cranmer*, pp. 384–5; H.A. Wilson (ed.), *The Order of the Communion, 1548: A Facsimile of the British Museum Copy* (London, 1908), pp. vii–xlii.
64. For these three terms, see J. Mattingly (ed.), *Stratton Churchwardens' Accounts, 1512–1578* (DCRS, New Series, 60, 2018), p. 162; Rose-Troup, p. 83; Carew, p. 63r.
65. TNA, STAC 7/7/12 (Tregose vs Penheliche et al.).
66. Arthurson, 'Fear and Loathing', p. 89.
67. Ibid.
68. For Killigrew's appointment as governor of Pendennis, see A.L. Rowse, *Tudor Cornwall: Portrait of a Society* (London, 1941; New York, 1969 edn), p. 247; for his claim for his expenses, see TNA, E 351/3538 (Account of J. Killigrew).
69. Arthurson, 'Fear and Loathing', p. 89; for Treffry and his position as captain of St Mawes, see TNA, REQ 2/25, no. 190; Rowse, *Tudor Cornwall*, pp. 247, 259.
70. TNA, SP 46/22, ff. 6, 24. See also Carew, p. 86.

71. *APC, II*, p. 535.
72. Carew, p. 98r.
73. G. Lefevre-Pontalis (ed.), *Correspondance politique de Odet de Selve: ambassadeur de France en Angleterre, 1544–49* (Paris, 1888), p. 328.
74. *FRDK*, p. 218.
75. Ibid., p. 219.
76. Carew, p. 98r; J. Speed, *The Historie of Great Britaine* (2nd edn, London, 1623), p. 1110; B.L. Beer (ed.), *The Life and Raigne of King Edward the Sixth, by John Hayward* (Kent, Ohio, and London, 1993), p. 75.
77. Lefevre-Pontalis, *Odet de Selve*, p. 328.
78. *FRDK*, pp. 217–18.
79. Ibid., p. 219.
80. Ibid.
81. Ibid.
82. Ibid.; Rose-Troup, p. 85.
83. *FRDK*, pp. 217–19.
84. Rose-Troup, p. 83.
85. R.N. Worth (ed.), *Calendar of the Plymouth Municipal Records* (Plymouth, 1893), p. 16.
86. Lefevre-Pontalis, *Odet de Selve*, p. 328. Letters from Godolphin 'and others in Cornewall', presumably sending word of the disturbances in the West, had reached the Council within three days of the initial trouble at St Keverne: see TNA, E315/257 (Account Book of the Court of Augmentations), f. 69v.
87. Arthurson, 'Fear and Loathing', p. 88.
88. WDRO, W/1 130 (Plymouth Receivers' Accounts), f. 246.
89. Arthurson, 'Fear and Loathing', p. 88.
90. *APC, II*, p. 198. See also TNA, E315/257, f. 71v.
91. Arthurson, 'Fear and Loathing', p. 88.
92. Ibid., p. 89.
93. Carew, p. 63r.
94. *FRDK*, p. 217.
95. *CPR, Edward VI, V*, p. 404; *TRP*, I, no. 308, p. 427.
96. *FRDK*, p. 217.
97. The men against whom the jurors decided there was insufficient evidence to proceed to a prosecution may well have been returned to prison, as five of them received pardons later in the year: see *CPR, Edward VI, I*, p. 275.
98. *APC, II*, p. 554.
99. The other two were James Roberts and William Amys: see *CPR, Edward VI, II*, p. 68; Rose-Troup, p. 89.
100. WDRO, W/1 130, ff. 248, 249r.
101. TNA, E 315/257, f. 81v.
102. *FRDK*, pp. 218–19. We must presume that the sixth man sent up to London in April had died, for whatever reason, in the Tower.
103. *FRDK*, p. 219.
104. TNA, E 344/19/15 (Geffrey's names appears in the list of clerics in Powder hundred).
105. W.D. Hamilton (ed.), *A Chronicle of England during the Reigns of the Tudors, from AD 1485 to 1559*, vol. II (Camden Society, New Series, 20, 1877), p. 4.
106. See *CPR, Edward VI, I*, p. 320.
107. Arthurson, 'Fear and Loathing', p. 91.
108. See, for example, Beer, *Rebellion and Riot*, p. 48; Speight, pp. 181–3.
109. A. Fletcher and D. MacCulloch, *Tudor Rebellions* (7th edn, Abingdon, 2020), p. 32.
110. *FRDK*, p. 219.

111. Ibid.
112. Arthurson, 'Fear and Loathing', pp. 85–6, 91.
113. Muller, *Gardiner*, p. 181.
114. TNA, E 351/3538; [W. Lynne], *The Thre Bokes of Cronicles ... [of] John Carion* (London, 1550), f. 274v.
115. Wilson, *Order of Communion*, pp. xxiii, xxvi.
116. Jones, pp. 79–80.
117. See W.J. Blake, 'The Rebellion of Cornwall and Devon in 1549', *JRIC*, vol. 18, part 1 (1910), pp. 171–7.

**Chapter 3: Outbreak: June 1549**

1. 2 & 3 Edward VI, c. 1, in G. Eyre and A. Strahan (eds), *Statutes of the Realm* (11 vols, London, 1810–28), IV, part 1, pp. 37–9.
2. D. MacCulloch, *Thomas Cranmer: A Life* (New Haven and London, 1996), pp. 410–21.
3. 2 & 3 Edward VI, c. 36, in Eyre and Strahan, *Statutes of the Realm*, IV, part I, pp. 78–93.
4. M.L. Bush, *The Government Policy of Protector Somerset* (London, 1975), p. 52.
5. 2 & 3 Edward VI, c. 36, in Eyre and Strahan, *Statutes of the Realm*, IV, part I, pp. 78–93. On the relief's likely repercussions in Devon, see J. Youings, 'The South-Western Rebellion of 1549', *Southern History*, 1 (1979), p. 106; E. Duffy, *The Voices of Morebath: Reformation and Rebellion in an English Village* (London and New Haven, 2001), p. 128.
6. Duffy, *Morebath*, pp. 111–28.
7. *CSPD, 1547–53*, p. 93; B.F. Cresswell, *The Edwardian Inventories for the City and County of Exeter* (London and Oxford, 1916), p. iii, passim; L.S. Snell (ed.), *Documents towards a History of the Reformation in Cornwall, No. 2: The Edwardian Inventories of Church Goods from Cornwall* (Exeter, 1955), pp. 6–7, passim.
8. *TRP*, 1, no. 327, p. 451.
9. Jones, p. 85.
10. Ibid., p. 86; R.C. Anderson (ed.), *Letters of the Fifteenth and Sixteenth Centuries* (Southampton, 1921), p. 66. I owe this latter reference to Daniel Spencer.
11. Jones, p. 87; D. Hoak, *The King's Council in the Reign of Edward VI* (1976; Cambridge, 2008 edn), pp. 35, 51.
12. On Herbert, see N.P. Sil, 'Herbert, William, First Earl of Pembroke (1506/7–1570)', in *ODNB*; O.L. Dick (ed.), *Aubrey's Brief Lives* (1949; London 1987 edn), pp. 221–3.
13. M.B. Davies, 'Boulogne and Calais from 1545 to 1550', *Bulletin of the Faculty of Arts at Fouad University*, 12 (1950), pp. 61–2. See also W.K. Jordan, *The Chronicle and Political Papers of King Edward VI* (London, 1966), p. 12.
14. Jones, p. 89.
15. Bod., Rawlinson MS, C.792, f. 1.
16. S. Mendyk, 'Hooker, John (c.1527–1601)', in *ODNB*.
17. Ibid.; D. MacCulloch, *Tudor Church Militant: Edward VI and the Protestant Reformation* (London 1999), p. 79.
18. Mendyk, 'Hooker', p. 960; J. Hooker, 'The Description of the Citie of Excester', in Holinshed, p. 1014.
19. Holinshed; DHC, ECA, Book 52, ff. 1–36; later published in W.J. Harte, J.W. Schopp and H. Taply-Soper (eds), *The Description of the Cittie of Excester, by John Vowell, alias Hoker: Volume II* (DCRS, Old Series, 19, 1919), pp. 55–96.
20. Bod., Rawlinson MS, C.792.
21. See J. Maclean (ed.), *The Life and Times of Sir Peter Carew, Knight* (London, 1857).
22. Holinshed, p. 1014.
23. Bod., Rawlinson MS, C.792, f. 1.

24. Holinshed, p. 1015.
25. For the visitors' order forbidding local clergymen to wear copes over their surplices, see Duffy, *Morebath*, p. 120.
26. Holinshed, p. 1015.
27. For the estimated population of Sampford Courtenay at this time, see J. Cornwall, *Revolt of the Peasantry, 1549* (London, 1977) p. 64.
28. Youings, 'South-Western Rebellion', pp. 116–17.
29. Rose-Troup, p. 133.
30. R. Hutton, *The Stations of the Sun: A History of the Ritual Year in Britain* (Oxford, 1996), pp. 244–5, 258.
31. Hoak, *King's Council*, p. 195; Hutton, *Stations*, p. 250. For a muttered threat by a Norwich apprentice in 1551 to rise against the rich men who had appropriated the former church-goods 'one Whitson Sondaye', see A. Wood, '"Poore men woll speke one daye": Plebeian Languages of Deference and Defiance in England, c.1520 – 1640', in T. Harris (ed.), *The Politics of the Excluded, c. 1500–1850* (Basingstoke, 2001), p. 87.
32. Hutton, *Stations*, pp. 249–50.
33. *CSPD, 1547–53*, p. 121.
34. Rose-Troup, Appendix E, pp. 427–9; DHC, Chanter, 14 (Bishop Veysey's Register, Volume I, 1519–51), f. 121.
35. DHC, Chanter, 14, f. 121; Pocock, p. 18.
36. Rose-Troup, p. 429.
37. Holinshed, p. 1015, marginal note.
38. Cornwall, *Revolt*, p. 66; T.L. Stoate (ed.), *Devon Lay Subsidy Rolls, 1543–45* (Bristol, 1986), p. 116.
39. KCC, KC/KCAR/6/2/140/08 SAC/66 (Sampford Courtenay Survey Book of 1568). The Underhills were still at 'Franckland' in 1616: see WCSL, DCRS/x/SAM, T.L. Stoate (transcriber), 'Sampford Courtenay Parish Registers' (typescript vol., 1988), p. 137.
40. D. MacCulloch and A. Fletcher, *Tudor Rebellions* (7th edn, London, 2020), p. 138.
41. Holinshed, p. 1015.
42. J. Youings, *Tuckers Hall, Exeter* (Exeter, 1968), pp. 10–11; DHC, ECA, Exeter Chamber Act Book 2 (1509–60), f. 133.
43. G. Oliver and P. Jones (eds), *A View of Devonshire in MDCXXX* (Exeter, 1845), p. 524.
44. Rose-Troup, p. 134; R. Whiting, *The Blind Devotion of the People: Popular Religion and the English Reformation* (Cambridge, 1989; 1990 edn), p. 221.
45. Holinshed, p. 1015.
46. Ibid.; Bod., Rawlinson MS, C.792, f. 2.
47. Holinshed, p. 1015.
48. Bod., Rawlinson MS, C.792, f. 3.
49. M. Bateson (ed.), *A Collection of Original Letters from the Bishops to the Privy Council, 1564* (Camden Society, New Series, 53, 1893), p. 69.
50. Bod., Rawlinson MS, C.792, f. 3.
51. Nothing is known for sure about William Hellyons beyond what Hooker tells us, but it has been suggested that he may conceivably be identifiable with the 'William Hillinges' who is noted to have owned two messuages in the parish of Northam in North Devon in 1549: see B.L. Beer, *Rebellion and Riot: Popular Disorder in England during the Reign of Edward VI* (2nd edn, Kent, Ohio, 2005), p. 223, n. 34; *CPR, Edward VI, III (1549–51)*, pp. 139–40; Stoate, *Lay Subsidy Rolls*, p. 103.
52. Holinshed, p. 1026.
53. Ibid.
54. Ibid.

55. BL, Anon., 'Ballad on the Defeat of the Devon and Cornwall Rebels, 1549' (printed fragment).
56. For 'Sampford More', see KCC, KC/KCAR/6/2/140/08, SAC/66.
57. DHC, ECA, Exeter Chamber Act Book, 2, f. 103; Hutton, *Stations*, pp. 313–14.
58. See Hutton, *Stations*, p. 315.
59. DHC, ECA, Exeter Chamber Act Book, 2, f. 103; C.R. Cheney and M. Jones, *A Handbook of Dates for Students of British History* (Cambridge, 2000), p. 79.
60. Bod., Rawlinson MS, C.792, f. 3.
61. Maclean, *Life*, p. 47; Holinshed, p. 1015.
62. A Privy Council order of 19 June noting that 'Mr Carew' had been given a warrant to pay for various arms probably related to Sir Wymond Carew, the receiver of the Duchy of Cornwall, rather than to Sir Peter or Sir Gawen: see *APC, II (1547–50)*, p. 292, index.
63. Holinshed, p. 1015.
64. *APC, II*, p. 292.
65. *CSPD, 1547–53*, p. 113; Pocock, pp. 8–10.
66. Pocock, pp. 8–10.
67. *CPR, Edward VI, II*, p. 251; D. Willen, *John Russell, First Earl of Bedford: One of the King's Men* (RHS Studies in History, 23, London, 1981), p. 70.
68. G. Redworth, *In Defence of the Church Catholic: The Life of Stephen Gardiner* (Oxford, 1990), p. 286.
69. Bod., Rawlinson MS, C.792, f. 2.
70. Maclean, *Life*, p. 48.
71. J. Walter, 'Grain Riots and Popular Attitudes to the Law: Maldon and the Crisis of 1629', in his *Crowds and Popular Politics in Early Modern England* (Manchester, 2006), p. 38.
72. Pocock, pp. 4–5.
73. For the argument that the Devon JPs may have succeeded in temporarily bringing the disorders under control prior to the arrival of the Carews, based on the phraseology of Somerset's letter of 26 June, see H.M. Speight, 'Local Government and the South-Western Rebellion of 1549', *Southern History*, 18 (1996), pp. 13–14.
74. Pocock, p. 38.
75. See A.L. Rowse, *Tudor Cornwall: Portrait of a Society* (1941; New York 1969 edn), p. 268; D. MacCulloch and A. Fletcher, *Tudor Rebellions* (4th edn, Harlow, 1997), p. 55.
76. Pocock, p. 39; J.G. Nichols (ed.), *Chronicle of the Grey Friars of London* (Camden Society, Old Series, 53, London, 1852), p. 59.
77. See Hutton, *Stations*, pp. 304–10; E. Duffy, *The Stripping of the Altars: Traditional Religion in England 1400–1580* (New Haven and London, 1992; 2005 edn), p. 460.
78. Pocock, pp. 26, 28, 29, 38.
79. Maclean, *Life*, p. 47.
80. Ibid.
81. Bod., Rawlinson MS, C.792, f. 2v.
82. Ibid.
83. Holinshed, p. 1016.
84. Ibid.
85. Longleat House, Thynne MSS, Sir John Thynne's Letter Book, vol. 2, f. 123r.
86. Maclean, *Life*, pp. 50–1; Speight, 'Local Government and the South-Western Rebellion', p. 12 (quotation).
87. Maclean, *Life*, p. 48.
88. Holinshed, p. 1016; Bod., Rawlinson MS, C.792, f. 3.
89. Bod., Rawlinson MS, C.792, f. 3v.
90. Holinshed, p. 1016; Bod., Rawlinson MS, C.792, f. 3.

91. Holinshed, p. 1022 (my italics). See also Maclean, *Life*, p. 51.
92. Bod., Rawlinson MS, C.792, f. 3.
93. DHC, ECA, Exeter Chamber Act Book, 2, f. 103v.
94. Ibid., ff. 103v–104; DHC, ECA, Exeter Mayor's Court Book, 81 (1545–57), ff. 179–80.
95. Bod., Rawlinson MS, C.792, f. 3.
96. Ibid., f. 3v.
97. Ibid., ff. 3v–4. Sadly, I can find no contemporary evidence to support Cotton's frequently repeated assertion that this acrimonious supper took place at the Mermaid Inn: see W. Cotton and H. Woollcombe, *Gleanings from the Municipal and Cathedral Records Relative to the History of the City of Exeter* (Exeter, 1877), p. 51.
98. Holinshed, p. 1017.
99. Bod., Rawlinson MS, C.792, f. 4v (my italics).
100. Ibid.
101. Ibid.
102. Maclean, *Life*, pp. 50–2.
103. Pocock, pp. 12–13. The second addressee is given here as 'Peter Courtenay', but this was probably a slip for 'Piers'.
104. Pocock, pp. 12–13.
105. Ibid.
106. Bod., MS Rawlinson MS, C.792, f. 4v.
107. R.M. Warnicke, 'Sheriff Courtenay and the Western Rising of 1549', in J. Bliss et al. (eds), *Aspects of Devon History: People, Places and Landscapes* (Exeter, 2012), pp. 143–8.
108. Holinshed, p. 1016.
109. Ibid., p. 1025.
110. TNA, SP 10/9, f. 48.
111. TNA, C 1/1289/66 (Bury vs Bury); TNA, C 78/9/48 (Chubbe vs Bury).
112. A. Travers (ed.), *Robert Furse: A Devon Family Memoir of 1593* (DCRS, New Series, 53, 2010), p. 32.
113. T. Risdon, *The Chorographical Description or Survey of the County of Devon* (Plymouth, 1811), p. 260.
114. Pocock, pp. 15–18.
115. Ibid.
116. Ibid.
117. For the keeping of an 'ancient charter' of the Cornish tinners in the steeple of Luxillian church, for example, see KK, 113, D.41, f. 49.
118. *A Message Sent by the Kynges Maiestie, to Certain of his People, Assembled in Devonshire* (London, 1549), sig. A3v.
119. Bod., Rawlinson MS, C.792, f. 5.
120. Ibid.
121. DHC, ECA, Book 55 ('The Freeman's Book'), f. 97v, marginal note.

**Chapter 4: Escalation: 1–15 July 1549**

1. Bod., Rawlinson MS, C.792, 'The Beginninge, Cause & Course of the Comotion ... in ... Devon and Cornewall ... Collected by John ... Hooker', f. 5.
2. Ibid., f. 6v. One of the Chamber men, John Wolcot, was definitely suspected of sympathising with the rebels: see Holinshed, p. 1019.
3. D. Willen, *John Russell, First Earl of Bedford: One of the King's Men* (RHS Studies in History, 23, London, 1981), pp. 68–9.
4. J. Youings, 'The City of Exeter and the Property of the Dissolved Monasteries', *RTDA*, 84 (1952), pp. 135–6.

5. Ibid., p. 123.
6. *A Copye of a Letter Containing Certayne Newes, & the Articles or Requestes of the Devonshyre & Cornyshe Rebelles* (London, 1549), sig. B.viii.
7. Bod., Rawlinson MS, C.792, f. 5; Youings, 'The City of Exeter', pp. 138–9.
8. Bod., Rawlinson MS, C.792, ff. 7v–8; Holinshed, p. 1019.
9. Holinshed, p. 1017; Speight, p. 218.
10. M. Stoyle, *Circled with Stone: Exeter's City Walls, 1485–1660* (Exeter, 2003), pp. 190–1; Holinshed, p. 1021.
11. Pocock, p. 18.
12. DHC, Chanter, 14 (Bishop Veysey's Register, Volume 1, 1519–51), f. 132.
13. Holinshed, p. 1021.
14. Bod., Rawlinson MS, C.792, f. 5v.
15. Ibid.
16. See J.A. Lynn, *Women, Armies and Warfare in Early Modern Europe* (Cambridge, 2008), passim.
17. It is interesting to note, in this context, that after the insurrection had been crushed, Reginald Mohun and two other Cornish gentlemen threatened to 'seke the extremity of lawe' against Agnes Winslade, the wife of the executed rebel leader John Winslade, 'whom they chardged to have been like offender as her husband was'. But the fact that Mohun and his allies levelled this charge against Agnes during the course of an attempt to seize the lands that John had previously settled on her must surely make us suspicious of their claim. See TNA, E 178/531 (inquisition as to the possessions of William Widesladd, 26 Elizabeth I).
18. Stoyle, *Circled with Stone*, pp. 75–8, 124–30, 188–9.
19. Bod., Rawlinson MS, C.792, f. 5.
20. *APC, V (1554–56)*, p. 112.
21. M.B. Davies (ed.), 'Boulogne and Calais from 1545 to 1550', *Bulletin of the Faculty of Arts of Fouad University*, 12 (1950), p. 62.
22. For the rebels' possession of ordnance, see Bod., Rawlinson MS, C.792, f. 5v; Holinshed, p. 1026.
23. Holinshed, p. 1018.
24. E. Duffy, *The Voices of Morebath: Reformation and Rebellion in an English Village* (New Haven and London, 2001), pp. 131, 134–41.
25. L. Toulmin-Smith (ed.), *The Itinerary of John Leland, in about the Years 1535–43: Parts I to III* (London, 1907), p. 239.
26. For Hooker's description of the protestors as the 'Sampford Courtney men', see Bod., Rawlinson MS, C.792, f. 2v.
27. There are many references to the earthwork known as the 'New Castle' in Exeter's medieval records: see, for example, DHC, ECA, Exeter Receiver's Roll, 1415/16.
28. For 'the Lammas Feyr, held in a place called Saynt Davyes Downe and Curlediche', see *L&P, XX*, 620 (4). See also J. and J.H. Wylie (eds), *HMC Report on the Records of the City of Exeter* (London, 1916), pp. 227–8; D.H. Pill, 'The Diocese of Exeter under Bishop Veysey' (MA dissertation, University of Exeter, 1963), p. 231.
29. For the rebels' carrying of 'crosses [and] banners' into the field during their later battles with Russell, see J. Foxe, *The First Volume of the Ecclesiastical History Containing the Actes and Monumentes* (London, 1570), p. 1499.
30. *CSPS, IX (1547–49)*, p. 397.
31. Rose-Troup, Appendix H ('La Responce du Peuple Anglois a leur Roy Edouard'), pp. 449-70; Anon., *A Message Sent by the Kynges Maestie, to Certain of his People Assembled in Devonshire* (unpaginated, London[?], *c.* 9 July 1549). For a copy of the *Message*, which has been mistakenly retitled to suggest that it was sent to the rebels of Devon *and* Cornwall, see Holinshed, pp. 1003–6.

32. A.R. Greenwood, 'A Study of the Rebel Petitions of 1549' (unpublished PhD thesis, University of Manchester, 1990), p. 23; Anon., *A Message*, passim. See also the discussion in Greenwood, 'Petitions', pp. 41–8.
33. A. Fletcher and D. MacCulloch, *Tudor Rebellions* (7th edn, Abingdon, 2020), p. 65; Greenwood, 'Petitions', p. 128.
34. Anon., *A Message*, [pp. 3r–v].
35. See F.W. Russell, *Kett's Rebellion in Norfolk* (London, 1859), pp. 40, 47, 68.
36. Pocock, p. 22.
37. Bod., Rawlinson MS, C.792, f. 7v.
38. J. Maclean (ed.), *The Life and Times of Sir Peter Carew* (London, 1865), p. 52. For confirmation of the fact that Russell 'lay longe' at Honiton, see C.L. Kingsford, *Two London Chronicles from the Collection of John Stow* (Camden Miscellany, Volume 12, London, 1910), p. 17.
39. Pocock, p. 22.
40. Ibid., pp. 22–3.
41. Bod., Rawlinson MS, C.792, f. 7.
42. Pocock, pp. 25–6; Bod., Rawlinson MS, C.792, f. 3v.
43. Pocock, p. 26; Holinshed, p. 1022; Speight, pp. 219–22.
44. Pocock, pp. 23–4.
45. TNA SP 10/9, no. 48 (transcribed in Rose-Troup, pp. 345–6); TNA, KB 8 17, items 1–13 (summarised in *FRDK*, pp. 221–2); Carew, pp. 63, 86, 98, 99v, 111v–112, 124, 155v; BL, Add MSS, 29,762 (William Hals's History of Cornwall), ff. 116v–118v; D. Gilbert, *The Parochial History of Cornwall: Founded on the Manuscript Histories of Mr Hals and Mr Tonkin* (4 vols, London, 1838), II, pp. 191–8.
46. See Rose-Troup, pp. 123–9. Hals's account is essentially a ragbag of information pulled together from the work of John Foxe and other published writers, though it may contain one or two fragments of genuinely independent material.
47. Hals's statement that John Milliton had been sheriff of Cornwall in 1549, for example, was followed by all historians of the rising until Helen Speight pointed out, as late as 1991, that the post had in fact been held in that year by Richard Chamond: see BL, Add MSS, 29,762, f. 117; Speight, pp. 104–5.
48. M. Stoyle, 'Fullye Bente to Fighte Oute the Matter: Reconsidering Cornwall's Role in the Western Rebellion of 1549', *EHR*, vol. 129, no. 538 (June 2014), pp. 554–65.
49. Bod., Rawlinson MS, C.792, f. 1.
50. TNA, E 351/3538 (Account of John Killigrew).
51. See *APC, II (1547–50)*, p. 162. On Killigrew and his father, see A.L. Rowse, *Tudor Cornwall: Portrait of a Society* (1941; New York, 1969 edn), pp. 85, 247–8, 293; A.C. Miller, *Sir Henry Killigrew: Elizabethan Soldier and Diplomat* (Leicester, 1963), pp. 5–9.
52. TNA, E 351/3538.
53. Ibid.
54. BL, Anon., 'Ballad on the Defeat of the Devon and Cornwall Rebels, 1549' (printed fragment).
55. See M. Stoyle, 'The Execution of "Rebel" Priests in the Western Rising of 1549', *JEH*, vol. 71, no. 4 (October 2020), p. 5; p. 12, fn. 51.
56. Carew, p. 124.
57. Gilbert, *Parochial History*, I, p. 88.
58. J.P.D. Cooper, 'Arundell, Humphrey, 1512/13–1550', in *ODNB*.
59. J. Chynoweth, *Tudor Cornwall* (Stroud, 2002), p. 179.
60. For Arundell as an 'unquiet' spirit, see, for example, Rowse, *Tudor Cornwall*, p. 263; J. Cornwall, *Revolt of the Peasantry 1549* (London, 1977), p. 60.
61. Speight, pp. 190–1.
62. Foxe, *Actes and Monumentes*, p. 1496.

63. On Arundell and the Mount, see BL, Add MSS, 29,762, f. 116v; Rose-Troup, pp. 99–100. Cornwall states that Arundell had led a band of foot soldiers at the siege of Boulogne in 1544, but does not provide a source: see *Revolt of the Peasantry*, p. 61.
64. TNA, SP 10/9, f. 48.
65. TNA, KB 8, no. 17, item 9; Speight, pp. 27, 91. See also Rose-Troup, pp. 100–1; Chynoweth, *Tudor Cornwall*, pp. 37, 84–5, 90–1, 112, 213–15.
66. It is interesting to note that Winslade's grandson went on to serve the king of Spain during the Elizabethan period: see C. Hayden, 'Tristram Winslade: The Desperate Heart of a Catholic in Exile', *Cornish Studies*, 20 (2012), pp. 32–62.
67. Rose-Troup, p. 100, n. 2.
68. TNA, SP 10/9, f. 48.
69. I. Arthurson, 'Fear and Loathing in West Cornwall: Seven New Letters on the 1548 Rising', *JRIC*, new series, vol. 3, parts 3–4 (2000), p. 89.
70. TNA, SP 10/9, f. 48.
71. *FRDK*, p. 222.
72. Carew, p. 86.
73. TNA, KB 8/17, f. 9.
74. Ibid.
75. M. Stoyle, 'Kill All the Gentlemen?: (Mis)representing the Western Rebels of 1549', *HR*, vol. 92, no. 255 (February 2019), pp. 50–72.
76. For Matilda Grenville, the daughter of John Bevill, see J.L. Vivian and H.H. Drake, *The Visitation of the County of Cornwall in the Year 1620* (London, 1874), p. 85.
77. Carew, p. 99v.
78. WDRO, W/1 130 (Plymouth Receivers' Accounts), f. 246.
79. TNA, E 351/3538.
80. TNA, C1/1216/55 (Ennys vs Playsted).
81. KK, CA/B35/27 (receipt signed by Thomas Treffry).
82. On Treffry, see Rowse, *Tudor Cornwall*, pp. 89, 228, 247, 249, 251; for Henderson's claim that Treffry remained loyal in 1549, see Henderson, *Essays*, p. 37.
83. Carew, p. 155v.
84. Ibid.
85. On Trewynnard, see J.J. Goring, 'Trewynnard, William', in S.T. Bindoff (ed.), *The House of Commons, 1509–1558* (3 vols, London, 1982), III, pp. 485–6.
86. TNA, STAC 5/T34, file 32 (Trewynnerd vs Newman and Hoppier).
87. Ibid.
88. Arthurson, 'Fear and Loathing', p. 91.
89. Ibid., pp. 79, 92.
90. The fact that, on 18 July, the councillors – having recently been apprised of the situation in Cornwall – were still instructing Russell to pass on orders to Godolphin strongly suggests that Sir William remained at liberty, whether in Pendennis or elsewhere: see Pocock, p. 33.
91. M. Stoyle, 'A Hanging at St Keverne: The Execution of Two Cornish Priests in 1549', *DCNQ*, vol. 52, part 1 (spring 2017), pp. 1–4.
92. Carew, pp. 111v–112.
93. BL, Cotton MS, Galba B.12, f. 114 (letter from Lord Russell, August 1549). See also BL, Harleian MS, 523 ('A book in 4to wherein are contained copies of divers letters from Sir Philip Hoby'), f. 51v.
94. Vivian and Drake, *Visitation*, p. 85; TNA, C1/1321/27 (Whetehyll vs Daryelle).
95. TNA, C1/1321/27.
96. For two recent military histories of the rising that consider how the rebel host may have been raised and armed in depth, see A. Hodgkins, 'They Would Yield to No Persuasions

... But Most Manfully Did Abide the Fight: A Military Assessment of the Western Rebellion', *RTDA*, 147 (2015), pp. 117–54, esp. pp. 121–32; E.T. Fox, *The Commotion Time: Tudor Rebellion in the West, 1549* (Warwick, 2020), esp. ch. 3, pp. 58–86.

97. Carew, p. 98.
98. Ibid., pp. 82v–83v.
99. Foxe, *Actes and Monumentes*, p. 1496.
100. For the Rosogan family, see Rose-Troup, p. 104; J.L. Vivian and H.H. Drake (eds), *The Visitation of Cornwall in the Year 1620* (London, 1874), p. 193.
101. TNA, STAC 2/28/70 (Mohon vs Arundell).
102. *TRP*, I, no. 339, p. 473. See also Pocock, p. 29.
103. Pocock, p. 33.
104. Ibid., p. 30.
105. Ibid., p. 33.
106. WDRO, W/1 130, ff. 254–5. On the Midsummer Watch, see R. Hutton, *The Stations of the Sun: A History of the Ritual Year in Britain* (Oxford, 1996), pp. 311–15.
107. WDRO, W/1 130, ff. 255r–v.
108. For Plymouth's lack of landward defences, see J. Barber, 'New Light on Old Plymouth', *Proceedings of the Plymouth Athenaeum*, iv (1973–79), pp. 55–66. For the Fort, see WDRO, W/1 130, ff. 246r–v, 248–9v; Carew, p. 99v. For the castle, see Barber, 'New Light', pp. 55–9; R. Higham, 'Public and Private Defence in the Medieval South-West', in R. Higham (ed.), *Security and Defence in South-West England before 1800* (Exeter, 1987), p. 45.
109. WDRO, W/1 130, ff. 255v, 257.
110. For the Council's instructions to Sir William Herbert, dated 23 July, to march to Russell's assistance with all speed, see TNA, SP10/8, f. 34.

**Chapter 5: Flood Tide: 15–31 July 1549**

1. Pocock, p. 27.
2. M.L. Bush, *The Government Policy of Protector Somerset* (London, 1975), p. 87; J. Cornwall, *Revolt of the Peasantry: 1549* (London, 1977), pp. 6–7, 90–3.
3. Pocock, p. 23.
4. C.L. Kingsford (ed.), *Two London Chronicles from the Collection of John Stow* (Camden Miscellany, Volume 12, London, 1910), p. 17.
5. Pocock, p. 23.
6. Ibid., p. 26. For the strength and composition of Grey's forces, see W.K. Jordan, *The Chronicle and Political Papers of King Edward VI* (London, 1966), p. 13; *CSPS, IX (1547–49)*, p. 406.
7. K. Halliday, 'New Light on the Commotion Time of 1549: The Oxfordshire Rising', *HR*, vol. 82, no. 218 (November 2009), pp. 655–76, esp. pp. 657, 669, 671–3.
8. TNA, SP 46/2, f. 19.
9. D. Loades, 'Kingston, Sir Anthony (c.1508–1556)', in *ODNB*.
10. See J.L. Vivian (ed.), *The Visitations of the County of Devon: Comprising the Heralds' Visitations of 1531, 1564 and 1620* (Exeter, 1895), p. 246.
11. TNA, SP 46/2, f. 21.
12. Kingston and his men may possibly have travelled down to Devon alongside other forces that Sir William Herbert had raised in Gloucestershire: see Pocock, p. 29.
13. See Anon. (ed.), *Grafton's Chronicle, or History of England* (2 vols, London, 1809), II, p. 519; Carew, p. 124.
14. For the classic account of this episode, see F.W. Russell, *Kett's Rebellion in Norfolk* (London, 1859); for Kett himself, see J. Walter, 'Kett, Robert (c.1492–1549)', in *ODNB*.
15. For the argument that the disturbances in Norfolk had little in common with the protests in Devon and Cornwall, and that it is misleading, in many ways, to describe

Kett's followers as 'rebels', see Russell, *Kett's Rebellion*, p. 3, n. 3; D. MacCulloch, *Tudor Church Militant: Edward VI and the Protestant Reformation* (London, 1999), p. 44.

16. For the list of articles that was eventually drawn up by the East Anglian protestors, entitled 'Kett's Demands Being in Rebellion', see D. MacCulloch and A. Fletcher, *Tudor Rebellions* (7th edn, Abingdon, 2020), pp. 161–3. For their use of the prayer book, see ibid., p. 91.
17. Pocock, p. 24.
18. D. MacCulloch, 'Kett's Rebellion in Context', in P. Slack (ed.), *Rebellion, Popular Protest and the Social Order in Early Modern England* (Cambridge, 1984), p. 41.
19. J. Strype, *Ecclesiastical Memorials Relating Chiefly to Religion . . . under King Henry VIII, King Edward VI and Queen Mary I, II, Part 1* (Oxford, 1822 edn), p. 276.
20. Pocock, p. 32.
21. Ibid., pp. 29, 23.
22. Ibid., p. 30.
23. Ibid., pp. 31–2, 34.
24. J. Maclean (ed.), *The Life and Times of Sir Peter Carew, Knight* (London, 1857), p. 52.
25. Bod., Rawlinson MS, C.792, 'The Beginninge, Cause & Course of the Comotion . . . in . . . Devon and Cornewall . . . Collected by John . . . Hooker', f. 7v.
26. Maclean, *Life*, p. 52.
27. See, for example, B.L. Beer, *Rebellion and Riot: Popular Disorder in England during the Reign of Edward VI* (2nd edn, Kent, Ohio, 2005), pp. 75–6.
28. TNA, SP 10/7, f. 41.
29. In his highly influential edition of a series of contemporary documents pertaining to the Western Rising, published in 1884, Nicholas Pocock assigned Russell's paper to June 1549, but did not explain why he had done so. Frances Rose-Troup, writing forty years later, noted in a neglected footnote that this date was evidently incorrect and suggested that the paper was instead a part of the lost letter that Russell is known to have sent to the Council on 18 July. See Pocock, pp. 11–12; Rose Troup, p. 243, n. 1. I suspect that, while Rose-Troup was nearly correct, the paper is in fact one of the 'articles of answere' which the councillors noted Russell to have enclosed with that letter: see Pocock, p. 30.
30. For support for the rebels in Dorset, Somerset, Wiltshire and Hampshire, see Pocock, pp. 40, 47; Rose-Troup, p. 407.
31. Maclean, *Life*, p. 52.
32. On Russell's 'extreme caution', see D. Willen, *John Russell, First Earl of Bedford: One of the King's Men* (RHS, Studies in History Series, 23, London, 1981), p. 72. On Carew's 'bold, active' and 'forceful' nature, see J. Wagner, *The Devon Gentleman: A Life of Sir Peter Carew* (Hull, 1998), p. 12.
33. For an excellent study of these petitions, which carefully reconsiders both their content and their chronology, see A.R. Greenwood, 'A Study of the Rebel Petitions of 1549' (unpublished PhD thesis, University of Manchester, 1990), part I, pp. 22–208.
34. TNA, SP 10/9, f. 48.
35. Pocock, p. 26.
36. Ibid.
37. For a discussion of this pamphlet and a transcription of the entire text, see Rose-Troup, 'Appendix H', pp. 441–70.
38. Greenwood, 'Petitions', p. 27.
39. Ibid., p. 27; Rose-Troup, p. 465; Halliday, 'Oxfordshire Rising', p. 666.
40. Rose-Troup, pp. 441–7; Greenwood, 'Petitions', p. 56 (quotation).
41. W.D. Hamilton (ed.), *A Chronicle of England during the Reigns of the Tudors from 1585 to 1559, by Charles Wriothesley, Windsor Herald* (2 vols, Camden Society, New Series, 11, 1875–77), II, p. 17.

42. Pocock, p. 33.
43. Ibid., p. 37.
44. There are a number of different drafts of this 'Answer': see TNA, SP 10/8, 5–8. Document No. 6, the most complete draft, is transcribed in full in Rose-Troup, Appendix G, pp. 433–40.
45. 'The King's Majestie's Answer' is incorrectly calendared in the *CSPD* under 8 July. For the true date of its composition, see Rose-Troup, p. 218; Greenwood, 'Petitions', p. 28; Stoyle, 'Fully Bent to Fight Out the Matter', p. 568.
46. For Somerset's authorship, see Rose-Troup, p. 218.
47. For summaries of the grievances that appear to have been raised in this supplication, see Rose-Troup, p. 218; Greenwood, 'Petitions', ch. 2, pp. 41–71.
48. TNA, SP 10/8, f. 6.
49. Pocock, p. 42.
50. Ibid., p. 37.
51. TNA, KB, 8/17, item 9. For 'Kestell', or 'Castell', see TNA, SP 10/7, f. 54; W.J. Blake, 'The Rebellion of Devon and Cornwall in 1549', *JRIC*, vol. 18, part 2 (1911), p. 323.
52. Pocock, p. 37.
53. Ibid., p. 42.
54. Ibid., p. 24.
55. *TRP*, I, no. 339, pp. 473–4.
56. Pocock, p. 29.
57. Ibid., p. 33.
58. Ibid., p. 41.
59. TNA, E 351/3538 (Account of J. Killigrew).
60. Anon., *A True Relation of a Brave Defeat Given by the Forces in Plimouth to Skellum Greenvile* (London, *c.* 18 February 1645), p. 4.
61. TNA, C1/1216/55 (Ennys vs Playsted).
62. Holinshed, p. 1018; for the possible identification of this individual as Richard Coffyn of Portlinch, see Rose-Troup, p. 103, n. 2.
63. BL, Anon., 'Ballad on the Defeat of the Devon and Cornwall Rebels' (printed fragment, 1549).
64. Pocock, p. 32.
65. WDRO, W/1 130 (Plymouth Receivers' Accounts), ff. 246, 248r–v, 253, 254–7.
66. M.A.S. Hume (ed.), *Chronicle of King Henry VIII of England* (London, 1889), p. 181.
67. Rose-Troup, p. 359, n. 1.
68. R.N. Worth (ed.), *Calendar of the Plymouth Municipal Records* (Plymouth, 1893), p. viii.
69. R.J. Skinner, 'The "Declaracion" of Ley: His Pedigree, Part II', *DCNQ*, vol. 37, part III (spring 1993), p. 102.
70. Pocock, p. 33. On Thomas Cotton's appointment as vice-admiral in May 1549, see C.S. Knighton and D. Loades (eds), *The Navy of Edward VI and Mary* (Navy Records Society Publications, 157, Farnham, 2011), p. 100, citing SP 10/7, no. 12.
71. WDRO, W/1 130, f. 257; Pocock, p. 33.
72. For Hooker's most fulsome account of the siege, see Holinshed, pp. 1018–22. For later accounts, see Rose-Troup, chs 12–13; Cornwall, *Revolt of the Peasantry*, ch. 5; M. Stoyle, *Circled with Stone: Exeter's City Walls, 1485–1660* (Exeter, 2003), pp. 78–80; Beer, *Rebellion and Riot*, pp. 57–61.
73. Bod., Rawlinson MS, C.792, ff. 6v–7.
74. Holinshed, p. 1021.
75. Bod., Rawlinson MS, C.792, ff. 8v–9.

76. Anon., 'Ballad on the Defeat of the Devon and Cornwall Rebels'.
77. Longleat House, Thynne MSS, vol. 2, f. 121v.
78. Rose-Troup, p. 380.
79. *APC, III (1550–1552)*, p. 231; A.L. Rowse and M. I. Henderson (eds), *Essays in Cornish History by Charles Henderson* (Oxford, 1935; Truro, 1963 edn), p. 196.
80. TNA, C1/1253/33 (Pomeroy vs Carsewell).
81. For Carvanell's self-description, in a petition to the king, as 'one of the yeomen of your grace's guard', see TNA, STAC, 3/1/46 (Carvanell vs Hawkyn). For the affair of the 'pope-holy pilgrimage', see A.L. Rowse, *Tudor Cornwall: Portrait of a Society* (1941; New York, 1969 edn), p. 231.
82. M. Hunkin, 'Resistance to the Edwardian Reformation: A Study of Religious Discontent in Devon and Cornwall during the Prayer Book Rebellion of 1549' (unpublished MA thesis, University of Southampton, 2001), p. 35; PRO, STAC 3/2/78 (Carvanell vs Esseball).
83. For the destruction of documents by protestors during the Middle Ages, see, for example, I.M.W. Harvey, *Jack Cade's Rebellion of 1450* (Oxford, 1991, 2010 edn), p. 125.
84. TNA, C 1/1368/79 (Morcombe vs Brownynge).
85. TNA, C 1/1276/1–4 (Wadland vs Gove).
86. E.H. Young, 'A Short Account of the Okehampton Market', *RTDA*, 57 (1926), p. 195.
87. D. MacCulloch, *Thomas Cranmer: A Life* (New Haven and London, 1996), p. 430.
88. E. Duffy, *The Voices of Morebath: Reformation and Rebellion in an English Village* (New Haven and London, 2001), p. 142.
89. J. Mattingly (ed.), *Stratton Churchwardens' Accounts, 1512–1578* (DCRS, New Series, 60, 2018), p. 92.
90. See R. Whiting, *The Blind Devotion of the People: Popular Religion and the English Reformation* (1989; Cambridge, 1991 edn), p. 76.
91. Duffy, *Morebath*, p. 139.
92. Ibid., p. 135.
93. Ibid., p. 138.
94. TNA, C1/1507/60 (Late bailiffs of Launceston vs Amadas).
95. TNA, SP 10/9, f. 48.
96. Pocock, pp. 34–5.
97. Bod., Rawlinson MS, C.792, ff. 8v–9.
98. Jordan, *Chronicle*, p. 14.
99. Pocock, p. 40.
100. 'R.L.', *A Copye of a Letter Containing Certayen Newes, & the Articles or Requestes of the Devonshyre and Cornyshe Rebelles* ([London], 1549). For a transcription of these articles, see Fletcher and MacCulloch, *Tudor Rebellions*, pp. 155–6.
101. Though, as Aubrey Greenwood notes, the list of nine articles published by John Foxe in 1570 – all of which relate to religion – may well be roughly contemporaneous with the Fifteen Articles and may even be 'a preliminary list submitted by one of the four camps during the compilation of the fifteen articles': see Greenwood, 'Petitions', pp. 35–8 (quotation p. 37). A variant copy of the original Fifteen Articles, with a sixteenth article added, was later printed in a tract now held at Corpus Christi College, Oxford: see Rose-Troup, pp. 222-3.
102. See, for example, Rose-Troup, ch. 14; Greenwood, 'Petitions', pp. 31–5, ch. 2; MacCulloch and Fletcher, *Tudor Rebellions*, pp. 65–9.
103. 'R.L.', *A Copye of a Letter*.
104. Ibid.; Pocock, p. 26.
105. 'R.L.', *A Copye of a Letter* (my italics).

106. Ibid.
107. WCSL, DCRS, X/SAM, T.L. Stoate (transcriber), 'Sampford Courtenay Parish Registers, 1558–1813' (typescript vol., 1988), pp. 1, 99, 125.
108. 'R.L.', *A Copye of a Letter.*
109. Blake, 'Rebellion of Cornwall and Devon', p. 193.
110. A view that is especially clearly expressed in Beer, *Rebellion and Riot*, pp. 61–2.
111. C. Hayden, 'Tristram Winslade: The Desperate Heart of a Catholic in Exile', *Cornish Studies*, 20 (2012), p. 52.
112. Bod., Rawlinson MS, C.792, f. 10.
113. Pocock, p. 32.
114. Jordan, *Chronicle*, p. 14. Russell's strength at this time is clearly much exaggerated in Rose-Troup, ch. 16 ('The Battle of Fenny Bridges'), pp. 253–61.
115. See Pocock, p. 44; Holinshed, p. 1002.
116. Holinshed, p. 1023.
117. Bod., Rawlinson MS, C.792, f. 10; Holinshed, p. 1023.
118. Bod., Rawlinson MS, C.792, f. 10; Holinshed, p. 1023.
119. Holinshed, p. 1023.
120. Bod., Rawlinson MS, C.792, f. 10v; Longleat House, Thynne MSS, vol. 2, ff. 123–4.
121. Bod., Rawlinson MS, C.792, f. 10v.

**Chapter 6: Defeat: August 1549**

1. J. Lock, 'Grey, William, Thirteenth Baron Grey of Wilton (1508/9–1562)', in *ODNB*; *CSPS, X (1550–52)*, p. 389 (quotation).
2. Bod., Rawlinson MS, C.792, 'The Beginninge, Cause & Course of the Comotion . . . in . . . Devon and Cornewall . . . Collected by John . . . Hooker', f. 10v.
3. Pocock, p. 26.
4. *CSPS, IX (1547–59)*, p. 406.
5. For the strength of the force that Grey led to Oxfordshire, see W.K. Jordan, *The Chronicle and Political Papers of King Edward VI* (London, 1966), p. 13. For the 200–400 horsemen led by Grey, see Pocock, pp. 23, 32. For Spinola and his Italian 'hagbutters', see TNA, E 101/76/35 (Documents subsidiary to the account of the treasurer of the Court of Augmentations), f. 97; TNA, SP 46/2, f. 31; *APC, II (1547–50)*, pp. 272, 298; Pocock, pp. 26, 29, 30–2; Holinshed, p. 1003. For the 1,000 'almaynes fotmen', see Pocock, p. 23.
6. Rose-Troup, p. 262, followed by most subsequent writers on the rebellion: see, for example, J. Cornwall, *Revolt of the Peasantry 1549* (London, 1977), p. 135; A. Hodgkins, 'They Would Yield to No Persuasions . . . But Most Manfully Did Abide the Fight: A Military Assessment of the Western Rebellion', *RTDA*, 147 (2015), p. 135.
7. For the disturbances in Bristol, see Jones, pp. 99–101.
8. S. Seyer, *Memoirs Historical and Topographical of Bristol and its Neighbourhood, Volume 2* (Bristol, 1823), p. 230.
9. Holinshed, p. 1023.
10. All of the 'Allemans footemen' eventually seem to have been despatched by the Council to assist the earl of Warwick against Kett's rebels, in fact: see *APC, II*, p. 316; TNA, SP 46/2, f. 36. In his recent military history of the rising, E.T. Fox has similarly concluded that none of the German infantrymen was sent to assist Russell in the West: see E.T. Fox, *The Commotion Time: Tudor Rebellion in the West, 1549* (Warwick, 2020), pp. 131–2.
11. C.L. Kingsford (ed.), *Two London Chronicles from the Collection of John Stow* (Camden Miscellany, Volume 12, London, 1910), p. 17.
12. Holinshed, p. 1003. For 'Jacques de Germiny' and his Burgundians, see TNA, SP 46/2, f. 50; *APC, II*, p. 347; Holinshed, p. 1003; Pocock, p. 62; M.B. Davies (ed.),

'Boulogne and Calais from 1545 to 1550', *Bulletin of the Faculty of Arts of Fouad University*, 12 (1950), p. 61.
13. According to the Welsh soldier Ellis Gruffydd, who ought to have known, de Germiny's men were drawn 'from Cleves and Burgundy': see Davies, 'Boulogne and Calais', p. 61.
14. For Petro Zanga and his Albanians, see TNA, SP 46/2, f. 60; *APC, II*, pp. 321, 329, 347; Pocock, p. 62.
15. See Pocock, p. 62, for a letter dated 18 August, in which the councillors asked for their thanks to be conveyed to de Germiny and Zanga for their services during the fighting of 3–6 August.
16. For William Grey and his 200 soldiers, see *APC, II*, p. 309; Pocock, p. 33; Jordan, *Chronicle*, p. 14.
17. Pocock, p. 32; Longleat House, Thynne MSS, vol. 2, f. 127.
18. Bod., Rawlinson MS, C.792, f. 10v. To these 2,500 men should probably be added the 'ccc straungers' whom 'Richmond Herald at Arms' was paid for 'conducting ... to my Lord Privy Seal' on 16 August; the identity of these foreign soldiers unfortunately remains obscure: see *APC, II*, p. 314. E.T. Fox has recently suggested that Russell may have been stronger still at the beginning of August, calculating that the royal army then numbered around 3,200 men: see Fox, *Commotion Time*, p. 128.
19. D. MacCulloch, *Thomas Cranmer: A Life* (New Haven and London, 1996), p. 439. For the full text of Cranmer's 'Answer to the Fifteen Articles of the Rebels', see J.E. Cox (ed.), *Miscellaneous Writings and Letters of Thomas Cranmer* (Cambridge, 1846), pp. 163–87.
20. See MacCulloch, *Cranmer*, p. 438.
21. For the full text of the 'Answer', see Pocock, pp. 141–93. Pocock originally ascribed this document to Udall, but fifty years later G. Scheurweghs suggested that it had, in fact, been written by Philip Nicolles, see G. Scheurweghs, 'On an Answer to the Articles of the Rebels of Cornwall and Devonshire (Royal MS. 18 B. XI)', *The British Museum Quarterly*, 8 (1933–34), pp. 24–5. More recently, Jonathan McGovern has put forward a convincing argument - based on the evidence of the handwriting of the original document - that Pocock's ascription to Udall was, in fact, correct; see J. McGovern, 'Nicholas Udall as Author of a Manuscript Answer to the Rebels of Devonshire and Cornwall, 1549', *Notes and Queries*, vol. 65, issue 1, March 2018, pp. 24-25.
22. Pocock, p. 181.
23. For evidence that Udall had read *A Message Sent by the Kynges Maiestie*, see Pocock, pp. 153, 163.
24. Ibid., p. 145.
25. For Udall's attacks on 'priests' and 'papists', see, for example, ibid., pp. 141, 146, 151, 152, 156, 190.
26. Ibid., p. 192.
27. Ibid., p. 191.
28. For this explanation of the rebels' turn of phrase, see MacCulloch, *Cranmer*, p. 430.
29. Pocock, p. 170.
30. Holinshed, p. 1015; J. Walter, 'Crown and Crowd: Popular Culture and Popular Protest in Early Modern England', in his *Crowds and Popular Politics in Early Modern England* (Manchester, 2006), p. 22.
31. B.L. Beer, *Rebellion and Riot: Popular Disorder in England during the Reign of Edward VI* (Kent, Ohio, 1982; 2nd edn, 2005), p. 168.
32. *TRP*, I, no. 344, p. 478.
33. Cox, *Writings of Cranmer*, pp. 179–80, 183.
34. Pocock, p. 172.
35. See Jones, pp. 33, 49, 58.
36. Carew, pp. 124, 111v; E. Duffy, *The Voices of Morebath: Reformation and Rebellion in an English Village* (New Haven and London, 2001), p. 135.

37. Pocock, p. 186.
38. Ibid., p. 145.
39. Ibid., pp. 156, 183.
40. Ibid., pp. 165, 170.
41. Ibid., p. 190 (my italics).
42. Ibid., p. 148.
43. Bod., Rawlinson MS, C.792, f. 10v.
44. Davies, 'Boulogne and Calais', p. 62.
45. Holinshed, p. 1023.
46. Longleat, Thynne MSS, vol. 2, f. 124.
47. Bod., Rawlinson MS, C.792, ff. 10v–11; Longleat, Thynne MSs, vol. 2, f. 124.
48. Holinshed, p. 1024.
49. Ibid.
50. Ibid.
51. For a brief account of Pomeroy, see Rose-Troup, pp. 103–4. For the claim made by the seventeenth-century writer John Prince that Pomeroy had been 'a commander in the wars under King Henry VIII in France', see J. Prince, *Danmonii Orientales Illustres: or The Worthies of Devon* (London, 1810), p. 649. Pomeroy's name certainly appears on a list of Devon gentlemen who had promised to assist Henry VIII in his third invasion of France, in 1544, in Sir Thomas's case, with a contingent of fifty 'footmen': see TNA, SP 1 185/58.
52. Holinshed, p. 1024.
53. Ibid., p. 1020.
54. Ibid., p. 1024.
55. Jordan, *Chronicle*, p. 14.
56. Holinshed, p. 1024.
57. Ibid.
58. Longleat, Thynne MSS, vol. 2, f. 127.
59. R.J. Skinner, 'The "Declaracion" of Ley: His Pedigree, Part II', *DCNQ*, 37 (1993), p. 103.
60. Ibid.
61. Holinshed, p. 1024.
62. Longleat, Thynne MSS, vol. 2, f. 124.
63. Ibid., f. 127.
64. Holinshed, p. 1024.
65. Ibid.
66. Skinner, 'Declaracion of Ley', p. 103 (my italics).
67. B.L. Beer (ed.), *The Life and Reign of King Edward the Sixth, by John Hayward* (Kent, Ohio and London, 1993), p. 82.
68. Jordan, *Chronicle*, p. 14. For Hayward's heavy reliance on Hooker's narrative and Edward's journal, see Beer, *Life and Reign*, pp. 14, 18.
69. Jordan, *Chronicle*, p. 14; Holinshed, p. 1024.
70. J. Foxe, *The First Volume of the Ecclesiastical History Containing the Actes and Monumentes* (London, 1570), p. 1499.
71. Ibid.
72. Bod., Rawlinson MS, C.792, f. 12v.
73. Holinshed, p. 1025.
74. Longleat, Thynne MSS, vol. 2, ff. 124r–v.
75. Ibid.; Holinshed, p. 1025.
76. Longleat, Thynne MSS, vol. 2, f. 124.
77. For Herbert's 'Welshmen', see Holinshed, p. 1025.
78. Ibid.; Longleat, Thynne MSS, vol. 2, f. 124.

79. Holinshed, p. 1025.
80. Ibid.
81. Pocock, p. 50.
82. W.D. Hamilton (ed.), *A Chronicle of England during the Reign of the Tudors, from AD 1485 to 1559, Volume II* (Camden Society, New Series, 20, 1877), p. 20.
83. Longleat, Thynne MSS, vol. 2, f. 121.
84. Pocock, p. 52.
85. For Sir Gawen's evident displeasure, see Longleat, Thynne MSS, vol. 2, f. 121.
86. Holinshed, p. 1025.
87. Davies, 'Boulogne and Calais', p. 62.
88. Longleat, Thynne MSS, vol. 2, f. 124. For 'public performances of pardon' in the aftermath of rebellions, see K.J. Kesselring, *Mercy and Authority in the Tudor State* (Cambridge, 2003), pp. 1–2, 22, 136, 157–61, 163–99. The fact that the churchwardens of Woodbury subsequently laid out 16s. 'for pardon for the whole parish' suggests that, in the wake of the Western Rebellion – just as in the wake of the later Northern Rebellion – pardons were extended to many 'who had not directly participated in the rising itself, but who had offered ... support': see DHC, Woodbury Churchwardens Accounts, PW1; K.J. Kesselring, *The Northern Rebellion of 1569: Faith, Politics and Protest in Elizabethan England* (Basingstoke, 2010), pp. 128–9. For evidence that the parishioners of Stratton in Cornwall similarly purchased a 'pardon' for their involvement in the rebellion, see J. Mattingly (ed.), *Stratton Churchwardens' Accounts, 1512–1578* (DCRS, New Series, 60, 2018), p. 92.
89. Longleat, Thynne MSS, vol. 2, f. 124.
90. Holinshed, pp. 1025–6.
91. Longleat, Thynne MSS, vol. 2, ff. 124–5. For rebel priests in Oxfordshire, Buckinghamshire and Norfolk in 1549, see K. Halliday, 'New Light on the "Commotion Time" of 1549: The Oxfordshire Rising', *HR*, vol. 82, no. 218 (November 2009), pp. 656, 662, 669–70, 675–6; Jones, pp. 166, 216–19, 228–9, 315; A. Wood, *The 1549 Rebellions and the Making of Early Modern England* (Cambridge, 2007), pp. 28, 170, 180.
92. TNA, C1/1369/11–20 (Martin vs Burnet).
93. *CSPS, IX*, p. 434.
94. Longleat, Thynne MSS, vol. 2, f. 121.
95. WDRO, 542/1 (Parish Register of St Budeaux, 1538–1656), f. 4.
96. Ibid.
97. The fact that the residents of Ashburton later recorded that they had laid out £10 for the service of 'the kyngs ma[jes]tie ayenst the rebells for the preservac[i]on of the townnys of Tottenes & Plymmouth by the comonndment of the lord of Bedford' certainly hints that a loyalist force may have passed through that town on their way to drive the insurgents out of Totnes and Plymouth in August 1549, while the fact that the townsmen of Totnes were later reimbursed some £700 'by them emprested to the Lord Pryvey Seale for his Majest[ie]s affayres' may perhaps point the same way: see Rose-Troup, p. 509; *APC, II*, p. 347.
98. Pocock, pp. 60–1.
99. WDRO, W1/1 130, ff. 256v–257.
100. BL, Cotton, Galba, B.12, f. 113v (Lord Russell's letter giving an account of the battle of Sampford Courtenay); Holinshed, p. 1026.
101. Bod., Rawlinson MS, C.792, f. 13v.
102. Longleat, Thynne MSS, vol. 2, f. 125.
103. BL, Cotton, Galba, B.12, f. 113v.
104. Ibid., f. 114.
105. Ibid.; Holinshed, p. 1026.

106. BL, Cotton, Galba, B.12, f. 114.
107. TNA, C1 1/1367/82 (Lowre vs Cruys).
108. BL, Cotton, Galba, B.12, f. 114.
109. Skinner, 'Declaracion of Ley', pp. 102–3.
110. Ibid., p. 103.
111. Prince, *Worthies*, p. 693.
112. The formal indictment of Arundell and Winslade was later to claim that they, together with 'other traitors', had killed 'divers of the king's lieges' at Launceston on 19 August before they were 'defeated and captured' on the same day: a statement which suggests that the Carews had encountered considerable resistance when they entered the town: see *FRDK*, p. 222. Russell's letter of 19 August clearly indicates that Arundell had already been apprehended before the Carews arrived on the scene, however – probably by some of the townsmen – while, in his own confession, Winslade was later to state that he had remained in Bodmin throughout the entire course of the insurrection, that he had been captured there and that he was 'at no fray': see TNA, SP 10, 9/48. Bearing this in mind, it seems sensible to regard the claims made in the indictment with some scepticism.
113. Longleat, Thynne MSS, vol. 2, f. 127.
114. Ibid., f. 127v.
115. BL, Harleian MSS, 523 ('A book in 4to . . . [of] letters from Sir Philip Hoby'), f. 52.
116. Bod., Rawlinson MS, C.792, f. 13v.
117. Holinshed, p. 1026.
118. Rose-Troup, p. 304.
119. TNA, SP 10 9/48; Rose Troup, p. 304, n. 3.
120. A.J. Jewers (ed.), *The Registers of the Parish of St Columb Major, Cornwall, from the Year 1539 to 1780* (London, 1881), p. 185.
121. TNA, E 351/3538 (Account of J. Killigrew).
122. TNA, E 199/6, item 52 (Inventory of the goods and chattels of Robert Raffe and John Wulcocke). See also M. Stoyle, 'A Hanging at St Keverne: The Execution of Two Cornish Priests in 1549', *DCNQ*, vol. 42, part 1 (spring 2017), pp. 1–4.
123. For a pro-government propaganda piece of late 1549, stating that the western rebels 'begane the laste yere, when they slew Bodye', see BL, Anon., 'Ballad on the Defeat of the Devon and Cornwall Rebels'. For Carew's observation that 'the last Cornish rebellion was first occasioned by one Kilter, and other his associates of . . . St Keveren, who . . . [killed] one Mr Body . . . and the yere following it grew to a general revolt', see Carew, p. 98.
124. Writing many years later, John Hayward was to claim that some of the rebels who had fled from Devon into Somerset had made their way to Bridgwater, and there 'endeavoured to set up the sedition againe': see Beer, *Life and Raigne*, p. 83. Whether this statement relates to the group who marched eastwards under Bury and Coffin, to another group of rebels who were reported to be assembled at Minehead towards the end of August, or whether both of these groups were the same remains unclear. For the rebels at Minehead, see Pocock, p. 66.
125. For the date of the engagement at Kingweston, see TNA, KB 8/17, item 8.
126. SHC, DD/X/LY 3 (Lyte commonplace book), f. 73.
127. 'Kingweston', in M. Siraut (ed.), *A History of the County of Somerset: Volume 10* (Woodbridge, 2010), p. 162.
128. Holinshed p. 1026; TNA, KB 8/17, item 8.
129. Rose-Troup, pp. 318–19.
130. *FRDK*, p. 222.
131. Rose-Troup, pp. 318–19.

**Chapter 7: Retribution: September 1549**

1. See Pocock, pp. 17–18.
2. Ibid., p. 54.
3. Ibid., p. 49.
4. For the description of Pomeroy as 'a simple gente' in a deposition of 1553, see J. Maclean (ed.), *The Life and Times of Sir Peter Carew, Knight* (London, 1857), p. 156. For an example of a captured rebel in the North of England being granted a special pardon 'for his simplicity' in the wake of the insurrection there in 1569, see J. Bellamy, *The Tudor Law of Treason* (1979; Abingdon, 2013 edn), p. 219.
5. Pocock, p. 63.
6. For Robert Paget, see ibid., pp. 53, 55, 62. For his relationship to his brother, see S.R. Gammon, *Statesman and Schemer: William, First Lord Paget – Tudor Minister* (Newton Abbot, 1973), p. 15.
7. Pocock, pp. 53, 55.
8. Ibid., p. 74. It is worth noting here that, on 31 August, a certain 'Jacobus Paget' was brought before the Council alongside two of the western rebel leaders and bound in a heavy recognisance, and that, on 14 December, the same man, now described as 'James Paget of London, gentleman', appeared before the Council and was bound over once again. See *APC, II (1547–50)*, pp. 320, 366. The connections, if any, that existed between James Paget, on the one hand, and Robert Paget and Sir William Paget, on the other, are yet to be elucidated.
9. For the capture of Maunder and Arundell, see BL, Cotton MSS, Galba, B.12 (Lord Russell's letter concerning the battle of Sampford Courtenay), ff. 113, 114.
10. Pocock, p. 63.
11. *FRDK*, p. 222; TNA, SP 10/9, f. 48.
12. BL, Harleian MSS, 523 (Hoby letter-book), f. 52. For William Winslade, see TNA, SP 10/8, f. 54; *APC, II*, p. 354.
13. For William Harris, see TNA, SP 10/8, f. 54; *APC, II*, p. 354. For the identification of 'Harries' as the eldest son of 'Sergeant Harryes', see S. Brigden (ed.), 'The Letters of Sir Richard Scudamore to Sir Philip Hoby, September 1549 to March 1555', in *Camden Miscellany: Number 30* (Camden Society, Fourth Series, 29, 1990), p. 89. For Sergeant John Harris, his residence at Hayne in Lifton parish, and the name of his eldest son, see G. Oliver and P. Jones (eds), *A View of Devonshire in MDCXXX, with a Pedigree of Most of its Gentry, by Thomas Westcote* (Exeter, 1805), p. 531; J. Prince, *Danmonii Orientales Illustres, or The Worthies of Devon* (London, 1810), pp. 468–9. For John Harris's service as recorder of Exeter between 1544 and 1548, see R. Izaacke, *Remarkable Antiquities of the City of Exeter* (2nd edn, London, 1723), part 1, p. 50.
14. For John Wise, see TNA, SP 10/8, f. 54; *APC, II*, p. 354. For the fact that he was Sergeant Harris's son-in-law, see Brigden, 'Scudamore', p. 89. For the marriage between Alice Harris, the daughter of John Harris of Hayne, and John Wise of Sydenham, esquire, see Oliver and Jones, *View of Devonshire*, pp. 531, 553.
15. Pocock, p. 66.
16. For the capture of Bury and Coffin at Kingweston, see TNA, SP 10/9, f. 48; Holinshed, p. 1026.
17. Holinshed, p. 1026.
18. TNA, SP 10/9, f. 48.
19. For a detailed discussion of the rack and the other implements of torture that were kept in the Tower, see Bellamy, *Treason*, pp. 109–21.
20. For a letter sent from the Council to Russell on 27 August, recalling Lord Grey and 'the strangers horsemen', see Pocock, p. 68.
21. Ibid., p. 64.
22. Brigden, 'Scudamore', pp. 73, 89.

23. A separate list of the prisoners who had been sent up to London – undated, but signed by Russell, Herbert and Grey – confirms that Scudamore had correctly identified all of the captives: see TNA, SP 10/8, f. 54. For Fortescue's first name, see *APC, II*, p. 354. It is possible that he was either one of the Fortescues of Preston in Ermington, or one of the Fortescues of Buckland Filleigh: see Oliver and Jones, *View of Devonshire*, p. 625; F.T. Colby, *The Visitation of the County of Devon in the Year 1620* (London, 1872), pp. 109–11. For a second contemporary letter confirming that 'the chief traytors of the West parties' had arrived at Westminster on 9 September, see Longleat House, Thynne MSS, vol. 2, f. 140. For a payment subsequently made to Lord Grey 'for his charges in bryngyng up to London [from] Excester Arundell with the others of the prisoniers [re] belles in the West Contrey', see TNA, E 101/76/35 (Documents subsidiary to the accounts of the treasurer of the Court of Augmentations), f. 124.
24. Brigden, 'Scudamore', p. 89.
25. Holinshed, p. 1027.
26. [W. Lynne], *The Thre Bokes of Cronicles, Whyche John Carion . . . Gathered* (London, 1550), p. cclxxv.
27. Brigden, 'Scudamore', p. 90. For the court's location at Westminster at this time, see *APC, II*, p. 320.
28. Brigden, 'Scudamore', p. 90.
29. Longleat House, Thynne MSS, vol. 2, f. 140. The halters may be said to have signified that the Ketts were already dead men, unless the king chose to pardon them.
30. Brigden, 'Scudamore', p. 88.
31. Ibid., p. 90.
32. *APC, II*, p. 354.
33. TNA, SP 10/8, f. 54 (my italics).
34. Ibid.
35. See Rose-Troup, p. 103, n. 2; J.L. Vivian and H.H. Drake (eds), *The Visitation of the County of Cornwall in the Year 1620* (London, 1874), p. 114. For a later reference to a member of this family as 'Thomas Castell, *alias* Kestell, of Kestell in Egloshayle', see WDRO, Plymouth Archives, 372/6/3/22.
36. D.E. Hoak, *The King's Council in the Reign of Edward VI* (Cambridge, 1976; 2008 edn), pp. 51, 61.
37. Pocock, p. 18.
38. S.B. House, 'Literature, Drama and Politics', in D. MacCulloch (ed.), *The Reign of Henry VIII: Politics, Policy and Piety* (London, 1995), pp. 185–6.
39. G.W. Bernard, *The King's Reformation: Henry VIII and the Remaking of the English Church* (New Haven and London, 2005), pp. 374–5.
40. See M.H. Dodds and R. Dodds, *The Pilgrimage of Grace, 1536–37, and the Exeter Conspiracy, 1538* (2 vols, Cambridge, 1915), II, chs 18–19.
41. *L&P, XII, 1*, p. 204.
42. See Bernard, *King's Reformation*, pp. 467–74, 489, 574–5.
43. For the proclamations of 14 June and 16 July ordering martial law against future rioters, see *TRP*, I, nos 334, 341, pp. 462–4, 475–6.
44. K. Halliday, 'New Light on the Commotion Time of 1549: The Oxfordshire Rising', *HR*, 82 (2009), pp. 657, 662; *CSPD, 1547–1553*, p. 127.
45. For the execution of Joyes, see *CPR, Edward VI, III: 1549–51*, p. 117. For the execution of the vicar of Barford in Oxfordshire at Aylesbury in August, see W.D. Hamilton (ed.), *A Chronicle of England during the Reigns of the Tudors . . . by Charles Wriothesley, Volume 2* (Camden Society, New Series, 20, 1877), p. 21.
46. 'R. L.', *A Copye of a Letter Containing Certayne Newes & the Articles or Requestes of the Devonshyre & Cornyshe Rebelles* (London, 1549), sig. B.vii verso.
47. Ibid., sig. B.viiiv.

48. Ibid., sigs A.iii, A.iiiv.
49. Ibid., sigs B.ii, B.iiv.
50. John Fry to Sir John Thynne, 16 August 1549, Longleat, Thynne MSS, vol. 2, ff. 124v–125.
51. Holinshed, p. 1026.
52. TNA C1/1369/19 (Martin vs Burnet, the answer of John Stampe).
53. TNA, E 199/6, item 52 (inventory of the goods of Robert Raffe and John Wulcocke).
54. J. Foxe, *The First Volume of the Ecclesiastical History Contayning the Actes and Monumentes* (London, 1570), p. 1496.
55. M. Stoyle, 'The Execution of Rebel Priests in the Western Rising of 1549', *JEH*, vol. 71, no. 4 (October 2020), pp. 759, 761.
56. For John Bochym, see BL, Add MSS, 29,762 ('[William] Hals's MSS of his Parochial History of Cornwall'), f. 59.
57. For Royse, see Stoyle, 'Rebel Priests', p. 759.
58. Brigden, 'Scudamore', p. 87.
59. For the priest Sir John Chaundeler, who led a rebel attack on Bury St Edmunds and who afterwards tried to stir up support for Kett in Essex, see B.L. Beer, *Rebellion and Riot: Popular Disorder in England during the Reign of Edward VI* (Kent, Ohio, 1982; 2nd edn, 2005), pp. 141–3, 147. His ultimate fate is unknown.
60. A recent claim that John Perin, the former abbot of Tavistock, was executed at some time between October 1549 and April 1550 for his part in the rebellion must be regarded, at least for the moment, as unproven: see E.T. Fox, *The Commotion Time: Tudor Rebellion in the West, 1549* (Warwick, 2020), pp. 83, 104, 182.
61. P.A.S. Pool, 'Cornish Parishes in 1753: IV, Stratton', *Old Cornwall*, vol. I, no. 11 (1966), p. 502; see also J. Mattingly (ed.), *Stratton Churchwardens' Accounts, 1512–78* (DCRS, New Series, 60, 2018), pp. 27 (and n. 178), 163 (and n. 50).
62. Mattingly, *Stratton Churchwardens' Accounts*, pp. 92, 163.
63. See Stoyle, 'Rebel Priests', table 3, p. 773; TNA, C 1/1387/14 (Tayllor vs Brayleghe).
64. DHC, Chanter, 14, Register of Bishop John Veysey, Volume 1 (1519–51), ff. 132v, 133r, 133v, 134r, 134v, 135r (Marystow).
65. Ibid., f. 135r.
66. Ibid., ff. 135r–v. I am indebted to Jonathan Vage for pointing out to me that a new scribe appears to have taken over the register at the foot of f. 135r.
67. Ibid., ff. 136r–9v.
68. I am extremely grateful to Jonathan Vage for confirming for me – from his extensive databases of West Country clergymen – that no further references to these men after 1549–50 are, at present, known to survive.
69. For the many executions of monks and other clerics that took place in the aftermath of the risings of 1536–37, see Dodds and Dodds, *The Pilgrimage of Grace*, II, chs 18–19.
70. TNA, C 1/1341/77 (Curtes vs stewards of Lydford).
71. It is not hard to imagine that the celebrated Sir Christopher Trychay – the parish priest of Morebath, on the borders of Exmoor – might have decided to adopt such a course of action during the turbulent summer of 1549, for example: see E. Duffy, *The Voices of Morebath: Reformation and Rebellion in an English Village* (New Haven and Yale, 2001), passim.
72. TNA, C 1/1341/77.
73. R.J. Skinner, 'The "Declaracion" of Ley: His Pedigree, Part II', *DCNQ*, 37 (1993), p. 103.
74. TNA, C 3/107/22 (Kemyshe vs Tewenneck).

75. Anon. (ed.), *Grafton's Chronicle, or History of England to Which Is Added his Table of the Bailiffs, Sheriffs and Mayors of the City of London* (2 vols, London, 1809), II, pp. 519–20.
76. C. Henderson, 'The Ecclesiastical History of the 109 Western Parishes of Cornwall', *JRIC*, new series, vol. 3, part 3 (1959), p. 452.
77. Pocock, p. 66. For an interesting account of the way in which John Chubbe of Ugborough, yeoman – later described as one who had been 'a great doer' in the rebellion and an 'under Captayne' under John Bury – set about obtaining his pardon in the wake of the rebels' defeat 'by ma[king] sute as well to dyverse men of honour as other[s] of worshippe and gave theym ... in rewarde for ther paynes ... [various] somes of money', see TNA, C 78/9/48 (Bury vs Chubb).
78. TNA, C 1/1272/49 (Tothill vs Stowell).
79. DHC, Chanter, 14, f. 132v.
80. For Blaxton's sustained record of religious conservatism, see T.F. Mayer and C.B. Walters (eds), *The Correspondence of Reginald Pole, Volume 4: A Biographical Companion – The British Isles* (Aldershot, 2008), pp. 61–6.
81. D&C, 3552 (Dean and Chapter Act Book, 1537–56), ff. 50v–51v.
82. Ibid.; Holinshed, p. 1021; D.H. Pill, 'The Diocese of Exeter under Bishop Veysey' (unpublished MA dissertation, University of Exeter, 1963), p. 335.
83. Pill, 'Veysey', p. 321.
84. J. Vowell, alias Hooker, *The Antique Description and Account of the City of Exeter, in Three Parts* (Exeter, 1765), p. 138.
85. *CPR, Edward VI, Volume IV, 1550–53* (London, 1926), pp. 36–7. For Coverdale's service with Russell in the West, see Pocock, p. 7, n. b, and p. 75; Holinshed, p. 1023.
86. DHC, ECA, Book 55 ('The Freeman's Book'), f. 134.
87. Hamilton, *Chronicle of England*, p. 20.
88. *CSPS, IX (1547–49)*, p. 432; Longleat House, Thynne MSS, vol. 2, f. 124. Edward VI himself later noted that at least 1,500 rebels had been killed during the fighting near Exeter: see W.K. Jordan (ed.), *The Chronicle and Political Papers of King Edward VI* (London, 1966), pp. 14–15.
89. TNA, C 1/1272/84 (Turpyn vs Denys).
90. For the discovery of 'a vast number of bones' on Clyst Heath when it was first ploughed, during the nineteenth century, which were judged to be the remains of those who had died in the fighting of 1549, see Rose-Troup, p. 276. A certain 'John Stevens of Witheridge' is another Devon man who is known, from a chance reference, to have been 'killed in the Rebellyon tyme': see J. Youings, 'Devon Monastic Bells', in T. Gray (ed.), *Devon Documents* (Tiverton, 1996), p. 213.
91. BL, Cotton, Galba, B.12, ff. 113–14.
92. M.B. Davies (ed.), 'Boulogne and Calais from 1545 to 1550', *Bulletin of the Faculty of Arts of Fouad University*, 12 (1950), p. 71; J. Stow, *A Summarie of Englyshe Chronicles* (London, 1565), p. 211.
93. Longleat House, Thynne MSS, vol. 2, f. 127.
94. Holinshed, p. 1027.
95. J. Stow, *The Annales of England* (London, 1592), p. 1006.
96. Pocock, pp. 40, 42.
97. Ibid., p. 42.
98. Ibid., p. 53.
99. Anon., *Grafton's Chronicle*, II, p. 519.
100. The man in question would appear to be one Nicholas Bowyer, who had previously served as mayor of Bodmin in 1536: see Rose-Troup, p. 309.
101. Anon., *Grafton's Chronicle*, II, pp. 519–20.
102. S. Rudder, *A New History of Gloucestershire* (Cirencester, 1779), p. 595.
103. Carew, p. 124.

104. Anon., *Grafton's Chronicle*, II, p. 520.
105. BL, Add MSS, 29,762, f. 118v. Frances Rose-Troup identifies the subject of Hals's anecdote as 'William Mayow', probably on the basis of the fact that a man of that name appears in the St Columb parish register: see Rose-Troup, pp. 104, 310, 499.
106. BL, Add MSS, 29,762, f. 118v.
107. M. Spriggs, 'Where Cornish Was Spoken and When: A Provisional Synthesis', *Cornish Studies*, 11 (2003), p. 239.
108. TNA, C 1/1216/55 (Ennys vs Playsted).
109. TNA, C 1/1367/82 (Lowre vs Cruys).
110. *TRP*, I, pp. 473–4.
111. TNA, C 1/1367/82.
112. Ibid.
113. TNA, C 1/1383/2 (Saundrye vs Bossyns).
114. A. Travers (ed.), *Robert Furse: A Devon Family Memoir of 1593* (DCRS, New Series, 53, 2010), p. 46.
115. Ibid., p. 135.
116. Ibid., p. 68.
117. TNA, C 1/1324/27 ([Unknown] vs Tottle).
118. Holinshed, p. 1025.
119. Davies, 'Boulogne and Calais', p. 62.
120. C.L. Kingsford (ed.), *Two London Chronicles from the Collection of John Stow* (Camden Miscellany, 12, London, 1910), p. 19.
121. Rose-Troup, p. 304, n. 3.
122. DHC, Consistory Court Book, 855B.
123. Pocock, pp. 66–8.
124. Ibid., p. 71.
125. Ibid., p. 75.
126. G. Scott Thompson, *Two Centuries of Family History: A Study in Social Development* (London, 1930), pp. 199–200.
127. Ibid., p. 200.

**Chapter 8: Aftershocks: October 1549 to January 1550**

1. For Wriothesley's dismissal, see *APC, II (1547–50)*, pp. 48–57; A.J. Slavin, 'The Fall of Lord Chancellor Wriothesley: A Study in the Politics of Conspiracy', *Albion*, vol. 7, no. 4 (winter 1975), pp. 265–86.
2. For the charges against Wriothesley, see *APC, II*, pp. 48–57 (quotation p. 57); for his readmission to the Council by early 1549 and his continued animus against Somerset, see D.E. Hoak, *The King's Council in the Reign of Edward VI* (Cambridge, 1976; 2008 edn), pp. 49–50; W.K. Jordan, *Edward VI: The Young King* (Cambridge, Massachusetts, 1968; 1971 edn), p. 71; Slavin, 'Fall of Wriothesley', p. 285.
3. See, for example, S. Adams et al. (eds), 'A Journall of Matters of State . . . [and] Certayne Brife Notes', in I. Archer et al. (eds), *Religion, Politics and Society in Sixteenth-Century England* (Camden Society, Fifth Series, Volume 22, 2003), pp. 53–4, 124.
4. On the rhetoric of commonwealth, see D. MacCulloch, *Tudor Church Militant: Edward VI and the Protestant Reformation* (London, 1999), pp. 122–6.
5. These two charges were subsequently to be specifically levelled at Somerset in the 'articles' drawn up against him by the Council in late 1549: see J. Stow, *Annales, or A Generall Chronicle of England* (London, 1631), p. 601.
6. Again, these charges were to be specifically made against Somerset in the articles: see ibid., p. 602.
7. See S.T. Bindoff, *Ket's Rebellion* (Historical Association Pamphlet, General Series, No. 12, London, 1949; reprinted in 1968), pp. 22–3; D. MacCulloch, *Thomas Cranmer: A*

*Life* (New Haven and London, 1996), p. 432; A. Fletcher and D. MacCulloch, *Tudor Rebellions* (7th edn, Abingdon, 2020), p. 93.

8. Bindoff, 'Ket's Rebellion', p. 11; E.H. Shagan, 'Protector Somerset and the 1549 Rebellions: New Sources and New Perspectives', *EHR*, 114 (February 1999), p. 62.
9. MacCulloch, *Cranmer*, p. 432; F.W. Russell, *Kett's Rebellion in Norfolk* (London, 1859), p. 202.
10. Pocock, p. 24.
11. Russell, *Kett's Rebellion*, p. 202.
12. TNA, SP 10/8, f. 31. For further evidence that it was supposed in Somerset's circle 'that the Lady Marie and her counsell were prvyey to' the rebellion in Norfolk, see S. Adams et al. (eds), 'A Journall of Matters of State', p. 58.
13. *CSPS, IX (1547–49)*, pp. 445–7.
14. For the date of the conversation between Van der Delft and Mary, see J.S. Berkman, 'Van der Delft's Message: A Re-appraisal of the Attack on Protector Somerset', *Bulletin of the Institute of Historical Research*, 53 (1980), pp. 247–8. I am not convinced by Berkman's suggestion that the conspiracy may have been hatched as early as June. For the religious opinions of these four men, see MacCulloch, *Tudor Church Militant*, pp. 52–3; Slavin, 'Fall of Wriothesley', p. 275; A. Boyle, 'Hans Eworth's Portrait of the Earl of Arundel and the Politics of 1549–50', *EHR*, vol. 117, no. 470 (February 2002), pp. 25–47; Hoak, *King's Council*, p. 252.
15. J.A. Muller (ed.), *The Letters of Stephen Gardiner* (Cambridge, 1933), p. 7.
16. P.Y. Stanton, 'Arundell, Sir Thomas (c. 1502–1552)', in *ODNB*. For another helpful pen-portrait of Arundell, see A.L. Rowse, *Tudor Cornwall: Portrait of a Society* (1941; New York, 1969 edn), pp. 219–22.
17. *APC, II*, p. 16.
18. Pocock, p. 38.
19. *APC, II*, p. 304. It is interesting to note that the other man who stood surety for Sir John at this time was Sir Thomas Stradling of St Donats in Glamorganshire, who was both a relative of the Arundells and a devoted adherent of the old faith. Stradling was later to note that he regarded both the rebellions of 1549 and Cranmer's eventual execution, under Mary, as punishments that had been visited on the archbishop for his blasphemy and impiety: see R.A. Griffiths, 'Stradling, Sir Thomas (c.1498–1571)', in *ODNB*; G.C.G Thomas, 'The Stradling Library at St Donats, Glamorgan', *National Library of Wales Journal*, vol. 24, no. 4 (1986), pp. 402–19, at p. 408.
20. *CSPS, IX*, pp. 467–70.
21. S.W. Singer (ed.), *The Life of Cardinal Wolsey, by George Cavendish . . . and Metrical Visions: Volume 2* (London, 1825), p. 126.
22. J. Ponet, *A Shorte Treatise of Politike Power* (London[?], 1556), pp. I iii, I iii verso.
23. P.Y. Stanton, 'Arundell, Mary [married names: Mary Radclife, countess of Sussex; Mary Fitzalan, countess of Arundel]', in *ODNB*.
24. *CSPS, IX*, p. 470.
25. On Southwell, see S. Lehmberg, 'Southwell, Sir Richard (1502/3–1564)', in *ODNB*. On his links with the Howards and with Mary, see D. MacCulloch, 'Kett's Rebellion in Context', *P&P*, 84 (August 1979), p. 54; D. MacCulloch, 'Kett's Rebellion in Context: A Rejoinder', *P&P*, 93 (November 1981), p. 171.
26. B.L. Beer, *Northumberland: The Political Career of John Dudley, Earl of Warwick and Duke of Northumberland* (Kent, Ohio, 1973), p. 13.
27. On Southwell's alleged collusion with the rebels in Norfolk, see MacCulloch, 'Rejoinder', pp. 171–2; Adams et al., 'A Journall of Matters of State', pp. 58–9; Skidmore, *Edward VI*, pp. 130–1.
28. For some intriguing suggestions as to the possible identity of the author, see Adams et al., 'A Journall of Matters of State', pp. 45–51.

29. Adams et al., 'Certayne Brife Notes', pp. 127–8.
30. Pocock, pp. 90–2.
31. Adams et al., 'Certayne Brife Notes', p. 133; Stow, *Annales*, p. 599.
32. Pocock, p. 116.
33. For these rumours, see, for example, Hoak, *King's Council*, p. 247; Adams et al., 'Certayne Brife Notes', p. 130; P.F. Tytler (ed.), *England under the Reigns of Edward VI and Mary* (2 vols, London, 1839), I, p. 209; J.G. Nichols (ed.), *Chronicle of the Grey Friars of London*, in *Camden Miscellany* (Camden Society, First Series, 53, 1851), p. 64.
34. Adams et al., 'Certayne Brife Notes', p. 135; Hoak, *King's Council*, p. 246.
35. G.N. Gibbons, 'The Political Career of Thomas Wriothesley, First Earl of Southampton, 1505–1550' (unpublished PhD thesis, University of Warwick, 1999), pp. 251–2.
36. Adams et al., 'Certayne Brife Notes', p. 131; *APC, II*, p. 332.
37. *APC, II*, p. 332.
38. S.M. Thorpe, 'Chamberlain, Sir Leonard (1504–61)', in S.T. Bindoff (ed.), *The History of Parliament: The House of Commons, 1509–58* (London, 1982), accessed via www.historyofparliamentonline.org, 10 July 2021.
39. Ponet, *Shorte Treatise*, pp. I iii, I iii verso. A subsequent passage in the text, which alludes to Arundell's eventual execution, makes it clear that Ponet was referring to Sir Thomas Arundell here rather than to the earl of Arundel.
40. Ponet, *Shorte Treatise*, p. I iii verso.
41. For the early modern use of the verb 'to whisk' in the sense of 'to hoax', see *OED*, accessed online, 15 December 2021.
42. Hoak, *King's Council*, p. 247.
43. Muller, *Letters*, pp. 440–1.
44. J. Bellamy, *The Tudor Law of Treason* (1979; Abingdon, 2013 edn), p. 98.
45. *FRDK*, p. 221.
46. MacCulloch, 'Kett's Rebellion', p. 74.
47. *APC, II*, p. 336.
48. Ibid., pp. 344–5; for the sending of the previous holder of this office, Sir Michael Stanhope, to the Tower, see ibid., p. 343.
49. MacCulloch, *Cranmer*, p. 447.
50. Ibid., pp. 447–8.
51. *TRP*, I, no. 352, p. 484.
52. MacCulloch, *Cranmer*, p. 450.
53. *APC, II*, pp. 352–3,
54. For the patchiness of the register when it comes to listing the names of the attendees, and for the fact that the list of councillors' names that appears in the printed calendar of the register under the date of 27 July – when the order relating to Arundell was first made – in fact relates to 1 November, when the original order was cancelled, see A.F. Pollard, *England under Protector Somerset: An Essay* (London, 1900), pp. 77–9.
55. *APC, II*, p. 354.
56. S. Brigden (ed.), 'The Letters of Sir Richard Scudamore', in *Camden Miscellany: Number 30* (Camden Society, Fourth Series, Volume 39, 1990), p. 89.
57. H. Robinson (ed.), *Original Letters Relative to the English Reformation … Chiefly from the Archives of Zurich* (2 vols, Cambridge, 1846–47), I, p. 69.
58. *CSPS, IX*, p. 470.
59. Ibid.; for the suggestion that it may well have been through Arundell himself that the conservative councillors had first 'informally raised … the possibility of a regency' with Mary, see Hoak, *King's Council*, p. 248.
60. *APC, II*, p. 354; Adams et al., 'Certayne Brife Notes', pp. 135–6. See also MacCulloch, *Cranmer*, p. 450.

61. *APC, II*, p. 362; Adams et al., 'Certayne Brife Notes', pp. 135–6.
62. For detailed discussions of the factional intrigues of early November 1549, see Hoak, *King's Council*, pp. 245–53; MacCulloch, *Cranmer*, pp. 449–50.
63. TNA, SP 10/9, no. 48.
64. Brigden, 'Scudamore', p. 92.
65. *FRDK*, p. 221.
66. Ibid.
67. Ibid., p. 222.
68. Ibid.
69. For social tensions in sixteenth-century East Anglia in general, see A. Wood, 'Poore Men Will Speke One Daye: Plebeian Languages of Deference and Defiance in England, 1520–1640', in T. Harris (ed.), *The Politics of the Excluded* (Basingstoke, 2001), pp. 69–92; for a significant passage in Bishop Rugge of Norwich's visitation articles of 1549, urging the visitors to enquire if there were any in the diocese who 'affirm all things to be common, or that there ought to be no magistrates, gentlemen or rich men in Christian realms', see Jordan, *Young King*, p. 325.
70. For the attendance of spectators at Tudor treason trials, see Bellamy, *Tudor Law of Treason*, pp. 133–7; for the rumours concerning Somerset's allegedly sinister intentions towards the social elite, see S.R. Gammon, *Statesman and Schemer: William, First Lord Paget – Tudor Minister* (Newton Abbot, 1973), p. 156; Pocock, p. 116.
71. Bellamy, *Tudor Law of Treason*, p. 44.
72. *FRDK*, p. 222.
73. M. Stoyle, '"Kill All the Gentlemen"?: (Mis)representing the Western Rebels of 1549', *HR*, vol. 92, no. 255 (February 2019), pp. 50–72.
74. *APC, II*, pp. 320, 356, 366.
75. Brigden, 'Scudamore', p. 94.
76. Ibid.
77. *CSPS, IX*, p. 477.
78. Brigden, 'Scudamore', p. 93.
79. Ibid., p. 96.
80. *APC, II*, pp. 362, 406; TNA E 101/76/36, f. 5. Shortly before this time, men under Hopton's command had been busily engaged 'about [the] execucion of certen traytors' at Uxbridge, Guildford and 'Waltham': see TNA, E 101/76/35, f. 159.
81. R. Virgoe, 'Hopton, Sir Ralph (c.1510–71) of Witham Friary, Somerset', in P.W. Hasler (ed.), *The History of Parliament: The House of Commons, 1558–1603* (London, 1981), accessed online, 15 December 2021 (unpaginated).
82. Russell, *Kett's Rebellion in Norfolk*, p. 161; *FRDK*, p. 221.
83. Brigden, 'Scudamore', p. 97
84. Ibid.
85. *APC, II*, p. 366.
86. *CPR, Edward VI, V (1547–53)*, pp. 338–9.
87. See, for example, Rose-Troup, p. 352; Rowse, *Tudor Cornwall*, p. 289.
88. Adams et al., 'Certayne Brife Notes', pp. 135–6.
89. *CSPS, IX*, p. 489; MacCulloch, *Cranmer*, p. 451.
90. Pocock, pp. 128–9.
91. Hoak, *King's Council*, p. 58.
92. Brigden, 'Scudamore', p. 107.
93. *CSPS, X (1550–52)*, p. 8.
94. For the imprisonment of Sir John Arundell and Southwell in the Fleet, see Ponet, *Shorte Treatise*, p. I iii verso; TNA, SP 46/58 (Reskymer papers), f. 139; Brigden, 'Scudamore', p. 114.

95. TNA, SP 46/58, f. 139.
96. The scholar who summarised Reskymer's letter in a calendar of SP 46, compiled in the 1960s, noted simply that it 'sends news of prisoners, including Sir John Arundell': see Anon., *Descriptive List of State Papers Supplementary (SP 46), Private Papers, Series I, 1535–1705* (List and Index Society, volume 33, London, 1968), p. 74.
97. Brigden, 'Scudamore', p. 114.
98. See G. Walker, *John Heywood: Comedy and Survival in Tudor England* (Oxford, 2020), p. 237.
99. Brigden, 'Scudamore', p. 114.
100. *APC, II*, p. 376; *CSPS, X*, p. 21; W.K. Jordan, *The Chronicle and Political Papers of King Edward VI* (London, 1966), p. 19.
101. Brigden, 'Scudamore', p. 114.
102. The dates that contemporary sources provide for the execution of the western rebels vary slightly, but 27 January – the date specified by Scudamore, Lynne and Gruffydd – seems the most likely to be correct.
103. Rose-Troup, p. 349.
104. A. Travers, *Robert Furse: A Devon Family Memoir of 1593* (DCRS, New Series, Volume 53, 2012), p. 65; TNA, C 78/9/48 (Chubbe vs Bury). For the dispute over money in which Margery Bury subsequently became embroiled with her dead husband's brother William, see TNA, C 1/1289/64–7 (Bury vs Bury).
105. See W.D. Hamilton (ed.), *A Chronicle of England during the Reigns of the Tudors . . . by Charles Wriothesley* (2 vols, Camden Society, New Series, 11, 1855–57), II, p. 32; C.L. Kingsford (ed.), *Two London Chronicles from the Collection of John Stow: Camden Miscellany, Volume 12* (London, 1910), p. 21; [Walter Lynne], *The Thre Bokes of Cronicles . . . Whyche John Carion . . . Gathered* (London, 1550), f. 276; M.B. Davies (ed.), 'Boulogne and Calais from 1545 to 1550', *Bulletin of the Faculty of Arts of Fouad University*, 12 (1950), p. 78.
106. Kingsford, *Two London Chronicles*, p. 21.
107. T. Cooper, *Cooper's Chronicle, Conteininge the Whole Discourse of the Histories . . . of this Realme* (London, 1560), f. 346v.
108. Nichols, *Chronicle of the Grey Friars*, p. 65.
109. J. Strype (ed.), *Memorial of the Most Reverend Father in God, Thomas Cranmer, Sometime Archbishop of Canterbury* (Oxford, 1812 edn), p. 875.
110. Ibid., p. 876.

## Conclusion

1. J. Norden, *Speculi Britanniae Pars: A Topographical and Historical Description of Cornwall* (London, 1728), p. 47.
2. Holinshed, p. 1016; A.L. Rowse, *Tudor Cornwall: Portrait of a Society* (1941, New York; 1969 edn), pp. 267, 271.
3. S. Adams et al. (eds), 'A Journall of Matters of State . . . [and] Certayne Brife Notes', in I. Archer et al. (eds), *Religion, Politics and Society in Sixteenth-Century England* (Camden Society, Fifth Series, Volume 22, 2003), p. 77. It is now clear that this dismissive description of the original rebel captains as 'Hick[s] and Tom[s]' – that is to say, as unlettered rustics, or persons of no account – was itself lifted from one of Hooker's earliest accounts of the rising, written in 1559, in which the Exeter chronicler had observed that, after the disturbances had begun, the protestors 'chose amonge them selfes diverse heckes & Tommes to be theire captaynes, & in warlike maner came to this Citie': see ECA, Book 55 (The Freeman's Book), f. 134.
4. Holinshed, p. 1018.
5. Pocock, p. 26.

6. BL, Anon., 'Ballad on the Defeat of the Devon and Cornwall Rebels' (printed fragment, London, 1549).
7. W.K. Jordan, *Edward VI: The Young King* (Cambridge, Massachusetts, 1968; 1971 edn), p. 468; J. Youings, 'The South-Western Rebellion of 1549', *Southern History*, I, (1979), p. 109.
8. Speight, p. 6.
9. See C. Hayden, 'Tristram Winslade: The Desperate Heart of a Catholic in Exile', *Cornish Studies*, 20 (2012), p. 34; C.J. Hayden, 'Tristram Winslade: An Elizabethan Catholic in Exile' (unpublished PhD thesis, University of Flinders, Australia, 2019), p. 31.
10. W.T. MacCaffrey, *Exeter, 1540–1640: The Growth of an English County Town* (1958; London, 1978 edn), p. 99; DHC, ECA, Exeter Chamber Act Book, 4 (1581–88), f. 35.
11. KCC, KC/KCAR/6/2/140/08 SAC/66 (Sampford Courtenay Survey Book of 1568).
12. A.J. Howard (ed.), *Devon Protestation Returns* (privately printed, 1973), pp. i, 80.
13. DHC, Quarter Sessions Rolls, Box 52 (Midsummer and Epiphany 1647), petition from the parishioners of Sampford Courtenay, midsummer 1647.

# BIBLIOGRAPHY


I MANUSCRIPTS

Bodleian Library, Oxford

Rawlinson MS, C.792, 'The Beginninge, Cause & Course of the Comotion or Rebellion in . . . Devon & Cornewall . . . Collected by John Vowell, Alias Hooker'.

British Library, London

Add MSS, 29,762, '[William] Hals's MSS of his Parochial History of Cornwall'.
Add MSS, 18,981, The Lady Mary's letter to Protector Somerset, 20 July 1549.
Cotton MSS, Galba B.12, Lord Russell's letter giving an account of the battle of Sampford Courtenay, 1549.
Cotton MSS, Otho, 11, Note of costs incurred in suppressing the Western Rising.
Cotton MSS, Vespasian, F.iii, Proclamation against Kett's rebels, 10 August 1549.
Harleian MSS, 352, 'Privy Council Acts, *temp* Edward VI'.
Harleian MSS, 523, 'A Book in 4to Wherein Are Contained Copies of Divers Letters from Sir Philip Hoby'.
Harleian MSS, 5827, 'A Discourse of Devonshire & Cornwall', by John Hooker.
Titus, F.VI, ff. 76–9, 'The Discription of ye Citie of Excestre Made and Done by John Vowell, al[ia]s Hoker'.

Dean and Chapter Archives, Exeter

D&C, 3551, Dean and Chapter Act Book (1521–36).
D&C, 3552, Dean and Chapter Act Book (1537–56).
D&C, 3688, List of Cornish clerics, *c.* 1536.

Devon Heritage Centre, Exeter

Chanter, 13, Register of Bishop Hugh Oldham, 1504–1519.
Chanter, 14, Register of Bishop John Veysey, Volume 1 (1519–1551).
Chanter, 15, Register of Bishop John Veysey, Volume 2 (1519–1551).
Consistory Court Book 855B.
Consistory Court Book 857.

Devon Quarter Sessions Rolls, Box 52 (Midsummer and Epiphany 1647).
ECA, Exeter Chamber Act Book, 1 (1509–38).
ECA, Exeter Chamber Act Book, 2 (1509–60).
ECA, Exeter Chamber Act Book, 3 (1560–81).
ECA, Exeter Chamber Act Book, 4 (1581–88).
ECA, Book 51 (John Hooker's Commonplace Book).
ECA, Book 52 (John Hooker's Ledger Book).
ECA, Book 54 (Richard Crossing's 'Catalogue . . . of the Antiquities . . . of Exeter', *c.* 1681).
ECA, Book 55 ('The Freeman's Book').
ECA, Mayor's Court Book, 81 (1545–57).
ECA, Mayor's Court Rolls, 1547–1550.
ECA, Miscellaneous Roll, 29 (papers relating to the parsonage of St Kerrian).
ECA, Miscellaneous Roll, 103 (papers relating to disputes between the cathedral and the city).
ECA, Receiver's Book, 1562–63.
ECA, Receiver's Roll, 1415–16.
ECA, Receivers' Vouchers, Box 1, accounts of William Hurst and John Blackaller, 1549.
ECA, Book 184b, list of former monastic properties in Exeter.
ECA, Miscellaneous Deeds 1464, conveyance of 20 May 1549.
4344A-99/PW1, Woodbury Churchwardens' Accounts, 1537–1792.

Exeter College, Oxford

MS 235 (John Prideaux's notes).

King's College, Cambridge

KC/KCAR/6/2/140/01/SAC/4-7, Sampford Courtenay manor court rolls, 1534–51.
KC/KCAR/6/2/140/08 SAC/66, Sampford Courtenay survey book of 1568.

Kresen Kernow, Cornish Record Office, Redruth

113, D41, Collections of Sampson Hill, 1657–1732.
CA/B35/27, Receipt signed by Thomas Treffry, 1549.

Longleat House, Wiltshire

Thynne MSS, Sir John Thynne's Letter Book, vol. 2.

The National Archives, London

C 1/1110/9–11, Carvanell vs Richard.
C 1/1216/55, Ennys vs Playsted.
C 1/1253/33–43, Pomeroy vs Carsewell.
C 1/1272/49, Tothill vs Stowell.
C 1/1272/78–82, Turpyn vs Turpyn.
C 1/1272/83–4, Turpyn vs Denys.
C 1/1273/55–6, Torner vs Smythe.
C 1/1276/1–4, Wadland vs Gove.
C 1/1289/64–7, Bury vs Bury.
C 1/1321/27, Whetehyll vs Daryelle.
C 1/1324/27, (Unknown) vs Tottle.
C 1/1341/77, Curtes vs stewards of Lydford.
C 1/1367/82, Lowre vs Cruys.
C 1/1368/79, Morcombe vs Brownynge.

C 1/1369/11–20, Martin vs Burnet.
C 1/1383/2, Saundrye vs Bossyns.
C 1/1387/14, Tayllour vs Brayleghe.
C 1/1507/60, Late bailiffs of Launceston vs Amadas.
C 3/107/22, Kemyshe vs Tewenneck.
C 3/224/55, Mayor of Exeter vs Carewe.
C 4/11/24, 'Divers persons' in Exeter vs Gybbys.
C 78/9/48, Chubbe vs Bury.
E 101/76/35, Documents subsidiary to the accounts of the treasurer of the Court of Augmentations, 36 Henry VIII to 3 Edward VI.
E 178/531, Inquisition as to the possessions of William Widesladd, 26 Elizabeth I.
E 199/6/52, Inventory of the goods and chattels of Robert Raffe and John Wulcocke.
E 315/257, Account Book of the Court of Augmentations.
E 351/3538, Account of J. Killigrew, paymaster of the works and fortifications of Scilly.
E 344/19/15, List of clerics in the diocese of Exeter, compiled for the clerical subsidy of 32 Henry VIII.
KB 8/17/1–9, Special oyer and terminer roll, 1549.
REQ 2/25/190, Petition of Thomas Treffry.
SP 1, State Papers, Henry VIII, General Series.
SP 10, State Papers, Domestic, Edward VI.
SP 16, State Papers, Domestic, Charles I.
SP 46/2, State Papers, Domestic, Supplementary, Miscellaneous letters and papers.
SP 46/22, State Papers, Domestic, Supplementary, Miscellaneous letters and papers.
SP 46/58, State Papers, Domestic, Supplementary, Reskymer Papers.
STAC 2/28/70, Mohon vs Arundell.
STAC 3/1/46, Carvanell vs Hawkyn.
STAC 3/2/14, Predyaux vs Seyntclere et al.
STAC 3/2/78, Carvanell vs Esseball et al.
STAC 5/T34/32, Trewynnerd vs Newman and Hoppier.
STAC 7/7/12, Tregose vs Penheliche et al.

North Devon Record Office, Barnstaple

B1/3972, Barnstaple Receivers' Accounts, 1389–1649.

Somerset Heritage Centre, Taunton

DD/X/LY 3, Lyte commonplace book, 1568–1638.

West Country Studies Library, Exeter

SXDEV/0001/RIS, 'A Chorographical Description of Devonshire ... Collected by the Travell of T.R. of Winscott, Gentleman'.
C. Fursdon, 'Transcript of the Bridford Parish Registers' (typescript vol., 1935).
T.L. Stoate, 'Transcript of the Sampford Courtenay Parish Registers, 1558–1813' (typescript vol., 1988).

West Devon Record Office, Plymouth

W/1 130, Plymouth Receivers' Accounts, *temp* Henry VII to Edward VI.
372/6/3/22, Bargain and sale by Thomas Castell, alias Kestell, of Kestell in the parish of Egloshayle, 1614.
542/1, Parish register of St Budeaux, 1538–1656.

II REPORTS OF THE HISTORICAL MANUSCRIPTS COMMISSION

Anon. (ed.), *Calendar of the Manuscripts of the Most Honourable the Marquis of Salisbury, Parts I–II* (London, 1883).
M. Blatcher (ed.), *Report on the Manuscripts of the Most Honourable the Marquess of Bath, Preserved at Longleat, Volume IV: Seymour Papers, 1532–1686* (London, 1968).
J.H. and J. Wylie (eds), *Report on the Records of the City of Exeter* (London, 1916).

III BOOKS

Anon., *The Order of the Communion* (London, 8 March 1548).
Anon., *A Message Sent by the Kynges Majestie, to Certain of his People, Assembled in Devonshire* ([London], 8 July 1549).
Anon., [*Ballad on the Defeat of the Devon and Cornwall Rebels*] (fragment, London, 1549).
Anon., *New Newes from Cornwall* (London, 27 October 1642).
Anon., *A True Relation of a Brave Defeat Given by the Forces in Plimouth to Skellum Greenvile* (London, *c.* 18 February 1645).
R. Carew, *The Survey of Cornwall, Written by Richard Carew of Antonie, Esquire* (London, 1603).
J. Cheke, *The Hurt of Sedition Howe Grevous It Is to a Communewelth* ([London], 1549).
T. Cooper, *Cooper's Chronicle, Conteininge the Whole Discourse of the Histories . . . of this Realme* (London, 1560).
J. Foxe, *The First Volume of the Ecclesiastical History Containing the Actes and Monuments* (London, 1570 edn).
—, *The First Volume of the Ecclesiastical History, Contayning the Actes & Monumentes* (London, 1576 edn).
E. Hall, *The Union of the Two Noble and Illustre Families of Lancastre & Yorke* (London, 1548; 1809 edn).
W.D. Hamilton (ed.), *A Chronicle of England during the Reigns of the Tudors, from AD 1485 to 1559, Volume II* (Camden Society, New Series, 20, 1877).
R. Holinshed, *The Third Volume of Chronicles* (London, 1587).
R. Izaacke, *Remarkable Antiquities of the City of Exeter* (2nd edn, London, 1723).
'R.L.', *A Copye of a Letter Containing Certayne Newes, & the Articles or Requests of the Devonshyre & Cornyshe Rebelles* ([London], 1549).
[W. Lynne], *The Thre Bokes of Cronciles, Whyche John Carion . . . Gathered* (London, 1550).
A. Nevil, *Norfolkes Furies, or A View of Ketts Campe* (London, *c.* 1625).
J. Norden, *Speculi Britanniae Pars: A Topographical and Historical Description of Cornwall* (London, 1728).
T. Norton, *To the Queenes Maiestes Poore Deceived Subiectes of the Northe* (London, 1569).
P. Nicolles, *The Copie of a Letter Sente to One Maister Chrispyne, Chanon of Exceter* (London, 1547).
[J. Ponet], *A Short Treatise of Politike Power* ([London], 1556).
'H. R.', *Haigh for Devonshire: A Pleasant Discourse of Sixe Gallant Marchants of Devonshire* (London, 1600).
J. Smythe, *Certain Discourses Written by Sir John Smyth, Knight* (London, 1590).
J. Speed, *The Historie of Great Britaine* (2nd edn, London, 1623).
J. Stow, *A Summarie of Englyshe Chronicles* (London, 1565).
—, *The Annales of England* (London, 1592).
—, *Annales, or A Generall Chronicle of England* (London, 1631).
J. Vowell, alias Hooker, *Catalog of the Bishops of Excester* (London, 1583).
—, *The Discription of the Cittie of Excester* (London, 1575).

—, *A Pamphlet of the Offices and Duties of Everie Particular Sworne Officer of the Citie of Excester* (London, 1584).
—, *The Antique Description and Account of the City of Exeter, in Three Parts* (Exeter, 1765).

## IV EDITIONS OF DOCUMENTS

S. Adams et al. (eds), 'A Journall of Matters of State ... [and] Certayne Brife Notes', in I. Archer et al. (eds), *Religion, Politics and Society in Sixteenth-Century England* (Camden Society, Fifth Series, Volume 22, 2003), pp. 35–136.
R. Anderson (ed.), *Letters of the Fifteenth and Sixteenth Centuries* (Southampton, 1921).
Anon. (ed.), *Journal of the House of Lords: Volume I, 1509–1577* (London, 1767).
Anon. (ed.), *Journal of the House of Commons: Volume I, 1547–1629* (London, 1802).
Anon. (ed.), *Grafton's Chronicle, or History of England, to Which Is Added his Table of the Bailiffs, Sheriffs and Mayors of the City of London* (2 vols, London, 1809).
Anon. (ed.), *The Chorographical Description or Survey of the County of Devon, by Tristram Risdon* (London, 1811).
Anon. (ed.), *Fourth Report of the Deputy Keeper of the Public Records* (London, 1843).
Anon. (ed.), *Calendar of the Patent Rolls ... Edward VI, Volumes I to V* (London, 1924–29).
Anon. (ed.), *Descriptive List of State Papers Supplementary (SP 46), Private Papers, Series I, 1535–1705* (List and Index Society, Volume 33, London 1968).
P.E. Barnes (ed.), *Memorials of the Most Reverend Father in God Thomas Cranmer ... by John Strype* (2 vols, London, 1853).
M. Bateson (ed.), *A Collection of Original Letters from the Bishops to the Privy Council, 1564* (Camden Society, New Series, 53, 1893).
B.L. Beer (ed.), *The Life and Reign of King Edward the Sixth, by John Hayward* (Kent, Ohio, and London, 1993).
W.J. Blake (ed.), 'Hooker's Synopsis Chorographical of Devonshire', *RTDA*, 47 (1915), pp. 334–48.
J.S. Brewer et al. (eds), *Letters and Papers, Foreign and Domestic, Henry VIII, Volumes 1–21* (London, 1880–1920).
S. Brigden (ed.), 'The Letters of Sir Richard Scudamore to Sir Philip Hoby, September 1549 to March 1555', in *Camden Miscellany: Number 30* (Camden Society, Fourth Series, 39, 1990), pp. 67–148.
J. Chynoweth et al. (eds), *The Survey of Cornwall, by Richard Carew* (DCRS, New Series, Volume 47, Exeter, 2004).
F.T. Colby (ed.), *The Visitation of the County of Devon in the Year 1620* (London, 1872).
J.P. Collier (ed.), *Trevelyan Papers prior to AD 1558* (Camden Society, Old Series, 67, 1856).
J.E. Cox (ed.), *The Works of Thomas Cranmer, Archbishop of Canterbury, Martyr, 1556* (2 vols, Cambridge, 1846).
— (ed.), *Miscellaneous Writings and Letters of Thomas Cranmer* (Cambridge, 1846).
B. Cresswell (ed.), *The Edwardian Inventories for the City and County of Exeter* (London and Oxford, 1916).
J.R. Dasent (ed.), *Acts of the Privy Council of England, New Series, Volume I, 1542–47* (London, 1890).
— (ed.), *Acts of the Privy Council of England, New Series, Volume II, 1547–50* (London, 1890).
— (ed.), *Acts of the Privy Council of England, New Series, Volume III, 1550–52* (London, 1891).
— (ed.), *Acts of the Privy Council of England, New Series, Volume V, 1554–56* (London, 1892).
M.B. Davies (ed.), 'Boulogne and Calais from 1545 to 1550', *Bulletin of the Faculty of Arts of Fouad University*, 12 (1950), pp. 1–90.
O.L. Dick (ed.), *Aubrey's Brief Lives* (London, 1949; 1987 edn).

A.G. Dickens (ed.), 'Robert Parkyn's Narrative of the Reformation', in A.G. Dickens, *Reformation Studies* (London, 1982), pp. 287–312.
G.R. Elton (ed.), *The Tudor Constitution: Documents and Commentary* (Cambridge, 1960; 1972 edn).
G. Eyre and A. Strahan (eds), *The Statutes of the Realm* (11 vols, London, 1810–28).
W. Frere and W. Kennedy (eds), *Visitation Articles and Injunctions: Volume II, 1536–58* (London, 1910).
F.J. Furnivall (ed.), *The Fyrst Boke of the Introduction of Knowledge, Made by Andrew Boorde* (London, EETS, 10, 1870).
J.A. Giles (ed.), *William of Malmesbury's Chronicle of the Kings of England* (London, 1847).
T. Gray (ed.), *Devon Documents* (Tiverton, 1996).
— (ed.), *The Chronicle of Exeter: 1205–1722* (Exeter, 2005).
W. Harte et al. (eds), *The Description of the Cittie of Excester, by John Vowell, alias Hoker: Volume II* (DCRS, Old Series, 19, 1919).
A.J. Howard (ed.), *Devon Protestation Returns* (privately printed, 1973).
P.L. Hughes and J.F. Larkin (eds), *Tudor Royal Proclamations: Volume I, The Early Tudors, 1485–1553* (New Haven and London, 1964).
M.A.S. Hume (ed.), *Chronicle of King Henry VIII of England . . . Written in Spanish by an Unknown Hand* (London, 1889).
— and R. Tyler (eds), *Calendar of State Papers, Spanish, Volume 9 (1547–1549)* (London, 1912).
A.J. Jewers (ed.), *The Registers of the Parish of St Columb Major, Cornwall, from the Year 1539 to 1780* (London, 1881).
W.K. Jordan (ed.), *The Chronicle and Political Papers of King Edward VI* (London, 1966).
J. Ketley (ed.), *The Two Liturgies, AD 1549 and AD 1552, Set Forth by Authority in the Reign of King Edward VI* (Cambridge, 1844).
J.N. King (ed.), *Voices of the English Reformation: A Source Book* (Philadelphia, Pennsylvania, 2004).
C.L. Kingsford (ed.), *Two London Chronicles from the Collection of John Stow* (Camden Miscellany: Volume 12; Camden Society, Third Series, 18, 1910).
C.S. Knighton (ed.), *Calendars of State Papers, Domestic Series of the Reign of Edward VI, 1547–53* (London, 1992).
— and D. Loades (eds), *The Navy of Edward VI and Mary* (Navy Records Society Publications, 157, Farnham, 2011).
G. Lefevre-Pontalis (ed.), *Correspondance politique de Odet de Selve: ambassadeur de France en Angleterre, 1544–49* (Paris, 1888).
R. Lemon (ed.), *Calendars of State Papers, Domestic Series, 1547–80* (London, 1856; Liechtenstein, 1967 edn).
J. MacClean (ed.), *The Life and Times of Sir Peter Carew, Knight* (London, 1857).
A.J. Malkiewicz (ed.), 'An Eyewitness Account of the Coup d'Etat of October 1549', *EHR*, 70 (1955), pp. 600–9.
J. Mattingly (ed.), *Stratton Churchwardens' Accounts, 1512–1578* (DCRS, New Series, 60, Woodbridge, 2018).
T. F. Mayer (ed.), *The Correspondence of Reginald Pole, 2, 1547–1554: A Power in Rome* (Farnham, 2003).
— and C.B. Walters (eds), *The Correspondence of Reginald Pole, Volume 4: A Biographical Companion – The British Isles* (Aldershot, 2008).
J.A. Muller (ed.), *The Letters of Stephen Gardiner* (Cambridge, 1933).
J.G. Nichols (ed.), *Chronicle of the Grey Friars of London* (Camden Society, Old Series, 53, 1852).
G. Oliver and P. Jones (eds), *A View of Devonshire in MDCXXX . . . by Thomas Westcote, Gent* (Exeter, 1845).
W. Page (ed.), *The Inventories of Church Goods for the Counties of York, Durham and Northumberland* (Surtees Society, Volume 97, 1896).

E. Peacock (ed.), 'On the Churchwardens' Accounts of the Parish of Stratton in the County of Cornwall', *Archaeologia*, 46 (1881), pp. 195–236.
D. Pickering (ed.), *The Statutes at Large: From the Thirty-Second Year of K. Hen. VIII to the Seventh Year of K. Edw. VI* (London, 1763).
N. Pocock (ed.), *Troubles Connected with the Prayer Book of 1549* (Camden Society, New Series, 37, 1884).
J. W. De La Pole (ed.), *Collections towards a Description of the County of Devon, by Sir William Pole of Colcombe and Shute, Knight* (London, 1791).
J. Prince, *Danmonii Orientales Illustres: or The Worthies of Devon* (London, 1810).
T. Risdon, *The Chorographical Description or Survey of the County of Devon* (London, 1811; Barnstaple, 1970 edn).
H. Robinson (ed.), *Original Letters Relative to the English Reformation* (2 vols, Cambridge, 1846).
M.M. Rowe (ed.), *Tudor Exeter: Tax Assessments 1489–1595, Including the Military Survey 1522* (DCRS, New Series, 22, 1977).
— and A.M. Jackson (eds), *Exeter Freemen, 1266–1967* (DCRS, Extra Series, 1, 1973).
S.W. Singer (ed.), *The Life of Cardinal Wolsey, by George Cavendish . . . and Metrical Visions: Volume 2* (London, 1825).
R.J. Skinner, 'The "Declaracion" of Ley: His Pedigree, Part II', *DCNQ*, vol. 37, part 3 (spring, 1993), pp. 101–6.
L.S. Snell (ed.), *Documents towards a History of the Reformation in Cornwall: No 1, The Chantry Certificates for Cornwall* (Exeter, n.d. [*c.* 1953]).
— (ed.), *Documents towards a History of the Reformation in Cornwall: No 2, The Edwardian Inventories of Church Goods from Cornwall* (Exeter, 1955).
T.L. Stoate (ed.), *Devon Lay Subsidy Rolls, 1524–27* (privately printed, Bristol, 1979).
— (ed.), *Devon Lay Subsidy Returns, 1543–45* (privately printed, Bristol, 1986).
L. Toulmin-Smith (ed.), *The Itinerary of John Leland, in or about the Years 1535–43: Parts I to III* (London, 1907).
A. Travers (ed.), *Robert Furse: A Devon Family Memoir of 1593* (DCRS, New Series, 53, 2010).
W.B. Turnbull (ed.), *Calendar of State Papers, Foreign Series, 1547–53* (London, 1861).
R. Tyler (ed.), *Calendar of State Papers, Spanish, Volume 10 (1550–1552)* (London, 1914).
P.F. Tytler (ed.), *England under the Reigns of Edward VI and Mary* (2 vols, London, 1839).
J.L. Vivian (ed.), *The Visitation of the County of Devon: Comprising the Heralds' Visitations of 1531, 1564 and 1620* (Exeter, 1895).
— and H.H. Drake (eds), *The Visitation of the County of Cornwall in the Year 1620* (London, 1874).
H.A. Wilson (ed.), *The Order of the Communion 1548* (Henry Bradshaw Society, Volume 34, London, 1907).
R.N. Worth (ed.), *Calendar of the Plymouth Municipal Records* (Plymouth, 1893).
T. Wright (ed.), *Three Chapters of Letters Relating to the Suppression of the Monasteries* (Camden Society, Old Series, 26, 1843).
C.D. Yonge (ed.), *The Flours of History . . . Collected by Matthew of Westminster* (2 vols, London, 1853).
J. Youings (ed.), *Devon Monastic Lands: Calendar of Particulars for Grants, 1536–1538* (DCRS, New Series, 1, 1955).

### V SECONDARY BOOKS

S. Alford, *Edward VI: The Last Boy King* (London, 2014).
B.L. Beer, *Northumberland: The Political Career of John Dudley, Earl of Warwick and Duke of Northumberland* (Kent State University Press, Ohio, 1973).

—, *Rebellion and Riot: Popular Disorder in England during the Reign of Edward VI* (rev. edn, Kent State University Press, Ohio, 2005).
J.G. Bellamy, *The Law of Treason in England in the Later Middle Ages* (Cambridge, 1970).
—, *The Tudor Law of Treason* (London, 1979; Abingdon, 2013 edn).
G.W. Bernard (ed.), *The Tudor Nobility* (Manchester, 1992).
—, *The King's Reformation: Henry VIII and the Remaking of the English Church* (New Haven and London, 2005).
—, *Who Ruled Tudor England: An Essay in the Paradoxes of Power* (London, 2022).
S.T. Bindoff, *Ket's Rebellion* (Historical Association Pamphlet, General Series, No. 12, London, 1949; 1968 edn).
—, *Tudor England* (Harmondsworth, 1950; 1958 edn).
J. Blundell, *Memoirs and Antiquities of the Town and Parish of Tiverton* (Exeter, 1712).
R.J.E. Boggis, *A History of the Diocese of Exeter* (Exeter, 1922).
S. Brigden, *New Worlds, Lost Worlds: The Rule of the Tudors, 1485–1603* (London, 2001).
M.L. Bush, *The Government Policy of Protector Somerset* (London, 1975).
'VC', *Odd Ways in Olden Days Down West: or Tales of the Reformation in Devon and Cornwall* (Birmingham, 1892).
P. Caraman, *The Western Rising, 1549: The Prayer Book Rebellion* (Tiverton, 1994).
C.R. Cheny and M. Jones, *A Handbook of Dates for Students of British History* (Cambridge, 2000).
B. Cherry and N. Pevsner, *The Buildings of England: Devon* (2nd edn, London, 1989).
J. Chynoweth, *Tudor Cornwall* (Stroud, 2002).
W. Cobbett, *A History of the Protestant Reformation in England and Ireland* (London, n.d.).
H.M. Colvin, *The History of the King's Works, Volume IV, 1485–1660, Part II* (London, 1982).
J.P.D. Cooper, *Propaganda and the Tudor State: Political Culture in the West Country* (Oxford, 2003).
J. Cornwall, *Revolt of the Peasantry 1549* (London, 1977).
W. Cotton, *An Elizabethan Guild of the City of Exeter* (Exeter, 1873).
— and H. Woolcombe, *Gleanings from the Municipal and Cathedral Records Relative to the History of the City of Exeter* (Exeter, 1877).
B.F. Cresswell, *Rambles in Old Exeter* (Exeter, 1927).
—, *A Book of Devonshire Parsons* (London, 1932).
C.S.L. Davies, *Peace, Print and Protestantism, 1450–1558* (London, 1982; 1984 edn).
A.G. Dickens, *The English Reformation* (London, 1964; 1965 edn).
R.W. Dixon, *History of the Church of England, from the Abolition of the Roman Jurisdiction, Volume III, 1549–53* (London, 1895).
M.H. Dodds and R. Dodds, *The Pilgrimage of Grace, 1536–37 and the Exeter Conspiracy, 1538* (2 vols, Cambridge, 1915).
E. Duffy, *The Stripping of the Altars: Traditional Religion in England, 1400–1580* (New Haven and London, 1992; 2005 edn).
—, *The Voices of Morebath: Reformation and Rebellion in an English Village* (New Haven and London, 2001).
—, *Fires of Faith: Catholic England under Mary Tudor* (New Haven and London, 2009).
—, *Saints, Sacrilege and Sedition: Religion and Conflict in the Tudor Reformations* (London, 2012).
—, *A People's Tragedy: Studies in Reformation* (London, 2020).
M. Dunsford, *Historical Memoirs of the Town and Parish of Tiverton in the County of Devon, Collected from the Best Authorities with Notes and Observations* (1790).
P. Edwards, *The Making of the Modern English State, 1500–1660* (Houndmills, 2001).
G.R. Elton, *Policy and Police: The Enforcement of the Reformation in the Age of Thomas Cromwell* (Cambridge, 1972; 1985 edn).

—, *Reform and Reformation: England, 1509–1558* (London, 1977; 1993 edn).
F.G. Emmison, *Tudor Secretary: Sir William Petre at Court and Home* (London, 1961).
E. Evenden and T.S. Freeman, *Religion and the Book in Early Modern England* (Cambridge, 2011; 2013 edn).
A. Fletcher and D. MacCulloch, *Tudor Rebellions* (Abingdon and London, 7 edns, 1968–2020).
E. Fox, *The Commotion Time: Tudor Rebellion in the West, 1549* (Warwick, 2020).
E.A. Freeman, *Historic Towns: Exeter* (London, 1887).
J.A. Froude, *History of England: From the Fall of Wolsey to the Death of Elizabeth: Volume V* (New York, 1870 edn).
H. Fulton (ed.), *Medieval Celtic Literature and Society* (Dublin, 2005).
J. Gairdner, *The English Church in the Sixteenth Century from the Accession of Henry VIII to the Death of Mary* (London, 1902; 1924 edn).
S.R. Gammon, *Statesman and Schemer: William, First Lord Paget – Tudor Minister* (Newton Abbot, 1973).
D. Gilbert, *The Parochial History of Cornwall: Founded on the Manuscript Histories of Mr Hals and Mr Tonkin* (4 vols, London, 1838).
E. Goldring, *Nicholas Hilliard: Life of an Artist* (New Haven and London, 2019).
T. Gray, *Strumpets and Ninnycocks: Name Calling in Devon, 1540–1640* (Exeter, 2016).
— (ed.), *Tudor and Stuart Devon: The Common Estate and Government* (Exeter, 1992).
J. Guy, *Tudor England* (Oxford, 1988).
C. Haigh, *English Reformations: Religion, Politics and Society under the Tudors* (Oxford, 1993).
I.M.W. Harvey, *Jack Cade's Rebellion of 1450* (Oxford, 1991; 2010 edn).
C. Henderson, *Essays in Cornish History*, ed. A.L. Rowse and M.I. Henderson (Oxford, 1935; 2nd edn, Truro 1963).
—, *A History of the Parish of Constantine* (Long Compton, 1937).
D.E. Hoak, *The King's Council in the Reign of Edward VI* (Cambridge, 1976).
W.G. Hoskins, *Devon* (London, 1954).
—, *Two Thousand Years in Exeter* (London, 1960; 1969 edn).
R. Hutton, *The Stations of the Sun: A History of the Ritual Year in Britain* (Oxford, 1996).
—, *A Brief History of Britain, 1485–1660* (London, 2010).
W.R.D. Jones, *The Mid-Tudor Crisis, 1539–63* (London, 1973).
W.K. Jordan, *Edward VI: The Young King* (Cambridge, Massachusetts, 1968; 1971 edn).
—, *Edward VI: The Threshold of Power* (London, 1970).
K.J. Kesselring, *Mercy and Authority in the Tudor State* (Cambridge, 2003).
—, *The Northern Rebellion of 1569: Faith, Politics and Protest in Elizabethan England* (London, 2010).
N. Key and R. Bucholz, *Sources and Debates in English History, 1485–1714* (Oxford, 2004).
F.A. Knight and L.M. Dutton, *Devonshire* (Cambridge, 1914).
S.K. Land, *Kett's Rebellion: The Norfolk Rising of 1549* (Ipswich, 1977).
E. Lega-Weekes, *Some Studies in the Topography of the Cathedral Close, Exeter* (Exeter, 1915).
C.D. Lindsay, *The Book of Plymouth* (Plymouth, 1938).
D. Linzey, *The Castles of Pendennis and St Mawes* (London, 1999).
S. Lipscomb, *1536: The Year that Changed Henry VIII* (Oxford, 2009).
C. Litzenburger, *The English Reformation and the Laity: Gloucestershire, 1540–1580* (Cambridge, 1997).
J. Loach, *Edward VI* (New Haven and London, 1999; 2002 edn).
D. Loades, *Two Tudor Conspiracies* (Cambridge, 1965; 2nd edn, Norwich, 1992).
—, *Politics and the Nation, 1450–1660: Obedience, Resistance and Public Order* (Brighton, 1974).
—, *The Mid-Tudor Crisis, 1545–65* (London, 1992).
—, *Essays in the Reign of Edward VI* (Dorchester, 1994).

— (ed.), *John Foxe and the English Reformation* (Aldershot, 1997).
J.A. Lynn, *Women, Armies and Warfare in Early Modern Europe* (Cambridge, 2008).
W.T. MacCaffrey, *Exeter, 1540–1640: The Growth of an English County Town* (London, 1958; 2nd edn 1978).
D. MacCulloch, *Thomas Cranmer: A Life* (New Haven and London, 1996).
—, *Tudor Church Militant: Edward VI and the Protestant Reformation* (London, 1999).
—, *All Things Made New: Writings on the Reformation* (London, 2016).
—, *Thomas Cromwell: A Revolutionary Life* (New York, 2018).
P. Marshall, *Heretics and Believers: A History of the English Reformation* (London and New Haven, 2019).
— (ed.), *The Impact of the English Reformation, 1500–1640* (London, 1997).
A.C. Miller, *Sir Henry Killigrew: Elizabethan Soldier and Diplomat* (Leicester, 1963).
J.A. Muller, *Stephen Gardiner and the Tudor Reaction* (London, 1926).
M. Nicholls, *A History of the Modern British Isles, 1529–63: The Two Kingdoms* (Oxford, 1999).
N. Orme, *Exeter Cathedral As It Was, 1050–1550* (Exeter, 1986).
—, *A History of the County of Cornwall, Volume II: Religious History to 1560* (The Victoria History of the Counties of England, Woodbridge, 2010).
P. Payton (ed.), *Cornwall in the Age of Rebellion, 1490–1690* (Exeter, 2021).
R. Pearse-Chope, *The Book of Hartland* (Torquay, 1940).
N. Pevsner, *The Buildings of England: Cornwall* (London, 1951).
D.H. Pill, *The English Reformation, 1529–1558* (London, 1973).
A.F. Pollard, *England under Protector Somerset: An Essay* (London, 1900; New York, 1966 edn).
—, *The History of England: From the Accession of Edward VI to the Death of Elizabeth, 1547–1603* (London, 1910).
A.W. Pollard and G.R. Redgrave (eds), *A Short Title Catalogue of Books Printed in England, Scotland and Ireland . . . 1475–1640* (London, 1986 edn).
R. Polwhele, *The History of Devonshire, Volume 1* (London, 1797; 2nd edn, Dorking, 1977).
H.F.M. Prescott, *Mary Tudor: The Spanish Tudor* (London, 1952; 2003 edn).
G. Redworth, *In Defence of the Church Catholic: The Life of Stephen Gardiner* (Oxford, 1990).
H. Reynolds, *A Short History of the Ancient Diocese of Exeter* (Exeter, 1895).
F. Rose-Troup, *The Western Rebellion of 1549: An Account of the Insurrections in Devon and Cornwall against Religious Innovations in the Reign of Edward VI* (London, 1913).
A.L. Rowse, *Tudor Cornwall: Portrait of a Society* (New York, 1941; London, 1969 edn).
S. Rudder, *A New History of Gloucestershire* (Cirencester, 1779).
F.W. Russell, *Kett's Rebellion in Norfolk* (London, 1859).
A. Ryrie, *The Age of Reformation: The Tudor and Stuart Realms, 1485–1603* (Harlow, 2009).
J.J. Scarisbrick, *The English People and the English Reformation* (Oxford, 1984; 1985 edn).
G. Scott-Thomson, *Two Centuries of Family History: A Study in Social Development* (London, 1930).
S. Seyer, *Memoirs Historical and Topographical of Bristol and its Neighbourhood, Volume II* (Bristol, 1823).
M. Siraut (ed.), *A History of the County of Somerset: Volume 10* (Woodbridge, 2010).
C. Skidmore, *Edward VI: The Lost King of England* (London, 2008).
P. Slack (ed.), *Rebellion, Popular Protest and the Social Order in Early Modern England* (Cambridge, 1984).
M. Stoyle, *West Britons: Cornish Identities and the Early Modern British State* (Exeter, 2002).
—, *Circled with Stone: Exeter's City Walls, 1485–1660* (Exeter, 2003).
—, *Water in the City: The Aqueducts and Underground Passages of Exeter* (Exeter, 2014).
J. Strype (ed.), *Ecclesiastical Memorials, Relating Chiefly to Religion and the Reformation of it . . . under King Henry VIII, King Edward VI and Queen Mary I, Volume II, Part 1* (Oxford, 1822 edn).

J. Sturt, *Revolt in the West: The Western Rebellion of 1549* (Exeter, 1987).
J. Sydney-Curtis, *Devonshire: Historical and Pictorial* (Southampton, n.d.).
G.M. Thomson, *Sir Francis Drake* (London, 1972; 1976 edn).
J.A.F. Thomson, *The Early Tudor Church and Society* (London and New York, 1993).
C. Torr, *Wreyland Documents* (Cambridge, 1910).
J. Wagner, *The Devon Gentleman: A Life of Sir Peter Carew* (Hull, 1998).
G. Walker, *John Heywood: Comedy and Survival in Tudor England* (Oxford, 2020).
A. Wall, *Power and Protest in England, 1525 to 1640* (London, 2000).
J. Walter, *Crowds and Popular Politics in Early Modern England* (Manchester, 2006).
R. Whiting, *The Blind Devotion of the People: Popular Religion and the English Reformation* (Cambridge, 1989; 1991 edn).
—, *Local Responses to the English Reformation* (Basingstoke, 1998).
D. Willen, *John Russell, First Earl of Bedford: One of the King's Men* (RHS Studies in History, 23, London, 1981).
P. Williams, *The Tudor Regime* (Oxford, 1979).
—, *The Later Tudors . . . England, 1547–1603* (Oxford, 1998).
A. Wood, *Riot, Rebellion and Popular Protest in Early Modern England* (Basingstoke, 2002).
—, *The 1549 Rebellions and the Making of Early Modern England* (Cambridge, 2007).
R.N. Worth, *A History of Devonshire* (London, 1886).
—, *History of Plymouth* (Plymouth, 1890).
J. Youings, *Tuckers Hall, Exeter: The History of a Provincial City Company through Five Centuries* (Exeter, 1968).
—, *The Dissolution of the Monasteries* (London, 1971).
—, *Early Tudor Exeter: The Founders of the County of the City of Exeter* (Inaugural Lecture, Exeter, 1974).
—, *The Penguin Social History of Britain: Sixteenth-Century England* (London, 1984; 1991 edn).

## VI ARTICLES

J.D. Alsop, 'Latimer, "the Commonwealth of Kent" and the 1549 Rebellions', *HJ*, vol. 28, no. 2 (June 1985), pp. 379–83.
I. Arthurson, 'Fear and Loathing in West Cornwall: Seven New Letters on the 1548 Rising', *JRIC*, new series, 2, vol. 3, parts 3–4 (2000), pp. 68–96.
J. Barber, 'New Light on Old Plymouth', *Proceedings of the Plymouth Athenaeum*, 4 (1973–79), pp. 55–66.
J.S. Berkman, 'Van der Delft's Message: A Reappraisal of the Attack on Protector Somerset', *Bulletin of the Institute of Historical Research*, 53 (1980), pp. 247–52.
G.W. Bernard, 'New Perspectives or Old Complexities?', *EHR*, vol. 115, no. 460 (February 2000), pp. 113–20.
W.J. Blake, 'The Rebellion of Cornwall and Devon in 1549', *JRIC*, vol. 18, part 1 (1910), pp. 147–96; and *JRIC*, vol. 18, part 2 (1911), pp. 300–38.
—, 'A History of Cornwall, 1529–39', *JRIC*, vol. 19, part 3 (1914), pp. 360–94.
A. Boyle, 'Hans Eworth's Portrait of the Earl of Arundel and the Politics of 1549–50', *EHR*, vol. 117, no. 470 (February 2002), pp. 25–47.
L. Boynton, 'The Tudor Provost Marshal', *EHR*, vol. 77, no. 304 (July 1962), pp. 437–55.
M.L. Bush, 'Protector Somerset and the 1549 Rebellions: A Post-Revision Questioned', *EHR*, vol. 115, no. 460 (February 2000), pp. 103–12.
W.H. Campbell, 'The Canons Resident of Exeter Cathedral, 1506–1561', *RTDA*, 146 (June 2014), pp. 121–44.
K.M. Clarke, 'The Carew-Mohun Chimney Piece', *DCNQ*, vol. 9, part 8 (1917), pp. 233–9.

J.P.D. Cooper, 'Arundell, Humphrey (1512–13 to 1550)', in *ODNB* (2004).
—, 'Carew, Sir Peter (1514(?)–1575)', in *ODNB* (2004).
—, 'Godolphin, Sir William (*b.* in or before 1518, *d.* 1570)', in *ODNB* (2004).
J. Cornwall, 'Kett's Rebellion: A Comment', *P&P*, 93 (November 1981), pp. 160–4.
B.F. Cresswell, 'The Church Goods Commission in Devon (1549–1552)', *RTDA*, 43 (1911), pp. 237–55.
C.S.L. Davies, 'Paulet, Sir Hugh, *b.* before 1510, *d.* 1573', in *ODNB* (2004).
E.F. Gay, 'The Midland Revolt and the Inquisitions of Depopulation of 1607', *TRHS*, new series, 18 (1904), pp. 195–244.
R.A. Griffiths, 'Stradling, Sir Thomas (c. 1498–1571)', in *ODNB* (2004).
K. Halliday, 'New Light on "the Commotion Time" of 1549: The Oxfordshire Rising', *HR*, vol. 82, no. 218 (November 2009), pp. 655–76.
C.J. Hayden, 'Tristram Winslade: The Desperate Heart of a Catholic in Exile', *Cornish Studies*, 20 (2012), pp. 32–62.
C. Henderson, 'Ecclesiastical History of the 109 Parishes in Western Cornwall', *JRIC*, new series, vol. 2, part 3 (1955), pp. 1–104, and part 4 (1956), pp. 105–210; and new series, vol. 3, part 2 (1958), pp. 211–382, and part 4 (1960), pp. 383–497.
A. Hodgkins, 'They Would Yield to No Persuasions . . . But Most Manfully Did Abide to the Fight: A Military Assessment of the Western Rebellion', *RTDA*, 147 (2015), pp. 117–54.
H. James, 'The Aftermath of the 1549 Coup and the Earl of Warwick's Intentions', *Bulletin of the Institute of Historical Research*, 57 (1989), pp. 91–7.
C.S. Knighton, 'Haynes [Heynes], Simon (d. 1552)', in *ODNB* (2004).
S. Lehmberg, 'Southwell, Sir Richard (1502–03 to 1564)', in *ODNB* (2004).
D. Loades, 'Kingston, Sir Anthony (c.1508–1556)', in *ODNB* (2004).
J. Lock, 'Grey, William, Thirteenth Baron Grey of Wilton (1508/9–1562)', in *ODNB* (2004).
D. MacCulloch, 'Kett's Rebellion in Context', *P&P*, 84 (August 1979), pp. 36–59.
—, 'Kett's Rebellion: A Rejoinder', *P&P*, 93 (November 1981), pp. 165–73.
—, 'Parliament and the Reformation of Edward VI', *Parliamentary History*, vol. 34, part 3 (2015), pp. 383–400.
R.B. Manning, 'Violence and Social Conflict in Mid-Tudor Rebellions', *JBS*, vol. 16, no. 2 (spring, 1977), pp. 18–40.
J. Mattingly, 'The Helston Shoemakers' Guild and a Possible Connection with the 1549 Rebellion', *Cornish Studies*, new series, 6 (1998), pp. 23–45.
J. McGovern, 'Nicholas Udall as Author of a Manuscript Answer to the Rebels of Devonshire and Cornwall, 1549', *Notes and Queries*, vol. 65, issue 1 (March 2018), pp. 24–5.
S. Mendyck, 'Hooker, John (c.1527–1601)', in *ODNB* (2004).
P.A.S. Pool, 'Cornish Parishes in 1753: IV, Stratton', *Old Cornwall*, vol. 6, no. 11 (1966), pp. 500–3.
F. Rose-Troup, 'Lists Relating to Persons Ejected from Religious Houses', *DCNQ*, 17 (January 1932–October 1933), pp. 81–96.
—, 'Lead from the Dissolved Religious Houses in Devon in 1549', *DCNQ*, vol. 19, parts 3–4 (July–October 1936), pp. 122–6.
A. Rowe, '1549–1949: A Tribute to Heroes', *The Cornish Review*, 2 (summer 1949), pp. 38–42.
G. Scheurweghs, 'On an Answer to the Articles of the Rebels of Cornwall and Devonshire (Royal MS 18 B. XI)', *The British Museum Quarterly*, 8 (1933–34), pp. 24–5.
E.H. Shagan, 'Protector Somerset and the 1549 Rebellions: New Sources and Perspectives', *EHR*, vol. 114, no. 455 (February 1999), pp. 34–63.
—, 'Popularity and the 1549 Rebellions Revisited', *EHR*, vol. 115, no. 460 (February 2000), pp. 121–33.
N.P. Sil, 'Herbert, William, First Earl of Pembroke (1506/7–1570)', in *ODNB* (2004).
C.A.J. Skeel, 'The Council of the West', *TRHS*, 4th series, 4 (1921), pp. 62–80.

A.J. Slavin, 'The Fall of Chancellor Wriothesley: A Study in the Politics of Conspiracy', *Albion*, vol. 7, no. 4 (winter, 1975), pp. 265–86.
H.M. Speight, 'Local Government and the South-Western Rebellion of 1549', *Southern History*, 18 (1996), pp. 1–23.
M. Spriggs, 'Where Cornish Was Spoken and When: A Provisional Synthesis', *Cornish Studies*, 11 (2003), pp. 228–69.
P.Y. Stanton, 'Arundell, Sir Thomas (c. 1502–1552)', in *ODNB* (2004).
—, 'Arundell, Mary [married name Mary Redcliffe] Countess of Sussex, Mary Fitzalan Countess of Arundell', in *ODNB* (2004).
M. Stoyle, 'The Dissidence of Despair: Rebellion and Identity in Early Modern Cornwall', *JBS*, vol. 38, no. 4 (October 1999), pp. 423–44.
—, 'Fullye Bente to Fighte Oute the Matter: Reconsidering Cornwall's Role in the Western Rebellion of 1549', *EHR*, vol. 129, no. 538 (June 2014), pp. 549–77.
—, 'A Hanging at St Keverne: The Execution of Two Cornish Priests in 1549', *DCNQ*, vol. 52, part 1 (spring 2017), pp. 1–4.
—, 'Kill All the Gentlemen?: (Mis)representing the Western Rebels of 1549', *HR*, vol. 92, no. 255 (February 2019), pp. 50–72.
—, 'Rebellion Repressed: The Recapture of Plymouth by Loyalist Forces in 1549', *DCNQ*, vol. 52, part 7 (spring 2020), pp. 191–5.
—, 'The Execution of Rebel Priests in the Western Rising of 1549', *JEH*, vol. 71, no. 4 (October 2020), pp. 755–77.
J. Taylor, 'Who Was William Hellyons?', *Devon Family Historian*, 157 (February 2016), p. 32; and 158 (May 2016), p. 23.
G.C.G. Thomas, 'The Stradling Library at St Donats, Glamorgan', *National Library of Wales Journal*, vol. 24, no. 4 (1986), pp. 402–19.
J. Walter, 'Kett, Robert (c. 1492–1549)', in *ODNB* (2004).
H.M. Whitley, 'The Church Goods of Cornwall at the Time of the Reformation', *JRIC*, vol. 25, no. 5 (1881), pp. 92–135.
M. Wolffe, 'Risdon, Tristram (c. 1580–1640)', in *ODNB* (2004).
J. Youings, 'The City of Exeter and the Property of the Dissolved Monasteries', *RTDA*, 84 (1952), pp. 122–41.
—, 'The Council of the West', *TRHS*, 5th series, 10 (1960), pp. 41–59.
—, 'The South-Western Rebellion of 1549', *Southern History*, 1 (1979), pp. 99–122.
E.H. Young, 'A Short Account of the Okehampton Market', *RTDA*, 57 (1926), pp. 187–225.

### VII CHAPTERS IN EDITED COLLECTIONS

S. Brigden, 'Youth and the English Reformation', in P. Slack (ed.), *Rebellion, Popular Protest and the Social Order in Early Modern England* (Cambridge, 1984), pp. 77–107.
J. Goring, 'Trewynnard, William', in S.T. Bindoff (ed.), *The House of Commons, 1509–1558* (3 vols, London, 1982), III, pp. 485–6.
T. Greeves, 'Four Devon Stannaries: A Comparative Study of Tin-Working in the Sixteenth Century', in T Gray (ed), *Tudor and Stuart Devon: The Common Estate and Government* (Exeter, 1992), pp. 39–74.
R. Higham, 'Public and Private Defence in the Medieval South West', in R. Higham (ed.), *Security and Defence in South-West England before 1800* (Exeter, 1987), pp. 27–49.
S.B. House, 'Literature, Drama and Politics', in D. MacCulloch (ed.), *The Reign of Henry VIII: Politics, Policy and Piety* (London, 1995), pp. 181–201.
O.J. Padel, 'Oral and Literary Culture in Medieval Cornwall', in H. Fulton (ed.), *Medieval Celtic Literature and Society* (Dublin, 2005), pp. 95–116.
R.M. Warnicke, 'Sheriff Courtenay and the Western Rising of 1549', in J. Bliss et al. (eds), *Aspects of Devon's History: People, Places and Landscape* (Exeter, 2012), pp. 143–8.

R. Whiting, 'For the Health of my Soul: Prayers for the Dead in the Tudor South West', in P. Marshall (ed.), *The Impact of the English Reformation 1500–1640* (London, 1997), pp. 121–42.

A. Wood, '"Poore Men Woll Speke One Daye": Plebeian Language of Deference and Defiance in England, c. 1520–1640', in T. Harris (ed.), *The Politics of the Excluded* (Basingstoke, 2001), pp. 67–98.

J. Youings, 'Western Rebellion of 1549', in R.H. Fritze (ed.), *Historical Dictionary of Tudor England, 1485–1603* (New York and London, 1991), pp. 540–1.

—, 'Devon Monastic Bells', in T. Gray (ed.), *Devon Documents* (Tiverton, 1996), pp. 210–13.

### VIII UNPUBLISHED THESES

J. Chynoweth, 'The Gentry of Tudor Cornwall' (unpublished DPhil thesis, University of Exeter, 1994).

G.N. Gibbons, 'The Political Career of Thomas Wriothesley, First Earl of Southampton, 1505–1550' (unpublished PhD thesis, University of Warwick, 1999).

A.R. Greenwood, 'A Study of the Rebel Petitions of 1549' (unpublished PhD thesis, University of Manchester, 1990).

C.J. Hayden, 'Tristram Winslade: An Elizabethan Catholic in Exile' (unpublished DPhil thesis, Flinders University, Australia, 2019).

M. Hunkin, 'Resistance to the Edwardian Reformation: A Study of Religious Discontent in Devon and Cornwall during the Prayer Book Rebellion of 1549' (unpublished MA thesis, University of Southampton, 2001).

A. Jones, 'Commotion Time: The English Risings of 1549' (unpublished PhD thesis, University of Warwick, 2003).

D.H. Pill, 'The Diocese of Exeter under Bishop Veysey' (unpublished MA thesis, University of Exeter, 1963).

H.M. Speight, 'Local Government and Politics in Devon and Cornwall, 1509–49, with Special Reference to the South Western Rebellion of 1549' (unpublished PhD thesis, University of Sussex, 1991).

### IX PAINTINGS

Jules Breton, *Le Pardon de Kergoat en Quéménéven en 1891* (1891).

# INDEX


abbeys and abbots 27, 40, 229
'abbey lands', the 116
Act of Relief of Sheep and Cloth, the 80, 106–7, 121–2, 156
Act of Royal Supremacy, the 26–7
Act of Six Articles, the 41, 53, 122, 133, 156, 175, 279
Act of Uniformity, the 80
actors, rebel captains compared to 90, 111, 187, 290
adultery 27
agrarian reform 75
agricultural workers 1, 87
Albania and the Albanians 146, 181, 183–4, 223, 226
'Alcibiades of England, the' *see* Dudley, John
aldermen 21, 30, 187, 272
ales *see* church ales
Alley, William, bishop of Exeter 93
Alsa, William, priest 233
altars 42, 53, 200
'alymanes' *see* Germans
ambassadors 62, 121, 204, 222, 242, 260, 263, 267, 275, 281; *see also* De Selve, Odet; Hoby, Sir Philip; Van der Delft, Francois
anchors 50
Andrews, John 172
angels 25
Angles, the 17
animals *see* cattle; dogs, horses; pigs; sheep; wolves
'Answer to the Commoners of Devonshire and Cornwall, the' 185–91
Anti-Christ, the 24
antiquarians 3, 11, 109, 126, 210, 234–5, 247, 289
Aragon, Catherine of, queen of England 21, 23, 27
archbishops 21, 26, 272; *see also* Cranmer, Thomas
archdeacons 39, 56, 117, 240
archers 196
armour 119, 194
arraignments 294
arrows *see* bows and arrows
'articles' (i.e., requests or demands) of the protestors 49, 121, 133, 145, 147, 154, 156–7, 175–8, 184–6, 188–90, 231, 258
artillery 18, 119, 138, 164, 184, 194, 198–9, 208–9
artisans 20
Arundel, earl of *see* Fitzalan, Henry
Arundell family, the 18, 40, 141, 225, 262, 286, 295–6
Arundell, Humphrey, gentleman and rebel captain 18, 27, 129–32, 140–1, 143–4, 150–1, 153, 156–8, 160, 164, 167, 173, 175–8, 203, 205, 208–12, 219–26, 228, 255–7, 260, 268–71, 277–81, 284–7, 290–1, 293–6
Arundell, Mary, gentlewoman 264
Arundell, Roger, gentleman 18, 27, 129–30

# INDEX


Arundell, Sir John, senior, gentleman 18, 27, 40–1, 130
Arundell, Sir John, junior, gentleman 18, 26–7, 40–1, 46, 99, 100, 130, 141, 224–5, 260–3, 274, 282–7, 291, 295–6
Arundell, Sir Thomas, gentleman 18, 26–7, 29–30, 40–1, 46, 99, 130, 224–5, 260–5, 267, 269–71, 273–5, 284, 286, 291–2, 295–6
Arwennack House, near Falmouth, Cornwall 19
Ashburton, Devon 13, 58
Ashenrydge, fish driver and rebel captain 112–13
ashlar *see* stone
Askew, Anne 228
assemblies, unlawful 30–1, 53, 57, 62–3, 90, 92–4, 100, 106, 112, 131, 141, 146, 230; *see also* riots
assizes 15, 37
Aston, in the diocese of Lichfield 74
Athelstan, king of Wessex 14
Atlantic Ocean, the 19
attorney 228
Aucher, Sir Anthony, gentleman 259
Augmentations, receiver of the court of 261
*Ave Maria*, the 39
Axminster, Devon 82

bailiffs 21, 72, 172–3
ballads and balladeers 95, 128, 163, 168, 235
banners 19, 33–6, 120, 132, 200, 210
'barkes' (i.e., barques) 128, 161
barns, burnt 101–3
Barnstaple, Devon 14, 204, 206, 233
Barow, John, priest 233
Barret, Roger, priest 177, 231, 233
barricades 107, 110, 135, 174–5, 192–4, 196, 198, 209
Barton, Elizabeth, mystic 25–6
Bath, earls of *see* Bourchier family
Bath, manor of, in North Tawton 91
Bath, Somerset 214
Bealbury, John 249
Beauchamp, John, gentleman 116
beds 250
beer 134
beheading *see* decapitation
bells and bellringing 56, 63, 132, 166; *see also* church bells
Benet, Richard, priest 233
Benet, Thomas, schoolmaster 24–5
Bere Ferrers, Devon 210
Berry, John *see* Bury, John
Berry Pomeroy, Devon 194
Bible, the 23, 28, 38, 187
Bideford, Devon 14, 162
bills, handwritten 24, 31, 54–5, 132, 156, 172–3; parliamentary 157; weapons and billmen 95, 197
biographies and biographers 42, 84, 185, 250
birds *see* geese
Bishop's Court Lane, Clyst St Mary, Devon 196
bishops 12, 21, 38–9, 41–2, 48, 52, 55–6, 58–9, 71, 73, 89, 93, 98, 117, 154, 170, 193, 229, 235–6, 241, 260, 275, 284
Bittadon, Devon 204, 233
Black Death, the 2
Blackaller, John, alderman and mayor of Exeter 30, 113
Blackdown Hills, the 11–12, 150
blacksmiths 33, 63
Blake, W.J., historian 177
blame 2, 31, 92, 102, 186, 210, 230–1, 251, 256–7
Blaxton, John, commissary 42, 89, 117, 240
Blewet, Sir Roger, gentleman 116
Blisland, Cornwall 131, 222
blockhouses 18
blood 63, 95, 101, 139, 175, 198, 244, 248, 279, 290
Bochim, Robert, priest 233
Bochym, Cornwall 233
Bochym, John 233
Bodinnick, Cornwall 135, 169
Bodleian library, Oxford 84–5, 105
Bodmin, Cornwall 15–18, 27, 129–34, 137, 141, 153, 156, 173, 176–7, 189, 212, 221–3, 245–6, 253, 290, 293
Bodmin Moor, Cornwall 15
Body, William, gentleman 56–7, 62–5, 67, 70–4, 95
Boleyn, Anne, queen of England 24–7, 229
bonds, financial 253
*Book of Common Prayer, the* 1, 3, 74, 80, 82, 85–6, 88–9, 91, 93, 98–9, 115, 121–2, 147, 156, 170–1, 175, 187–8, 258, 284, 292
Boorde, Andrew, author 16

Bosavern in St Just, Cornwall 169
Boson family, of West Penwith 249
Bossins, Thomas 249
Bottreaux Castle, Cornwall 239
boulders 20
Bourchier family, the 14
Bourchier, John, earl of Bath 45, 233
Bow, Devon 13, 250
bows and arrows 118–19, 136, 165, 172, 179
Bowyer, mayor of Bodmin 245
Brankin, James, ship owner 161
Bray, Henry, mayor of Bodmin 176–7, 221–3, 245
bread 23, 41, 167, 200
Breton language, the 16
bridges 12–14, 70, 104, 178–81, 191–3, 197–9, 226, 287, 291, 293
Bristol 182
Britons, Ancient 14, 17
Brittany and the Bretons 16, 31, 35, 169
Brook, tenement in Sampford Courtenay 90
Brown, John, parson of Langtree 235
Bruton, Somerset 214
Bucer, Martin, theologian 171
bulwarks 60, 193, 195–6, 200, 209
Burgundy and the Burgundians 183–4
burning, of barns and houses 60, 102–3, 131, 174, 195, 197; of heretics 24, 41
Bury, John, gentleman and rebel captain 108, 176, 203, 212–14, 223–4, 226, 228, 256, 277, 280, 286–7
Bury, Margery, gentlewoman, wife of John 108, 287
Bushy Leaze, Kingsweston, Somerset 214

Calais, France 119, 183, 191, 203
Cambridge, Cambridgeshire 259
'camping time, the' 148
camps and camping 109, 120, 129, 132, 138, 148, 160, 167, 171–2, 175, 177, 182–3 189–91, 193, 199–200, 202, 207–9, 212, 231–3, 258–9, 290–1, 293
candles 22, 35, 42, 206
candlesticks 200
cannons 138, 162–3
canons 22, 32, 37, 42, 47, 50, 53–5, 116–17, 166–7, 175, 229, 231, 240–1, 270
Canterbury, Kent 25
  archbishop of 21, 26, 45, 202; *see also* Cranmer, Thomas
captains, rebel 4, 6–7, 89, 91, 108, 111–14, 118, 123, 129, 131–2, 135, 141, 152, 158, 162, 164, 167, 169, 171–3, 176–7, 187, 190, 193–4, 199, 201, 207, 210, 212, 219–26, 230, 248, 256–7, 265, 271, 274–6, 278–9, 286, 290, 296–7
cardinals 32, 56, 175, 260
Carew family 87, 176, 179
Carew, George, archdeacon of Totnes 240
Carew, Richard, antiquarian 15–18, 20, 59, 63, 65, 67, 126, 129, 132–6, 138–9, 140–1, 246–7, 289
Carew, Sir Gawen, gentleman 43, 46, 52, 55, 96–7, 100–2, 104–5, 107–8, 112, 124–5, 128, 168, 179, 202–5, 210–11, 240
Carew, Sir George, gentleman 43
Carew, Sir Peter, gentleman 42–3, 50–2, 55, 66, 84, 93, 96–7, 100–8, 112, 124–5, 128, 150, 152, 164, 173, 202–3, 207, 210–12, 240, 286
Carew, Sir William, gentleman 42
carpenters 31
  construct gallows 206
Carpyssacke, Uryn [?], fisherman 33–7, 39, 60
Carrick Roads, Cornwall 18
Carvanell, Alexander 169
Castell, clerk, and secretary to Humphrey Arundell 158, 224, 226, 228
Castle Canyke, Cornwall 129
castles 12, 14–15, 18–19, 55, 60–1, 67, 111, 120, 127, 129, 133–40, 143–4, 160–2, 164, 189, 205–6, 210, 227, 239, 248, 250, 281
Catholics and Catholicism 5, 21–3, 41, 53, 178, 231, 237–8, 263, 265, 268, 270, 273, 290, 294, 297; *see also* 'papists'
cattle 120, 251
Cavendish, George, poet 263, 267
Cecil, William, 1st Baron Burghley 259
'certayne brief notes' (document) 266–8, 283
Chagford, Devon 13
chains, persons hanged in 37, 204, 229–30, 233, 281; used by the rebels, to fortify town and villages 101

chalices 28
Chamber of Exeter, the 12, 53, 55, 96, 103, 114–16, 118, 165
Chamberlain, Leonard, esquire 269, 281
Chambers, Richard, servant to Simon Haynes 32–3, 38
chancels 187
Chancery, court of 239, 250
Channel, the 181
chantries and chantry priests 22, 53, 58
chantry commissioners 58, 91
chapels 19
chaplains 72
Chard, Somerset 150–1
Charles V, king of Spain and Holy Roman Emperor 32
charters, stolen by the rebels 169
chests, broken up 251
children 28, 39, 44–5, 86, 110, 214, 264, 296; *see also* infant baptism
Chipping Norton, Oxfordshire 230
choir books 42
Christ, Jesus 23–4, 34–5, 39, 41, 50, 187
  passion of 155
  wounds of 33–4
christenings *see* infant baptism
Christmas day 284
Christmas games 176, 187
Chubbe, John, yeoman and rebel 'under captain' 108
church ales 88–9, 94
church bells, ringing of 56
church goods 22, 24, 28, 48, 55–7, 62, 81–2
'church holy days' 27, 29, 34–5, 39
church houses 94–5
church jewels and treasures *see* church goods
church steeples and towers 30, 111, 119, 163, 170
  monks, priests and rebels hanged from 146, 204, 213, 229–30, 233, 281
churches 1, 4, 12, 14–15, 19, 22, 24, 27–31, 35, 38–9, 48, 55–9, 62, 73, 85, 87, 89–90, 94, 111–12, 120, 170, 171, 200, 213–14, 237
  prisoners held in 108–9, 201
churchwardens 21, 65, 81
  accounts of 171–2
churchyards 95, 292, 297
clerks 89, 224
Cleves, Anne of, queen of England 41
cliffs 20
closet, clerks of the 89
cloth-making 12–13, 20, 56, 80, 82, 106, 121, 156
clothes and clothing 30–1, 138, 229, 247; *see also* coats, French hoods, smocks and vestments
Clowance 57
Clyst Heath, Devon 12, 198–201, 297
Clyst Honiton, Devon 12
Clyst, River, Devon 12, 193, 197–8
Clyst St Mary, Devon 104, 107, 110, 127, 192–9, 220
coats, red 146, 183
cob 87
Coffin, rebel captain 135, 162, 212–14, 223–6, 228
Coffin family, of Portledge, Devon 162
Collaton, Agnes 29
Cologne, Germany 83
Columbjohn, Devon 91
commissaries 42, 89, 117, 240
commissioners 4, 20, 29, 39, 46, 49–50, 58, 62–3, 68, 70, 91
common councillors 272–3
common land 75, 80–1, 95
'commons', the 20, 65, 67, 82, 104, 112, 124, 153, 155, 166, 242–3, 253, 267–8
'Commonwealth', rebellion of 258
'Commonwealth', rhetoric of 256
'commonwealths', rebel captains in Kent referred to as 146, 258–9
communion in both kinds 59
Comptroller of the Household, the 269–70, 275
conspiracy and conspirators 36, 40, 85, 263–72, 275, 286, 292
constables 21, 69, 103, 132, 140, 250, 277
Constantine, Cornwall 16, 64–5, 67
convocation 25, 27
Copplestone, Devon 13
cords, prisoners tied up with 214
corn 13, 251
'Cornish Commotion' of 1548, the 4, 6, 58–75, 81, 122, 133–4, 137, 139, 163–4, 188, 213, 230, 285, 289, 292–3
Cornish cultural difference 4, 14, 17, 23, 35, 39, 73, 138, 157, 176, 189, 292–3
Cornish language 16, 19, 38–9, 48–9, 57, 59, 73–4, 138, 157, 188–9, 292
Cornish rising, of 1497, the 33, 36, 60

Cornwall and the Cornish 1, 2, 4–7, 11, 14–16, 19–21, 23, 28– 29, 33, 39–41, 46–8, 50, 56, 62–3, 65–7, 69, 71, 74, 81, 91, 99, 113, 125–30, 132–3, 135, 141–2, 145, 149, 151, 153, 155–6, 158–61, 163–4, 167, 169, 171–3, 175–80, 185, 188, 190–1, 203–5, 207, 209, 210, 212–13, 215, 222, 225, 230–1, 233–5, 238–9, 244, 247–9, 251, 253–4, 279–80, 282, 285, 290–1, 295–6
  archdeaconry of 39, 56
  commission of the peace of 46
  deputy receiver of the duchy of 127
  sheriff of 55, 68, 282
  undersheriff of 69
  *see also* West Cornwall and the West Cornish
*Cornwall, Survey of* 15, 59, 126, 140, 289
Corpus Christi, feast of 100
Cotton, Thomas, vice-admiral of the Narrow Seas 164
Council of the West, the 40
Council of Twenty-Four, the *see* Chamber of Exeter, the
couriers 147
Court, the 18, 42, 46, 96, 261–2, 267, 269, 288
Courtenay family 39, 87–9
Courtenay, Edward, 1st earl of Devonshire 282
Courtenay, Gertrude, marchioness of Exeter 25–6, 40
Courtenay, Henry, marquess of Exeter 26, 30–2, 39–40, 87, 282
Courtenay, John, gentleman 116, 165–6
Courtenay, Sir Peter 46
Courtenay, Sir Piers 100, 104–8, 116, 146
Courtenay, Sir William, of Powderham 146
Coverdale, Miles, cleric 193, 241
Cowley Bridge, Devon 13
craft corporations 96, 103
Cranmer, Thomas, archbishop of Canterbury 26, 41, 45–6, 59, 80, 155, 184–6, 188–9, 202, 272, 275
Crediton, Devon 1, 13, 100–3, 106–7, 110, 112, 120, 124, 128, 169, 207, 290
  buildings at, burnt 102–3, 174
Creed, the 38–9
Cresswell, Beatrix, historian 3
Crewkerne, Somerset 82
Crispin, Richard, cathedral canon 24, 47, 49–52, 55, 175, 231, 240, 270, 292
Cromwell, Thomas, vicar-general 26–9, 33, 36–41, 56, 278
Croppe, Thomas 66, 164
cross-dressing 31
crosses and crucifixes 22, 28, 31, 62, 120, 142, 171, 200, 235, 290
crowds 25, 35, 95, 98, 203, 286
Crowne, Thomas 164
Cullompton, Devon 82
curates 22, 59, 74, 204, 233
Curtes, John, priest 237–9
Cury, Cornwall 233

dances and dancing 187
Dartmoor 13, 58, 87
Dartmouth, Devon 14, 52
Daryette, John, yeoman 140
Davies, Gilbert, publisher 126
De Germiny, Captain Jacques 183–4, 203, 251
De Selve, Odet, French ambassador 62–3, 71, 73
Dean and Chapter of Exeter Cathedral, the 12, 23, 32–3, 37, 42, 46, 55, 103, 115, 240–1
  canons of 32, 42, 47, 50, 53–5, 116–17, 166–7, 175, 231, 240–1, 270
  chapter house of 38
  manors belonging to 240–1
  precentor of 240
  treasurer of 54
Dean Prior, Devon 109, 250
deans 12, 23, 32, 37–9, 42, 46, 50
decapitation 229, 287, 296
dedication feasts 27–9, 34–5
deeds, stolen by the rebels 169–70
Denys, Philip, gentleman 238
Denys, Sir Thomas, gentleman 24, 25, 30–1, 46, 104–9, 242, 250
depositions 136, 271
Derby, earl of *see* Stanley, Edward
desertion 161
'development', early twenty-first century, engulfs the East Devon countryside 297
devil, the 177
devils 200

Devon, county of 1, 2, 6–7, 11, 13, 20–1, 23, 39–40, 43, 46, 50, 52, 58, 80–2, 85, 87–8, 93, 96–101, 103, 106, 108–9, 112–13, 117, 119, 120–3, 125, 127–30, 132–3, 140–1, 143–9, 151–4, 156–7, 159–60, 162, 164, 167–8, 171–3, 177–8, 182–3, 185, 190–1, 194, 196, 202–7, 210–12, 215, 222, 225, 228, 230–5, 237–9, 242–4, 248, 250–1, 254–5, 257, 259, 286, 290, 292–3, 296–7
  sheriff of 43, 50
Devonshire, earl of *see* Courtenay, Edward
'diets' 97
Dillon, Robert, soldier 119
dinners 29, 69, 245
dioceses 12, 21–2, 38–9, 49–51, 55–6, 58–9, 74, 89, 235, 237, 240–1
disease and sickness 273, 280, 288; *see also* Black Death
disembowelling 69–70, 287
disguises 30–1
divisions 40, 43, 107, 188, 260, 267, 292
documents, stolen and destroyed 169–70, 251
dogs, Anglo-Saxons equated with 17
doors 24, 29, 54, 63, 227, 246
Dorset, county of 40, 99, 124, 145, 148, 150–1, 178–9, 183, 197, 214, 261, 291
Dorset, marquess of *see* Grey, Henry
Dover, Kent 183
Dowriche, Thomas, gentleman 279
Drake's Island *see* St Nicholas Island
dramatic performances *see* interludes; pageants; stage plays
drink 206; *see also* beer; wine
drums and drummers 194
Dudley, John, first earl of Warwick, later duke of Northumberland 43, 150, 234, 255–6, 259–60, 263–7, 270, 272–3, 275–8, 280–4, 294, 296
Duffield, Bernard, steward 116, 165–6
Duffield, Frances, daughter of Bernard 166
Duffy, Eamon, historian 80, 120, 171
Dussindale, Norfolk 266

East Anglia 112, 147–8, 150, 170, 189, 191, 226, 234, 255, 258–9, 271, 277, 296
East Ogwell, Devon 210
Easter 59, 61, 73–4, 81
Edward VI, king of England 1, 4, 5, 7, 27, 44–5, 47–8, 52–3, 56, 60, 64, 72, 75, 79, 86, 88, 100, 104, 115, 121–3, 129, 134, 137, 152–5, 164, 171, 178, 186, 196, 199, 226, 238, 250, 256, 259, 261–3, 267–70, 273, 289
  chronicle or journal of 174, 181, 183, 195
  surveys captured rebel leaders 226
Edwards, Henry, servant to Sir William Godolphin 47
Elizabeth I, queen of England 17, 44, 93, 238–9
elections 43
Ely, bishop of *see* Goodrich, John
enclosure 75, 80–1, 257
  protests and riots against 75, 81–2, 97, 147, 189, 214
English Civil War, the 2
English language 16, 23, 28, 38, 39, 59, 73–4, 122, 157, 176, 188–9, 292
Ennys, Thomas, of Gluvias, Cornwall 134–5, 137, 162, 248
entrails, burnt 69, 215
epistles 38, 51
'espials' *see* spies
Esseball, John 169
Essex, county of 147, 258, 260
estuaries 18, 61
ethnicity 16–17
eucharist, the 41
Europe, reformation in 23
evangelicals 24–6, 32, 38, 41, 43–6, 49–50, 52–53, 58, 71–72, 74, 79–80, 83–4, 86, 95–6, 104, 108, 115–16, 128, 185, 193–4, 224, 230, 234, 257–8, 260, 264–5, 268, 272–6, 280–1, 283–4, 287–8
'evidences' (i.e., legal documents), stolen and destroyed by the rebels 170
executions and executioners 6, 26, 27, 32, 37–8, 40–1, 68–70, 74, 87, 89, 108, 128, 147, 163, 198, 204, 206, 213–15, 221–2, 229–30, 233–8, 243–8, 252, 263, 276, 281–8, 293, 295, 297; *see also* burnings; decapitation; hangings; hanging, drawing and quartering

executor-councillors 44
Exe, River, Devon 13, 108, 212
Exeter 1, 3, 12–13, 20, 24, 26, 29–33, 37, 42, 53–4, 60–1, 83–5, 91, 100–5, 107–9, 112–21, 126–8, 149, 160, 163, 166–7, 173–5, 177–8, 189, 192–5, 199–203, 205–7, 214, 223, 225, 232, 261, 291–3, 296–7
  boundaries of 55
  city walls of 12, 84, 118–20, 165–6, 201–2, 242, 290
  common bell of 166
  diocese of 49–51, 240–1
  magistrates of 12, 100
  marchioness of, *see* Courtenay, Gertrude
  marquess of, *see* Courtenay, Henry
  mayor of 53–4, 107, 113–14, 166–7, 202
  mayor's court of 52, 103
  places in
    Bishop's Palace 21, 117
    Black Friars, house of 39–40, 115–16, 166
    Cathedral 12–13, 21, 37, 39, 42, 53–4, 270
    Cathedral Close 13, 38, 55, 116–18
    Chapter House 38, 118
    East Gate 12, 53
    Grey Friars, house of 39
    Guildhall 31, 114, 118, 166
    Longbrook Valley 120
    North Gate 13
    Rougemont Castle 12, 120, 250
    St David's parish 13
      New Castle in 120
      St David's Down in 13, 120, 167, 172, 189
    St Edmund's parish church 119
    St Nicholas Priory 29–30, 55, 118
    St Sidwell's fee 53
    St Sidwell's parish 12, 55
      St Sidwell's church in 108, 119
    South Gate 195
    Southernhay 120
      St John's Fields in 202
  recorder of 222
  siege of 2, 4–5, 83, 113, 117–18, 120, 141, 144–5, 164–5, 167, 177, 180, 191, 201–2, 212, 219, 233, 240–2, 251, 290
  streets of 54, 194
Exmoor 13, 81
Exmouth, Devon 242
fabrics *see* silk; velvet; woollen-cloth
factions and factionalism 5, 40, 43, 52, 58, 108, 115, 125, 194, 255, 261, 266, 272, 275–6, 280–1, 283, 284, 294
faggots, used to burn traitors' entrails 69
fairs 15, 120
Fal, River, Cornwall 18–19
Falmouth, Cornwall 18, 60
farms, farming and farmers 13, 21, 80, 87, 90, 159, 296
feasts and festivals 22, 27, 34–6, 39, 74, 88, 91, 94, 96, 100, 122, 187–8, 246; *see also* dedication feasts
fences, pulled down 81
Feniton, Devon 52, 178–9
Fenny Bridges, Devon 12, 178
  battle of 179–81, 191–2, 291, 293
fields 92, 119, 193, 296
'Fifteen Articles', the 175–7, 185–6, 189–90
fines 2, 210, 237–8, 250, 263
fingers, broken 138
fire 25, 75, 101, 102–3, 195, 197, 215
First World War, the 3
fish-drivers 112
Fisher, John, bishop of Rochester 229
fishermen and fishing 14, 16, 19, 34, 37
Fitzalan, Henry, 12th earl of Arundel 260, 264, 283–4
Five Wounds of Christ, device of 34
food 16, 107, 136, 167, 202, 206, 251; *see also* bread; mutton
Fortescue, William, rebel captain 224–6, 274
fortifications 104, 107, 127, 134, 143, 161, 193, 195, 198–200
forts 18–19, 134, 143, 162
Fosse Way, the 11, 82, 174–5
Fowey, Cornwall 135
Fowey Moor *see* Bodmin Moor
Fox, servant to Sir Hugh Pollard 102–3
Foxe, John, historian 130, 141, 199–200, 233–4
France and the French 41–2, 62, 121, 127, 153–4, 194, 228; *see also* Brittany; Calais; Normandy; Paris; Tréport
Francis, Sir William, gentleman 196
Frankland, tenement in Sampford Courtenay 90
French ambassador, the *see* De Selve, Odet
French hoods 247
friars and friaries 22, 25

Frog Lane, Clyst St Mary, Devon 196
Frome, Somerset 81, 213, 215
Fry, John, gentleman 101–3, 180, 192, 197, 201, 203–4, 207, 232, 235, 242–3
funerals 22, 108
furse 25, 194
Furse, John 250
Furse, Margaret, wife of John 250
Furse, Philip, yeoman 109
Furse, Robert, yeoman 109, 250, 286

gallows 37, 68–70, 206, 230, 233, 235, 245–7, 285
games *see* Christmas games; May games; Midsummer games
gaols *see* prisons
Gardiner, Stephen, bishop of Winchester 52–3, 72–3, 98, 122, 260–2, 264, 270
garrisons 127–8, 130, 138, 140, 160–2, 191
gates 12, 13, 15, 53, 61, 70, 113, 119, 138, 195, 226
geese, allegedly to be taxed 110
Geffrey, Martin, clerk of St Keverne 63–4, 69–70, 230
Genoa and the Genoese 182
gentlemen 16, 20–1, 24, 26, 33, 36, 40–2, 46, 57, 60, 62, 65–8, 70–1, 75, 84, 89, 92–3, 99, 101–4, 107–9, 112–13, 115, 125, 127, 129–30, 132–3, 136–7, 142, 150, 161–2, 165, 169, 175–6, 179, 183, 196, 201–2, 206–7, 210, 214, 222–3, 225, 231–2, 238–40, 250, 253–6, 259, 267, 271, 277–80, 282, 285, 287, 290, 294–6
Germany and the Germans 146, 148, 171, 181–2
gibbets 287
Gibbs, William, of Feniton 52, 203, 286–7
Glandfeld, Elizabeth 29–30
Glevyan, Cornwall 247
Gloucestershire, county of 146, 149, 201, 246
Gluvias, Cornwall 134, 248
Godolphin family, the 40–1
Godolphin, Sir William, senior, gentleman 19, 29, 33–7, 40–1, 46–8, 60
Godolphin, Sir William, junior, gentleman 41–2, 47, 57, 65–7, 70–1, 127–8, 137, 139, 227, 253, 282–3, 285, 295
Godolphin House, Breage, Cornwall 19, 33, 40, 57
Goodrich, John, bishop of Ely 275, 281
gorse 20
'gospellers' (i.e., evangelicals) 258, 262, 268
'Governours of the [rebel] campes', the 177, 231, 233
Grade, Cornwall 60
Grafton, Richard, chronicler 244–7
grand juries 68–9
granite 13, 15, 19–20, 87
grass 13, 214
graves 242
gravestones 297
graziers and grazing 13, 80
Great Master, the 260
Grenville, Matilda, wife of Sir Richard 133
Grenville, Sir Richard, gentleman 41–2, 46, 65–7, 116, 133, 138–40, 161
Green Hill Cross, Sampford Courtenay, Devon 208
Greenwood, Aubrey, historian 294
Grey, Henry, marquess of Dorset 275, 281
Grey, William, 13th Baron Grey de Wilton 145–6, 149, 154, 173, 180–4, 191, 198, 200, 202, 207–9, 212, 223–4, 226, 230, 232, 243, 251
Greystone Bridge, on the River Tamar 14
Groom of the Stool, the 269, 273
Gruffydd, Ellis 119, 191, 203, 243, 251
guilds 15, 22, 53, 58
guildhalls 12, 31
Gulval, Cornwall 233
guns and gunners 120, 145, 161, 164, 182, 184, 192, 200, 208
gunpowder 119, 137

'hackbutters' *see* harquebusiers
Hales, John 75
Hals, William, antiquarian 126, 129, 247
halters 226, 246
Hamble, Hampshire 34
Hampshire 58, 147, 178
Hampton Court 267
hangings 37, 60, 68, 70, 146–7, 155, 202, 204, 213–15, 221, 229–30, 233–5, 238, 242, 244–7, 281, 296
hanging, drawing and quartering 68, 70, 215, 230, 280, 287
Harberton, Devon 47
'harness' 82, 108

harquebuses and harquebusiers 119, 145, 149, 181–2, 196, 208
Harper, William, priest 89–90
Harris, Alice 222
Harris, John, gentleman 222–3
Harris, William 222, 224, 226, 274
Harrys, Thomas and John, gentlemen 169
Hartland Abbey, Devon 27
Harvey, Anthony, gentleman 90–1, 93, 106, 107
Hatherleigh, Devon 170
havens 18, 50
hay 136
Hayden, Cheryl, historian 295
Hayne, Devon 222
Haynes, Simon, dean of Exeter 32–3, 37–9, 42, 46, 51–2
Hayward, John, historian 198–9
heads, set upon bridges, gates and poles 69–70, 287
heaths 12, 198–201, 297
Heavitree, Devon 25, 199
hedges 196, 199, 200, 208
'hedge gentry' 21
Helland, Cornwall 18, 27, 129
Hellions, William, gentleman or yeoman 94–6, 101, 297
helmets 196
Helston, Cornwall 37, 55, 61–6, 69, 72, 75, 86
Helston Down, Cornwall 61
henchmen 42
Henderson, Charles, historian 135
Henry VII, king of England 33
  statue of 12
Henry VIII, king of England 4, 11, 12, 14, 17, 21, 23–7, 32, 35, 40–5, 48, 52–3, 64, 72, 86–7, 89, 91, 104, 122, 133, 146, 228–30, 260–3, 268, 278–9, 280
  French wars of 194
  last will and testament of 44
  matrimonial difficulties of 25–7, 32
  wives of *see* Aragon, Catherine of; Boleyn, Anne; Cleves, Anne of; Parr, Catherine; Seymour, Jane
Herbert, Sir William, first earl of Pembroke 81–2, 149, 201–3, 206–11, 223, 227, 238, 240, 251, 267
heresy and heretics 23–7, 41–3, 53, 72, 95, 115, 122–3, 168, 170–1, 175, 194, 228
Hertfordshire 75, 189
'Hicks and Toms', rebels described as 290
hillforts 129
Hinton St George, Somerset 42, 82, 106, 123, 196
Hoby, Sir Philip, English ambassador to the Holy Roman Empire and Flanders 222, 224, 226, 234, 276, 279–82, 284–5
Holcombe Burnell, Devon 24
Holinshed, Raphael, chronicler 83, 183
Holmes, Thomas, yeoman 131–2, 222–6, 228, 256, 271, 277, 280, 285–7, 295
Holwell, John 117
holy days, *see* feasts and festivals
Honeychurch, hamlet near Sampford Courtenay, Devon 90
Honiton, Devon 12, 123–5, 141, 144–5, 150–2, 160, 170, 173–4, 178, 180–4, 191–2, 291
Hooker, John, chronicler 3, 29–30, 82–109, 111–20, 122–7, 150, 152, 162, 164–7, 173–4, 177–80, 182, 184, 187, 191–203, 206, 209, 212, 225, 232, 241–3, 251, 290
Hooper, John 274
Hopton, Sir Ralph, gentleman 281
horses and horsemen 69, 71, 92, 97, 101, 118, 145–7, 149–50, 179, 181–4, 192, 196–8, 201, 203, 206, 209, 211, 214, 223, 226, 251, 285
horse flesh, eaten by the defenders of Exeter 167
House of Commons, the 297
houses 87, 119–20, 160, 195, 211, 281, 284
  attacked 63, 245
  burned and threatened to be burned 131, 174, 195, 197
  rifled and pillaged 137, 168–70
Howard, Margaret 261
Howard, Thomas, 3rd duke of Norfolk 229, 261–2, 264–5, 270, 282
hue and cry 132, 215
hurdles 285–6
husbandmen 64

iconoclasm and iconoclasts 29–30, 39, 73, 261
'idols' and idolatry 28, 31, 48, 128
images, religious 4, 22, 28, 31, 34–5, 39, 42, 48, 58–9, 62–3, 73–4

imperial ambassador, the *see* Van der Delft, Francois
indictments 54, 62, 64–5, 68, 70–2, 126, 132–3, 139, 214, 276–7, 279–80, 293–4
industry 12–13, 19, 80, 251
infant baptism 22, 110, 121–2, 156, 205
injunctions 28, 38, 39, 48–9, 52, 58, 171
inns 13
interludes 90–1, 94, 187–8, 290
interrogations 5, 24, 57, 66, 69, 108, 110, 131, 153, 212, 219–21, 223, 227–8, 262, 271, 283
inventories 55–7, 81, 170, 213, 233
  stolen and destroyed by the rebels 170
Ireland and the Irish 2, 297
Irish, Edmund, smith 63, 69
Iron Age, the 129
iron clamps 69
islands 19, 134
Italy and the Italians 32, 42, 83, 145, 149, 182–4, 196, 208; *see also* Genoa and the Genoese

Joseph, Michael, blacksmith and rebel captain 33
Joyes, Henry, vicar of Chipping Norton 230
judges, royal 15, 277
juries *see* grand juries
justices of the peace 12, 15, 20, 30–1, 40, 46, 57, 65, 90–4, 98–100, 102, 104–8, 116, 130–1, 133, 139, 156, 172, 250, 253–4, 261, 296

keeps 15, 133
Kenninghall, Norfolk 259, 265
Kent, county of 88, 147, 150, 191, 258–9
  'Nun of' *see* Barton, Elizabeth.
Kerrier, hundred of Cornwall 19, 33, 37, 61, 65, 71–3, 137
Kett, Robert, rebel captain 112, 123, 147, 173, 226, 258, 265, 270–1, 276–81, 296
Kett, William 226, 276–7, 280–1
Kett's Rebellion 147, 234, 265–6, 271, 277, 294
kidnapping 169
Kilkhampton, Cornwall 41, 133
Killigrew, John, junior, gentleman 60-1, 74, 127, 134–5, 137, 161–2, 213
Killigrew, John, senior, gentleman 18–19, 60–1, 127, 134–5, 137, 161
Kilter, John 65, 67
Kilter, William, husbandman 64–5, 67–8
King's Bench, court of 277
King's Nympton, Devon 91
Kingston, Devon 197
Kingston, Mary, wife of Sir Anthony 146
Kingston, Sir Anthony, gentleman 146–7, 153, 201, 209, 238–9, 244–8
Kingsweston, Somerset 214–15, 223
knight marshal, the 281
knives 63
Knyvett, Sir Thomas, gentleman 271
Kympe, Roger 249
Kyrton *see* Crediton

labourers 86, 90, 112
ladders 246, 287
Lammas Fair 120
Land's End, the, Cornwall 11, 14, 20, 127
languages *see* Breton; Cornish; English; Latin
Lanherne House, Cornwall 18, 27, 40–1, 99, 130, 141, 224–5, 260, 286, 295–7
landsknechts 182
Langtree, Devon 235
Latimer, Hugh, theologian 26
Latin 23, 28, 59, 87, 157, 176, 178, 284
laughter 229
Launceston, Cornwall 14–15, 27, 68, 138, 172, 210–12, 214, 221–2, 243
Launceston Castle 15, 67, 138–9, 210
law, civil 83
lawsuits 130, 172, 204
lawyers 21, 28, 62, 136, 276–8, 294
'leades' *see* roofs
leases, lost in the rebellion 170
Lee, Henry 177
Leland, John, antiquarian 11–18
Lelant, Cornwall 238
Lethbridge family of Sampford Courtenay 297
letters 30, 33, 36–8, 40, 47, 51, 53–62, 66–7, 69, 71–2, 102, 106–7, 109–11, 121, 123–4, 141–3, 145–7, 149, 151–3, 155–9, 164, 173–4, 176–8, 183, 185, 192, 204–7, 209, 213, 220–1, 223, 226, 229, 231–2, 235, 243–5, 252–3, 259, 261, 267, 270, 273, 276, 281, 284–5, 291

Ley, Henry, gentleman 196–8, 210, 238
libels *see* bills, handwritten
'liberties' 53–4
Lichfield 74
'lights' *see* candles
Lincolnshire 71, 87, 96
linguistic boundaries 16
Liskeard, Cornwall 140, 249
Lithbridge, protestor at Sampford Courtenay 94
Littleham, Devon 242
Livery Dole, place of execution, in Heavitree, Devon 25
Lizard Peninsula, Cornwall 33, 37, 60–1, 137, 233, 292
lodgings 16, 63, 281
'Lollards' 22–3
London 1, 3, 5–6, 12, 15, 17, 38, 42–3, 46–7, 49–50, 53–8, 62, 67, 69–70, 72–4, 79, 86, 95–6, 100, 104, 106, 109–10, 121, 128, 141, 145, 152–3, 155, 159, 171–2, 175, 177–8, 183–7, 191, 202, 204, 221, 223–6, 230–1, 242, 244, 251, 254–6, 259–60, 262, 265, 267–8, 270, 272–3, 279, 285, 291, 294
  aldermen of 187, 273
  common councillors of 273
  mayor of 273
  places in
    Blackfriars 224
    Bridge 70, 287
    Farringdon Street 226
    Fleet Bridge 226
    Fleet Prison 42, 52, 226, 228, 274, 284–6
    Ludgate 226
    Smithfield 70
    St Paul's 186, 202
      dean of 50
    Tower Hill 285
    Tower of London 6, 40, 50, 70, 73, 98, 108, 126, 129–31, 175, 221, 223–4, 228, 231, 240, 256, 262, 264, 268–71, 274, 276, 281–6, 295–6
      constable of 69, 277
      lieutenant of 281
    Tyburn 230, 285–7
  plays banned in 187–8
'London Lords, the' 267–8, 271
Looe, Cornwall 212
loopholes 101
Lord Chancellor, the *see* Wriothesley, Thomas
Lord Privy Seal, the *see* Russell, John
Lord St John *see* Paulet, William
Lord's Prayer, the 48
Louth, Lincolnshire 87
Lower, William, gentleman 248–9
Lower Incott, tenement in Sampford Courtenay 90
loyalists 3, 38, 60–1, 72, 95–6, 102, 108–9, 113, 116, 118, 128, 133–8, 140, 142–4, 155, 160–6, 168–9, 179, 183, 185, 192, 197, 201, 203–10, 227, 232–5, 238, 241, 248–51, 253–5, 260, 291, 293
Luson, William, chancellor of Exeter Cathedral 117
Luther, Martin, theologian 23
Lutherans 25
Lynne, Walter, chronicler 74, 225
Lyster, Sir Richard 277
Lyte, Henry, gentleman 214

Man, Edward, vicar of Tregony, Cornwall 239
Manaccan, Cornwall 213, 233
manors 91, 286–7
maps 214
Marches, Council of the 21
maritime trade 14, 20
mariners 63–4
market crosses 235
market houses 235
markets and marketplaces 1, 12–13, 15, 64, 72, 100, 103, 123, 140, 170, 214
marriages 22, 26, 83, 146
martial law 204, 206, 229–30, 232–3, 244
Mary, the Lady, daughter of Henry VIII and eventually queen of England 21, 32, 44, 89, 148, 237–8, 248, 259–60, 262, 264–6, 268, 270, 272, 275, 292
  viewed as a potential regent 6, 7, 292
*Mary Rose*, the, warship 43
Marystow, Devon 222, 236
Mason, Hugh, of Grade, Cornwall 60–1, 131
Mason, Sir John 228
mass, the 23, 59, 87–8, 90, 100, 121, 200, 237–8, 268, 273
massacres 199–200

Maunder, shoemaker and rebel captain 112–13, 207, 221–3
May, Dr William, dean of St Paul's, London 50
May games 88, 187
mayors 21, 30–1, 52–4, 65, 103, 107, 113–14, 142–3, 164, 166–7, 176–7, 202, 221–2, 245–7, 272
Mayow, of Glevyan 247–8
members of parliament 21, 43, 52, 136, 274
memories 2, 17, 39, 48, 82, 129, 211, 247
Meneage, the, Cornwall 33, 72–3, 137, 213
mercenaries 2, 145, 149, 154–5, 181, 183
merchants 14, 21, 83
Merthen, in Constantine, Cornwall 67
*Message sent by the Kynges Majestie, A* 121–3, 153, 185
messengers 147, 159, 178, 248
*Metrical Visions* 263
Midlands, the 75, 81, 182, 241
Midsummer games 91, 187–8, 287
Midsummer watch, the 142
Milliton, John, gentleman 55, 57, 69
mills and millers 12, 239, 246–7; *see also* windmills
minstrels 91
miracles 48
Mohun, Reginald, gentleman 135, 169
Mohuns Ottery, Devon 42, 124, 150
monasteries 22, 32
  dissolution of 27, 29, 39, 56
monks 22, 25, 33, 229
  hanged as traitors 32, 229
moors 13–15, 58, 87, 209
Morebath, Devon 81, 171–2, 189
Moreman, John, priest 24, 50, 52, 55, 83–4, 175, 231, 240, 270
Moreton, Simon, priest 128–9, 235
Morshead, John 250
Morton, Gabriel, priest 238
Mount's Bay, Cornwall 19, 47
'mounts' (i.e., earthen fortifications) 119
Mourton, James, priest 233
MPs *see* members of parliament
Mullion, Cornwall 63
murder 63–4, 67–8, 71, 74, 95, 125, 136, 200, 210, 280, 285
'murmering' 58–9
musters 61, 119, 142
mutton 134
Myller, Alice 29
'Narrow Seas', the 164
National Archives, the 233
New Hall, Essex 260
'new fashions' 64, 72, 95
'new learning', the 25, 45, 47, 50, 52, 69, 116, 148, 240
'new preachers' 73
new service *see Book of Common Prayer*, the
Newman, Margaret 137
Newton Abbot, Devon 210
Nicolles, Philip, controversialist 46–7, 49–52, 292
night watches 96, 103, 119
nobles 18, 20, 23, 32, 40, 43, 255, 261, 267, 282
Norden, John, antiquarian 289, 291
Norfolk, county of 112, 123, 147–8, 173, 226, 234, 255, 258–9, 265, 276–8, 281–2
  duke of *see* Howard, Thomas
Normandy 43
Normans, the 120
North, Sir Edward 228
North Lew, Devon 237
North Tawton, Devon 91
Northaw, Hertfordshire 75, 189
Northern Ireland 2
Northumberland, duke of *see* Dudley, John
Norwich, Norfolk 147, 281
'Nun of Kent', the *see* Barton, Elizabeth
nuns 22, 25

'Oak of Reformation', the 112, 173
oaths 35, 297; *see also* Protestation, the (1641)
Okehampton, Devon 13–14, 170, 207
Okehampton Castle 14
'old learning, the' 41, 265
'old sort, the' 272, 282–3, 288
oral tradition 129, 247
*Order of Communion, the* 59, 73–4, 188, 292
ordnance *see* artillery
Otter, River, Devon 12, 179
Ottery St Mary, Devon 174–5, 178
Owen, ap, gentleman, 209
Oxford, Oxfordshire 83–4
Oxfordshire 146–9, 154, 181–3, 213, 230, 232
oyer and terminer, commissions of 67–9, 139, 277

Padstow, Cornwall 16
pageants 91, 229
Paget, Robert 220–1,
Paget, Sir William, gentleman 221, 269–70, 275
Painswick, Gloucestershire 246
painters and painting 22, 33–6, 48
palaces 21, 97, 117, 121, 226, 265
pamphlets 49–52, 121, 153–4, 185
panniers 118
pans, used to 'seeth' quartered limbs 215
'papists' and popery 40, 74, 79, 87, 126, 148, 165, 186, 230, 232, 257–8, 261, 280
pardons
  remissions of punishment 25, 32, 67–8, 70, 75, 99, 105, 147, 185, 191, 203, 205, 207, 210, 212, 214, 220, 235, 239–40, 242, 251–3, 257–9, 274
  religious festivals 35
'Pardon Monday' 35
Paris, France 153–4
parish registers 234
parliament, acts of 26–7, 29, 41, 58–9, 79–80, 122, 133, 156, 175, 279
parliaments 20, 52–3, 79–80, 121, 274; *see also* 'Reformation Parliament', the
Parr, Catherine, queen of England 89, 261
Parr, William, marquis of Northampton, 260
parsons 59, 204, 210, 233, 235–8
Pater Noster, the 28, 38–9
Paul, Cornwall 47
Paulet, Sir Hugh, gentleman 42, 46, 82, 106, 196–7, 202, 211–14, 223, 240, 243
Paulet, William, Lord St John 260, 269, 283
Payne, John 247–8
peasants 242
Peckham, Sir Edward, gentleman 268–9
*Pedn an laaz see* Land's End
peers *see* nobles
Pelynt, Cornwall 131, 212
Pembroke, earl of *see* Herbert, Sir William
Pendennis Castle, Cornwall 18–19, 60–1, 127, 134, 140, 212, 227
  governor of *see* Killigrew, John, senior
  siege of 134–5, 137, 144, 155, 160–2, 164, 169, 205, 213, 248
Pengersick Castle, Cornwall 55, 57
Pennycross, near Plymouth, Devon 211
Penryn, Cornwall 28, 134
Penwith, hundred of Cornwall 19, 56–7, 62, 65, 70–1, 137, 169, 249
Penzance, Cornwall 19, 128
petitions and petitioning 68, 105, 121–2, 134, 139–40, 144, 152–3, 155–7, 159, 172, 175–6, 188, 190, 237, 239, 247–8, 250, 297
pigs 110, 288
pikes 29, 197
pilgrims and pilgrimage 19, 23, 31–2, 34–5, 37, 39, 48, 146, 169, 229, 237, 294
Pilgrimage of Grace, the 31–2, 34–5, 37, 146, 229, 237, 294
pillaging *see* robbery and pillaging
Pilton, Devon 204, 233
pioneers 200, 208
'placards' *see* bills
plate, silver 28, 55–6, 249
plays and players *see* actors and stage-plays
Playsted, Stephen 248
plough-chains 101
Plymouth, Devon 14, 65, 69, 134, 142–4, 155, 161, 163–4, 170, 175, 196, 205–6, 211, 238
  'Black Book' of 65, 163
  guildhall in 69, 142
  high cross in 142
  mayor of 65, 142, 164
  rebels driven out of 205, 211
  receivers' accounts of 66, 68, 142, 163, 206
  'spoyled' by the rebels 163, 170
Plymouth Castle, siege of 143–4, 162, 164, 205–6, 210
Plymouth Hoe, gallows constructed at 68, 163
Plymouth Sound 134
Plympton, Devon 13
poets 263, 288
Pole, Reginald, churchman 23, 32, 175
poles, heads and quarters impaled on 69
'politiques' 260
Pollard, John, archdeacon 117
Pollard, Sir Hugh, gentleman 46, 90–3, 102, 104–5, 108
Pomeroy, Richard, gentleman 169
Pomeroy, Sir Thomas, gentleman 194–5, 212, 220, 222–3, 274

Ponet, John 264–5, 267, 269–70, 273
Pope, Tamsine 205
pope, the 21, 24–6, 28, 32, 230
popery *see* 'papists'
population statistics 16, 20, 87
ports 14, 16, 120, 201
portreeves 21, 247
Portledge, Devon 162
Poundstock, Cornwall 128–9, 235
Powderham, Devon 146
*praemunire* 25
prayers and praying 22–3, 25, 34, 38, 48; *see also Ave Maria*; Creed; Lord's Prayer; *Pater Noster*
prayer books 26, 74, 80; *see also Book of Common Prayer*
'Prayer Book Rebellion, the' *see* Western Rising
preaching and preachers 24, 28, 39, 42, 49–50, 72–3, 83, 155, 175, 193, 231, 241
pregnancies 130
priests 1, 22, 38, 47–8, 59, 63, 70, 74, 83, 85–7, 90, 132, 148, 156–8, 186, 204, 230, 237–9, 249
  accused of being stirrers of rebellion 63, 66, 69, 88–9, 137, 146, 204, 229, 231–5, 239
  attainted 234, 236
  executed 69, 128–9, 146, 213, 233–7, 247, 293–4
  fined 239–40
  hunted down 204
  lampooned on stage 229
  menaced 237–8, 241
  participate in Pilgrimage of Grace 32, 229, 237, 294
  questioned 230
  ransomed 238
  serve as 'Governours' of the rebel camps 231, 233
  slain in the field 204, 232, 235–7, 293–4
Prince, John, antiquarian 210
printers 49, 51, 225
priories 29, 30, 55, 118, 229–30
prisons 15, 30–1, 40, 42, 52, 56–7, 133, 138–9, 226, 284
prisoners 66, 94, 107–9, 115, 129–30, 133, 136–40, 166, 168, 170, 175, 197, 201–2, 205, 210, 214, 221–5, 231–2, 242–4, 251, 253, 255, 257, 262, 268–9, 271, 276, 279, 282, 285, 295
  discharged 73, 274, 284
  executed 198, 199, 247
  given as 'gifts' 203
Privy Chamber, the 273, 284
Privy Council, the 42, 44–5, 48, 53–4, 56–8, 62, 65–9, 73, 81, 88–9, 96–7, 99–100, 106, 110, 123, 144–5, 148–50, 152–3, 155, 169, 179, 181, 186, 202, 207, 209, 220–3, 226, 228, 231, 252, 255–6, 258–60, 262, 267–8, 272–5, 277–84, 288
  register of 273–4, 282–3
privy councillors, the 54–8, 62, 66, 70, 73, 75, 79, 96–9, 103, 106–7, 109–11, 116–17, 121, 123–5, 141–3, 145–9, 151–2, 154–60, 164, 173–4, 181–2, 184, 187, 212, 219–21, 223, 230–1, 243, 251–2, 262, 264, 267–8, 270–1, 273–5, 281, 283–4
  divisions among 44, 269
Privy Seal, Lord *see* Russell, Lord John
processions, religious 35, 48, 100
proclamations 26, 64, 72, 81, 141–2, 159–60, 188, 215, 230, 249, 252, 257, 267, 273
'protestants' 45, 53, 87, 130, 275, 289, 294, 297
protests 1–6, 30–1, 34, 55, 58–9, 62, 70, 74–5, 82, 84–5, 87–95, 97–9, 102–4, 107, 109, 129, 132–30, 143, 155, 176, 186–7, 190, 214, 229, 231, 237, 257–9, 289–90, 295
Protestation, the (1641) 297
provost marshals 147, 204, 239, 244–7
pulpits 24, 26
Pyder, hundred of Cornwall 65
Pyers, John, mariner of St Keverne 63, 66, 69–70
Pyne, Joan 251
pyxes 200

quarter sessions 12, 16, 64
'quarters', displayed on gates, posts and public buildings 69–70
queens *see* Aragon, Catherine of; Boleyn, Anne; Cleves, Anne of; Parr, Catherine; Seymour, Jane

rack, the 228
Raddon, Devon 109
Raffe, Robert, priest 213, 233
Raleigh, Walter, gentleman 108
ramparts 101–2, 200
'rampires' *see* bulwarks
ransoms 203, 210, 238, 248–51
Raynes, Dr, bishop of Lincoln's chancellor 71
Reading, Berkshire 183
'rebels', protestors described as 2–3, 5, 63, 65, 74–5, 94, 105, 125, 158, 171
receivers' accounts 66, 68, 142, 163, 206
recognisances 262, 274
Reede, Joan, rioter 29
regnal years 79
Reeve, Joan, rioter 29
'Reformation Parliament', the 24
Reskymer, John, gentleman 67, 70, 72, 285
Reskymer, William, gentleman 285, 295
*Responce du Peuple Anglois, La* 153–5
Resseygh, John, yeoman 64
Revelation, book of 229
rewards 48, 202–3, 206, 210–11, 238, 241, 245, 249, 261, 266, 286
Reynell, Richard 210–11
Rich, Sir Richard 228
Richmond Palace, Surrey 97, 121
rings, stolen 138
riots and rioters 29–31, 54–5, 57–60, 63–4, 75, 81, 97, 118, 189, 261
roads 11, 13–15, 17–19, 82, 101, 104, 107, 120, 170, 174, 192, 194, 196, 199–200, 204, 207–9
  Roman 11, 82, 174–5
robbery and pillaging 2, 118, 125, 135–7, 139–40, 163, 168–70, 179, 192, 250–3
Rochester, Kent 229
rocks 50
Rogers, Mr, of the privy chamber 284
Rome and the Romans 175, 229
rood lofts 22, 29, 171
rood screens 22
roofs 111, 226
ropes, captured rebels bound with 248
rosary beads 48
Roscarrock, Richard, gentleman 279
Rose-Troup, Frances, historian 126–7, 292, 294
Rosogan, James 140–1, 213
Rosogan, John 140–1
Rowland, Edmond 250
Rowse, A.L., historian 290
royal supremacy, the 26–8, 32
Royse, Robert, priest 234
rumours 28, 33, 47, 82, 110, 166, 268, 273–5, 278, 282, 284, 287
  ordered to be spread against the protestors 125, 168
Russell, Lord John 5, 40–1, 43, 97–8, 100, 105–6, 109–10, 115–17, 121, 123–5, 141–53, 155, 157–60, 164–8, 170, 173–5, 178–86, 191–204, 206–12, 214, 219–24, 226–8, 230, 231–3, 235, 238–40, 242–4, 248–55, 257–8, 262, 267, 274, 286, 291, 293

'sacramentarians' 41
saddles 226, 236
St Aubyn, Thomas, gentleman 57
St Budeaux, Devon 205
St Buryan, Cornwall 19
St Cleer, Cornwall 234, 236
St Columb Major, Cornwall 141, 213, 247
St Erth, Cornwall 136
St Germans, Cornwall 179
St Ives, Cornwall 238, 247
St John's Eve 142
St Just-in-Penwith, Cornwall 169
St Just-in-Roseland, Cornwall 70
St Keverne, Cornwall 33–6, 60–5, 69–70, 72–3, 87, 131, 137, 213, 233, 289
St Lawrence, guild of (in Ashburton, Devon) 58
St Mawes Castle, Cornwall 19, 61, 135, 140, 162, 169
  captain of *see* Treffry, Thomas
St Michael the archangel, feast of 96
St Michael's Mount, Cornwall 19, 47, 71, 128, 130, 160
  siege of 136–40, 211, 213
St Nicholas Island, Devon 134, 139, 143, 162
St Thomas, near Exeter, Devon 204, 213, 233
St Veep, Cornwall 233
St Winnow, Cornwall 65
saints 22–4, 28, 31, 35, 42
saints' days 22, 35
Salisbury plain, Wiltshire 178
Saltash, Cornwall 134
Salter, William 239

Sampford Courtenay, Devon 1, 2, 4–5, 85–96, 98, 100, 102, 109–10, 112–13, 119–23, 127, 156, 173, 176–7, 204–9, 212–14, 221–2, 230, 233, 243, 245, 248, 266, 290, 292, 296
 church house of 94–5
 manor of 297
 parish church of 1, 87, 90, 112
  tower of 109–11
 'Sandford More' in 95
Sandford, Devon 279
Sawley Abbey, Lancashire 229
Saxons, the 14
schools and schoolmasters 24, 83, 185
Scilly, Isles of 127–8
Scotland and the Scots 45, 79, 145, 181–2, 265
scouts 207
scribes 79, 235–7
scripture 24, 33, 39, 50, 59
Scudamore, Sir Richard, gentleman 224–6, 234, 276, 279–82, 284–5, 295
Seagar, William, labourer and rebel captain 86–7, 89–90, 111–13, 176, 296
seas, wild, encompass the West Country 19, 50
secretaries 158, 224, 227–8, 259, 271
Sennen, Cornwall 19
serjeants-at-law 222
sermons 26, 39, 47, 73, 108, 155, 186, 193
servants and serving men 32, 36, 47–8, 56, 58, 62, 101–2, 108, 119, 176, 179, 212, 214, 225, 233, 246–7, 250–1, 253, 259, 263, 265–6, 269, 273, 282, 286, 296
Seymour, Edward, earl of Hertford, later duke of Somerset 4, 5, 43–6, 48, 52–4, 58, 62, 67, 69, 71–2, 74–5, 79–80, 86, 88, 97, 102–3, 105–6, 109–11, 115, 121, 127, 139, 143–8, 153, 156–9, 161, 163–4, 175–6, 178, 184, 202, 219, 221, 223, 228, 230, 252–3, 255–60, 262–73, 276, 278–80, 283–4, 290–3
Seymour, Jane, queen of England 27, 44
Shaftesbury, Dorset 99, 261
sheep and sheep-farming 13, 80, 82, 106, 110, 121, 156
sheepskins, rebel captains compelled to ride on 226
Sherborne, Dorset 151
sheriffs 20, 24, 43, 50, 55, 68–9, 88, 100, 105, 108, 116, 146, 165, 214, 281–2
ships and shipping 16, 50, 120, 135, 161–2, 164, 206; *see also* 'barkes'
shoemakers 112, 221–2
*Shorte Treatise of Politike Power, A* 264
shovels 29
shrines 23, 48
sieges *see* Exeter; St Michael's Mount; Pendennis Castle; Plymouth Castle; Trematon Castle
silk 118
Silverton, Devon 108, 203
Slader, Mark, gentleman 90–1, 93
Sloman, John, rebel captain 176, 296
Smith, John, billman 197
Smith, Sir Thomas 228
smiths *see* blacksmiths
smocks, gentlewomen stripped to 138
Smyth, Robert, gentleman 179–80
social radicalism 259, 280
social tensions 16, 170, 277, 292, 294–5
soldiers 2, 32, 42, 45, 61, 82, 119, 124, 127–8, 134, 137, 145–9, 161, 179–84, 191, 193, 197–8, 201, 203, 208, 213, 243, 249, 251–2
Somerset
 county of 11, 13, 40, 81–2, 100, 123–4, 148, 151, 178–9, 183, 196–7, 207, 211–15, 291
 first duke of *see* Seymour, Edward
Somerton, Somerset 214
South Hams, the, Devon 14, 175, 206, 211
Southampton 34, 37, 161
 first earl of *see* Wriothesley, Thomas
Southron, Thomas, treasurer of Exeter Cathedral 54, 117
Southwell, Sir Richard 264–5, 268–71, 275, 281, 284
Southey, Hugh, tailor 296
Spain and the Spanish 32, 41, 178
Speight, Helen, historian 295
Spenser, William 249
spies 147, 158, 174
 hanged 244
Spinola, Captain Paulo Baptist 182–4, 196
'spoyling' *see* robbery and pillaging
'spykes' 29
stage plays 90–1, 111, 187–8
stakes 24–5

Stanley, Edward, third earl of Derby 229
Stannaries, Lord Warden of 40
Stannary towns 13
stewards 82, 116, 165
sticks 25, 248
'stirs' 1, 2, 4, 36, 57, 60–1, 63, 66–7, 75, 81, 89–91, 96, 98, 107, 116, 126, 128, 146, 148, 150, 170, 219, 228, 231–2, 255, 257, 290, 296
stone 12, 87, 235; *see also* granite
stones, hurled at iconoclasts, by women of Exeter 29, 30
  hurled over castle walls, by prisoners 67
  hurled at loyalist soldiers, by rebels 196
Stow, John, chronicler 243
Stowell, letter writer 109
Stowell, John, priest 239–40
'strangers' 99, 145–6, 149, 155, 183, 206, 251
Strasbourg, France 83
Stratton, Cornwall 171, 234–5
  church rood-loft in, restored by the rebels 171
streets 24, 29, 54, 166, 194, 226, 286
stripping 24, 32, 138
sub-priors 229
'Submission of the Clergy', the (1531) 25
subsidies 90
suburbs 12–13, 15, 53, 108, 116, 119–20, 165, 201
Sussex, county of 147
supplications *see* petitions
surveys 15, 56, 57, 59, 90, 126, 140, 289, 297
Swimbridge, Devon 250
Switzerland and the Swiss 273
swords 7, 38, 172, 185, 190, 197, 199, 212, 232, 244
Sydenham, in Marystow, Devon 222

Tailboys, Lady Margaret, wife of Sir Peter Carew 96
tailors 86, 89, 112, 177, 296
Tamar, River 5, 14, 18, 128, 160, 205, 211, 233, 254, 291
tar, severed limbs coated with 215
tavern signs, rebels hanged from 247
taverns 27, 247
Tavistock, Devon 13–14, 43, 69
Tavistock Abbey, Devon 40
Tawstock, Devon 14
taxes and taxation 20, 45, 80, 82, 107, 121–2
'Ten Articles', the (1536) 27–8
Ten Commandments, the 28, 39, 48
tenements 90, 297
Tewennecke, John 239
Thames Valley 191
thatch 87
theology and theologians 26, 47, 50, 52, 83
Thomas, William, mariner 63, 69
Thorverton, Devon 109
Thynne, Sir John, steward 82, 102, 192, 203–4, 207, 211, 214–15, 232, 243
timber 198, 229
tin-miners ('tinners') 1, 13, 19
tin works 13, 19–20
Tiverton, Devon 82
Tompson, John, priest 177, 231
Tong, Dr Roger, king's chaplain 72–3
tools 29
Topsham, Devon 201
Torrington, Devon 14, 172, 177
torture 223, 228, 248
Tothill, Robert 239–40
Totnes, Devon 14, 175
  archdeacon of 240
'town versus gown' disputes 54
translators 16, 225
transubstantiation, doctrine of 23, 41, 53, 122
Travers, Captain 196
treason and traitors 26–7, 31, 37, 41, 60, 63, 67–70, 87, 105, 112, 123, 132, 142, 146, 153, 159, 163, 165, 169, 211, 213, 222–4, 226, 228–30, 235, 238, 242–4, 249, 252, 254, 257, 262, 268, 270–1, 277–83, 285–6, 288–91
trees
  climbed by children 214
  cut down to form barricades 107, 174, 198
  rebels hanged from 246
  *see also* 'Oak of Reformation', the
Treffry, Thomas, captain of St Mawes Castle 61, 135
Tregarrick, hamlet in Pelynt, Cornwall 131, 213, 251
Treglosacke, John, fisherman 34, 37
Tregonwell, Dr John, lawyer 28–30
Tregony, Cornwall 239

Trelawney, John, gentleman 169
Trematon Castle, Cornwall 140, 160–1, 189
siege of 133–4, 138–9
Tréport, Normandy, attacked by the English 43
Trevanion, John 239
Trevanyon, Hugh, gentleman 130, 169
Trevian, Pasco, mariner 64, 68
Trewinnard, in St Erth, Cornwall 136
Trewynnard, William, gentleman 136–37
trials 5–6, 64, 67–9, 72, 126, 139, 158, 204, 230, 275–81, 294
Tribo, John William, mariner of St Keverne 63, 69
trivets 215
trumpets and trumpeters 194, 206
Truro, Cornwall 17–19, 70, 127, 134, 239
Trychay, Sir Christopher, vicar of Morebath 172
Tucker, Martha, wife of John Hooker 83
turf 20
Turpyn, John 242
Turpyn, William 242
Tywardreath, Cornwall 40

Udall, Nicholas, dramatist 185–91
Ugborough, Devon 108
Underhill family, of Sampford Courtenay 90, 297
Underhill, William/Thomas, tailor and rebel captain 85–7, 89–90, 111–13, 176–7, 209, 219–20, 296
undersheriffs 69, 250

Van der Delft, Francois, imperial ambassador 121, 204, 242, 260, 263–4, 266, 270, 275, 280–1, 284
velvet 118
Vermigli, Pietro Martire ('Peter Martyr') 83
vestments, clerical 87
Veysey, John, bishop of Exeter 12, 21, 38–9, 42, 48, 56, 89, 117, 240
register of 170, 235–6, 241
scribe of 235–7
vicars 1, 47, 59, 137, 171–2, 204, 213, 230, 233, 235, 238–9
vicars general 27, 42
visions 25, 84, 263
visitations 27, 46, 49–50
visitors 16, 25, 28, 30–1, 38, 46, 49–50, 83, 87–8

wagons 194
waits *see* minstrels
Wales and the Welsh 6, 17, 119, 178, 191, 201, 203, 206, 209, 251
Wannell, Thomas 250
wards, administrative 12
warders and warding 57, 117, 119, 211
warrants 48, 97, 123, 132, 158, 171, 173, 211, 233, 249, 253
Warter Priory, Yorkshire 229
Warwick, first earl of *see* Dudley, John
Warwickshire 42
watches and watching 54–5, 96, 103, 117, 119, 201; *see also* Midsummer watch
Watton Priory, Yorkshire 230
Webber, William 169
Wells, Somerset 214
Welsh, Robert, vicar of St Thomas 204, 213, 232-3
'West Britons', the 14
West Cornwall and the West Cornish 4, 16–17, 19, 36–7, 48, 57, 59, 62, 65, 73, 91, 127–8, 133, 137, 139, 160, 163, 188, 212, 230, 285
West Penwith, Cornwall 19
Western Rising 3–6, 11, 82–114, 119, 126, 141–2, 144, 146, 161, 182, 187, 213, 225, 234, 255, 257, 260, 265, 285, 289–90, 292, 294–6
Westminster 16, 53, 69–70, 226–7, 230, 277
Hall 277–8, 280
Matthew of, chronicler 16
Weston Peverell, Devon 211
Whetehyll, Jane 139
Whetehyll, Robert, esquire 139–40
'whisking' 270
Whit Monday 1, 85, 88, 297
Whitsun 80, 85, 88
holidays 88
week 85, 91
wills, destroyed by the rebels 170
Wilton, Herefordshire 181, 183
Wiltshire, county of 81–2, 149, 151, 178, 291
windmills 192–3, 198
windows 22, 30, 48
wine 23, 69

Winkleigh, Devon 208
Winslade, John, gentleman 131–2, 140–1, 158, 173, 178, 203, 212–13, 219, 222–4, 228, 251, 256, 277–80, 286–7, 290–1, 293–4
Winslade, Tristram 178
Winslade, William 222, 226, 274, 296
Winter, Thomas, illegitimate son of Cardinal Wolsey 56
Wise, John, gentleman 222–4, 226, 236, 274
Wolcock, John, priest 137, 213, 233
Wolsey, Cardinal Thomas 260, 263
wolves, Sir William Herbert's men compared to 82
women 6, 16, 24–5, 29–31, 35–6, 83, 108, 118–20, 130, 133, 136, 138–9, 146, 166, 171, 187, 222, 228, 247, 250–1, 261, 264, 269, 287, 297
wood 13, 25, 215; *see also* sticks
Wood, Alexander, gentleman 90–1, 93
Woodbury, Devon 192–3
Woodbury Hill, Devon 198
woods 14, 130
woollen-cloth 80
worms 40
Wotton, Nicholas 268
wounds and wounding 136, 179, 194, 197, 211
Wriothesley, Thomas, earl of Southampton 45, 169, 187, 228, 256, 260, 262–5, 267–70, 272–5, 280–1, 283–4
Wymondham, Norfolk 147, 281

yeomen 21, 64, 90, 94, 108–9, 131–2, 140, 147, 225, 250, 286, 290, 296
yeomen of the guard 169
York, Yorkshire 229
York, archbishop of 21

Zanga, Captain Petro 183–4, 223, 226
Zurich, Switzerland 273